Advancing Geographic Information Science

The Past and Next Twenty Years

EDITED BY

HARLAN ONSRUD and WERNER KUHN

GSDI ASSOCIATION PRESS

Advancing Geographic Information Science: The Past and Next Twenty Years
Harlan Onsrud and Werner Kuhn (Editors)
Compilation © 2016 by GSDI Association Press / 946 Great Plain Ave. PMB-194,
Needham, MA
02492-3030, USA

Front cover photo credit: Sun and Moon Together on the Tay by Ross2085 (CC BY 2.0)
Back cover photo credit: Bass Harbor Lighthouse Acadia by Robbie Shade (CC BY 2.0)

ISBN 978-0-9852444-4-6

Contents

2

PART THREE: Extended Abstracts

4

Foreword

This book is the result of invited and solicited submissions to an institute on **Advancing Geographic Information Science: The Past and Next Twenty Years.** A core goal of the institute was to review the research challenges of the past twenty years and discuss emerging challenges of the next twenty.

The summer of 2015 marked the twenty-year anniversary of first of two **International Early-Career Scholars Summer Institutes in Geographic Information.** These early GIScience conferences were jointly funded by the U.S. National Science Foundation (NSF) and the European Science Foundation (ESF) and held in Wolfe's Neck Maine in 1995 and at Villa Borsig in Berlin Germany in 1996. The series of continuing Vespucci Institutes arose from and were modeled after the successful institutes held in 1995 and 1996.

In celebration of the success of the early institutes, participants in those institutes invited a new generation of early career scholars to join with them in an anniversary institute. It was co-organized by the Vespucci Initiative and the NCGIA sites of Maine, Buffalo and Santa Barbara and held in Bar Harbor, Maine, 29 June thru July 3, 2015.

As in the past, the participants were equally divided among senior and early career scholars. Senior scholars were invited while early career scholars competed through a paper submission process. The full chapters contained in this book were subjected to a peer refereeing and revision process prior to inclusion in the publication. The review board consisted primarily of scholars that participated in the Institutes twenty years ago.

In keeping with tradition, the Institute supported interactions among senior and early career scholars by (a) utilizing active presentation, discussant and audience sessions, (b) scheduling outdoor activities and social events throughout the week to allow for informal one-on-one and small group discussions and (c) incorporating within the program a research proposal development competition. The program may be viewed at http://giscienceconferences.org/vespucci2015week2/.

We thank the authors of the chapters, the peer review board, and all participants in the Institute for their considerable efforts and constructive criticisms of the ideas and works of each other. We also thank the GSDI Association Press for its willingness to publish this book as a whole and the individual chapters under a Creative Commons Attribution 4.0 License. This allows all to use the materials presented to their own best advantage facilitating the advancement of science.

Harlan Onsrud and Werner Kuhn (Editors)

About Editors

Harlan Onsrud is Professor of Spatial Information Science and Engineering in the School of Computing and Information Science at the University of Maine and a research scientist with the National Center for Geographic Information and Analysis (NCGIA). His research and teaching focuses on the analysis of legal, ethical, and institutional issues affecting the creation and use of digital databases and the assessment of the social and societal impacts of spatial and tracking technologies. He is past president and past Executive Director of the Global Spatial Data Infrastructure Association (GSDI), past-president and fellow of the University Consortium for Geographic Information Science (UCGIS), and past Chair of the U.S. National Committee (USNC) on Data for Science and Technology (CODATA) of the National Research Council. He has participated in several U.S. National Research Council studies related to spatial data and services and has been funded as a Fulbright Specialist in Law with assignments in Australia and Germany.

Werner Kuhn holds the Jack and Laura Dangermond Endowed Chair in Geography at the University of California, Santa Barbara, where he is professor of Geographic Information Science. He is also the director of the Center for Spatial Studies at the University of California Santa Barbara (UCSB). His main research and teaching goal is to make spatial information and computing accessible across domains and disciplines. Before joining UCSB in late 2013, Kuhn was a professor of Geoinformatics at the University of Münster, Germany, where he led MUSIL, an interdisciplinary semantic interoperability research lab. Kuhn is a leading expert in the area of geospatial semantics and especially known for his work on Semantic Reference Systems as well as on interaction metaphors for Geographic Information Systems. He is a co-founder of the Vespucci Initiative for Advancing Science through Geographic Information and of the COSIT (Conference on Spatial Information Theory) Series.

6

Introduction

The advancement of geographic information science (GIScience) involves wide ranging facets that intersect with numerous other science domains. The tools and theories of GIScience actively contribute to the advancement of other science domains while at the same time GIScience benefits substantially from the insights gained in working across and among numerous science domains.

The first part of this book consists of several co-authored chapters that look back in time at the progress made by GIScientists over the past twenty years. They also address emerging challenges that should be addressed by GIScientists or by the scientific community as a whole.

At the conference in which the chapters in this book were critiqued and discussed, the sessions in which materials were presented and discussed included those on Semantics and Reasoning, Spatial Relations and Properties, Network and Probabilistic Approaches, Feature Detection and Digital Mapping, Movement and Change, Geo-ontologies for Linked Data, Rethinking Principles and Approaches, Data and Services, and Resource Tracking and Management. However, many scientific breakthroughs within the field have come not from narrowly constrained specialties but from intersections within the discipline and with other disciplines. In this spirit, rather than categorize the contributions to this volume as we did at the recent institute sessions, the editors chose to publish the peer-reviewed articles in this volume in alphabetical order. Extended abstracts are presented in a similar arrangement. In this manner we hope that readers are able to better make connections among thinking and diverse perspectives through these contributions and within the broad field that has come to be known as geographic information science.

8

Contributions of GIScience over the Past Twenty Years

Max J. Egenhofer[1], Keith C. Clarke[2], Song Gao[2], Teriitutea Quesnot[3], W. Randolph Franklin[4], May Yuan[5], and David Coleman[6]

1 School of Computing and Information Science and National Center for Geographic Information and Analysis, 5711 Boardman Hall, University of Maine, Orono, ME 04469-5711, USA

2 Department of Geography, 1720 Ellison Hall, University of California, Santa Barbara, Santa Barbara, CA 93106-4060, USA

3 Centre for Research in Geomatics, Laval University, 1055 Avenue du Séminaire, Pavillon Louis-Jacques Casault, Quebec City, QC G1V 0A6, Canada

4 Department of Electrical, Computer & Systems Engineering, 6026 JEC, Rensselaer Polytechnic Institute, 110 8th St, Troy, NY 12180, USA

5 School of Economic, Political, and Policy Sciences, The University of Texas at Dallas, 800 W Campbell Road, Richardson, TX 75080-3021, USA

6 Department of Geodesy and Geomatics Engineering, University of New Brunswick, P.O. Box 4400, E3B 5A3, Fredericton, NB, Canada

Abstract: This paper summarizes the discussions related to the panel "Contributions of GIScientists (or GIScience) over the past Twenty Years" at the 2015 Vespucci Institute. Reflections about the past not only provide an account of what occurred, but also may serve as a basis for comparison when in the future somehow related scenarios arise. Such histories may be detailed enumerations of chronological events or, more analytically, analyses of interactions that enabled or caused specific developments. The purpose of this paper is to account for some key developments in the academic field of geographic information science over the past twenty years (i.e., since 1995) and to assess some of the impact of these developments. The panel in Bar Harbor, moderated by David Coleman, included two invited presentations (by Max Egenhofer and Keith Clarke), and responses by two early career panelists (Song Gao and Teriitutea Quesnot), and by two senior panelists (Randolph Franklin and May Yuan).

Keywords: Emergence of GIScience; short recent history; outlets of GIScience research; publication ranking; selected highlights of GIScience research; contributions to other disciplines; research topics that have disappeared; recently emerging topics.

1   Introduction

Geographic information system (GIS) as the term and concept preceded geographic information science. The term geographic information system is widely attributed to Roger Tomlinson's Canadian Geographic Information System [88]. The concept spread over its first twenty years to sizeable software systems whose principal goal was to perform computerized mapping.

The first Big Book [64] included a chapter by Coppock and Rhind [10], entitled "The History of GIS," which described primarily the roles of different organizations in developing computerized mapping systems. To contrast this history's focus on vector representations, Foresman [28] provided a complementary history of GIS from the raster perspective. A third approach—The GIS History Project [62]—aimed at a critical examination of the history of GIS. All these efforts highlight that a single history about geographic information is unlikely to represent fully the many different facets and linkages that geographic information systems have.

As this paper focuses on developments since the two International Early Career Summer Institutes in Geographic Information [11, 12], the examination and reflection on geographic information science is limited here to new insights gained since the mid 1990s.

This chapter summarizes the main ideas and remarks that emerged from both the panelists (i.e., the authors) and the audience during the first panel session. Specifically, this panel reviewed the emergence of GIScience (Section 2), and its recent history (Section 3). Panelists analyzed the proliferation of the terms GIS and GIScience throughout the literature (Section 4) and examined the journal and competitive conferences that are dedicated to GIScience (Section 5) and the most frequently cited articles in some outlets (Section 6). Selected research highlights and contributions to other disciplines are discussed in Sections 7 and 8, respectively. Finally, the change of topics in the research landscape (Section 9) and recently emerging topics (Section 10) are discussed. The chapter closes with conclusions in Section 11.

2   The Emergence of Geographic Information Science

The term *Geographic Information Science* emerged in the early 1990s. Goodchild's keynote address at the Fourth International Symposium on Spatial Data Handling introduced ideas of some science behind the systems [32]. This approach was very much in response to concerns expressed by Abler [1] that geographic information systems were theory-poor, yet in the long term the success of such a field would require strong theoretical underpinnings.

The introduction of a term that distinguished the systems from the science marked the start of this transition. While Goodchild's initial choice was *Spatial* Information Science (possibly in line with the Symposium's name), the longer version of the essay published in the *International Journal of Geographical Information Systems* (IJGIS), replaced *spatial* with *geographical* information science [34]. The minor discrepancy between geographical and geographic had already been addressed by Abler [1] during the emergence of the NCGIA, attributing the difference to the British (geographical) vs. US (geographic) linguistic intricacies and the IJGIS's preferences (Goodchild's 1991 keynote at EGIS had used the term Geographic Information Science [33]). Goodchild [36] reflects on twenty years of progress, including these historical accounts in Geographic Information Science. The twenty-one research initiatives of the National Center for Geographic Information and Analysis (NCGIA), which fuelled much research publication in the GIS field between 1988 and 1996, can be seen as a first comprehensive GIS research agenda (www.ncgia.ucsb.edu/research/initiatives.html).

Geographic Information Science was quickly adopted as a popular term in academia, as it promotes scientific endeavors beyond technological GIS applications. The broader adoption of geographic information science was evident by the establishment of the (US) University Consortium for Geographic information Science (UCGIS). In 1997, the flagship journal, IJGIS, changed its name from the *International Journal of Geographical Information Systems* to the *International Journal of Geographical Information Science*.

Then editor-in-chief Peter Fisher highlighted that the name change was only after the 24th character (not counting blanks) so that future volumes would still be most likely shelved in libraries in close proximity, when sorted alphabetically. A few years later, the journal *Cartography and Geographic Information Systems* also adopted the science term, changing to *Cartography and Geographic Information Science*. With the initiation of the *International Conference on Geographic Information Science* in 2000, the term Geographic Information Science gained further prominence within the scientific community, as this biennial conference series caters on the many components of this interdisciplinary field and its intricacies. The conference series' acronym (GIScience) became a popular way to refer to the field, distinguishing it from its systems (GISs).

3 A Short Recent History of Geographic Information Science

Depending on when one wants to pinpoint the birth of geographic information science, any of its histories may start between 1990 and 1992. The reflection on the early 1990s through mid 2010s captured in this section develops from an earlier focus on a somewhat longer time frame [18] during which the *game changers* contributed to the formation of geographic information science, such as Vannevar Bush's *As We May Think* [5], Tomlinson's Canadian Geographic Information Systems [88], Tobler's Computer Movie Simulating Urban Growth [86], Hägerstrand's Time Geography [46], Dutton's Symposium on Data Structures for Geographic Information Systems [15], Pat Hayes's Naive Physics Manifesto [48], Peucker's TINs [73], Tomlin's Map Algebra [87], Guttmann's R-tree [45], and Abler's vision about the US National Center for Geographic Information and Analysis [1].

Although held only a week prior to Goodchild's 1990 keynote [32], the NATO Advanced Study Institute on Cognitive and Linguistic Aspects of Geographic Space [66] became the foundation of the cognitive and computational aspects of geographic information science. Together with the *Conference on Spatial Information Theory* (COSIT) series and the *Journal of Spatial Cognition and Computation*, a subfield was created that had high impact on geographic information science overall. Twenty-five years later the critique as to whether Las Navas's Lakoffian credo was more an advancement or an impediment to bringing other approaches on board [7] is up for debate.

By 1992 the first traces of micro-sensors started to make an impact on the field as not only GPS-based location (albeit crude at that time) emerged. The Active Badge Location Systems [91] pioneered sensor-based location techniques to track people movement in building complexes. Coupled with the advent of the World-Wide Web, location data can be quickly disseminated across space. Negroponte's visionary account of a Being Digital [72] within a society started a novel perspective, also on sharing spatial data digitally, instantaneously. Only shortly afterwards, the visions of location sensors, the Web, and novel space-time interactions came together in the concept of Digital Earth [41]. Access to scientific and cultural data with respect to the sphere would enable global collaboration.

In addition, the virtual reality, augmented reality, and visualization technologies more broadly pushed for immersive digital environments. The Virtual LA project [51] added the facet that the traditional map based conveyance of geographic information could be accomplished in a way that allows users to experience space more like they were immersed in that space. In addition, the opportunity of combining photo-realistic renderings of infrastructure with simulations about non-static objects and events started to bring the community outside of its confines.

The setting of networked sensors [24] provided the backbone for real-time data collections of distributed phenomena. Geosensor networks [82] highlight the particular challenges that arise with static and mobile sensor colonies that are spatially distributed. The amount, complexity, and diversity of datasets that arise within such geosensor networks have fuelled the contemporary focus on spatial big data [79].

At the beginning of the millennium, the focus shifted towards the meaning of data. The Semantic Web [4] provided a vision that the Web also needs logic in order to make automatic inferences about the data. A critical role in this setting is reserved for ontologies—specifications of conceptualizations [43]. Semantics and ontologies were further specified within the context of geographic information, yielding such concepts as the Geospatial Semantic Web [17] and Ontology-Driven GIS [27].

A new development in the recent history of geographic information science is the concept of volunteered geographic information [35], which puts a focus on spatial data collections that are community-driven rather than conducted and controlled by a single authority. As such volunteered data sets do not necessarily follow a prescribed format, they have the potential of great variability (e.g., quantitative vs. qualitative) and accuracy. Volunteered datasets to which masses of users contribute have the enormous prospectus of timely, up-to-date access to spatial information about phenomena that undergo rapid change.

4   Proliferation of the Terms GIS and GIScience

The terms *GIS* and *GIScience* have become increasingly popular within the scientific world, not only within its own field. In order to quantify such a development, we used Scopus, the abstract and citation database of peer-reviewed literature to query the number of publications that contain the keyword GIS or GIScience between 1991 and 2015 (Figure 1). The annual summary counts reveal for phases:

1. Up to 1995, annual counts were less than 1,000.
2. Between 1996 and 2000 the use of the two terms increases modestly to just below 1,300.
3. Between 2001 and 2010, the counts essentially quadrupled to roughly 6,000 occurrences annually.
4. Since 2010, this count has plateaued at roughly 6,000 annual occurrences of the terms GIS and GIScience.

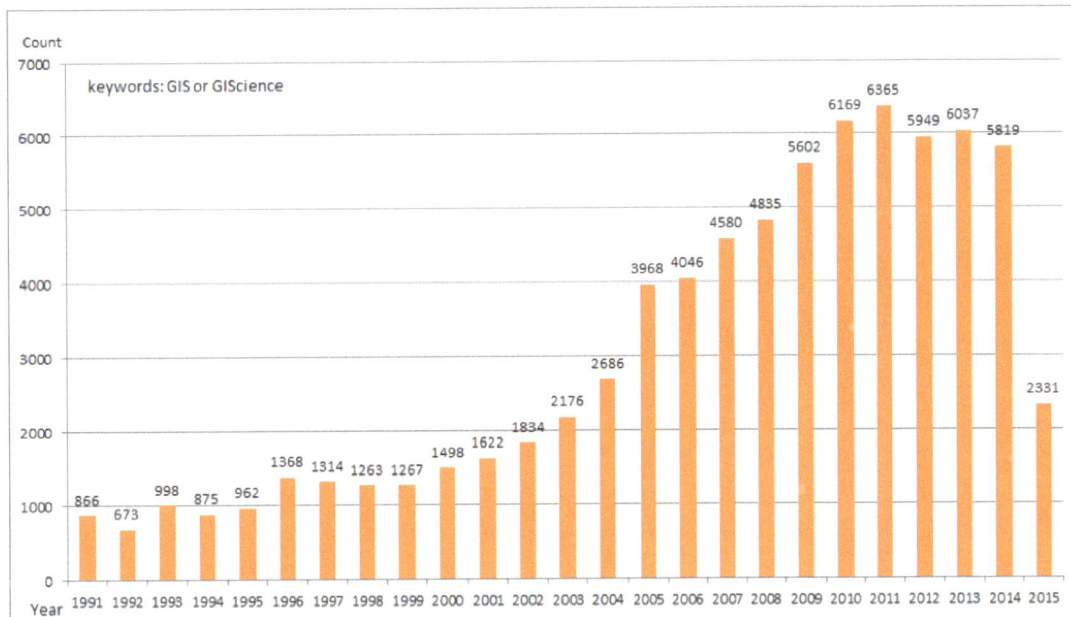

Figure 1: Total number of publications with the keywords GIS or GIScience, based on a Scopus query for the years 1991 through 2015, executed in July 2015.

5   The Outlets of Geographic Information Science over the last Twenty Years

The landscape of the outlets that cater to advances in geographic information science and geographic information systems has changed quite dramatically over the last twenty years. In 1995, the *International Journal of Geographical Information Systems* (IJGIS) was the only journal that targeted GIS research as its primary goal. A year later, *Transactions in GIS* published its first issue. At the *First International Conference on Geographic Information Science* (GIScience 2000), a panel on journals that were interested in recruiting papers on research in geographic information science was crowded with editors of sixteen journals (Table 1).

Table 1: Journals represented at the editors' panel at GIScience 2000.

Annals of the AAG
Cartographica
Cartography and Geographic Information Science
Computers and Geosciences
Computers, Environment and Urban Systems
Environment and Planning B
Geographic Information Sciences
Geographical Analysis
Geographical Systems
GeoInformatica
Geomatica
International Journal of Geographical Information Science
Networks and Spatial Economics
Spatial Cognition and Computation
Transactions in GIS
URISA Journal

A study of GIScience journals, published in 2008 [8], started with 121 journals, reduced them to 84 that were deemed more core to GIScience, ultimately focusing on a subset of 54 in an attempt to rank them. This means the core outlets for GIS and GIScience research more than tripled over eight years. More recently, further reputable outlets have appeared, such as the *Journal on Spatial Information Science, ACM Transactions on Algorithms and Systems, Earth Science Informatics*, and *Open Geospatial Data, Software and Standard*.

The landscape of regularly scheduled conferences that cater to geographic information science research has seen less volatility. Launching a new journal may be less involved than sustaining a conference series on a regular basis. The global distribution of the events over the last 20 years highlights over the years a focus on Europe and North America.

In the mid 1990s, the Spatial Data Handling Symposia (SDH) dominated the field of theoretical contributions to GIS (Section 5.5). Autocarto continues as a viable cartographically-oriented supplement to GIScience, and the AAG meetings included selected sessions related to GIS research.

In the early 1990s, two new conferences series adopted the computer scientists' rigor of fully refereed full papers for conferences with the biennial Symposia on *Large Spatial Databases (SSD)* and the *Conference on Spatial Information Theory (COSIT)* (Section 5.2), with proceedings published in Springer's Lectures Notes in Computer Science (LNCS) series and a single-track conference program. Both established themselves as venues for focused work in specific subfields of geographic information science. The annual *ACM Workshops on Geographic Information Systems*, which also had a rigorous reviewing system, attracted only small audiences, however.

In order to provide a forum for a more encompassing perspective of geographic information science research, the biennial conference series on Geographic Information Science, dubbed *GIScience*, started in 2000 (Section 5.1). With the formation of *ACM SIGSPATIAL* (Section 5.4)—a Special Interest Group with a focus on the acquisition, management, and processing of spatially-related information—in the early 2000s, ACM GIS became the SIG's annual meeting of that SIG, drawing large crowds to the presentations of fully refereed papers on systems issues in GIS.

Specialized meetings with a focus on a subfield of GIScience continue on *Spatial Accuracy*, *Spatial Cognition*, *GeoComputation* (Section 5.6), *Web and Wireless GIS*, and *Digital Earth*. Regional GIS meetings (e.g., *GISRUK* in the UK, *AGIT* in Austria, *GeoInfo* in Brazil) complement the conference landscape.

The GIScience Conferences portal giscienceconferences.org is a comprehensive archive of these events.

5.1   GIScience

The first International Conference on Geographic Information Science was held in Savannah (Georgia, USA) in October 2000. It was hosted by NCGIA, UCGIS, and the AAG. This conference aimed to bring together GIScience researchers from a wide variety of disciplines, including cognitive science, computer science, engineering, geography, information science, mathematics, philosophy, psychology, social sciences, and statistics. In order to focus on fundamental GIScience advances papers that deal with applications of Geographic Information Systems were systematically discouraged. This multi-track conference brings around 300 researchers every two years. Since 2002, GIScience has been offering both fully refereed papers as well as extended abstracts that were screened by program committee members. This mixture catered to the different disciplinary preferences in the computational and the geographic fields of GIScience. Paper sessions are usually preceded by workshops and tutorials and followed by a poster session.

5.2   COSIT

The initiation of the series of Conferences on Spatial Information Theory (COSIT) was preceded by the international conference "From Space to Territory: Theories and Methods of Spatio-Temporal Reasoning", which was held in Pisa (Italy) in 1992. It is at times referred as COSIT 0. The first COSIT meeting was held in 1993 as an interdisciplinary biennial European conference on the representation and processing of information about geographic space. COSIT changes its venue every two years, and so far has been held in Australia, Austria, France, Germany, Italy, Switzerland, the UK, and the US. The COSIT conferences cover multiple fields of interests, such as the cognitive aspects of geographic information, the ontology of space, cartography, and behavioral geography. COSIT is a single-track conference. It includes a doctoral colloquium, workshops, tutorials, and poster presentations. Full papers have been published in the LNCS series. Between 100 and 130 researchers participate in COSIT every two years.

5.3   AGILE

The mission of the Association of Geographic Information Laboratories for Europe (AGILE) is to "promote academic teaching and research on GIS at the European level and to stimulate and support networking activities between member laboratories." This mission is notably achieved through an annual research conference that systematically takes place in Europe. AGILE's conference series on Geographic Information Science started in 1998 in Enschede (Netherlands) and clearly became a European reference in the area of GIScience. This conference focuses on research areas related to GIScience, from spatial cognition to geodesign, through health and medical Informatics. Full articles are published in Springer's Lecture Notes in Geoinformation and Cartography, whereas short papers are included in different electronic proceedings.

5.4   ACM SIGSPATIAL

The ACM SIGSPATIAL International Conferences on Advances in Geographic Information Systems is nowadays a series of symposia and workshops. It brings together researchers and developers specialized in GIS and other systems based on geospatial data. ACM SIGSPATIAL clearly emphasizes the technical aspects of geographic information systems (e.g., algorithms, database systems, and geometric computations). This annual conference is typically sponsored by such companies as ESRI, Google, Oracle, and Microsoft. ACM SIGSPATIAL is organized around paper and demo sessions as well as Ph.D. showcases. Topics addressed during ACM SIGSPATIAL cover numerous research areas (e.g., currently Big Spatial Data, GPU and Novel Hardware Solutions, Spatial Data Analytics, and Web and Real-Time Applications). Proceedings are published by ACM.

5.5   Spatial Data Handling

The international symposium on Spatial Data Handling (SDH) began in Zurich (Switzerland) in 1984. It is the key meeting of the International Geographical Union (IGU) Commissions on Geographical Information Science and on Modeling Geographical Systems. SDH is a well-know biennial research forum in the field of GIScience. It brings together geographers, cartographers, computer scientists, and other GIScientists every two years. The latest SDH (16th) was held in Toronto in October 2014 jointly with the ISPRS Technical Commission II Symposium.

5.6   GeoComputation

The GeoComputation meetings started in 1996 in Leeds (UK) as an annual conference centered on geographic analysis, statistics, modeling, and computation algorithms for geospatial data. GeoComputation takes place every alternate year with the GIScience conference since 2002. This is a classic conference where workshops, paper sessions, and poster presentations are proposed.

6   Systematic Analyses of Publications

The development of a scientific community relies on many researchers and key players' contributions to this domain. A past analysis of social and spatial networks aimed at identifying patterns of collaborations among researchers, universities, and institutions in GIScience [2]. The results revealed to what degree individual trajectories (change of affiliations) of researchers impact the formation of a network of the GIScience communities. Citation counts remain a key currency when assessing the impact of research. André Skupin presented a citation analysis of the GIScience literature at the 2008 symposium, which identified Peter Burrough, Mike Goodchild, and Max Egenhofer as the three most-cited researchers in GIScience [36]. These results might be biased, however, because of the bibliographic datasets used in the analysis.

In a complementary analysis, Keßler et al. demonstrated how to semantically annotate and interlink bibliographic datasets using Linked Data technology and enable complex queries [49]. One such query showed that by 2012 only seventeen researchers had published full papers at ACM GIS, COSIT, and GIScience conferences, and another five have met this criterion in the meantime (Table 2). Most of them either have a background in computer science or collaborate with computer scientists.

Table 2: The seventeen researchers who published at least one full paper in each of the three conference series ACM GIS, COSIT, and GIScience by 2012 [52], plus the five who joined this club by 2015.

Benjamin Adams	Krzysztof Janowicz	Andrea Rodríguez
Christophe Claramunt	Christopher B. Jones	John Stell
Matthew P. Dube	Werner Kuhn	Egemen Tanin
Matt Duckham	Lars Kulik	Jan Oliver Wallgrün
Max J. Egenhofer	Ross S. Purves	Stephan Winter
Leila De Floriani	Martin Raubal	Michael Worboys
Andrew U. Frank	Kai-Florian Richter	
Mark Gahegan	Claus Rinner	

In order to complement the previous review and assessment, we employed two analyses based on 2015 data. The first analysis focuses on the most frequently cited articles in key outlet (Section 6.1). The citation searches focused on two journals and two refereed conferences. The second analysis looked at the development of the most prominent terms used in the publications of a conference series over seven consecutive events (Section 6.2).

6.1 Most Frequently Cited Papers in Selected GIScience Outlets

Occasionally, journal editors have published citation counts of their top-rated articles in editorials of their journal [26, 57]. These counts show that typically, publications must have been disseminated for some time before they collect significant numbers of citations. Also, more dated publications have a greater opportunity to collect more citations. While these side effects seem to favor mostly dated work, novel seminal work often rises quickly into the top of the charts.

Here we used Google Scholar to identify the ten most frequently cited articles in five different GIS and GIScience outlets: (1) *The International Journal of Geographical Information Science*, and its predecessor *The International Journal of Geographical Information Systems* (IJGIS), (2) *Transactions in GIS* (TG), (3) the series of conferences on spatial information theory (COSIT), and (4) the GIScience conference series.

Among these four samples, the IJGIS citation counts are the highest (Table 3). IJGIS has the longest history of the four (published since 1987) and the highest frequency. Three of its top-ten papers appeared in 1995, the year of the first Young Scholars Institute. Four of the top cited papers appeared during the pioneering years of geographic information science. Only one of the top ranked papers—a survey article—appeared after 2000. The top-ten articles are mostly methodological, focusing on novel theories and models. IJGIS's most frequently cited article relates to advances in theory, in particular the modeling of spatial relations, one of the five bullets in the NCGIA solicitation [1].

The top citation counts for TG include an article from the TG's inaugural issue in 1996, and most of the remainder from the early 2000s (Table 4). A rapidly rising paper from 2010 relates to the emerging theme of volunteered geographic information, while the most frequently cited paper in TG addresses ontologies, one of the topics that are emerged in recent years (Section 10.1). Unlike in the other samples publications, topics related to the geographies of the information society [80] are more prominently represented in TG's top ten.

The COSIT conference series (Table 5), including the 1992 meeting in Pisa, reveals very high citation counts in its early years (1992–1995), and another peak in 1999. Cognitive, computational, and conceptual work is fairly balanced among the top COSIT papers. Like with the IJGIS, COSIT's most frequently cited paper focuses on the modeling of spatial relations.

The GIScience conference series (Table 6) has the shortest history among the sampled outlets as it started with full papers only in 2002. Nine of its top-ten papers are from the first two LNCS volumes covering Geographic Information Science. Its top ranked article deals with landmarks, a topic that also fared well among the COSIT papers.

Table 3: The ten most frequently cited articles published in the *International Journal of Geographical Information Science/Systems*, based on Google Scholar.

Title	Authors	Year published	Cited by as of August 2015
Point-set topological spatial relations	Egenhofer and Franzosa	1991	1,808
The GARP modelling system: problems and solutions to automated spatial prediction	Stockwell	1999	1,185
Integrating multi-criteria evaluation with geographical information systems	Carver	1991	891
Loose-coupling a cellular automaton model and GIS: long-term urban growth prediction for San Francisco and Washington/Baltimore	Clarke and Gaydos	1998	858
Geographical information science	Goodchild	1992	858
Kriging: a method of interpolation for geographical information systems	Oliver and Webster	1990	784
Integrating geographical information systems and multiple criteria decision-making methods	Jankowski	1995	667
GIS-based multicriteria decision analysis: a survey of the literature	Malczewski	2006	637
An event-based spatiotemporal data model (ESTDM) for temporal analysis of geographical data	Peuquet and Duan	1995	605
Interpolating mean rainfall using thin plate smoothing splines	Hutchinson	1995	551

Table 4: The ten most frequently cited articles published in *Transactions in GIS*, based on Google Scholar.

Title	Authors	Year published	Cited by as of August 2015
Using ontologies for integrated geographic information systems	Fonseca, Egenhofer, Agouris, and Câmara	2002	507
Integrating dynamic environmental models in GIS: the development of a dynamic modelling language	Wesselung, Karssenberg, Burrough , and van Deursen	1996	286
GI science, disasters, and emergency management	Cuttler	2003	226
Critical issues in participatory GIS: deconstructions, reconstructions, and new research directions	Elwood	2003	212
A new GIS-based solar radiation model and its application to photovoltaic assessments	Śúri and Hofierka	2004	202
Quality assessment of the French OpenStreetMap dataset	Girres and Touya	2010	196
On the use of weighted linear combination method in GIS: common and best practice approaches	Malczewski	2000	180
Use of information technology for community empowerment: transforming geographic information systems into community information systems	Ghose	2001	175
Integration of space syntax into GIS: new perspectives for urban morphology	Jiang and Claramunt	2002	176
Technical Note: A GIS-coupled hydrological model system for the watershed assessment of agricultural nonpoint and point sources of pollution	Di Luzio and Srinivasan	2004	165

Table 5: The ten most frequently cited papers published in the proceedings of the *Conference on Spatial Information Theory* (including COSIT 0), based on Google Scholar.

Title	Authors	Year published	Cited by as of August 2015
Using orientation information for qualitative spatial reasoning	Freksa	1992	648
Naive geography	Egenhofer and Mark	1995	600
Cognitive maps, cognitive collages, and spatial mental models	Tversky	1993	526
Scale and multiple psychologies of space	Montello	1993	416
Reasoning about gradual changes of topological relationships	Egenhofer and Al-Taha	1992	399
People manipulate objects (but cultivate fields): beyond the raster-vector debate in GIS	Couclelis	1992	389
The nature of landmarks for real and electronic spaces	Sorrows and Hirtle	1999	358
Network and psychological effects in urban movement	Hillier and Iida	2005	287
Elements of good route directions in familiar and unfamiliar environments	Lovelace, Hegarty, and Montello	1999	285
Pictorial and verbal tools for conveying routes	Tversky and Lee	1999	280

Table 6: The ten most frequently cited papers published in the fully-refereed proceedings of the *GIScience*, conference series based on Google Scholar.

Title	Authors	Year published	Cited by as of August 2015
Enriching wayfinding instructions with local landmarks	Raubal and Winter	2002	381
The SPIRIT spatial search engine: architecture, ontologies and spatial indexing	Jones, Abdelmoty, Finch, and Fu	2004	165
From objects to events: GEM, the geospatial event model	Worboys and Hornsby	2004	164
Project Lachesis: parsing and modeling location histories	Hariharan and Toyama	2004	168
Analyzing relative motion within groups oftrackable moving point objects	Laube and Imfeld	2002	125
Transmitting vector geospatial data across the Internet	Buttenfield	2002	123
Modeling the semantics of geographic categories through conceptual integration	Kuhn	2002	91
GeoVSM: An integrated retrieval model for geographic information	Cai	2002	59
Semi-automatic ontology alignment for geospatial data integration	Cruz, Sunna, and Chaudhry	2004	57
What is the region occupied by a set of points?	Galton and Duckham	2006	57

6.2   The Evolution of Terms in the GIScience Conference Series

The seven LNCS volumes of full papers published biennially in the GIScience meetings since 2002 provide a relatively concise opportunity to examine how specific terms were a focus in these articles of a period of twelve years. The word clouds for the titles and keywords of all full papers in these seven conferences (Figure 2) present some spatialization of the text strings. Authors used consistently the terms *spatial* and *data* in high frequency (although not necessarily in combination). Also *information* and *science* appear prominently throughout the years. Spatial is used consistently more frequently than geographic or geospatial. In recent years, the terms *ontology*, *indoor*, and *dynamic* emerged.

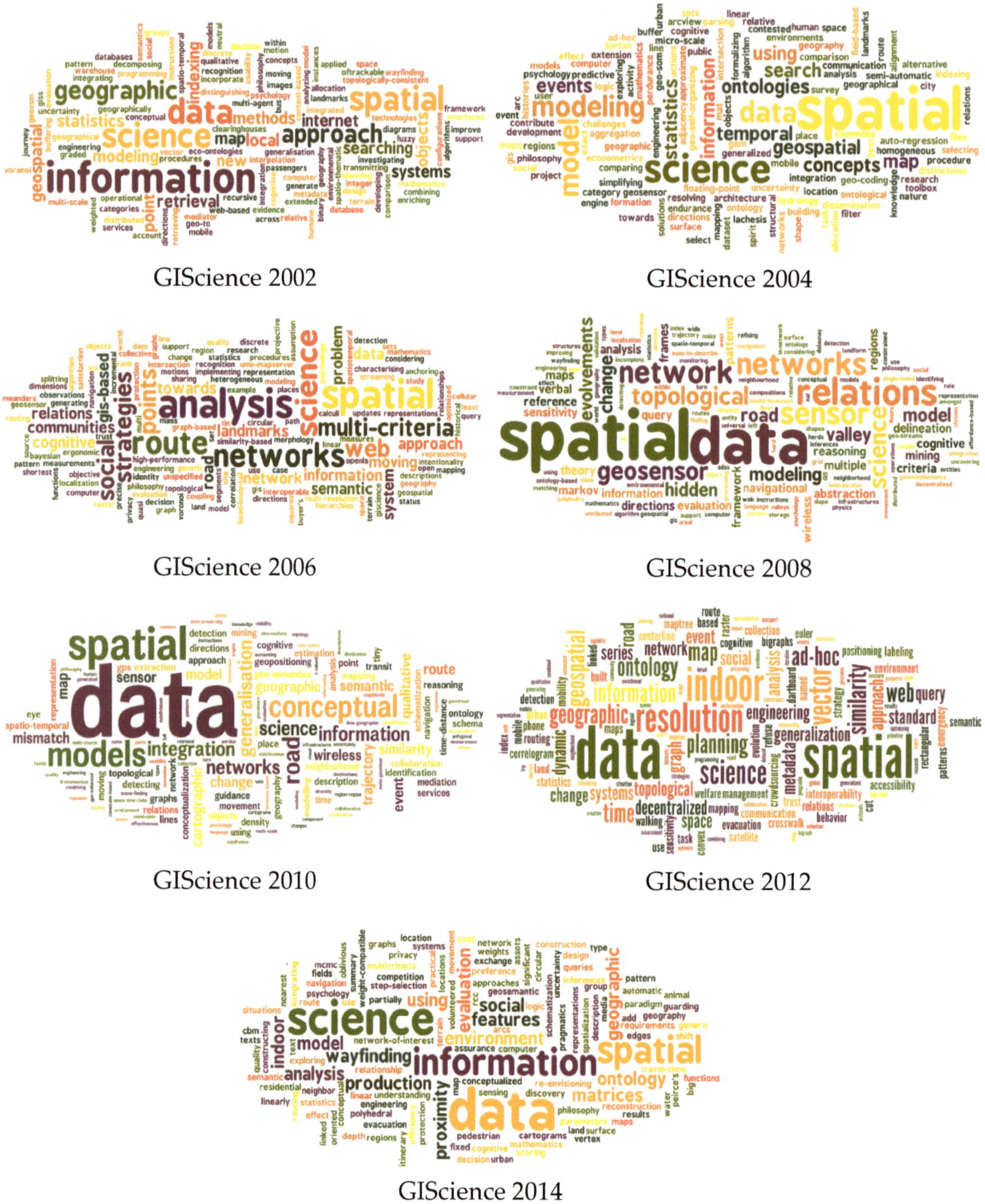

GIScience 2002

GIScience 2004

GIScience 2006

GIScience 2008

GIScience 2010

GIScience 2012

GIScience 2014

Figure 2: Word clouds of full papers of the GIScience conference 2002–2014.

7 Selected Research Highlights

7.1 Advances in Theory

As the core concept of GIScience is to study the *science behind the systems*, great efforts have been made towards advances in geographic information theories, such as models for spatial relations [19, 21, 29, 42, 74] and uncertainty in geographic data and GIS analysis, which exists in the whole process of data acquisition, geographical abstraction, representation, processing and visualization [94]. The studies of uncertainty help researchers and decision makers make better use of complex, multi-dimensional spatial data with regard to quality control that needs special handling, cleaning, and processing. Fisher discussed the critical causes and conceptual models of uncertainty in spatial data with a number of real-world examples [25]. Methods to visualize uncertainty information on maps were proposed and summarized [60, 62]. Longley *et al.* suggested five general dimensions of uncertainty in GIS data [59], namely, attribute accuracy, positional accuracy, logical consistency, completeness and lineage. Achievements in this field advance scientific analysis for geographic data.

7.2 The Cognitive World

UCGIS's research challenge on "Cognition of Geographic Information" investigates the understanding of human perception, memory, reasoning and communication toward spatial phenomena. Four of the former NCGIA research initiatives were dedicated to this theme (I2: Languages of Spatial Relations, I10: Spatiotemporal Reasoning in GIS, I13: User Interfaces for GIS, and I21: Formal Models of the Common Sense Geographic Worlds). In the same vein, the NCGIA's Varenius Project included a specific topic on "Cognitive Models of Geographic Space" [67]. The book *The Cognition of Geographic Space* [53] and the UCGIS research agenda on *Cognition of Geographic Information* [71] provide a clear overview of the main contributions done before the establishment of GIScience in 1992. These reviews notably include the concept of cognitive maps [14], theories of human spatial knowledge [78] and its acquisition from direct experience, languages, and maps [84, 85]. Recent advancements in the area of cognitive GIScience fall into the categories of (1) human factors of GIS, (2) geovisualization, (3) navigation systems, (4) cognitive geo-ontologies, (5) geographic and environmental spatial thinking and memory, and (6) cognitive aspects of geographic education [70].

7.3 The Computational World

Spatial is special [16]. The storage of geographic data needs to handle not only the attributes but also the geometry information. In addition, the rates of geographic data generation were becoming far greater than that of the capabilities for the effective processing, storage, manipulation and analysis of such datasets. Thus new approaches to GIS data models, structures, management, queries and algorithms have been developed in the computational world to advance GIS-based computing and applications [76, 78].

7.4 The Social World

The NSF-funded National Center for Geographic Information and Analysis (NCGIA) helped establish a global standard core curriculum in GIS [39]. This NCGIA Core Curriculum was expanded from a set of hard copy lesson plans to various versions of an on-line shared curriculum, which fuelled the teaching of GIS, both within the discipline as well as the dissemination to many fields that use GIS in their domain analyses. At the same time, the expansion of textbooks at all levels in the field has been extraordinary. An important recent development has been the creation and subsequent improvement of the Geographic Information Science and Technology Body of Knowledge (www.aag.org/bok) [13]. This detailed specification of the core concepts and skill sets necessary for study and proficiency in GIS has influenced the Department of Labor's job specifications and descriptions, and is now supported by substantial online tools and an online ontology (http://gistbok.org/). In recent years the availability of online social networks and VGI outlets has led to a sub-field of GIS that studies social interactions via the Internet and the World Wide Web, using such tools as the geotags in Flickr, place names in tweets, and geocodes in Foursquare, Google+, and others. These activities often involve "big data" applications over millions or billions of records, challenging the limits of traditional desktop GIS [47].

8   Contributions of GIS to other Disciplines

GIS has made contributions to various domains in computer science, such as computational geometry. Geographers, such as at the Census, have been creating tools to process large databases since before the term *computational geometry* was even used in this context. One GIS contribution is to provide particularly hard problems with large datasets that need workable, fast solutions. An example is label placement on maps.

Another contribution within computer science is to the database domain. Spatial data types have been brought into mainstream databases with geospatial data model and query language support (e.g., Geodatabase, Oracle Spatial, PostgreSQL), as well as providing spatial indexing and spatial join methods [44]. However, more research is needed to improve support for network and field data, as well as spatial stream query processing [6, 77, 78].

In addition, the visualization of geographic information also draws a lot of attention from the computer scientists. Research of representation, visualization-computation integration, interfaces, cognitive/usability issues in geovisualization should be addressed in these crosscutting challenges [61]. Efforts have been made to foster a capable and integrated science and engineering community to conquer these challenges.

This influence of GIS is in the tradition of mathematics and physics where the big theoretical advances and conceptual unifications respond to applied problems. For example, in physics, Newton's theory of gravity described and unified both the orbit of the moon and the trajectories of small thrown objects. In GIS, the problem of overlaying two maps with almost coincident edges that cause slivers and rounding errors motivates the study of robust geometric algorithms in Computational Geometry. This crosscutting influence has great potential to continue into the future, when various 2D GIS algorithms may extend into 3D. For instance, overlaying maps in GIS in 2D provides techniques that can lead to overlaying 3D triangulations, a new approach that has benefits in the domains of Computer Aided Design and computational fluid dynamics.

Countless application domains have benefitted from GIS spatial analysis over the past twenty years. The two Big Books [58, 64] offer detailed accounts for many areas, but more recent advancements continue to ignite new cross-fertilizations, some of which we address here.

In regional planning and urban studies, GIS has been widely applied as an analysis and modeling tool to support decision-making [93], and as a simulator for urban growth [9].

Advancements in GIS also enabled GeoDesign as an emerging sub-field of landscape architecture that is supported by spatial decision analytical tools and illustrates using science in design as well as design in science [3]. Also, GIScience brings spatial analysis and statistics, as well as other location intelligence components, to facilitate traditional social science research, such as migration, demographics, crime analysis [49], and spatiotemporal access to urban opportunities [56].

In digital humanities, the development of geographic information retrieval spatial search, and digital gazetteer research has contributed to the new form of geolibrary [38]. The scientometrics community also addressed the importance of geospatial components in the scientific analysis of bibliographic data in order to identify institutional and international research collaboration and citation impact patterns [30].

GIS has led the spatial turn in health studies, in which spatial data, analysis, and global health research will be systematically incorporated for creating new discovery pathways in science [75]. This facilitates opportunities for new interdisciplinary research in which GIScientists to collaborate with medical scientists on research funded by the National Institutes of Health.

9 Changes of Topics in the Research Agenda of Geographic Information Science

Over the past twenty years, the research agenda in geographic information science has gone through a variety of iterations (Table 7), starting with Goodchild's initial list. The University Consortium for Geographic Information Science established in 1996 a list of ten research priorities [89]. The Varenius Project of the National Center for Geographic Information and Analysis [37] concisely formulated three research thrusts—cognitive [67], computational [20], and societal issues [80]. UCGIS updated its research priorities in 2004 and augmented them by another four challenges [63].

Table 7: Major priorities in GIScience research.

Goodchild [34]	Data collection and measurement Data capture Spatial statistics Data modeling and theories of spatial data Data structures, algorithms, and processes Display Analytical tools Institutional, managerial, and ethical issues
UCGIS [89]	*Research Priorities*: Spatial data acquisition and integration Distributed computing Extensions to geographic representations Cognition of geographic information Spatial analysis in a GIS environment Future of the spatial information infrastructure Uncertainty in spatial data Interoperability of geographic information Scale GIS and society
Varenius [37]	Strategic Areas for Geographic Information Science Research Cognitive models of geographic space Computational methods for representing geographic concepts Geographies of the information society
UCGIS [63]	*Research Challenges*: Spatial data acquisition and integration Cognition of geographic information Scale Extension to geographic representations Spatial analysis and modeling in a GIS environment Uncertainty in geographic data and GIS-based analysis The future of the spatial information infrastructure Distributed and mobile computing Interoperability GIS and society: interrelation, integration, and transformation
UCGIS [63]	*Emerging Themes*: Geographic visualization Ontological foundations for GIScience Remotely acquired data and information in GIScience Geospatial data mining and knowledge discovery

The major topics and priorities of GIScience research have changed over time. Some of them disappeared or were less developed than other topics, while new topics have also emerged. It is interesting to see how these research topics have been changed with regards to the twenty-one NCGIA research initiatives (http://www.ncgia.ucsb.edu/research/initiatives.html), which focused on the basic research on geographic analysis utilizing GIS and brought all parts of the GIS community to lay out appropriate research agenda. The topics of data modeling and theories of spatial data seem to be well studied with the achievements of vector, raster, and hybrid models in GIS. The geo-atom model, which represents the association between space-time point and property, can be taken as one of the generic forms for geographic information representations and combine discrete objects and continuous fields [40]. The research on geospatial data structures and modeling are related to the initiatives of "accuracy of spatial databases" and "multiple representations."

10 Topics that Recently Emerged in the GIScience Research Agenda

A series of new topics emerged recently in GIScience. Many of the are technology-driven or aimed at the development of new technologies, such as crowd-based solutions; spatial analysis of social media data; high-performance computing and the cloud; open-source solutions and software mashups; web-based mapping applications; location-based services and mobile computing; embedded solutions (e.g., within GPS routing systems), sensor-networks and their integration into real-time GIS; and integration of spatial and temporal processes into GIS functionality. We elaborate on four research threads (Sections 10.1-10.4) that are currently most prominent.

10.1 Ontologies in GIS

The study of ontologies in GIS bridges the gap between implementation and human conceptual modeling for representing geospatial phenomena and their analysis. Although it was not listed in the original research initiatives, it did play an increasing role in the series of core GIScience conference topics, as shown in the word cloud visualization of GIScience conference topics (Figure 2). Ontology plays an important role in knowledge organization and information integration. The use of ontologies in GIS development has been widely discussed in related research [27, 68], but relatively few studies have addressed the design of the user interface based on semantic integration [55]. Semantic reference systems were suggested for solving semantic interoperability issues, especially to ground geospatial semantics in physical processes and measurements [54]. With the advent of Semantic Web and Linked Data, research on *geospatial semantics* is valuable for GIScientists interested in semantics research as well as knowledge engineers interested in spatiotemporal data exploration [50].

10.2 Volunteered Geographic Information

The emergence of volunteered geographic information [35] and community mapping engaged the fast growth of citizen science. The research on credibility, geoprivacy and other societal implication issues become more and more important as the growth of ubiquitous location awareness devices and crowdsourcing studies on geospatial Web [23, 83].

10.3 Spatial Big Data

Recently, as the context for geographic research evolves from a data-scarce to a data-rich or big-data environment, a *data-driven geography* [66] is emerging that describes large volumes of data with a geospatial component (including structured, semi-structured, and unstructured data) for various aspects of environment and society as is being created by millions of sensors constantly, in a variety of formats such as remotely sensed imagery, GPS logs, maps, blogs, videos, audios, and photos [31]. This trend sheds new light on spatial modeling and geographic knowledge discovery, and brings about innovative developments in GIScience. The topic of *spatial big data* has emerged as one of the research challenges for advancing GIS in a new era.

10.4 CyberGIS

With the advancement of representative cloud computing systems, clusters and grids, high performance computing infrastructures have attracted increasing attention for GIScientists and geographers as a way of solving data-intensive, computing-intensive,and access-intensive geospatial problems [92]. The emerging concept of *CyberGIS,* which synthesizes cyberinfrastructure, spatial analysis, and high-performance computing, provides not only a promising solution to aforementioned geospatial problems as a cloud service but also facilitates a community-driven and participatory approach to achieve scientific breakthroughs across geospatial and other communities [90].

11 Conclusions

Twenty years after the first Young Scholars Summer Institute in Geographic Information, we reviewed the advances in the field. The field is still vibrant and continues to reinvigorate itself with new challenges. Awareness of GIS and Geographic Information Science has increased significantly, and the academic field has matured with a much wider set of outlets for the dissemination of research results. Progress in Geographic Information Science has come through seminal work, but inside and outside of the field, which reflects its interdisciplinary character. Frequently, new technology has required novel approaches to dealing with spatial data and communicating spatial information. Over the last 20 years, the Web and mobile computing have provided unprecedented new opportunities, to which the GIScience research community responded with the development of a plethora of new methods. It is critical that the community is led by the formulation of big intellectual challenges, like those presented in the NCGIA solicitation [1], and the visions of a geographic information science [34], a Naive Geography [22], a Digital Earth [41], a geospatial semantic web [17], or the volunteered geographic information [35].

Acknowledgments

The panelists are grateful to the organizers of the 2015 Vespucci Summer Institute and the Institute's support provided by the US Bureau of the Census and by ESRI. Max Egenhofer's work is partially supported by NSF grants IIS-1016740 and IIS-1527504. Keith Clarke acknowledges support from the National Science Foundation via the I-UCRC program and the Spatio-temporal Innovation Center. Song Gao is supported by a Jack & Laura Dangermond Travel Scholarship and thanks his Ph.D. advisory committee Krzysztof Janowicz, Michael F. Goodchild, and Helen Couclelis from the Department of Geography at the University of California, Santa Barbara. Teriitutea Quesnot is supported by the Social Sciences and Humanities Research Council of Canada (SSHRC) and the Geothink.ca project and he thanks his Ph.D. advisor Stephane Roche from the Geomatics Department at Laval University. Randolph Franklin is supported by the National Science Foundation under Grant No. IIS-1117277. May Yuan's work is partially supported by NSF grant OCI-0941501. David Coleman's research is supported by the Natural Sciences and Engineering Research Council of Canada.

References

[1] ABLER, R. F. The National Science Foundation National Center for Geographic Information and Analysis. International Journal of Geographical Information System 1, 4 (1987) 303–326.

[2] AGARWAL, P., BÉRA, R., AND CLARAMUNT, C. A social and spatial network approach to the investigation of research communities over the World Wide Web. In GIScience 2006: Proceedings of the Fourth International Conference on Geographic Information Science, N. Xiao, M.-P. Kwan, M. Goodchild, S., Eds., (Berlin, 2006), Springer, LNCS vol. 4197, pp. 1–17.

[3] BATTY, M. Defining geodesign (= GIS+ design?). Environment and Planning B: Planning and Design 40, 1 (2013), 1–2.

[4] BERNERS-LEE, T., HENDLER, J., AND LASSILA, O. The semantic web. Scientific American 284, 5 (2001): 28–37.

[5] BUSH, V. As we may think. The Atlantic Monthly. 176, 1 (1945), 101–108.

[6] CÂMARA, G., EGENHOFER, M. J., FERREIRA K., ANDRADE, P., QUEIROZ, G., SANCHEZ A., JONES, J., AND VINHAS, L. Fields as a generic data type for big spatial data. In GIScience 2014: Proceedings of the Eighth International Conference on Geographic Information Science, M. Duckham, E. Pebesma, K. Stewart, and A. Frank, Eds., (Berlin, 2014), Springer, LNCS vol. 8728, pp. 159–172.

[7] CÂMARA, G. Revisiting research agendas in geographic information science, Keynote, Vespucci Week in Advancing GIScience, Bar Harbor, ME, http://www.dpi.inpe.br/gilberto/present/gcamara_vespucci_2015.pptx

[8] CARON, C., ROCHE, S., GOYER, D., AND JATON, A. GIScience journals ranking and evaluation: an international delphi study. Transactions in GIS 12, 3 (2008), 293-321.

[9] CLARKE, K. C., AND GAYDOS. Loose-coupling a cellular automaton model and GIS: long-term urban growth prediction for San Francisco and Washington/Baltimore. International Journal of Geographical Information Science 12, 7 (1998), 699–714.

[10] COPPOCK, J. T., AND RHIND, D. W. The history of GIS. In Geographical Information Systems: Principles and Applications, D.J. Maguire, M.F. Goodchild, and D.W. Rhind, Eds. Longman, 1991, pp. 21–43.

[11] CRAGLIA, M., AND COUCLELIS, H., Eds., Geographic information research: Bridging the Atlantic. Taylor & Francis, 1997.

[12] CRAGLIA, M., AND ONSRUD, H., Eds., Geographic Information Research: Transatlantic Perspectives. CRC Press, 1998.

[13] DIBIASE, D., DEMERS, M., JOHNSON, A., KEMP, K. K., LUCK, A. T., PLEWE, B., AND WENTZ, E. Introducing the first edition of geographic information science and technology body of knowledge. Cartography and Geographic Information Science 34, 2 (2007), 113-120.

[14] DOWNS, R. M., AND STEΛ, D. Cognitive maps and spatial behavior: process and products. In Image and Environment: Cognitive Mapping and Spatial Behavior, R. M. Downs and D. Stea, Eds. Aldine Press, Chicago, pp. 8-26, 1973.

[15]   DUTTON, G. First International Advanced Study Symposium on Topological Data Structures for Geographic Information Systems, Vol.1-8, Harvard University, Cambridge, MA, 1978.

[16]   EGENHOFER, M. J. What's special about spatial?—database requirements for vehicle navigation in geographic space. ACM SIGMOD Record 22, 2 (1993), 398-402.

[17]   EGENHOFER, M. J. Toward the semantic geospatial web. In GIS '02: Proceedings of the 10th ACM International Symposium on Advances in Geographic Information Systems (New York, NY, USA, 2002), ACM Press, pp.1–4.

[18]   EGENHOFER, M. J. A future history of geographic information science (Keynote), GeoInfo 2014, (Campos do Jordão, Brazil, 2014), http://www.spatial.maine.edu/~max/FutureHistory.mov.

[19]   EGENHOFER, M. J., AND FRANZOSA, R. F. Point-set topological spatial relations. International Journal of Geographical Information Systems 5, 2 (1991), 161-174.

[20]   EGENHOFER, M. J., GLASGOW, J., GUNTHER, O., HERRING, J. R., AND PEUQUET, D. J. Progress in computational methods for representing geographical concepts. International Journal of Geographical Information Science 13, 8 (1999), 775-796.

[21]   EGENHOFER, M. J., AND HERRING, J. R. Categorizing binary topological relations between regions, lines, and points in geographic databases, Tech. Rep., Department of Surveying Engineering, University of Maine, 1990.

[22]   EGENHOFER, M. J., AND MARK, D. M. Naive geography. In: COSIT 1995: Proceedings of the International Conference on Spatial Information Theory: A Theoretical Basis for GIS, A. U. Frank and W. Kuhn, Eds. (Berlin, 1995), pp. 1-15.

[23]   ELWOOD, S. Geographic information science: emerging research on the societal implications of the geospatial web. Progress in Human Geography 34, 3, 2010, 349–357.

[24]   ESTRIN, D., GOVINDAN, R., HEIDEMANN, J., AND KUMAR, S. Next century challenges: scalable coordination in sensor networks. In MobiCom '99: Proceedings of the 5th Annual ACM/IEEE International Conference on Mobile Computing and Networking (New York, NY, USA, 1999), ACM Press, pp. 263–270.

[25]   FISHER, P. F. Models of Uncertainty in Spatial Data. Geographical Information Systems 1, (1999), 191–205.

[26]   FISHER, P. F. Citations to the international journal of geographical information systems and science: the first 10 years. International Journal of Geographical Information Science 15 (2001), 1–6.

[27]   FONSECA, F. T., EGENHOFER, M. J., AGOURIS, P., AND CÂMARA, G. Using ontologies for integrated geographic information systems. Transactions in GIS 6, 3 (2002), 231–257.

[28]   FORESMAN, T. W. Ed. The History of Geographic Information Systems: Perspectives from the Pioneers. Prentice Hall, Chicago, 1998.

[29]   FRANK, A. U. Qualitative spatial reasoning about distances and directions in geographic space. Journal of Visual Languages & Computing 3, 4 (1992), 343-371.

[30]   FRENKEN, K., HARDEMAN, S., AND HOEKMAN, J. Spatial scientometrics: towards a cumulative research program. Journal of Informetrics 3, 3 (2009), 222–232.

[31]   GAO, S., LI, L., LI, W., JANOWICZ, K., AND ZHANG, Y. Constructing gazetteers from volunteered big geodata based on Hadoop. Computers, Environment and Urban Systems (in press).

[32]   GOODCHILD, M. F. Spatial Information Science. In Fourth International Symposium on Spatial Data Handling (Zurich, 1990) vol. 1: pp. 3–14.

[33]   GOODCHILD, M. F. Progress on the GIS Research Agenda. In EGIS: Proceedings of the Second European GIS Conference (Utrecht: The Netherlands, 1991), EGIS Foundation, pp. 342–350.

[34]   GOODCHILD, M. F. Geographical information science. International Journal of Geographical Information Systems 6, 1 (1992), 31–45.

[35]   GOODCHILD, M. F. Citizens as sensors: the world of volunteered geography. GeoJournal 69, 4, (2007), 211–221.

[36]   GOODCHILD, M. F. Twenty years of progress: GIScience in 2010. Journal of Spatial Information Science 1, (2010), 3–20.

[37]   GOODCHILD, M. F., EGENHOFER, M. J., KEMP, K. K., MARK, D. M., AND SHEPPARD, E. Introduction to the Varenius project. International Journal of Geographical Information Science 13, 8 (1999), 731-745.

[38]   GOODCHILD, M. F., AND HILL, L. Introduction to digital gazetteer research. International Journal of Geographical Information Science 22, 10 (2008), 1039–1044.

[39]   GOODCHILD, M. F., AND KEMP K. K. NCGIA education activities: the core curriculum and beyond. International Journal of Geographical Information Systems 6, no. 4 (1992): 309-320.

[40]   GOODCHILD, M. F., YUAN, M., AND COVA, T. J. Towards a general theory of geographic representation in GIS. International Journal of Geographical Information Science 21, 3, (2007): 239–260.

[41]   GORE, A. The digital earth: understanding our planet in the 21st century. Australian surveyor 43, 2 (1998), 89–91.

[42]   GOYAL, R., AND EGENHOFER, M. J. The direction-relation matrix: a representation of direction relations for extended spatial objects. UCGIS Annual Assembly and Summer Retreat (Bar Harbor, ME, USA, 1997), http://www.spatial.maine.edu/~max/DRM.pdf.

[43]   GRUBER, T. R. Toward principles for the design of ontologies used for knowledge sharing. International Journal of Human-Computer Studies 43, 5, (1995), 907–928.

[44]   GÜTING, R. H. An introduction to spatial database systems. The VLDB Journal 3, 4, (1994), 357–399.

[45]   GUTTMAN, A. R-trees: A dynamic index structure for spatial searching. In SIGMOD '84: Proceedings of the 1984 ACM SIGMOD International Conference on Management of Data (New York, NY, USA, 1984), ACM Press, pp. 47–57.

[46] HÄGERSTRAAND, T. What about people in regional Science? Papers in Regional Science 24, 1 (1970), 7–24.

[47] HAN, S.Y., TSOU M.-H., AND CLARKE, K. C. Do Global Cities Enable Global Views? Using Twitter to Quantify the Level of Geographical Awareness of US Cities. PloS one 10, 7 (2015).

[48] HAYES, P. J. The naive physics manifesto. In Expert Systems in the Micro-Electronic Age, D. Michie, Ed., Edinburgh University Press, Edinburgh, UK, 1979, pp. 242–270.

[49] HIRSCHFIELD, A., BROWN P., AND TODD, P. GIS and the analysis of spatially-referenced crime data: experiences in Merseyside, UK. International Journal of Geographical Information Systems 9, 2 (1995), 191–210.

[50] JANOWICZ, K., SCHEIDER, S., PEHLE, T., AND HART, G. Geospatial semantics and linked spatio-temporal data—past, present, and future. Semantic Web 3, 4 (2012), 321–332.

[51] JEPSON, W., LIGGETT, R., AND FRIEDMAN, S. Virtual modeling of urban environments. Presence—Teleoperators and Virtual Environments 5, 1 (1995), 72–86.

[52] KESSLER, C., JANOWICZ, K., AND KAUPPINEN, T. Spatial@linkedscience—exploring the research field of GIScience with linked data. In GIScience 2012: Proceedings of the Seventh International Conference on Geographic Information Science, N. Xiao, M.-P. Kwan, M. Goodchild, and S. Shekhar, Eds., (Berlin, 2012), Springer, LNCS vol. 7478, pp. 102–115.

[53] KITCHIN, R., AND M. BLADES. The Cognition of Geographical Space. I. B. Taurus Publishers, 2001.

[54] KUHN, W. Semantic reference systems. International Journal of Geographical Information Science 17, 5 (2003), 405–409.

[55] KUHN, W. Geospatial semantics: why, of what, and how? Journal on Data Semantics III (2005), 1–24.

[56] KWAN, M. P. Gender and individual access to urban opportunities: a study using space–time measures. The Professional Geographer 51, 2 (1999), 210–227.

[57] LEES, B. G. 25 Volumes of the international journal of geographical information science. International Journal of Geographical Information Science 25, 1 (2011), 1–5.

[58] LONGLEY, P. A., GOODCHILD, M. F., MAGUIRE, D. J., AND RHIND, D. W. Geographical Information Systems: Principles, Techniques, Applications and Management. John Wiley & Sons, 1999.

[59] LONGLEY, P. A., GOODCHILD, M. F., MAGUIRE, D. J., AND RHIND, D. W. Geographic Information System and Science. John Wiley & Sons, 2005.

[60] MACEACHREN, A. M. Visualizing uncertain information. Cartographic Perspectives 13 (1992), 10–19.

[61] MACEACHREN, A. M., AND KRAAK, M. J. Research challenges in geovisualization. Cartography and Geographic Information Science 28, 1 (2001), 3–12.

[62] MACEACHREN, A. M., ROBINSON, A., HOPPER, S., GARDNER, S., MURRAY, R., GAHEGAN, M., AND HETZLER, E. Visualizing geospatial information

uncertainty: what we know and what we need to know. Cartography and Geographic Information Science 32, 3 (2005), 139–160.

[63] MCMASTER, R. B., AND USERY, E. L., Eds. A Research Agenda for Geographic Information Science. CRC Press, 2004.

[64] MAGUIRE, D. J., GOODCHILD, M.F., AND RHIND, D. W., Eds., Geographical Information Systems: Principles and Applications, Longman, 1991.

[65] MARK, D. M., CHRISMAN, N., FRANK, A. U., MCHAFFIE, P. H., AND PICKLES, J. The GIS history project. UCGIS Summer Assembly. Bar Harbor, ME, http://www.ncgia.buffalo.edu/gishist/bar_harbor.html, 1997.

[66] MARK, D. M., AND FRANK A. U. Cognitive and Linguistic Aspects of Geographic Space. Kluwer, NATO ASI Series D, Vol. 63, 1992.

[67] MARK, D. M., FREKSA, C., HIRTLE, S. C., LLOYD, R., AND TVERSKY, B. Cognitive models of geographical space. International Journal of Geographical Information Science 13, 8 (1999), 747-774.

[68] MARK, D. M., SMITH, B., EGENHOFER, M. J., AND HIRTLE, S. C. Ontological foundations for geographic information science. In A Research Agenda for Geographic Information Science, R. B. MacMaster and E. L. Usery, Eds. CRC Press, 2004, pp. 335–350.

[69] MILLER, H. J., AND GOODCHILD, M. F. Data-driven geography. GeoJournal 80, 4 (2015), 449–461.

[70] MONTELLO, D. R. Cognitive research in GIScience: recent achievements and future prospects. Geography Compass 3, 5 (2009), 1824-1840.

[71] MONTELLO, D. R., AND FREUNDSCHUH, S. Cognition of geographic information. In A Research Agenda for Geographic Information Science, R. B. MacMaster and E. L. Usery, Eds. CRC Press, 2004, pp. 61–91.

[72] NEGROPONTE, N. Being Digital. Alfred A. Knopf Inc., 1995.

[73] PEUCKER, T. K., FOWLER, R. J., LITTLE, J. J., AND MARK, D. M. The triangulated irregular network. In American Society of Photogrammetry, Digital Terrain Models Symposium (St. Louis, MO, USA, 1978), pp. 516–540.

[74] RANDELL, D. A., CUI, Z, AND COHN, A. G. A spatial logic based on regions and connection. In KR '92: Proceedings of the 3rd International Conference on Principles of Knowledge Representation and Reasoning, B. Nebel, C. Rich, and W. R. Swartout, Eds. (Morgan Kaufmann, 1992), pp. 165-176.

[75] RICHARDSON, D. B., Volkow, N. D., KWAN, M. P., KAPLAN, R., GOODCHILD, M. F., AND CROYLE, R. T. Spatial turn in health research. Science 339, 6126 (2013): 1390.

[76] RIGAUX, P., SCHOLL, M., AND VOISARD, A. Spatial databases: with application to GIS, Morgan Kaufmann, 2001.

[77] RODDICK, J. F., HOEL, E., EGENHOFER, M. J., PAPADIAS, D., AND SALZBERG, B. Spatial, temporal and spatio-temporal databases-hot issues and directions for PhD research. ACM SIGMOD Record 33, 2 (2004), 126–131.

[78] SHEKHAR, S., CHAWLA, S., RAVADA, S., FETTERER, A., LIU, X., AND LU, C. T. Spatial databases—accomplishments and research needs. IEEE Transactions on Knowledge and Data Engineering 11, 1 (1999), 45–55.

[79] SHEKHAR, S., GUNTURI, V., EVANS, M. R., YANG, K. Spatial big-data challenges intersecting mobility and cloud computing. In MobiDE '12: Proceedings of the Eleventh ACM International Workshop on Data Engineering for Wireless and Mobile Access, (New York, USA, 2012), ACM Press, pp. 1–6.

[80] SHEPPARD, E., COUCLELIS, H., GRAHAM, S., HARRINGTON, J. W., AND ONSRUD, H. J. Geographies of the information society. Cognitive models of geographical space. International Journal of Geographical Information Science 13, 8 (1999), 797-823.

[81] SIEGEL, A. W., AND WHITE, S. H. The development of spatial representations of large-scale environments. Advances in Child Development and Behavior 10 (1975), 9-55.

[82] STEFANIDIS, A., AND NITTEL, S., Eds., GeoSensor Networks. CRC Press, 2004.

[83] SUI, D., ELWOOD, S., AND GOODCHILD, M. F., Eds. Crowdsourcing geographic knowledge: volunteered geographic information (VGI) in theory and practice. Springer, New York, 2012.

[84] TAYLOR, H., AND TVERSKY, B. Spatial mental models derived from survey and route descriptions. Journal of Memory and Language 31, 2 (1992), 261-292.

[85] THORNDYKE, P., AND HAYES-ROTH, B. Differences in spatial knowledge acquired from maps and navigation. Cognitive Psychology 14, 4 (1982): 560-589.

[86] TOBLER, W. R. A computer movie simulating urban growth in the Detroit region. Economic Geography 46 (1970), 234–240.

[87] TOMLIN, C. D. Geographic Information Systems and Cartographic Modeling. Prentice-Hall, 1990.

[88] TOMLINSON, R. F. A geographic information system for regional planning. In: G.A. Stewart (ed.) Symposium on Land Evaluation, Commonwealth Scientific and Industrial Research Organization, Melbourne, Australia, 1968.

[89] UCGIS , Research priorities for geographic information science. Cartography and Geographic Information Science 23, 3 (1996), 115-127.

[90] WANG, S., ANSELIN, L., BHADURI, B., CROSBY, C., GOODCHILD, M. F., LIU, Y., AND NYERGES, T. L. CyberGIS software: a synthetic review and integration roadmap. International Journal of Geographical Information Science 27, 11 (2013), 2122–2145.

[91] WANT, R., HOPPER, A., FALÇAO, V., AND GIBBONS, J. (1992) The active badge location system. ACM Transactions on Information Systems 10, 1 (1992), 91–102.

[92] YANG, C., GOODCHILD, M. F., HUANG, Q., NEBERT, D., RA SKIN, R., XU, Y., BAMBACUS, M., AND FAY, D. Spatial cloud computing: how can the geospatial sciences use and help shape cloud computing? International Journal of Digital Earth 4, 4 (2011), 305–329.

[93] YEH, A. G. Urban planning and GIS. In P. A. Longley, M. F. Goodchild, D. J. Maguire, and D. W. Rhind, Eds., John Wiley & Sons, 2005, pp. 877-888.

[94] ZHANG, J., AND GOODCHILD, M. F. Uncertainty in Geographical Information. CRC Press, 2002.

Technological and Societal Influences on GIScience

Stephan Winter[1], Xavier Lopez[2], Francis Harvey[3], Benjamin D. Hennig[4], Myeong-Hun Jeong[5], Timothy Trainor[6], and Sabine Timpf[7]

1 Department of Infrastructure Engineering, The University of Melbourne, Australia
2 Oracle Corp., USA
3 Leibniz-Institute for Regional Geography and University of Leipzig, Germany
4 School of Geography and the Environment, Oxford University, UK
5 CyberGIS Center for Advanced Digital and Spatial Studies, UIUC, USA
6 US Census Bureau, Washington DC, USA
7 Department of Geography, University of Augsburg, Germany

Abstract: This paper highlights and critically reflects on some of the most significant technological and societal influences on GIScience over the last 20 years, or since its inception. For the purpose of this book, which in the following chapters begins to sketch out likely paths for future directions of GIScience, one conclusion of this chapter can be taken for granted: In the next 20 years again significant external factors from technology and society will shape GIScience. This paper summarizes the discussions related a panel on the topic at the 2015 Vespucci Institute. The panel in Bar Harbor, moderated by Stephan Winter, included two invited presentations (by Xavier Lopez and Francis Harvey), and responses by two early career panelists (Benjamin D. Hennig and Myeong-Hun Jeong), and by two senior panelists (Tim Trainor and Sabine Timpf).

Keywords: Geographic information science, spatial information science, spatial information technology, GIS and society, neogeography.

1   Introduction

This chapter highlights and critically reflects on some of the most significant technological and societal influences on GIScience over the last 20 years. The question whether, and if so, to what extent, technological and societal influences have impacted on GIScience, or helped shaping GIScience, is worth putting forward and thinking about in a volume that explores challenges for GIScience in the next 20 years.

The question is a fundamental one. When we consider the last 20 years, it offers us a better vantage of where we stand now and to think about the future. Also, it offers a vantage to reflect on the idea that any science is independent from technological changes or societal impact: Shouldn't science be the quest for underlying truths or laws that sustain any technological and societal influence? A romantic view, but a common view. We know that GIScience – as many other sciences, but in contrast to logic and mathematics – is an empirical science [19, 7, 8, 9], and empiricism is always driven by technological possibility as well as societal interest. This statement can be observed in physics as much as in geography, and thus holds for GIScience as well. Take privacy as an example. Privacy has come up as an issue on the research agenda only recently, and is a social issue: Technology exposes more and more of our movements, activities and thoughts such that a societal response for privacy protection is needed. As much as this response will apply regulations and legal enforcements, it will also rely on new knowledge and proof of techniques such as encryption and location obfuscation. Where we are will always influence what we know.

And yet, also empirical research should reveal over time a body of knowledge that holds over larger periods of time, i.e., is neither bound to particular technology (in times where technologies change so quickly, or innovation rates are exponential, as indicated by Moore's "Law" [14]), nor to a particular constitution of society. Its "laws" are statements which have been and can always be again confirmed by evidence. For example, research on people's ability to deal with vague spatial concepts, such as 'downtown' or 'Mt Everest', or on our ability to represent and reason with this vague knowledge in information systems, should have a considerably longer half-life than on people's views of where 'downtown London', 'the Alps' or 'Mt Everest' are.

Fortunately we know well from geography that different points of view help us gain a better scientific understanding. Critical thinking, instead of taking on one position, considers multiple positions, thus gaining deeper insights and developing more robust solutions. This chapter offers some of these thoughts. It is a result of a panel discussion on technological and societal influences on GIScience at the Vespucci's Summer Institute in GIScience 2015. The discussion was inspired by two presentations, which are summarized here. However, this chapter transforms this discussion by reflecting on the relationship between society, technology and GIScience as perceived today and felt to impact in the future. For the purpose of this book, one conclusion of this chapter can be taken for granted: In the next 20 years again significant technological and societal influences will shape GIScience.

2   The impact of technological change on GIScience

Over 500 years ago printing revolutionized the production (technological change) and accessibility (social change) of maps (Fig. 1). About 50 years ago computers became mature enough to allow people such as McHarg [13], Tomlinson [20], Fisher [6], Chrisman [2] and so many others to think about transforming maps for the information age.

Figure 1: The world first printed map, printed by Lucas Brandis in Lübeck [15].

And just above 20 years ago, with maturing database technology, artificial intelligence and understanding of spatial statistics, the term geographic information science was coined [8]. So while it is no surprise that technological change impacts on a field of knowledge it is still worth considering which technologies that came up over the past 20 years disrupted a linear development, or evolution, of the body of knowledge in GIScience. And while GIScientists have, and will continue to make significant, sometimes even disruptive contributions to society and knowledge, the following list concentrates on the external forces that have taken place in information technology and have influenced GIScience. This list has to stay selective, and thus, subjective.

- Evolving IT Platforms: Over the last 20 years, the underlying IT platforms used in GI Science have evolved profoundly from PCs to workstations, web services to mobile computing; and more recently, to Big Data (Hadoop) platforms hosted on the cloud. These IT platforms have transformed the underlying tools, data and techniques that GIScientists apply day to day.

- Databases: in the mid-1990s, commercial database vendors such as Ingres, Informix, IBM and Oracle introduced spatial databases. By incorporating spatial types, indexes and spatial query into a relational database, it was now possible to incorporate location analysis directly into mainstream IT operational and analytical applications. Over time, spatial databases supported richer spatial types including 2D vectors, to include raster data, planar topology, network topology, TINs, 3D vector models, and point clouds, thereby offering high-performance computing to applications using these spatial types.

- Free & Open Source Software: Young students and researchers of GI Science today are blessed with a rich assortment of mature open source and free GI technology. Products such as Linux, Java, Postgres, GeoTools, and MapServer are mainstream technologies for GI Scientists and professionals alike.

Researchers avail themselves to tools that are easy to acquire, adapt, and use. This was not necessarily the case in the era of commercial desktop GIS. Costs to academic departments have decreased while the range of tooling continues to grow.

• Spatial Data Infrastructures: In the 1990s and 2000s, the policy concept of National Spatial Data Infrastructures (NSDI) took hold throughout hundreds of developed and developing countries. National governments, in particular, began to recognize the importance of sharing public sector investments in spatial data broadly across the society and economy. While the promised infrastructures are late in coming – pieces exist but it is not yet a smooth experience –, key activities such as spatial data standards, public dissemination mandates, capacity building, relaxed intellectual property rights, and inter-organizational coordination have been closely studied and influenced by GI Scientists. Today's political emphasis on 'open data', 'open gov', and 'linked open data' have been enabled by these early efforts to make government spatial data more openly shareable.

• Global Positioning System: In May 2000, the U.S. Air Force eliminated 'selective availability', the intentional degradation of GPS signals for non-military purposes. This measure improved the precision of GPS signals to about 1 meter, making it feasible to develop broad range of precision surveying, navigation, and mobile location services. The adoption of GPS exploded across all sectors creating new research opportunities for understanding crowd-sourced movement of entities; management and analysis of massive streams of location data; and exploring predictive location behavior based on historical tracking patterns.

• Sensor Data Collection: the mainstream use of GPS signals for positioning, coupled with the miniaturization of low cost field sensors, ushered in the rapid use of sensor data collection at the turn of the century. Biologists tracked wildlife, trucking companies tracked and regulated the performance of their trucks, meteorologists used stationary sensors in the land, oceans, and atmosphere to monitor the environment. Sensors have crossed over into mainstream consumer use with the release of wearable devices. GI scientists continue to be advanced users of location-enabled sensors, and innovators in the use of Big Data sensor streams.

• World Wide Web: The most transformative technology innovation of this last period was the advent of the World Wide Web in 1993. While the Web transformed nearly all sectors of computing, it had a profound impact on the GI community. Before the Web, nearly all work done by GI Scientists was constrained to desk- top systems; after the Web most projects and research is oriented to or exploit the networked nature of the Web. The open standards, formats, and protocols introduced by the W3C, resulted in radical restructuring of how information was transported and published across the Internet. The Web enabled the rapid trans- formation from desktop and client/server platforms to Web Services, creating a foundation for a new class of Web mapping services.

• Web Mapping Services: In 1996, Barry Glick, a University of Buffalo Ph.D. graduate working at Donnelley, introduced MapQuest, a ground-breaking Web mapping service using government created data. MapQuest, and later services from AOL, Microsoft, ESRI, and Google provided mainstream Web users with the power to display maps, search features, geocode addresses, generate driving directions via Web browsers. Over time, these platforms enabled businesses, government agencies and citizens the ability to upload and display their own features on background map tiles. The underlying techniques pioneered by Glick and others – caching of map tiles, in-memory-based routing, crowd-sourced mapping – continue to make Web mapping services ubiquitous.

• Mobile Computing: Between 1999 and 2005, the promise of wireless location-based services (LBS) had been widely promoted. Japanese and European wireless providers brought early innovation in delivering powerful GPS enabled 3G phones. A constraint to these early mapping services were the proprietary nature of wireless carrier services that also blocked access to Web content. However, by 2006 US carriers had upgraded their 3G networks coinciding with Apple's release of the iPhone 3G smart phone. This device enabled app developers and users to directly access Web content creating a powerful smart phone platform that delivers GI services to nearly every mobile phone user globally. More recently, mobile application environments using HTML5 show promise in solving device-specific constraints within the World Wide Web.

• Social media & crowd-sourced data: By mid-2000, a new generation of open source Web and mobile computing services re-invented how mapping content was created. Citizen volunteers, field scientists, activists and amateur mappers began to generate and contribute spatial feature content to a new generation of Web mapping services, like Google Maps, OpenStreetMaps, and DBPedia. Michael Goodchild referred to this phenomena as volunteered geographic information [10]. Within a decade, the use of crowd sourced map data has challenged the role of government and commercial sector in the provisioning of vector mapping features.

• Linked Data: Linked Data is an evolution of by Tim Berners Lee's Semantic Web vision first introduced in 1999 [1]. Building on W3C standards and Web services, Linked Data focuses on the large scale integration and reasoning of data collections on the Web. Unfortunately, the dearth of formal ontologies, and immaturity of early RDF and SPARQL specifications slowed uptake of the Semantic Web. By 2011 these standards had matured and the availability of open source linking vocabularies, combined with a vast ecosystem of web mapping services, affords an opportunity to realize Tim Berners Lee's vision of a Web of geospatial features that introduces a potential area of research for GI Science.

• From data scarcity to data deluge: Over time – a process rather than a disruptive event – through spatial data infrastructures, open data initiatives and sensor data collection, GIScience is now confronted with unprecedented data volume, variety, and velocity. These advanced technologies not only bring forth computational innovation such as geospatial optimization and simulation, but also yield actionable insight from big data. GIScience therefore seeks today to resolve problems of dealing with and analyzing heterogeneous spatial data, integrating and synthesizing diverse data sources, and orchestrating collaboration, rather than data collection and pre-processing.

3 Societal influence on GIScience

With advancing geospatial technologies, and not least heavily supported by the increasing possibilities of the Internet, a revived interest in maps can be observed in recent years. Changing technologies and the revival of public interest in mapping led to the emergence of a large number of untrained cartographers producing maps and geographic data visualizations in the online world as well as contributing to the technological advances themselves. Corresponding to the list above, three underlying social outcomes can be identified immediately:

- Location data becomes mainstream: Map consumption and production moves from specialists to enthusiasts, and into everyday life.

- Democratization of tools and services: The combination of open source tools and Web services has broadened the developer base as much as the user base for simple and free mapping tools and apps that create, analyze and exploit spatial data.

- Open data initiatives: While free and public domain spatial data has been a feature of the US GI marketplace for a long time, other countries had different policies and values. But over the last two decades also European mapping and statistical agencies have reversed previous restrictive data dissemination policies and are now promoting open data initiatives for selected datasets. The growing availability of government-sourced open data is now driving a range open data services.

The growing availability of map data has made society aware of the limitations of navigation systems geared towards cars, and sparked a (still growing) interest in derivatives of navigation data for bicycles, pedestrians, public transport, wheelchairs or strollers. The drive towards individualized products not only had an impact on type or precision of geographic data but also engendered research on individual cognitive differences in, e.g., wayfinding or map perception. At the same time, prosumers are starting to contribute to datasets and products [10, 18]. However, as the revived interest in geodesign shows, prosumers have the right to expect more of GIScience, especially in terms of integrating the knowledge gained through analyzing and mapping geodata back into the original disciplines such as landscape design, forestry management or navigation.

In geography such trends have been identified by speaking of a methods-oriented 'neogeography' [21]. Neogeography is understood as combining cartographic techniques and GIS and bridging the gap between users and developers. The more recent field of neocartography[1] is seen even more broadly by looking beyond academia and science. It sees the described developments from the perspective of the cartographic community and does not exclude the untrained amateurs from changes in cartography and GIScience.

---

[1] http://neocartography.icaci.org/

4   Perceived Constants

With the attempts to define GIScience in the literature (e.g., [8, 12, 11]) also attempts to define its research agenda came along. Thus, one approach to think about constants – challenges that have not gone away – is comparing these research agendas over time: an approach that is not new [12], and perhaps too obvious with a 20 year anniversary [11]. Similarly to research agendas also the evolution of a body of knowledge [4] reveals constants, or core elements. Some challenges that we perceive as significant staying with GIScience are listed in the following paragraphs.

Merging disparate data sets on its own is not too difficult. Making them work together seamlessly is more challenging. Tools are beginning to help with that challenge. Data integration means more than joining two or more data sets. Data integration can create new data with new meaning, even if it is not yet clear how this can happen and what are its effects.

Over time, spatial data have been made increasingly useful through organized and disciplined standards (metadata), through helpful tools (vendors and open source software), and through increasing amounts of needed, and in some cases, unintended geospatial data (SDIs, VGI). Also over time, the precision and accuracy of geospatial data has increased. Finer and finer resolutions have provided information that allows data exploration at levels significantly greater than 20 years ago, but this trend has not stopped yet. It begs also the question of data quality, a topic that has been well researched and published, but which has not been applied to most of the data that is used. Simple (and sometimes untrue) statements appear in metadata catalogs, but in the end feature-level data quality is needed to be able to answer that question accurately. Once the "goodness" or fitness for use of the pieces can be determined, then more general statements about the quality of data sets can be determined.

Many phenomena GIScientists study range over several spatial scales. Within geography the range might be smaller than in physics, but it still goes from smaller than a person to the whole world. Although the field is aware of this fact and numerous papers have been written on this topic, there is as yet no definite body of wisdom how to deal with multi-scaled systems or phenomena or how to deal with coupled systems spanning over different levels of scale.

Maps and existing approaches to mapping emphasize static properties or geographic forms, whereas geographers and ecologists are often more interested in mapping the process(es) that produced these forms. While maps (*plural*) help with this endeavor, the field needs to agree upon a handling of (geo-)process in order to get at the original research questions behind the representation. Mathematical and more recently agent-based simulations have brought a notion of process into the field that differs radically from the notion of a geoprocess – however an integration of these two approaches would ultimately benefit GIScience.

Another constant, although an underrated, is ethics. Ethics accounts for the values of our engagements in science and helps formulate our choices, values and responsibilities. In Geographic Information it covers all aspects from what is observed (or not), who has access, for which purposes is it used, and how is it communicated, and concerns system design [16, 17, 3] as much as people building or using these systems [5]. As a constant charge for reflection and responsibility, ethical questions do also change with societal values over time (as they are different between societies).

5   Relationship between technology, society and GIScience

After reflecting on the opening question – the question whether, and if so, to what extent, technological and societal influence have impacted GIScience, or helped shape GIScience, is worth putting forward and thinking about in a volume that explores challenges for GIScience in the next 20 years – it is quite clear that this chapter scratches the surface of many influences, both of technology and society. It answers the opening question positively: the field has been heavily influenced by these external factors. Perhaps what is always going to be most important is not the degree of completeness in the reflections, but the degree they enable GIScience to develop and progress through critical thinking.

Fast technological progress meant that the field had to adapt the handling of geodata/geoinformation to this progress, from static to streams, from scarce to big, from unstructured to structured and semantically rich data, from vector to raster to linked data. Over this progress it seems that the same questions have been asked repeatedly, always within a different data paradigm, and that we were ever adapting algorithms to these new paradigms. The field thus seldom got to the point to ask what the data was being used for and how to support the 'handling' of data in prosumer contexts, illustrating that with technological and societal influences (changes) some questions remain constant.

References

[1]   BERNERS-LEE, T., HENDLER, J., and LASSILA, O. The semantic web. Scientific American 284, 5 (2001), 34–43.

[2]   CHRISMAN, N. Exploring Geographic Information Systems. John Wiley & Sons, New York, 1997.

[3]   CRAMPTON, J. The ethics of GIS. Cartography and Geographic Information Systems 22, 1 (1995), 84–89.

[4]   DIBIASE, D., DEMERS, M. N., JOHNSON, A., KEMP, K., TAYLOR LUCK, A., PLEWE, B., and WENTZ, E. A. Geographic Information Science and Technology Body of Knowledge. Association of American Geographers, Washington, D.C., 2006.

[5]   DIBIASE, D., HARVEY, F., GORANSON, C., and WRIGHT, D. The GIS professional ethics project: Practical ethics for GIS professionals. In Teaching Geographic Information Science and Technology in Higher Education, D. J. Unwin, K. E. Foote, N. J. Tate, and D. DiBiase, Eds. John Wiley and Sons, Chichester, UK, 2012, pp. 199–209.

[6]   FISHER, P. F., and UNWIN, D. Re-presenting GIS. John Wiley & Sons Ltd, Chichester, 2005.

[7]   GOLLEDGE, R. G., and AMEDEO, D. On laws in geography. Annals of the Association of American Geographers 58, 4 (1968), 760–774.

[8]   GOODCHILD, M. F. Geographical information science. International Journal of Geographical Information Systems 6, 1 (1992), 31–45.

[9]   GOODCHILD, M. F. The validity and usefulness of laws in geographic information science and geography. Annals of the Association of the American Geographers 94, 2 (2004), 300–303.

[10]   GOODCHILD, M. F. Citizens as sensors: The world of volunteered geography. GeoJournal 69 (2007), 211–221.

[11]   GOODCHILD, M. F. Twenty years of progress: GIScience in 2010. Journal of Spatial Information Science 1, 1 (2010), 3–20.

[12]   MARK, D. M. Geographic information science: Defining the field. In Foundations of Geographic Information Science, M. Duckham, M. F. Goodchild, and M. F. Worboys, Eds. Taylor & Francis, London, 2003, pp. 3–18.

[13]   MCHARG, I. L. Design with Nature. Natural History Press, Garden City, NY, 1969.

[14]   MOORE, G. E. Cramming more components onto integrated circuits. Electronics Magazine (1965).

[15]   NN. Rudimentum noviciorum sive Chronicarum et historiarum epitome. Lucas Brandis, Lübeck, 1475.

[16]   ONSRUD, H. J. Ethical issues in the use and development of GIS. In Proceedings from GIS/LIS 97 (1997), American Society for Photogrammetry and Remote Sensing and American Congress on Survey and Mapping.

[17]   ONSRUD, H. J., and LOPEZ, X. Intellectual property rights in disseminating digital geographic data, products and services: Conflicts and commonalities among EU and US approaches. In European Geographic Information Infrastructures: Opportunities and Pitfalls, P. A. Burrough and I. Masser, Eds., vol. 5. Taylor and Francis, London, 1998, pp. 153–167.

[18]   RICHTER, K.-F., and WINTER, S. Citizens as database: Conscious ubiquity in data collection. In Symposium on Spatial and Temporal Databases (SSTD), D. Pfoser, Y. Tao, K. Mouratidis, M. Nascimento, M. Mokbel, S. Shekhar, and Y. Huang, Eds., vol. 6849 of Lecture Notes in Computer Science. Springer, Berlin, 2011, pp. 445–448.

[19]   SCHLICK, M. Allgemeine Erkenntnislehre, Vol. 1 of Naturwissenschaftliche Monographien und Lehrbücher. Verlag von Julius Springer, Berlin, 1918.

[20]   TOMLINSON, R. Thinking about GIS: Geographic Information System Planning for Managers. ESRI Press, Redlands, CA, 2003.

[21]   TURNER, A. Introduction to Neogeography. O'Reilly, Sebastopol, CA, 2006.

Emerging Technological Trends likely to Affect GIScience in the Next Twenty Years

Silvia Nittel[1], Lars Bodum[2], Keith C. Clarke[3], Michael Gould[4], Paulo Raposo[5], Jayant Sharma[6], Maria Vasardani[7]

[1]School of Computing and Information Science, University of Maine, Orono, ME 04469, USA
[2]Department of Development and Planning, Aalborg University, DK-9000 Aalborg, Denmark
[3]Department of Geography, UC Santa Barbara, Santa Barbara, CA 93106-4060, USA
[4]ESRI and University Jaume I, Spain
[5]Department of Geography, Pennsylvania State University, PA, USA
[6]Oracle USA Inc., Nashua, NH, USA
[7]The University of Melbourne, Department of Infrastructure Engineering, Parkville 3010, Victoria, Australia

Abstract: This article summarizes the discussions related to the panel "Emerging Technological Trends likely to Affect GIScience in the Next 20 Years" at the 2015 Vespucci Institute. The panel in Bar Harbor, moderated by Silvia Nittel, included two invited presentations (by Michael Gould and Lars Bodum), and responses by two early career panelists (Paulo Raposo and Maria Vasardani), and by two senior panelists (Jayant Sharma and Keith Clarke).

Keywords: Technological future developments, real-time sensor streams, decentralized spatial computations, geovisual analytics, geoprivacy, place, user interfaces.

1   Introduction

The scope of GIScience is understood in different ways; one of its definitions is the "science of geographic information." This includes collecting, modelling, understanding, integrating, analysing, and processing geographic information to understand the geographic world around us better. Mark [41] cites another definition from a US National Science Foundation report: "The basic research field that seeks to redefine geographic concepts and their use in the context of geographic information systems."

Similar to the field of "information science," geographic information science is influenced by novel technological developments that create new types of data; in geographic information science this includes novel technology of observing the world at different levels of detail, the ability to process data at huge throughput, make results immediately available and share it widely.

Novel technologies have contributed to the making of Geographic Information Systems (GIS) since the very beginning. These include raster data processing from remote sensing, geometric data representation and processing from Computer Aided Design (CAD), relational and object/relational database technology from mainstream IT, webmapping borrowed from mainstream web technology, and the list goes on. Novel technology also impacts GIScience and enables or inhibits emerging applications.

In this article, we ask a few fundamental questions and attempt to look into a crystal ball, predicting which technological developments are most likely to change the landscape of GIS by enabling novel applications and usage of geographic information, and therefore, challenge GIScience to develop new scientific concepts, models and theories.

2 Technological Influences

2.1 Networked Sensors and Real-time GIS

The last two decades have seen unprecedented advances in the development of small-scale sensor devices, inexpensive, small computing platforms and almost ubiquitous wireless communication access [44][21]. While the promise of these technological developments still is mostly harvested in research labs under pilot implementations, its widespread use is one of the significant technological influences that is highly likely to affect GIScience, once platforms are robust, inexpensive and easy to program, and training is wide-spread among students. Today, high school students are programming sensor applications with Arduinos [13] to live streaming data [58][16], and the next generation of college students and scientists will be much more familiar with this technology. This technology will allow us to continuously monitor the world, at much higher spatial and temporal densities than ever before. Furthermore, this information is available for processing or simply visualization in near real-time [1, 45], [46]. While the computing platforms will likely be few and widely used [13, 30, 36], similar to computer operating systems today, the powerful and at the same time problematic aspect will be a large variety of commercial-off-the-shelf sensor devices for different purposes. Likely, in this Internet-of-Things [3, 23] and sensor web environment, sensor data streams will be widely shared, however, not all will be collected under uniform circumstances, which will pose new challenges for analysis and integration. Sensor nodes will range from stationary sensors, to autonomous vehicles collecting data to even humans acting as sensors. Applications domains are precision agriculture, environmental event detection, extreme weather, personal safety, personal health, medical applications, energy-efficient living, and many others.

Overall, one can confidently state that in the next 20 years, GIS will become live, and help to answer new questions such as 'what is happening near me in real-time?' or 'what is happening in geographic space in real-time?' [7][14][15]. To truly leverage such a ubiquitous sensing infrastructure, research advances are necessary to enable easy access, sharing, and search of this conglomerate of sensor data based on time, space, parameter(s) and higher-level information such as events and patterns [71]. As WWW technology [6] once enabled a wave of unprecedented information sharing, the creation of an interoperability platform with open source software will enable a similar potential for geographic information, however, also not without drawbacks (e.g. geoprivacy, see Section 2.4). Being able to observe different kinds of new phenomena in geographic space in real-time requires advanced concepts of space-time theory, and software needs to be able to deal with continuous time. Novel algorithms for existing spatio-temporal methods are necessary that can cope with the scale and velocity of these sensor data streams [45]; this will affect analysis, visualization as well as our reaction to the available information.

2.2   Autonomous Data Collection and Analysis

Related to real-time sensor data collection is the special domain of vehicles that autonomously move in space, may it be on the ground, in the air or in the water. Several types of autonomous and semi-autonomous vehicles are already in frequent use, such as drones, unmanned aerial vehicles (UAVs), and self-driving cars. Each of these machines collects data about its constantly-changing surroundings, and also interprets these in real-time to make navigation decisions. Many collect data for later analysis. Two of the most pronounced changes to GIScience we expect to see in the near future are an increase in the *volume* of data collected via autonomously-navigating vehicles, and an increased research focus on *automated and distributed interpretation* of spatial data. Most data will likely continue to be collected by remote sensors on these vehicles. Geo-computation, using immediately collected data onboard UAVs and the like, will likely prompt a bridging of GIS, remote sensing, photogrammetric, and signal processing methods [26]. An increasing research emphasis on how computer vision methods apply directly to geographic information seems likely in the years to come. Promising methods in use today include geographic object-based image analysis [7], making use of techniques from throughout remote sensing and computer vision [67]. The use of decentralized computing [17, 63] will likely increase, in part as a means to process very large data sets, but also in part to manage distributed collection, storage, and dissemination, and provide localized, and immediate reaction to events. Processing these data will require automated abstraction and generalization [9].

2.3   People as Sensors and Intuitive Geographic Information Systems

In the last decade, we have seen large contributions from people to data observation and collection through the rising availability of location-aware technology and smartphones. Volunteer GIS and Citizen Science project make types of data collection feasible that are difficult to collect with automated mechanisms, such as sensors [49]. However, the promise of volunteered information across all sectors of the geographic information economy also mandates the *intuitive* geographic information capture, exchange and reasoning as emerging fields of research. Such information is especially crucial in emergency management, but also in other functions that depend on the interaction between people and their 'smart' environment, such as using a smartphone application, performing a general internet search, or talking to an autonomous vehicle. Place is a central concept in these spatially enabled environments, as the available digital networks, mobility, and modern geo-communication techniques are changing the way people talk about places and interact. Recent approaches to the modern concept of 'digital environments' are advocating the place-based networks instead of the areal spaces, especially when it comes to cities [4, 11]. These ideas also challenge the more traditional spatial models of GIS with the layer-cake view of the world, in favor of a networked cupcakes view of a place-based GIS [55].

When it comes to urban intelligence, [4] identify many key contributors—networks, movements and sensors amongst others. It is apparent then that geospatial intelligence is a primary resource and GIScience can aid in the development of social infrastructure and the engagement of non-experts in spatial practices. Mobile positioning technologies can be customized to the individual and provide more user-friendly, intuitive interfaces (see Section 2.6). Accordingly, methods that validate information acquired using these technologies and ensure their integration with other geographic data sources are necessary [25]. GIScience will also play a major role when it comes to supporting the digital dimension of smart environments. In the digital city model, for example, there are multiple, interconnected components of the city's infrastructure, such as transportation or cadastral, that will require open access to multiple technological platforms that can address the needs of citizens and other private or public companies and organizations [54]. Finally, geo-collaboration and public participation GIS are aspects of GIScience that can cement the participative dimension of a digital, smart environment [28].

As mentioned before, modern digital spaces will be comprised more of networks of places, where places are connected through information fluidity [42]. In these environments, citizens are involved in the production of place-based information, which is self-staged by people's words and perception. It is important then, that the notion of place is somehow formalized, in order to make it available to GIScience theories and computing systems, as well as for scientific reasoning [69]. Its formalization will improve urban intelligence by allowing participants to decrypt senses of places and their complex relationships, on both physical and digital levels. [33] discusses many of the foundational concepts, such as ontologies related to building platial concepts in GIScience. However, the power that the concept of place has when it comes to describing and understanding societal dynamics comes at the price of bigger complexity when trying to formalize it, especially due to its inherent vagueness (e.g. boundaries, description, localization), more so in digital environments [29].

2.4   Privacy Needs and Control over Data

The GIScience of 20 years ago favoured spatially aggregated data (e.g. into census tracts and counties), samples of points and other distributions (e.g. well data, weather stations, pixels) and standard statistical analytical methods based on the Gaussian assumptions of lack of autocorrelation and sample independence. Today, data are "big," characterized by volume, variety and velocity. This is particularly true of web service data, location based services and social media. This amount of data is expected to multiply, with the exploding use of automated, real-time data collection to be expected in the next 20 years. Today's typical datasets may have millions of records, be instantaneous in time and include metric and non-metric information, such as text, links and similarity measures. Positional and temporal accuracy and precision are unprecedented, largely because of the success of the various Global Navigation Satellite Systems, particularly the Global Positioning System, and the ubiquity of mobile devices that make use of them, such as smartphones. A consequence of this trend is that individual records can now be associated with unique personal identifying information such as social security numbers, street addresses or precise locations and times. Sensitive geographical information can easily be "reverse geocoded," meaning that malicious, commercial and law enforcement users can now integrate data to points, to individuals and their behavior [2]. This is particularly critical in health records, criminal and law enforcement records, when sites need protection (such as children's schools and homes, endangered species breeding sites, or archaeological remains), or when revealing individual locations would be gross violations of personal privacy [18].

In parallel, GIScience has seen a change in the issue of ownership of geospatial information. Twenty years ago, many geographical datasets remained proprietary-- copyrights and patents protected the creators of geographic information. In the United States, important copyright rulings established that facts about the surface of the earth, as represented on maps, were not subject to copyright, only the particular form of organization of their means of management or display. Over time, federal and increasingly state and local governments have used the Freedom of Information Act and the Internet to make public data universally accessible, and not insignificantly to also reduce the costs of distribution to essentially zero. While some detailed street and navigational databases remain protected by patent and copyright, increasingly there is an expectation that such data are also a public good that should be universally available. The growth of online mapping services, volunteered geographic information datasets such as openstreetmap.org and Wikimapia, and government data redistribution clearing houses such as data.gov and geoplatform.gov; plus the placement of huge amounts of satellite data into the public domain (e.g. Landsat) and the rise of Google maps, Apple maps, Here, and other services increasingly mean that people use such open data, almost regardless of ownership. Increasingly, such data are contributed to the public domain, along with the tools to handle and transform them into useful information. The expectation is that in the future most, if not all, detailed geographic information will be in the public domain, accurate and documented, searchable and linked, and that acquisition of such data will be effortless and free.

The ubiquity of such data, however, will place the onus of future GIScience on the creation and application of policy and tools for the protection of personal geospatial privacy. The current state of affairs provides no such provision, and has been discussed with some alarm [14, 43]. The status and issues surrounding geoprivacy today are summarized by [51] and [61]. Some recent political reports have examined the implications of big data for privacy, in particular the report "Big Data: Seizing Opportunities, Preserving Values." This report was the first to acknowledge that big data can "create an asymmetry of power" between data providers and users, and that software now can easily reverse data anonymity. The report reviews the pertinent legal history and key rulings and laws and provides case studies in health care, education, homeland security, and law enforcement. The implications of this report are that the U.S. Constitution's Fourth amendment protects people, not places; that people are entitled to a "reasonable expectation of privacy," that there is a need to protect against insider threats, and that consumers have little understanding of the potential loss of privacy, individual and collective. As GIScience moves into the future, these legal implications beg more attention be paid to the legalities of geospatial data and privacy. Current methods of masking and aggregation cannot always protect privacy [5, 20, 34, 35, 48] and better technical means will be necessary. A current focus on the imagery collected from small drones and UAVs has become the issue of today, but this is really only the tip of the iceberg as far as the future is concerned.

GIScience will need to establish principles for determining geospatial privacy rights. Critical to understanding the difference behind geospatial data is that its value depends almost entirely on use. Malicious, illegal or unintended negative consequences for individual privacy are possible once such data are aggregated over time and space. Currently, policy on data privacy has been focused on the consent of the user at the point of data collection. However, there is a spectrum of uses just as there is a spectrum of personal attitudes toward consent for each of these uses. The "who" and the "how" of these unintended uses are important: *who* needs consent to use the data beyond its original purpose and *how* will it be used. A first principle of fair geospatial privacy is that individual consent is necessary from each individual to the data user for each and every additional use beyond that for which the data was acquired. Secondly, geospatial data should be used with respect for the rights, dignity, personally identifiable information and identity of the person to whom the data relates—geospatial applications should respect basic human rights. This should include the constitutionally recognized rights of privacy within one's home or place of residence. Thirdly, it should be recognized that there are tangible benefits, both to individuals, organizations and society, of making available personal geospatial information—the right to enjoy these benefits should be protected against exploitation, illegal activity, and unwarranted denial. The right of the individual to make consensual trade-offs for surrendering privacy in exchange for information benefits should not be denied to that individual.

2.5   Geovisual Analytics

We expect that the field of geovisualization and geovisual analytics will be significantly influenced by large and real-time geographic data and the development of inexpensive, novel user interfaces such as head mounted displays.

2.5.1   Geovisual Analytics

Much of the GIS community has focused on geovisualization and geovisual analytics since their introduction [40]. While in other domains such business visual analytics has become a new powerful way to integrate different ways of visualization and statistical analytics to understand data, visualization has always been an integral part of dealing with geographic data. Until recently, geovisualization applications developed throughout academia and private industry have generally focused on large datasets describing past or recent events. A few frequent application areas have been in *public health* [31, 38, 53], *disaster relief* [10, 65], *demographic analysis* [60, 62], *environmental monitoring and climate change* [39, 56], and *data-rich "smart cities"* [19, 57]. The near future is likely to see interest in using geovisualization techniques to analyze these and other themes increase. An intensifying interest in geovisualization seems particularly likely given the increasing ubiquity of sensors and the volumes of data these produce. Geovisualizations of real-time data will probably become more commonplace, particularly in time-sensitive scenarios such as disaster relief, and applications for which real-time data are readily available, such as social media [66] or news events [50].

2.5.2   Novel Geographic Information User Interfaces

Throughout the history of Geographic Information Science, a number of different computer interfaces have been tested and tried out for the visualization of geographic information. Only a few have been successful enough to deliver a result for users that were qualitatively decent. Even though we have lived through almost 50 years of technological development since the first geographic information systems were introduced, the preferable interface is still the 2D flat monitor. First generations came in monochrome versions. In early 1980's the first personal computers were produced by IBM and others and the hardware included a Colour Graphics Adapter (CGA) that were able to show 4 colours simultaneously out of a palette of 16 colours. Combining these developments with the immediate fame of the computer mouse and by introducing real graphical user interfaces in the operating systems of personal computing in mid 1980's, this solution made the way for a real success for the 3:4 ratio computer monitor. With a few changes to the specs, such as the aspect ratio and incredible improvements in the resolution, the speed of the rendering and the number of colours, this interface is still the predominant for most of the geovisualization done today [47]. But what will happen in the future? Will we see alternative computer interfaces get a larger share of the market or will we continue to rely on the flat monitor? Among a long list of more or less successful technologies there are a few interesting technologies that will be discussed in this chapter.

- Stereoscopy
- 3D displays
- Head Mounted Displays, projected walls and CAVEs (VR)
- Mobile screens (touch sensitive screens)

2.5.3   Stereoscopy

Stereoscopy is an old technology that has shown to be very useful for geovisualization purposes. Stereoscopy is the name of the 3D effects that are created when specific technology delivers two different images that present the correct perspective for each eye. These 3D effects can be simulated with modern technologies either by use of active or passive stereo. Active stereo makes use of an emitter that synchronizes the output from the graphics processing unit (GPU) with active shutter-glasses that open and close with a frequency of 60 Hz or more. For professional use, this is still the most popular technology and very reliable to integrate with high performance computer technology. Passive stereo works with polarized glasses where the computer also processes two images but with different polarization so that each eye can focus on the image with the correct perspective. The passive stereo method has gained immense popularity since 2005 after the movie industry adapted the technology and made it a part of their regular market. Stereoscopy will continue to be an important technology for geovisualization purposes, but it will still require specific hardware at both ends (GPUs and glasses) and therefore the use will probably still be limited to image-related purposes. In many of the solutions mentioned later in this chapter, stereoscopy is an important element of the technology in use.

2.5.4   3D Displays

The first few years after 2000 brought out a range of manufacturers of computer displays that came up with new technologies simulating 3D viewing without the use of glasses. This technological development was made possible because of the potential for a real break-through of these solutions in normal TV sets. Even though many producers of 3D TVs made huge investments in this field, the general breakthrough in the market never came. The technology used in the different display types varies from holographic imaging technology to the more common integral imaging technology. There is still a lot of research in this field and 3D displays are still being developed, but it seems to be very difficult to make it into a commercial success. Very few applications within geovisualization have been developed for this type of interface [22].

2.5.5   Head Mounted Displays, projected walls and CAVEs (VR)

The combination of geovisualization and Head Mounted Displays (HMD) goes back to the very early years of the developments within Virtual Reality (VR). Even though the term VR was coined much earlier and there were a few experimental success stories such as I. Sutherlands: The Sword of Damocles [64], the real break-through of the technology came much later. Between Sutherlands' first HMD in 1968 and the generation of commercial VR solutions in the beginning of 1990s there were a few interesting projects that promoted new computer interfaces for the use within geovisualization. The Aspen Movie Map from 1977 was the very first example of a hypermap that showed the possibilities of a videodisc delivering video to the user with reference to a position on the map [37]. Even though the project was ground-breaking in many ways, the interface to the geographic visualisation was still made available through 2D monitors.

From 1990 the scientific computer workstations began to be so powerful that it was possible to process several simultaneous images for projected walls. That made the way for new computer interfaces such as the Panorama with three overlapping and digitally stitched images or the famous CAVE from the Electronic Visualization Laboratory (EVL) at University of Illinois at Chicago [12]. The hardware solutions were in some of the applications combined with stereoscopic vision. These immersive VR interfaces – even though they were very expensive – became very popular for a period in history from 1995 until around 2005. In the same period, some of the important scientific progress of geovisualization in VR was made around the world. One of the more prestigious examples came from a team of researchers in Delft, NL, led by Edward Verbree [32, 70]. Another interesting application made possible by the projected walls principle was the GeoWall also created at University of Illinois at Chicago [27]. With a stereoscopic back-projection the wall was used as interface for both regular desktop GIS applications and with more sophisticated high resolution digital earth applications such as Google Earth from Google or iView3D from IVS.

An interesting side-kick to the development of projected interfaces is the tangible solutions. The most prominent applications of this type of interface were created by the Tangible Media Group at Media Lab, MIT, led by Hiroshi Ishii. One of the most interesting cases was an application called Urp for urban planning purposes, where changes in the urban terrain model were made with the bare hands and by moving small objects – creating virtual shadows and indicating planning zones and other demarcations [68].

In later years (2013-2015) new hardware solutions have been launched and promoted as possible new interfaces to geovisualization. These are developed with a focus on gaming and are sold directly to end-users. It is still too early to say what kind of impact these cheaper VR solutions will have on the geovisualization domain. Very few tests have been made so far and it still seems like the traditional VR problems occur also with these cheaper products. Among the problems are the difficulties to establish the correct orientation due to the limited viewing angle, and simulation sickness after using the HMD. In both cases the effects caused by these problems have very different individual influences on the users. It means that two users can have two very different experiences using the HMD [27].

2.5.6   Mobile Screens (touch sensitive screens)

More focus will be on mobile solutions in the future. Both tablets and phones will become both larger in size and resolution. Tablets will probably attract more attention because they fit the demands of traditional geovisualization users. They will be launched in larger models (>12" and retina) and the direct interface through touch sensitive screens will make it possible to add more functionality to the applications and change the way you manipulate a geovisualization directly or indirectly with your hands or with a stylus. This will be very interesting for developers of geovisualization applications because of the potential larger markets [15]. Such interfaces can also accommodate modes frequently used by people when trying to communicate geographic information, such as sketch elements drawn on a base-map, called sketch-maps [8], and accompanying natural language descriptions [59].

2.5.7   The Future for computer interfaces for geovisualization

Considerable amounts of resources will still be invested into the research field of alternative computer interfaces for geovisualization in the coming years. Especially the distributed systems that works in combination with a tablet or a smartphone will have a real possibility to change the game as it looks today. The easy access to developer tools and the open APIs means that more developers will contribute to the growth in the number of applications. Larger tablets (> 12") from the hardware producers with new input devices (stylus) and advanced touch sensitivity will make the way for new geovisualization applications.

The problems related to the use of stereoscopic HMDs – even those launched as cheaper alternatives these years – seem to remain unsolved and prevent a real breakthrough of VR interface to the geovisualization applications. It seems to be difficult, amounting almost to impossible, to avoid the physical impacts such as simulation sickness from very close focusing and stereoscopic adjustments to the human eyesight. If these effects will not be eliminated, then a break-through of this technology will not take place at all.

3   Conclusions

In this article, we have attempted to predict which technological developments are most likely to change the landscape of GIS and challenge GIScience to develop new scientific concepts, models and theories in the next 20 years. Naturally, the future is notoriously difficult to predict, and surprise technological inventions might steer the field into a different direction. However, we are fairly confident to say that we see several likely technologies, that will influence GIScience fundamentally: there are sensors and smart environments, autonomous data collection and in-place processing, availability and searchability of geographic information and the significant problem of geoprivacy, and simpler, more intuitive human computer interfaces for GIS.

References

[1]   Ali, M. et al.: Real-time spatio-temporal analytics using Microsoft StreamInsight. Proceedings of the 18th SIGSPATIAL International Conference on Advances in Geographic Information Systems - GIS '10. pp. 542–543 ACM Press, New York, New York, USA (2010).

[2]   Armstrong, M.P. et al.: Geographically masking health data to preserve confidentiality. Stat. Med. 18, 5, 497–525 (1999).

[3]   Atzori, L. et al.: The Internet of Things: A survey. Comput. Networks. 54, 15, 2787–2805 (2010).

[4]   Batty, M. et al.: Smart cities of the future. Eur. Phys. J. Spec. Top. 214, 1, 481–518 (2012).

[5]   Beresford, A.R., Stajano, F.: Location privacy in pervasive computing. IEEE Pervasive Comput. 2, 1, 46–55 (2003).

[6]   Berners-Lee, T., Connolly, D.: Hypertext Markup Language (HTML), http://tools.ietf.org/html/draft-ietf-iiir-html-00.

[7]   Blaschke, T.: Object based image analysis for remote sensing. ISPRS J. Photogramm. Remote Sens. 65, 1, 2–16 (2010).

[8]   Boschmann, E.E., Cubbon, E.: Sketch Maps and Qualitative GIS: Using Cartographies of Individual Spatial Narratives in Geographic Research. Prof. Geogr. 66, 2, 236–248 (2014).

[9]   Burghardt, D. et al.: Abstracting Geographic Information in a Data Rich World:Methodologies and Applications of Map Generalisation. Springer (2012).

[10]   Charvat, K. et al.: Spatial Data Infrastructure and Geovisualization in Emergency Managemento Title. In: Pasman, H.J. and Kirillov, I.A. (eds.) Resilience of Cities to Terrorist and other Threats. pp. 443–473 Springer (2008).

[11]   Chourabi, H. et al.: Understanding smart cities: An integrative framework. 45th Hawaii International Conference on System Science (HICSS), 2012. pp. 2289–2297 IEEE, Maui, HI (2012).

[12]   Cruz-Neira, C. et al.: Surround-screen projection-based virtual reality: the design and implementation of the CAVE. Proc. SIGGRAPH '93. 135–142 (1993).

[13]   D'Ausilio, A.: Arduino: A low-cost multipurpose lab equipment, (2012).

[14]   Dobson, J.E., Fisher, P.F.: Geoslavery. IEEE Technol. Soc. Mag. 22, 1, (2003).

[15]   Doellner, J.: Service-Oriented Geovisualization for Geodesign. Proceedings of Digital Landscape Architecture. pp. 43–45 Herbert Wichmann Verlag, VDE VERLAG GMBH, Zurich, Switzerland (2014).

[16]   Duckham, M. et al.: Challenges to Using Decentralized Spatial Algorithms in the Field: The RISERnet Geosensor Network Case Study. SIGSPATIAL Newletter, Spec. Issue "Geosensor Networks." 7, 2, 14–21 (2015).

[17]   Duckham, M.: Decentralized Spatial Computing; Foundations of Geosensor Networks. Springer (2013).

[18]   Duckham, M., Kulik, L.: Location privacy and location-aware computing. In: Drummond, J. et al. (eds.) Dynamic & mobile GIS: Investigating change in space and time. pp. 34–51 CRC Press, Inc., Boca Raton, FL, USA (2006).

[19]   Dykes, J. et al.: Editorial - GeoVisualization and the Digital City, (2010).

[20]   El Emam, K., Dankar, F.K.: Protecting Privacy Using k-Anonymity. J. Am. Med. Informatics Assoc. 15, 5, 627–637 (2008).

[21]   Estrin, D. et al.: Instrumenting the world with wireless sensor networks. 2001 IEEE International Conference on Acoustics, Speech, and Signal Processing, (ICASSP '01). pp. 2033 – 2036 IEEE Computer Society, Salt Lake City, UT , USA (2001).

[22] Fattal, D. et al.: A multi-directional backlight for a wide-angle, glasses-free three-dimensional display. Nature. 495, 348–351 (2013).

[23] Gershenfeld, N. et al.: The Internet of things. Sci. Am. 291, 4, 76–81 (2004).

[24] Gong, J. et al.: Real-time GIS data model and sensor web service platform for environmental data management. Int. J. Health Geogr. 14, 2, (2015).

[25] Goodchild, M.F., Li, L.: Assuring the quality of volunteered geographic information. Spat. Stat. 1, 110–120 (2012).

[26] Granshaw, S.I., Fraser, C.S.: Editorial: Computer Vision and Photogrammetry: Interaction or Introspection? Photogramm. Rec. 30, 149, 3–7 (2015).

[27] Henriksen, S., Midtbø, T.: Investigation of Map Orientation by the Use of Low-Cost Virtual Reality Equipment. In: Sluter, C.R. et al. (eds.) ies Lecture Notes in Geoinformation and Cartography. pp. 75–88 Springer (2015).

[28] Johnson, P.A., Sieber, R.E.: Situating the Adoption of VGI by Government. In: Sui, D. et al. (eds.) Crowdsourcing Geographic Knowledge. pp. 65–81 Springer Netherlands (2013).

[29] Jones, C.B. et al.: Modelling vague places with knowledge from the Web. Int. J. Geogr. Inf. Sci. 22, 10, 1045–1065 (2008).

[30] Kahn, J.M. et al.: Next Century Challenges : Mobile Networking for " Smart Dust ." Proceedings of the 5th annual ACM/IEEE international conference on Mobile computing and networking. pp. 271–278 ACM (1999).

[31] Khan, K. et al.: Spread of a novel influenza A (H1N1) virus via global airline transportation., (2009).

[32] Kraak, M.-J. et al.: Virtual Reality, The New 3-D Interface for Geographical Information Systems. In: Câmara, A.S. and Raper, J. (eds.) Spatial Multimedia and Virtual Reality. pp. 131–136 Taylor & Francis (1999).

[33] Kuhn, W.: Core concepts of spatial information for transdisciplinary research. Int. J. Geogr. Inf. Sci. 26, 12, 2267–2276 (2012).

[34] Kwan, M.-P. et al.: Protection of Geoprivacy and Accuracy of Spatial Information: How Effective Are Geographical Masks?, (2004).

[35] Leitner, M., Curtis, A.: A first step towards a framework for presenting the location of confidential point data on maps—results of an empirical perceptual study. Int. J. Geogr. Inf. Sci. 20, 7, 813–822 (2006).

[36] Libelium: Waspmote, http://www.libelium.com/products/waspmote/.

[37] Lippman, A.: Movie-maps: An application of the optical videodisc to computer graphics. ACM SIGGRAPH Comput. Graph. 14, 3, 32–42 (1980).

[38] Luan, H., Law, J.: Web GIS-Based Public Health Surveillance Systems: A Systematic Review. ISPRS Int. J. Geo-Information. 3, 2, 481–506 (2014).

[39] Luo, W. et al.: Web-Based Visualization of the Global Change Assessment Model. Workshop on Visualisation in Environmental Sciences (EnvirVis). , Cagliari, Italy (2015).

[40] MacEachren, A.M.: How Maps Work: Representation, Visualization and Design. (1995).

[41] Mark, D.: Geographic Information Science: Critical issues in an emerging crossdisciplinary research domain. J. Urban Reg. Inf. Syst. Assoc. 12, 1, 45–54 (2000).

[42] Mitchell, W.J.: City of Bits. MIT Press (1996).

[43] Monmonier, M.: Spying with Maps: Surveillance Technologies and the Future of Privacy. University of Chicago Press, Chicago (2002).

[44] Nittel, S.: A survey of geosensor networks: Advances in dynamic environmental monitoring. Sensors. 9, 7, 5664–5678 (2009).

[45] Nittel, S.: Real-time Sensor Data Streams. SIGSPATIAL Newletter, Spec. Issue "Geosensor Networks." 7, 2, 22–28 (2015).

[46] Nittel, S. et al.: Real-time Spatial Interpolation of Continuous Phenomena using Mobile Sensor Data Streams. SIGSPATIAL'12: Proceedings of International Conference on Advances in Geographic Information Systems (ACM-GIS). , Redondo Beach, CA (2012).

[47] Nyerges, T.L. et al.: Cognitive Aspects of Human-Computer Interaction for Geographic Information Systems. Kluwer Academic Publishers (1995).

[48] Olson, K.L. et al.: Privacy protection versus cluster detection in spatial epidemiology. Am. J. Public Health. 96, 11, 2002–2008 (2006).

[49] Paulos, E. et al.: Citizen science: Enabling participatory urbanism. Urban Informatics: community Integration and Implementation. pp. 1–16 (2008).

[50] Peuquet, D.J. et al.: A Method for Discovery and Analysis of Temporal Patterns in Complex Event Data. Int. J. Geogr. Inf. Sci. 29, 9, 1588–1611 (2015).

[51] Pomfret, K.D.: Summary of Location Privacy in the United States. in. In: Janssen, K. and Crompvoets, J. (eds.) Geographic Data and the Law: Defining New Challenges. Leuven University Press.

[52] Resch, B. et al.: Real-Time Geo-awareness – Sensor Data Integration for Environmental Monitoring in the City. 2009 International Conference on Advanced Geographic Information Systems & Web Services. pp. 92–97 Ieee (2009).

[53] Robinson, A.C. et al.: Designing a web-based learning portal for geographic visualization and analysis in public health, (2011).

[54] Roche, S.: Geographic Information Science I: Why does a smart city need to be spatially enabled? Prog. Hum. Geogr. 38, 5, 703–711 (2014).

[55] Roche, S.: Geographic information science II: Less space, more places in smart cities. Prog. Hum. Geogr. (2015).

[56] Roth, R.E. et al.: The Competitive Analysis Method for Evaluating Water Level Visualization Tools. In: Vondrakova, A. et al. (eds.) Modern Trends in Cartography. pp. 241–256 Springer (2014).

[57] Sagl, G. et al.: Contextual Sensing: Integrating Contextual Information with Human and Technical Geo-Sensor Information for Smart Cities. Sensors. 15, 7, 17013–17035 (2015).

[58] Sanchez, L. et al.: SmartSantander: The meeting point between Future Internet research and experimentation and the smart cities. Future Network & Mobile Summit (FutureNetw). pp. 1–8 , Warsaw, Poland (2011).

[59] Schlaisich, I., Egenhofer, M.J.: Multimodal Spatial Querying: What People Sketch and Talk About. in 1st International Conference on Universal Access in Human-Computer Interaction. pp. 732–736 Lawrence Erlbaum (2001).

[60] Schuermann, R.T., Chow, T.E.: Geovisualization of Local and Regional Migration Using Web-mined Demographics. Int. Arch. Photogramm. Remote Sens. Spat. Inf. Sci. XL, 2, 93–97 (2014).

[61] Shanley, L.A. et al.: Tweeting Up a Storm The Promise and Perils of Crisis mapping. Photogramm. Eng. Remote Sens. October 2013, 865–879 (2013).

[62] Skupin, A., Hagelman, R.: Visualizing demographic trajectories with self-organizing maps. Geoinformatica. 9, 2, 159–179 (2005).

[63] Stefanidis, A., Nittel, S.: GeoSensor Networks. CRC Press, Inc. (2004).

[64] Sutherland, I.E.: A head-mounted three dimensional display. Proceedings of the December 9-11, 1968, fall joint computer conference, part I on - AFIPS '68 (Fall, part I). p. 757 ACM Press (1968).

[65] Tomaszewski, B.: Geographic Information Systems (GIS) for Disaster Management. CRC Press, Inc., Boca Raton, FL, USA (2014).

[66] Tsou, M.-H.: Research Challenges and Opportunities in Mapping Social Media and Big Data. Cartogr. Geogr. Inf. Sci. 42, sup1, 70–74 (2015).

[67] Turek, F.: Machine Vision Fundamentals, How to Make Robots See. NASA Tech Briefs Mag. 35, 6, 60–62 (2011).

[68] Underkoffler, J., Ishii, H.: Urp: A luminous-tangible workbench for urban planning and design. Proceedings of the SIGCHI conference on Human factors in computing systems: the CHI is the limit. pp. 386–393 ACM (1999).

[69] Vasardani, M., Winter, S.: Place Properties. In: Onsrud, H. and Kuhn, W. (eds.) Andvancing Geographic Information Science. GSDI Press (2015).

[70] Verbree, E. et al.: Interaction in virtual world views-linking 3D GIS with VR, (1999).

[71] Wang, D. et al.: Active complex event processing over event streams. Proc. VLDB Endow. 4, 10, 634–645 (2011).

Emerging Societal Challenges Likely to Affect Geographic Information Science in the Next Twenty Years

Laxmi Ramasubramanian[1], Helen Couclelis[2], and Terje Midtbø[3]

1 Department of Urban Policy and Planning, Hunter College, CUNY,
695 Park Avenue, New York, NY 10065, USA
2 Department of Geography, 1720 Ellison Hall, University of California, Santa Barbara,
Santa Barbara, CA 93106-4060, USA
3 Geomatics, Norwegian University of Science and Technology,
N-7491 Trondheim, Norway

Abstract: This paper summarizes the discussions of the panel "Emerging Societal Challenges Likely to Affect GIScience in the Next Twenty Years" at the 2015 Vespucci Institute. Major drivers of change are likely to include demography, urbanization, climate, and digital technologies. The panel in Bar Harbor, moderated by Laxmi Ramasubramanian, included two invited presentations (by Helen Couclelis and Terje Midtbø), and responses by two early career panelists (James Campbell and Jeon-Young Kang), and by two senior panelists (Aileen Buckley and Stéphane Roche).

Keywords: Societal challenges, demography, urbanization, climate, digital technologies.

1   Introduction

The objective of Panel 4 was aptly summarized in its title; however, most panel participants tacitly acknowledged that the task of predicting the societal changes and challenges relevant to geographic information science in the next two decades was too ambitious. Both invited speakers thus chose to considerably narrow the scope of their remarks in order to encourage a more focused discussion.

In their presentations, Terje Midtbø and Helen Couclelis both loosely adopted a 'social construction of technology' (SCOT) perspective, which emphasizes the tight recursive coupling between societal change and technological change, and the inability to predict the outcomes of the resulting complex feedback processes. By doing so, the speakers sidestepped any ambition to develop an inventory of relevant future societal changes and challenges. Indeed, Midtbø implied that attempting to do so would be akin to making predictions by peering into a crystal ball. Couclelis made a similar point concerning even those societal trends that are already on the horizon. Still, it was easy for the seven panel members to agree on the fact that most future societal changes and challenges relevant to GIScience and technologies are likely to stem from a small number of already well-established domains of global significance. Four of these broad and interconnected areas that are the sources of more specific drivers of change are: demography, urbanization, climate, and digital technologies.

1.1 Demography

The world's population is projected to continue growing rapidly in the next twenty years. However, population growth is predicted to occur unevenly, with much of Europe and Japan facing population declines, while parts of Africa and Asia would be experiencing significant increases. A consequence of the population declines already observed and anticipated in many developed countries will be an altered age structure with disproportionately large (and growing) population percentages being above 65 years of age.

1.2 Urbanization

The world is becoming increasing urban and already, since about 2006, over half of the world's population lives in cities. This trend is set to continue in the next twenty years, with the majority of the earth's population eventually living in a city or an urban exclave adjoining a major city. Rapid urban growth has impacts on infrastructure, food systems, public health, and governance, while cities in parts of the world where populations are declining still have to deal with crumbling and obsolete infrastructure. In some regions, trans-border immigration increases urbanization pressures.

1.3 Climate

Global climate changes are apparent, and while a general warming trend across the planet is predicted, regional-level changes are much less well understood, complicating prediction and political action. Seasonal variations are likely to intensify (hotter summers, colder winters) with severe weather events increasingly creating natural disasters (fires, floods, dust storms) and other challenges for human habitation. Coastal communities, where the majority of the earth's populations lives, are likely to be vulnerable to increased sea-level rise and more frequent flooding.

1.4 (Digital) Technologies

We have already witnessed the rise of a generation of people who were born and have reached adulthood in a world where most everything depends on technology. These first digital natives and all those who will follow will live lifestyles that take for granted a seamless interface and round-the-clock communion with the digital world and its hardware peripherals. Distinguishing needs from fads, providing and keeping up to date the necessary technological infrastructure, safeguarding security, safety and equity, and anticipating the most critical societal changes will not be simple. While this is currently true primarily of technologically advanced countries, the rest of the world is not far behind.

2 Societal Challenges

2.1 The importance of data

Central to the SCOT perspective is the notion that societal needs can lead to the development of new technology, just as existing technology can be harnessed toward the resolution of new societal challenges. Either way, at any point in time, the available data play a critical role in forging the connection between technology and society. In his presentation titled *"Twenty Years from Today..."* Terje Midtbø stressed that *data* constitute a third integral part of the society-technology dialectic. He then gave examples of societal challenges that are likely to affect GI science contributions over the next twenty years, provided that the necessary data can be obtained in the quantity, quality, and locational accuracy needed. These examples are representative of the drivers of change stemming from the four broad problem domains mentioned above.

Older populations: People especially in western countries are living longer but not without the burdens of old age. Among other things, the elderly and disabled more generally would benefit from better indoor navigation possibilities. Despite ongoing efforts to map interior spaces, there is still a lack of indoor navigational technology that can compete with the outdoor satellite systems when it comes to availability, standardization and accuracy. To this end better models of the indoor environment are needed that can become the basis for visualizations specifically tailored to people with reduced sight or mobility, and for other approaches to navigational guidance using auditory or tactile cues. Such methods would be part of what has been called 'welfare technology', and most of these would require constant streams of live data that can only be provided by networks of sensors.

Bioengineering is another field that largely depends on sensors that are built in, or are in close connection with the human body. Thanks to emerging bioengineering technologies, parts of the body and its functions will be able to be repaired, replaced or extended with the help of artificial sensors, restoring sight, hearing, the sense of touch or smell, etc. These built-in 'tools' could extend the functionality of the human body past the frailties of old age or trauma. For example, a navigational implant may interact with a suitable model of the world and help people move safely and efficiently in both indoor and outdoor environments.

Safer mobility in urban areas and beyond: Safer and more efficient mobility is supported by the development of autonomous vehicles and vessels. There is much ongoing work on making cars safer to reduce human injuries and loss of life as well as economic losses. Car accidents are usually caused by human failure, and by making cars autonomous the expectation is that the number of accidents will be greatly reduced. There is also ongoing research on how to make ships autonomous in order to make conveyance of goods more cost-effective and to reduce very costly losses of both cargo and vessels. Research and development in both these areas is undertaken by big industries, and in both cases geographic information methods and data are essential. Appropriate models must be built and algorithms for handling different situations must be developed, but again, models and algorithms are of little use without live streams of geocoded data.

Natural disasters: New ways of monitoring natural hazards through the use of sensor networks will also play an increasing role when it comes to public safety. Pilot projects show that it is now possible to issue accurate, localized early warnings for a number of different natural disasters, such as floods, landslides and earthquakes, whether caused by climate change or not. Knowledge that such technological capabilities exist creates demands from local communities for more sensors and more monitoring of potential dangerous phenomena in close proximity.

The promise and problem of sensors: The technological developments mentioned above would help mitigate several already existing and emerging societal challenges. They also clearly challenge GI science itself to come up with new ways of thinking as well as with new tools. But the fact that these developments all depend on nearly ubiquitous networks of sensors gives pause. Monitoring everything can easily turn into surveillance of everyone. Will we be tracking every human being, whether outdoors or indoors, while monitoring city traffic, or the unsteady slope behind your house, or when checking for possibly accident-causing toys left behind on grandmother's floor? For most people this sounds absurd. We do not want this kind of surveillance. Nevertheless, where should the balance be struck between providing needed societal services and protecting people's' privacy? There will certainly be some critical ethical boundaries to be debated and defined.

2.2   The importance of flexibility and adaptive capacity

Following Terje Midtbø, Helen Couclelis presented a paper entitled *"Faster Horses": emerging societal challenges and GI science*. The title refers to a quote attributed to Henry Ford, speaking of his game-changing Model T car: "If you had asked people what they wanted, they would have said 'faster horses'". The point is that people have difficulty predicting disruptive innovations, even if related 'emerging trends' had been visible for quite some time, as was the case with the diffusion of the automobile.

Even harder to predict are emerging societal trends with respect to their implications for geographic information science. The principle of the social construction of technology (SCOT) mentioned earlier, which posits a dialectical relationship between technological development on the one hand and societal transformation on the other, makes prediction futile. Being the sum of theoretical perspectives on a class of software tools, GI science is a prime example of this dynamic: the tools must be adapted to the changing use needs, but changing use needs challenge the possibilities afforded by the tools at any one time. Furthermore, GI science is evolving based on field-internal trends as well as on wider technological and societal influences, making it impossible at this point to tell whether this evolution will be at the rather mundane wolf-to-dog scale, or whether, within the 20-year time horizon considered, it will perhaps yield something quite extraordinary such as the dinosaur-to bird transformation.

For the purposes of this presentation, Couclelis chose a rather narrow but realistic illustration of the problem: GI science in relation to emerging societal trends that will likely challenge metropolitan governments in the industrialized world in the next couple of decades. There are two main aspects to this discussion. The first aspect concerns the local governments - traditional major users of GI technologies - that must serve the evolving needs of urban life and society; the second aspect has to do with the new technological and other developments that affect urban life modes and societal relations. In standard urban geography and planning taxonomies, the aspects of urban life for which local governments are responsible fall into the following seven domains: home, work, commerce, health, education, recreation, and transportation/ communication. This classification served urban planning and services well as long as there was a reliable correspondence between the spaces (urban land uses) on the one hand, and the placing and timing of activities on the other. But the convenient symmetry between where you are and what you are doing started disintegrating once communication became separated from transportation. A major and growing challenge for local governments is thus the continuing breakdown of traditional place-activity connections brought about by ICTs, as these accelerate on their asymptotic pursuit of 'anything anywhere any time'.

In addition to this major but already decades-old challenge of the dislocation of activity, there are numerous emerging ones that local governments must already deal with. De Souza et al. (2015) present an up-to-date catalog and discussion that includes the following six recent developments: (1) UAVs and air space, (2) automated vehicles, (3) artificial intelligence innovations, (4) peer-to-peer platforms, (5) data privatization, and (6) the growing numbers of fragile and conflict states. As a thought experiment, one might set up a matrix of the seven aspects of urban life mentioned above, versus the six areas of new challenges discussed in De Souza et al. (2015). (Table 1). For each cell of that matrix one may then seek to identify societal challenges in the purview of local government, and in particular those where GI technology is likely to be of help. Thus, for example, one issue at the intersection of 'Health' and 'Automated Vehicles' might be the possibility of health-restricted individuals (e.g. the elderly and handicapped) using their own vehicles in large numbers, thus forcing the reduction of special transportation services and impacting those not wealthy enough to own a car. Rethinking the provision of such services in a changed technological and social environment would be a task where GI science and technology could greatly help. Clearly, the hardest of all societal challenges for local governments will be found along the last column of 'Urbanizing Fragile and Conflict States'. This is a reminder of how much this brief, narrowly focused presentation cannot cover, though aspects of these challenges, such as international refugee flows and terrorist networks affect metropolitan areas in even the most advanced countries.

Aspects of Urban Life	Emerging Disruptive Technologies					
	1	2	3	4	5	6
Home						
Work						
Commerce						
Health		X				
Education						
Recreation						
Transportation						

Table 1. Aspects of urban life versus emerging disruptive technologies and other challenging developments (see above for numbering).

So, where to GI science in a fast-changing world filled with unreliable societal trends and unpredictable developments? In the face of deep uncertainties, flexibility and adaptive capacity are key. Rather than striving to meet some specific research agenda, GI science must be rethought so as to be able to evolve, adapt to, and anticipate emerging needs and circumstances. This way GI science will be what it should be, at all times: user-oriented, problem centered, and multi-perspectival.

3   Discussion and Conclusions

The discussants and commentators on the panel emphasized the need to avoid being distracted by hypothetical problems and be pragmatic about the use and value of GI science to address serious and immediate concerns. They recommended the systematic consideration of both basic human needs (e.g., at the level of individuals and small groups) but also of more complex social needs (e.g., at the level of urban management, participation in government and governance). Both Roche and Buckley emphasized the importance of working closely with other disciplines, arguing that GI science contributes a unique and necessary, but not in itself sufficient perspective on the problem at hand. Campbell reminded the group of the imperative never to lose sight of the question of ethics, as each response to a new societal challenge, based on different theoretical framings, methodological approaches, and data sources, creates its own new set of ethical challenges.

Participants on the panel as well as the audience seemed divided between those who argued that the GI science community has a responsibility to propose new tools and solutions to help intervene through action – i.e. to offer our expertise to directly serve society, and others who wondered whether such thoughts and beliefs might overestimate the importance of our field to the point of hubris. The discussion was lively, but ultimately inconclusive.

To close: It is a foregone conclusion that societies are changing and will continue to do so in the next twenty years under the drivers of demographic shifts, rapid urbanization, climate change, and technological developments, among others. While the explosive rise of digital technologies and the geoweb has resulted in advances that empower individuals and groups greatly, major geopolitical and societal divides persist or are being intensified by these technologies, ensuring that breakthroughs and innovations will continue being distributed unevenly. The role that GI scientists can and should play is far from clear, with many in this scholarly community viewing themselves as fairly focused subject matter experts, qualified to participate in collaborative problem solving endeavors, while others strive for an active role as motivators, advocates, or influencers of science-driven and evidence-based policy changes benefiting society. Either way, GI scientists must recognize that even the most narrowly technical of our work may eventually have wide-ranging societal and ethical implications.

References

[1]   Desouza, K, Swindell, D, Smith, K.L, Sutherland, A, Fedorschak, K, and C. Coronel, 2015. Local government 2035: Strategic trends and implications of new technologies. Issues in Technology Innovation, No. 27, May 2015. Washington, D.C: The Brookings Institution.
http://www.brookings.edu/research/papers/2015/05/29-local-government-strategic-trends-desouzaxx

From Body of Knowledge to Base Map: Managing Domain Knowledge through Collaboration and Computation

Sean C. Ahearn [1] and André Skupin [2]

1 Center for Advanced Research of Spatial Information, Department of Geography, Hunter College, New York, NY 10065 USA
2 Center for Information Convergence and Strategy, Department of Geography, San Diego State University, San Diego, CA 92182, USA

Abstract: This paper describes an approach and technology for operationalizing a body of knowledge for domain knowledge management. The system enables collaboration, exploration, and exploitation of domain knowledge through a front-end visual wiki, an ontology-driven knowledge base and Web services. The service-based architecture enables applications that allow knowledge artifacts to be related to domain concepts through inference, and such inferred relationships to be visualized. Essential to the design and operation of the system are such notions as *reference system* and *base map* borrowed from traditional mapping. This includes the idea of a domain base map onto which any domain artifact can be projected. We hypothesize that this type of system can help to break down traditional boundaries, such as between educators, students, researchers, and professionals.

Keywords: Ontology, knowledge domains, reference systems, base maps, visualization, wiki, collaboration, body of knowledge.

1 Introduction

There is a critical need to improve the construction and dissemination of knowledge within and across the many communities that constitute a knowledge domain. Scientific research, academic education, technical training, and professional practice are driven by seemingly disparate concerns, and there tends to be little interaction between these sub-communities. As a result, cutting-edge research is often slow to transition into professional practice, while educational activities and materials often do not represent the current state of research and practice. Similar inefficiencies characterize the matching of software tools to related research insights, students' aspirations to curricular options, and educational programs to workplace needs. Alternatively, what if undergraduate curricula and textbooks co-existed in the same knowledge ecosystem with research publications, software documentation, job advertisements, and grant proposals? What if a student learning an analytical software tool would have ready access to a set of research studies in which similar tools were recently used? What if she would also be shown a list of current job openings requiring mastery of associated skills, reinforcing the real-world relevance of curricular content? What if she could then compare her skill levels in different areas of the knowledge domain with those required by the jobs of interest to her to see how well she matched the various positions available? And, finally, what if that knowledge ecosystem was organically changing as the field evolved? The discussion below demonstrates how the *BigKnowledge® Body of Knowledge* system (*BK-BoK*™) extends the work of Ahearn et al [1] to afford the vision underlying these questions and provide a framework for building improved knowledge ecosystems.

The metaphor of an ecosystem is gaining acceptance as a way of modeling how a community produces and consumes knowledge [6, 8]. An ecosystem consists of a multitude of participants that interact synergistically – by creating, moving, and consuming resources – for the success of the system and themselves. In a knowledge ecosystem, the participants include *actors* (people and institutions), *activities* (the tasks that actors perform, such as employment, education, and research), and *artifacts* (the products of actors' activities, including published and unpublished documents (Figure 1).

These *domain elements* interact in the ecosystem by producing, sharing, and using knowledge about the domain, including theoretical *concepts*, demonstrable *skills*, and knowledge-bearing *resources*. A form of knowledge ecosystem does of course already exists for any given discipline, consisting of the hundreds of thousands of relevant people, institutions, products, and publications. The problem is that the inefficient state of current knowledge ecosystems, as suggested earlier, impedes the diffusion of knowledge (ideas, algorithms, practices, etc.) and the integration of distributed knowledge into a more effective whole.

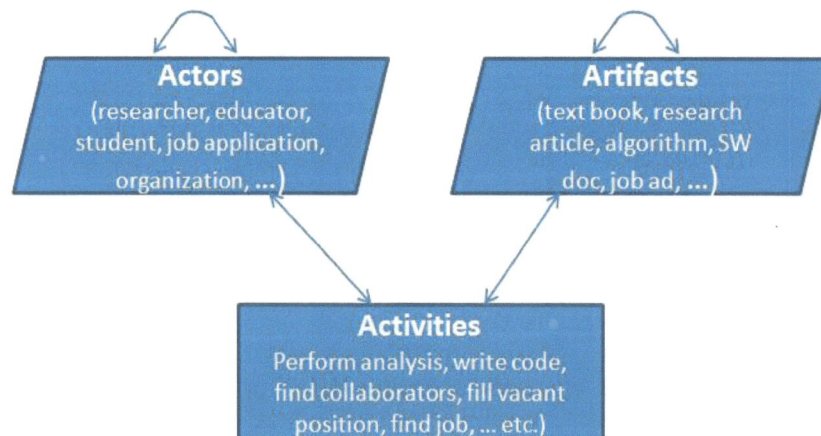

Figure 1. Knowledge Ecosystem

A number of initiatives have addressed aspects of this problem with the creation of formalized "bodies of knowledge." For example, the *Geographic Information Science and Technology Body of Knowledge* (*GIS&T BoK*) [7] was developed to provide: (i) a resource for course and curriculum planning; (ii) a basis for comparison of education programs; (iii) a foundation for professional certification, program accreditation, and articulation agreements; and (iv) a resource for HR professionals. Published in 2006, it was a landmark accomplishment in the field [12], but as a framework for actual implementation it has been somewhat limited in use [8] because of a lack of formalization.

Contemporary ontologies provide a formal and computationally supported approach for capturing domain concepts and their relationships. Examples include the *Cognitive Atlas* (http://www.cognitiveatlas.org) for cognitive science, the *Indiana Philosophy Ontology* project (http://inpho.cogs.indiana.edu), the *Software Engineering Body of Knowledge* (*SWEBOK*, http://swebok.org), the *ACM Computing Classification System* (*CCS*, http://www.acm.org/about/class/2012) and the *Semantic Web Applications in Neuromedicine* ontology (*SWAN*, http://www.w3.org/TR/hcls-swan) [6]. All of these initiatives are ambitious, but they tend to have a fairly narrow scope with respect to integration and application. For example, there seems to be little interaction between the *ACM/IEEE-CS Computer Science Curricula 2013* (designed for education), *SWEBOK* (designed for professional practice), and the *ACM CCS* (designed for research publications), even though they have a great deal in common, including overlaps in sponsoring organizations.

2 Relationships and Knowledge Pathways

Ahearn et al. [1] presented a foundational approach for capture, storage, and exploitation of domain concepts, their relationships, and related knowledge artifacts. Since then, further work has expanded the underlying meta-ontology to include a richer set of concept relationships. They now encompass broader (super-concept), narrower (sub-concept), pre-requisite, post-requisite, and similarity relationships (Figure 2). Note that *pre-requisite, post-requisite* and *similar* can be weighted, reflecting relationship strength. The expansion in the types of relationships affords the generation of different "views" or "pathways" through the knowledge base. Those pathways are ultimately navigated through related pairs of concepts. A *taxonomic pair* represents a broader-narrower relationship. A *prerequisite pair* is a relationship that reflects the fact that one concept depends on another; that is, one must understand and be competent in Concept A (to some degree) before one can understand and be competent in Concept B. Finally, there is the *similarity pair*, in which participating concepts share a similar meaning. These pair-wise relationships are a feature of the knowledge ontology and once discovered, should be encoded in the domain knowledge base. A *knowledge pathway* is than an ordered sequence of any number of concepts, traced through the network of concept pairs in the pursuit of particular objectives. For example, a particular course may first cover Concept X, then Concept A, then Concept D, then Concept F. The sequential movement of each domain element (such as a book, a course, or a student) through the domain can thus be represented as a unique pathway through the domain ontology. Of particular relevance for educational applications are networks of pre-/post-requisites, which can be exploited for high-level curricular planning (e.g., course articulation), but also form backbone structures for designing highly personalized, yet competency-oriented, educational experiences.

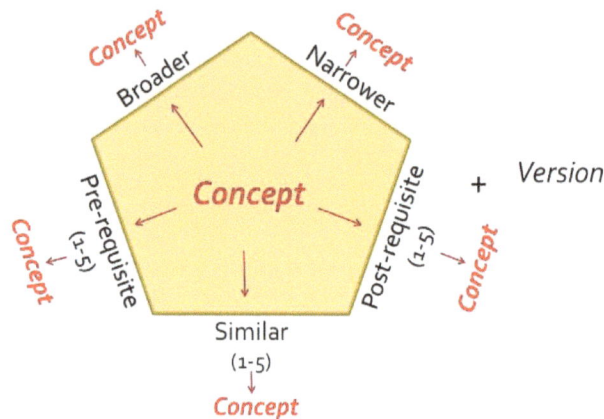

Figure 2. Concept Relationships

3 Collaborative Input and Bottom-up Design

Capturing knowledge is a central challenge for any system that aspires to develop and maintain a formalized Body of Knowledge. The knowledge captured is intended to reflect the collective knowledge of the community. The community therefore needs to be able to participate in improving and updating the standard. This is in direct contrast to the "top-down" approach of committees of experts that have created the standard bodies of knowledge in most domains (e.g., [7]). Since a "top-down" approach cannot always accurately reflect the collective knowledge of the entire community, a more inclusive approach is to use a wiki service that relies on crowd sourcing for the revision of the domain ontology. This allows anyone in the community to propose changes, debate those proposals, and collaboratively come to consensus. An implementation of this type of approach was discussed in [1], with additional editorial and access mechanisms added since. The editing environment now involves four different types of users: viewer (non-authorized user), contributor (authorized user), editor and super-user. Viewers can browse the network of concepts, skills, and resources. Logged-in contributors can make proposals to add or modify concepts, relationships, skills, and associated resource artifacts. Editors are tasked with determining which of the additions/changes proposed by contributors should be added to the authoritative knowledge base. Determination of acceptance is made based on the contributions related to a given concept by the various "contributors" that have weighed in and requires a consensus of the editors responsible for, and have approved access to, that part of the BoK. Super-users manage accounts.

The visual Wiki enables the user to have two views of the data: a *synoptic view* in which the entire knowledge space is visible and a *focal view* that shows a particular concept in its relational context (Figure 3). Using either view, changes can be made to the system by contributors and editors can approve or reject proposed changes.

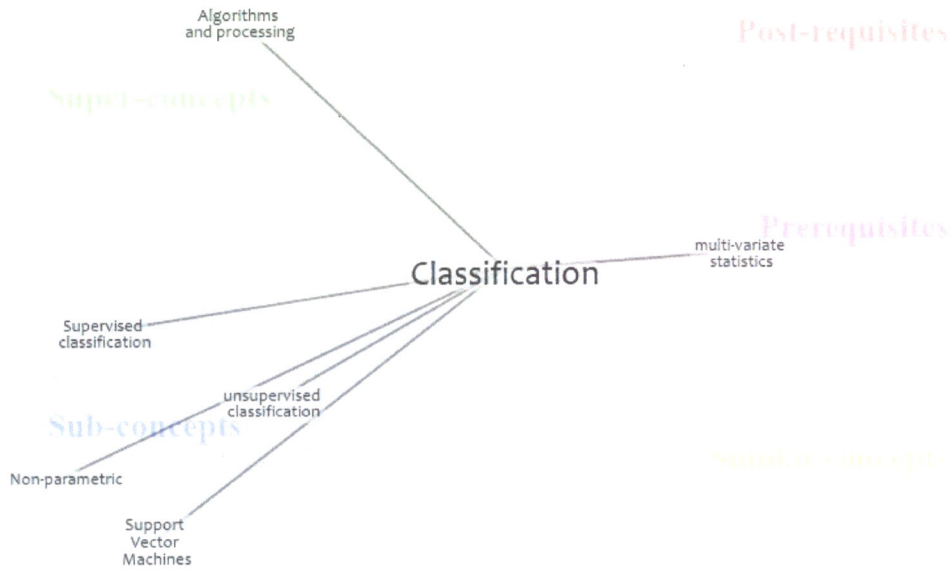

Figure 3. Focal View in Visual Wiki

4 System Architecture

The **BK-BoK** system is composed of these main components: a visual Wiki (**BoKWiki**), an ontology store (**BoKOnto**), and a series of BoK web services that can be ingested by other applications, as demonstrated by a visualization application (**BoKVis**) (Figure 4).

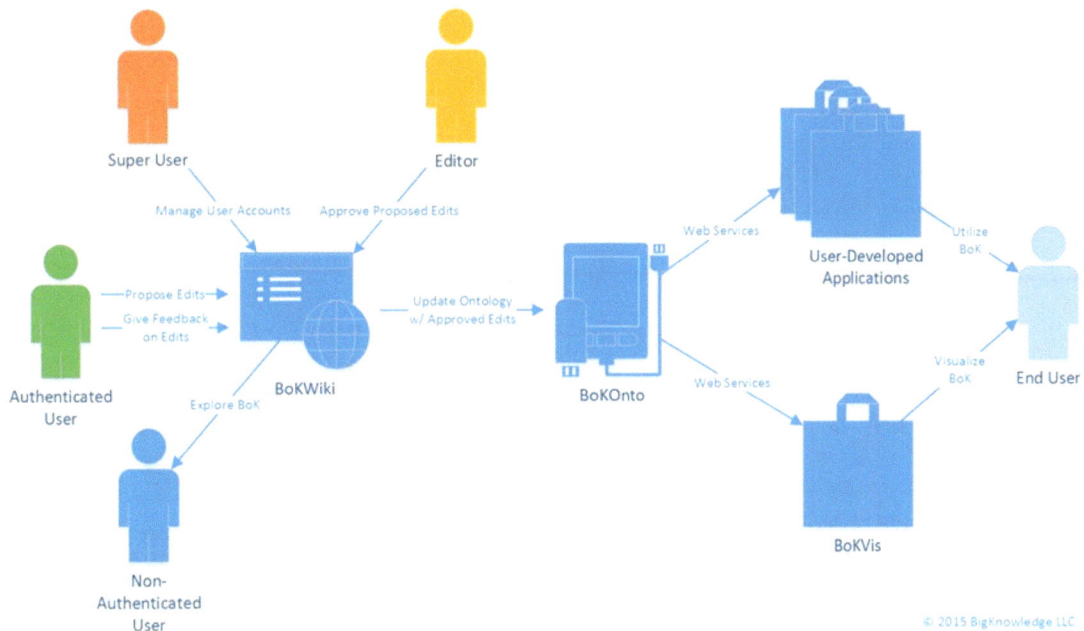

Figure 4. *BK-BoK* System Architecture

BoKWiki is the environment in which the knowledge space can be explored by a viewer of the system, in which a contributor can make suggestions for new concepts, new relationships or to edit existing ones, and in which editors can approve changes made by the contributors. Upon approval, which is triggered by an editor, a service is called for moving modifications over to *BoKOnto*. If such edits involve the assertion of new concepts, then the initial versions of corresponding concepts, properties, and relationships are stored in triple form. Likewise, changes that are made to existing concepts result in the generation of new triples, with the modified concept being explicitly linked to its preceding version. In this manner, all changes are version-managed and changes to the BoK over time can be tracked and analyzed. This permits the creation of a view of the BoK for any date in time.

BoKOnto holds the authoritative version of the BoK in form of a triple store. The domain ontology is exposed through various Web services that enable the domain ontology to be exploited in user-provided applications. Services range from simple text queries of ontology content to more advanced inference operations, but also include a services for retrieval of the complete BoK in a range of formats.

5   BoK to Base Map

The notion of a base map has long been central to the practice of cartography and GIS. It is meant to provide a stable, foundational spatial platform, onto which thematic layers can be projected. Such projections are effectively locational inferences derived from entities represented in certain foundational reference systems. For example, a geographic phenomenon can be mapped onto the base map by first determining its location in latitude and longitude (i.e., the foundational reference system) and then determining its location in the projected space of the base map (i.e., locational inference). Analogously, when a base map is created for a knowledge domain, then one can, for any given knowledge artifact, actor, or activity [1], first determine its location in the knowledge reference system and then infer the phenomenon's location in the base map. How can such knowledge reference systems and base maps be created? The following outlines two approaches, one directly based on a formally defined domain BoK and its prescribed ontological structure, the other based on mining of domain artifacts. Hybrid approaches are possible as well, such as when Bodies of Knowledge themselves are subjected to content analysis [1].

5.1   From BoK to Base Map

Ahearn et al. [1] introduced a service-oriented architecture for representing domain knowledge structures, initially in relation to the 2006 Geographic Information Science and Technology Body of Knowledge [7]. This approach expanded the scope of not only how one could *update* and *maintain* any BoK on an on ongoing basis, but also how and for which purposes a BoK could *operationalized*. A key contribution of that effort was the transfer of geographic and cartographic principles to the *contextualization, mapping* and *visualization* of a knowledge domain ontology. By conceptualizing a formally defined body of knowledge (an ontology) as the foundation of a "spatial reference system," arbitrary knowledge artifacts can be readily related to this domain reference system, and thereby to each other.

In terms of visualization, this reference system approach links up with the notion of a base map that in a visual context is kept relatively simple (Figure 5), but provides the ability to perform inference and overlays derived from user queries (Figure 6) or even whole knowledge artifacts.

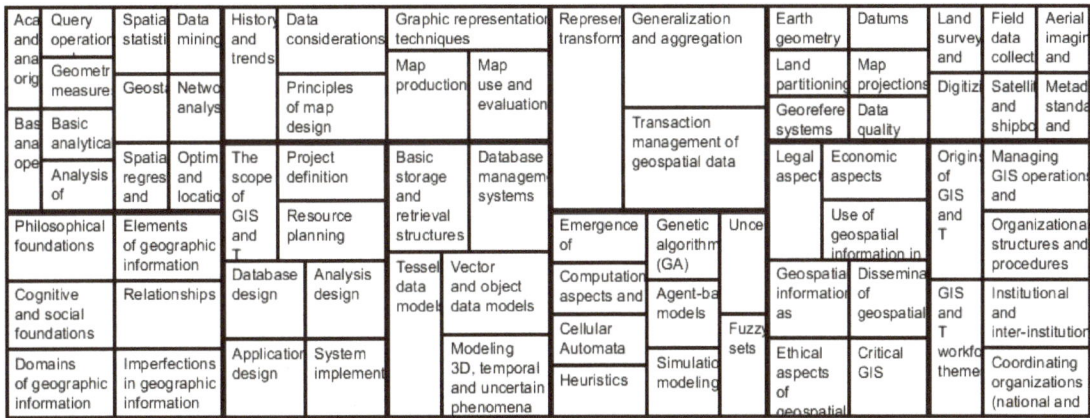

Aca and ana orig	Query operation	Spatial statisti	Data mining	History and trends	Data considerations	Graphic representation techniques		Represen transform	Generalization and aggregation		Earth geometry	Datums	Land survey and	Field data collect	Aerial imagin and
	Geometr measure	Geost	Netwo analys		Principles of map design	Map production	Map use and evaluation				Land partitioning	Map projections	Digitiz	Satelli and shipbo	Metad standa and
Bas ana ope	Basic analytica										Georefere systems	Data quality			
	Analysis of	Spatial regres and	Optim and locatio	The scope of GIS and T	Project definition	Basic storage and retrieval structures	Database managem systems		Transaction management of geospatial data		Legal aspect	Economic aspects	Origin of GIS and T	Managing GIS operations and	
Philosophical foundations	Elements of geographic information				Resource planning			Emergence of	Genetic algorithm (GA)	Unce	Use of geospatial information in			Organizationa structures and procedures	
				Database design	Analysis design	Tessell data model	Vector and object data models	Computation aspects and	Agent-ba models		Geospatial informatio as	Dissemina of geospatial	GIS and T workfo theme	Institutional and inter-institution	
Cognitive and social foundations	Relationships							Cellular Automata		Fuzzy sets					
Domains of geographic information	Imperfections in geographic information			Application design	System implement		Modeling 3D, temporal and uncertain phenomena	Heuristics	Simulatio modeling		Ethical aspects of geospatial	Critical GIS		Coordinating organizations (national and	

Figure 5. Simple base map derived from a BoK and implemented as treemap. GIS&T BoK hierarchy is ingested live from a BK-BoKOnto Web service.

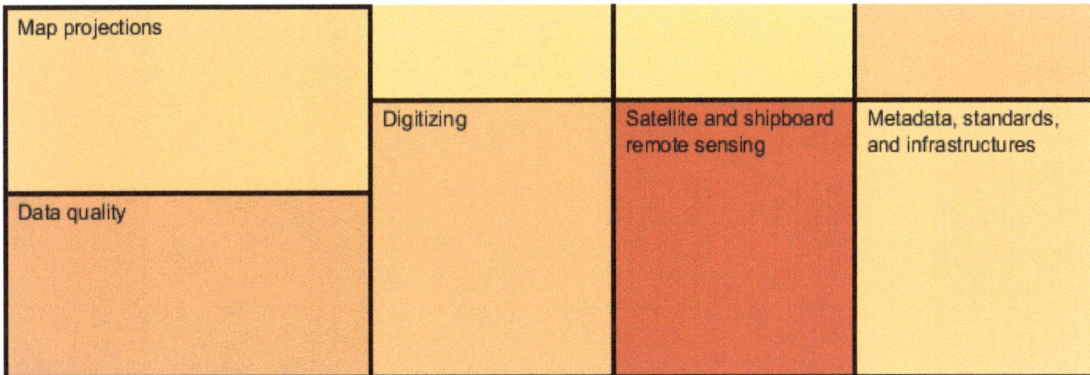

Figure 6. Visualization derived from two different BoK Web services: BoK concept hierarchy service and topic inference service. Overlaid is a query for "remote sensing", with higher red color value indicating a stronger similarity match of the concept to the query. Lower red color values indicate a weaker match.

A domain ontology based approach allows extending domain knowledge projection beyond domain *concepts*. For example, one can link up with domain-specific skills, as illustrated in the ranked listing of GIS&T skills in response to a query for "remote sensing" (Figure 7). Notice that the query phrase does not have to be verbatim contained in the skills description. Instead of performing client-side text matching, an inference service is invoked, whose results are then displayed.

The combination of a knowledge reference system approach with base mapping and inference services also enables more complex knowledge-algebraic operations, such as the explicit comparison of two courses (Figure 8) or of two persons or of an individual's expertise vis- à-vis the stated requirements of a job. These kinds of projection and overlay operations enables user applications that operate on the knowledge spaces that we intellectually and productively "inhabit" [1].

| Explain the principle of multibeam bathymetric mapping |
| Explain the concept of data fusion in relation to remote sensing applications in GIS and T |
| Differentiate push-broom and cross-track scanning technologies |
| Differentiate between active and passive sensors, citing examples of each |
| Select the most appropriate remotely sensed data source for a given analytical task, study area, budget, and availability |
| Discuss the consequences of increasing and decreasing resolution |
| Describe an application of hyperspectral image data |
| Explain the concepts of spatial resolution, radiometric resolution, and spectral sensitivity |

Figure 7. Snippet of interactive visualization that ingests BoK concept hierarchy service and topic inference service in a scrollable list display. Shown are not concepts, but skills retrieved and sorted in response to a query for "remote sensing". Only the very top of the ranking is shown in figure, identifying the best matching learning objectives.

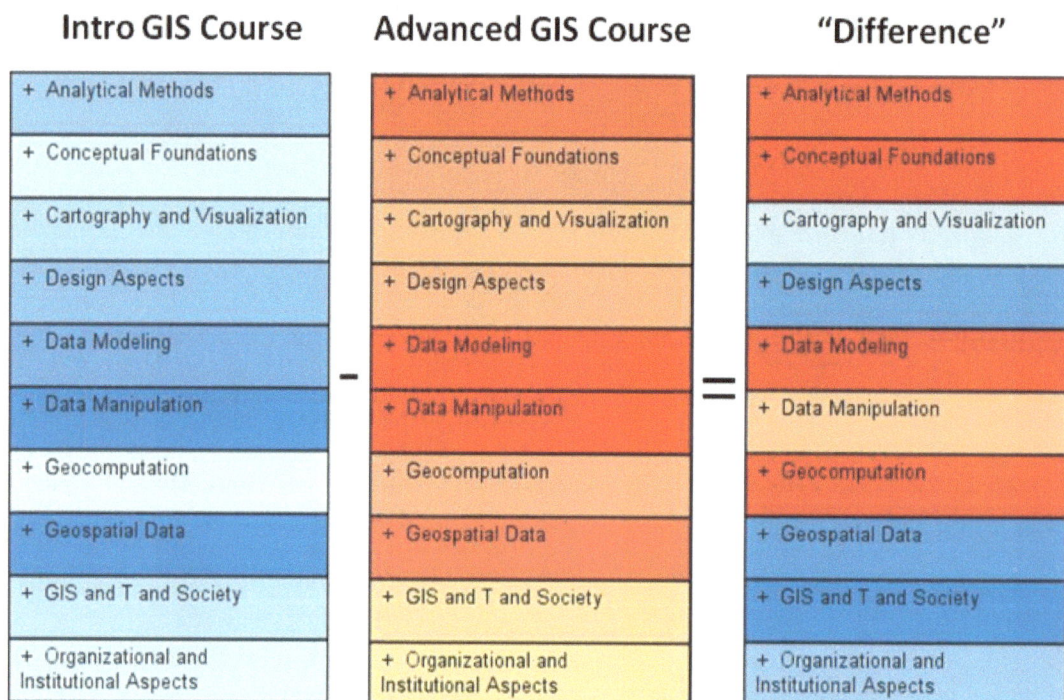

Figure 8. Knowledge algebra operation applied to two GIS courses in a reference system derived from the GIS&T BoK and projected onto a coarse domain base map through natural language inference. For individual courses, darker colors indicate a better match to a GIS&T BoK knowledge area. In the course "difference" overlay, a divergent color scheme indicates that dark blue topics (e.g., "Geospatial Data") are more strongly associated with the Intro GIS class, while the dark red topics (e.g. "Geocomputation") are associated with the Advanced GIS class.

5.2 From Knowledge Artifacts to Base Map

The reference system and base map notions introduced by [1] are applicable even when no formal domain ontology exists or if its current content does not reflect the evolution of the domain. In that case, content mining comes to the fore and could be applied to any collection of domain artifacts, including knowledge canonized in text book form (figure 9a) and formal (Figure 9b) and informal collections (Figure 9c) of domain writings.

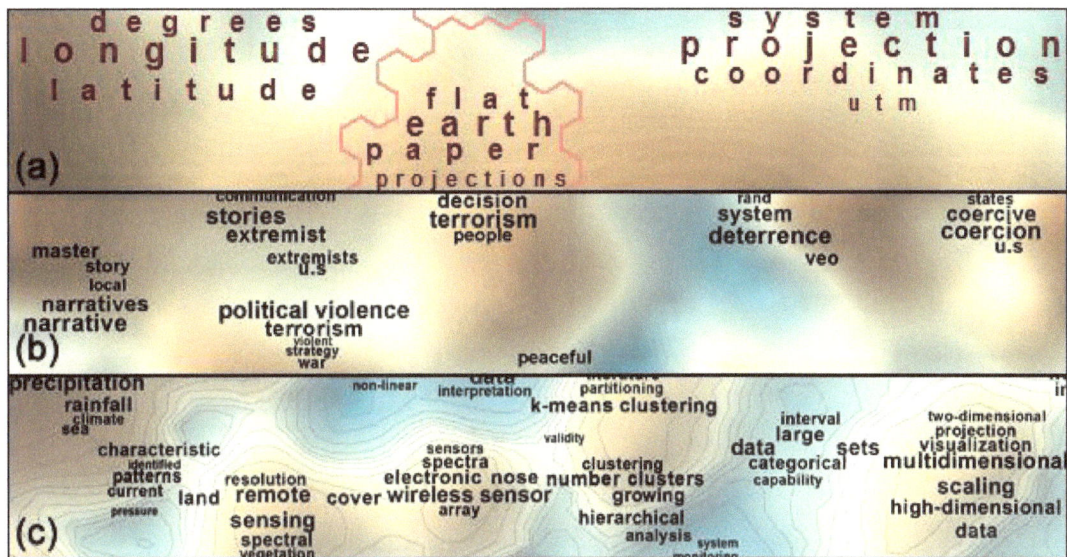

Figure 9. Snippets of base maps derived from domain artifacts for three different domains and artifact types: (a) GIS textbook, (b) an edited collection of research papers on violent extremism, (c) corpus of independently authored research papers on self-organizing maps. Contours, coloring, and hill shading derived using a term dominance landscape approach [15, 17].

These base maps and underlying reference systems can reflect recent advances in domain knowledge that have not yet been captured in a formal manner in a BoK. By projecting an existing BoK into such an artifact-derived reference system, it becomes possible to either confirm the continued relevance of topics already contained in a BoK or detect new domain structures (indicated by significant base map / reference system structures void of coverage by the existing BoK) or even help identify concepts as being outdated or deprecated within the domain. Intelligent use of natural language processing – as opposed to simple string matching – can ensure that this works even in the presence of common domain language issues, like synonyms (e.g., "conformal" and "angle-preserving") and homonyms (e.g., "map" in different domains). Another, mostly unexplored possibility, consists of using this "book to base map" approach to identify key concepts and structures as a starting point in the creation of a completely new BoK, especially for novel domains, in which there is a lack of canonized knowledge resources.

6   Discussion and Conclusion

Catalysts for creative thought and the emergence of new ideas are still something of a mystery. As Salman Rushdie once said "a little bit of this and a little bit of that is how new ideas come into the world". More and more we see that the old paradigm of disciplinary and sub-disciplinary silos that don't interact, is fading. In fact we had an early sense of the power of interdisciplinary research when such scientists like Amar Bose and Noam Chomsky were crowded out of their space at MIT and placed in a barely serviceable edifice called *Building 20*. A heterogeneous group of researchers from different disciplines were working in a cramped space that "forced solitary scientists to mix and mingle" [10]. This resulted in some of the most innovative research in decades. What does the new *Building 20* look like? Is it an abstract space in which diverse constituencies can act based on shared knowledge? What would it take to conceptualize, structure, and populate a single space (Figure 10) in which domain actors, from students to educators, researchers and professionals, can act and interact in a manner that is more efficient and, yes, catalytic, than allowed by current knowledge ecosystems?

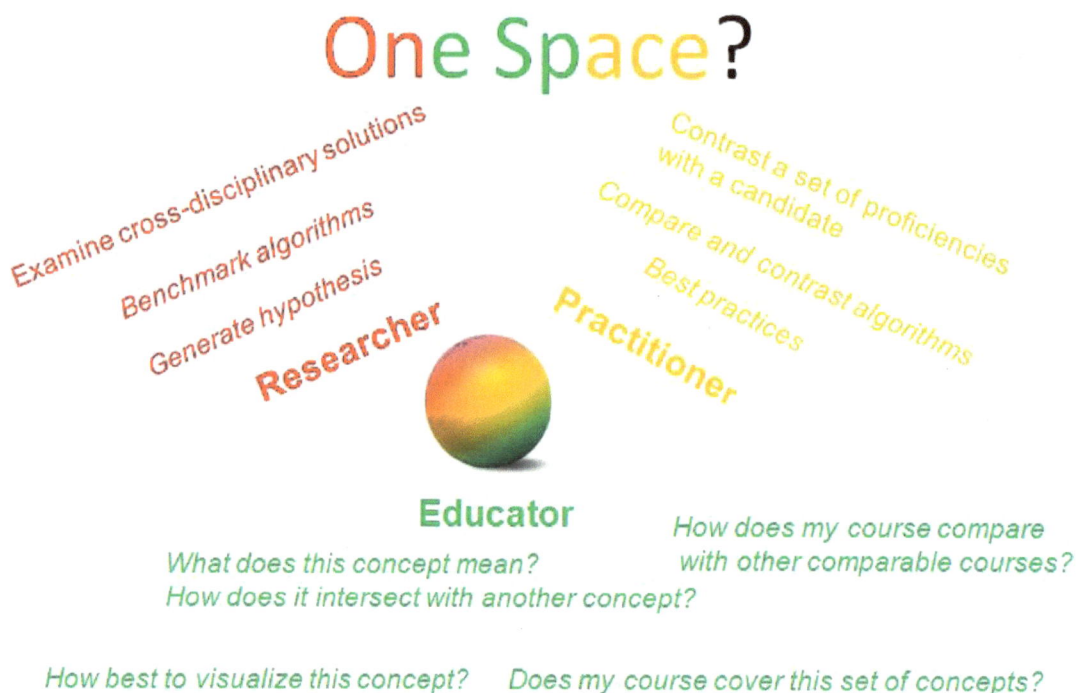

Figure 10. One Space for Education, Research, and Practice

6.1   Making Space for Knowledge

We believe that underlying such a shared space must be a knowledge reference system that simultaneously supports encapsulating canonized domain knowledge, helps to uncover novel or hidden knowledge, and supports computational inference (e.g., relating arbitrary domain artifacts to each other), all in an environment whose spatiality can be made tangible through visualization.

Cartography, geography, and geographic information science have a key role to play in conceptualizing and implementing this vision, but they can also catalyze the injection of key ideas into efforts of computer scientists, information scientists, and non-geographic domain specialists. For example, the *base map* notion is being increasingly adopted in information visualization ([3-5][14]), in a marked departure from common practices in that domain. That the *base map* and *reference system* concepts are sometimes conflated raises the need for GIScientists to clarify how measurement, projection, distortion, and standardization can be usefully addressed in any domain that is attempting to be spatialized in the broadest sense. That effort can itself result in new techniques [16] and new interdisciplinary collaborations [17].

Canonization of domain knowledge through formal processes of concept elicitation and structuring – the creation of a Body of Knowledge – is a useful step towards operationalizing these ideas. This requires involving broad constituencies, in order to foster a *sense of place* within the resulting knowledge spaces, lest those spaces should remain "foreign lands" even for domain insiders. Wikification is a key strategy for capturing the breadth of domain concepts and for generation buy-in from the community. Another requirement is for the resulting knowledge structures to be made accessible to domain services, from human resource management to coordination of research activities. If a BoK is to form the sustainable heart of a domain knowledge ecosystem, then it has to be accessible through a variety of means and for many purposes, from knowledge management to exploration and analytics. The *BK-BoK* system discussed in the article provides such a framework, since it provides a front-end visual wiki (*BokWiki*), an ontology-driven knowledge base (**BoKOnto**), and a service-based architecture for enabling applications.

6.2   Putting Domain Knowledge to Work for Education

Almost without exception, most BoKs have typically been created with the explicit and exclusive goal of supporting tasks in education, especially curricular planning. This has included efforts in the GIS&T domain [11-13]. Though [1] presented a vision significantly expanded beyond this, education and training is an arena where an overtly knowledge-centric approach to integration of actors, artifacts, and activities, including an elaboration of canonized and emergent practices, shows particular promise.

A range of novel education applications can be envisioned, involving numerous elements of higher and vocational education, from faculty and administrators to students and the learning infrastructure, such as courseware. An operationalized domain knowledge reference system allows breaking down traditional barriers in the knowledge ecosystem. What if the theory-laden, long-term approaches of *education* and the hands-on, short-term view of *training* could be represented in a single space? What if core concepts could be explicitly linked to hands-on tools and real-world *practices*? For example, how could students quickly find mappings between the concept of "functional distance," a GIS software tool for computing "cost distance," and a map of hospital service areas published by a county health and human services agency? Other types of mappings supported by a reference system and base map approach include course articulation and course equivalency, which can now be represented in overtly spatial terms, by identifying overlaps and gaps.

The explicit linking of concepts, skills, tools, and literature through ontological relationships allows tracking students' progress in a number of ways. For example, instructors could project individual performance results into the knowledge space to identify which tasks students found especially challenging and take note of the associated prerequisite concepts. This would create a new dynamic in pedagogy: interactive, expansive, and comprehensive. The ability to project learning outcomes into a common space also allows comparison of different instructional modes, such as traditional lecture-lab approaches versus the various forms of flipped learning [2].

References

[1]   AHEARN, S.C., ICKE, I., DATTA, R., DEMERS, M.N. PLEWE, B., AND SKUPIN, A. (2013) Re-engineering the GIS&T Body of Knowledge. International Journal of Geographical Information Science 27(11), 2227-2245.

[2]   BISHOP, J.L. AND VERLERGER, M.A. (2013) The Flipped Classrom: A Survey of the Research. ASEE Annual Conference and Exposition, June 23-26, 2013, Atlanta, Georgia.

[3]   BÖRNER, K. (2010) Atlas of Science: Visualizing What We Know. MIT Press.

[4]   BÖRNER, K. (2015) Atlas of Knowledge: Anyone Can Map. MIT Press.

[5]   CHEN, C., CRIBBIN, T., MACREDIE, R., AND MORAR, S. (2002) Visualizing and Tracking the Growth of Competing Paradigms. Journal of the American Society for Information Science and Technology 53(8): 678-689.

[6]   CICCARESE, WU, E., WONG, G., OCANA, M., KINOSHITA, J., RUTTENBERG, A., AND CLARK, T. (2008). The SWAN biomedical discourse ontology, Journal of Biomedical Informatics 41:739–751.

[7]   DIBIASE, D., DEMERS, M., JOHNSON, A., KEMP, K., TAYLOR LUCK, A. PLEWE, B. AND WENTZ, E., eds. (2006) Geographic Information Science and Technology Body of Knowledge. Association of American Geographers.

[8]   FOOTE, K. E., et al. "GIS&T in higher education: Challenges for educators, opportunities for education." Teaching geographic information science and technology in higher education (2012): 3-15.

[9]   GAO, Y., KINOSHITA, J. , WU, E., MILLER, E., LEE, R., SEABORNE, A., CAYZER, S., CLARK, T. (2006) SWAN: A distributed knowledge infrastructure for Alzheimer disease research, ScienceDirect, Web Semantics: Science, Services and Agents on the World Wide Web, 4:222-228.

[10]   LEHRER, J. (2012) GROUPTHINK: The Brainstorming Myth. The New Yorker 87(46): 22-27.

[11]   PRAGER, S., AND PLEWE, B. (2009) Assessment and Evaluation of GIScience Curriculum using the Geographic Information Science and Technology Body of Knowledge, Journal of Geography in Higher Education, 33: 46-69.

[12]   PRAGER, S. (2011) Using the GIS&T Body of Knowledge for Curriculum Design: Different Design for Different Contexts. In: Unwin, D.J., Foote, K.E., Tate, N.T., and DiBiase, D. (Eds.) Teaching Geographic Information Science and Technology in Higher Education. Chichester, UK: John Wiley & Sons, Ltd. 63-80.

[13]   RIP, F. (2008) GIS&T Body of Knowledge: basis for e-learning, certification and curriculum planning? Proceedings of the Eleventh Annual AGILE Conference.

[14]   SKUPIN, A. (2000). From metaphor to method: Cartographic perspectives on information visualization. In IEEE Symposium on Information Visualization (InfoVis 2000), IEEE: 91-97.

[15] SKUPIN, A. (2004) The World of Geography: Visualizing a Knowledge Domain
      with Cartographic Means. Proceedings of the National Academy of Sciences. 101
      (Suppl. 1): 5274-5278.

[16] SKUPIN, A. (2009). Discrete and continuous conceptualizations of science:
      Implications for knowledge domain visualization. Journal of Informetrics, 3(3):
      233-245.

[17] SKUPIN, A., BIBERSTINE, J. R., AND BÖRNER, K. (2013). Visualizing the topical
      structure of the medical sciences: a self-organizing map approach. PloS ONE,
      8(3), e58779.

Towards a Theory of GIS Program Management

Jochen Albrecht

Department of Geography, Hunter College, CUNY, 695 Park Ave, New York, NY 10065, USA

Abstract: After a brief flurry of monographs on business and organizational aspects of GIS in the 1990s, little attention has been paid to a systematic approach in support of GIS Program management. Most existing efforts in both public and private enterprises are based on anecdotal evidence. This chapter outlines a range of research questions and the beginning efforts to study modern GIS management practices and help develop a body of knowledge that can be used for the accreditation of GIS Programs and the certification of GIS Program managers.

Keywords: Enterprise GIS, strategic planning, cost benefit evaluation, human resources, funding, governance, capability maturity model, management competency model.

1 Introduction

GIS has grown up. We do not need to explain the acronym anymore; everybody knows what it is and everybody seems to be using it. Or so they think. Text books of the late 20th century spent a lot of time defining GIS; definitions that show little resemblance to how GIS users in 2015 understand GIS. Many current GIS applications are as easy to use as writing an email on a mobile device and the end user is well-shielded from the 'S' in GIS, the system that was all-important in the definitions of the 1990s. This chapter aims to provide academic support for the people who build and maintain such systems; not the programmers who help us to create ever faster indexes on unstructured data but the people who build the infrastructure that the easy to use applications depend on.

Every organization that has multiple GIS users has de facto a GIS Program [1]. If the users get their work done and are not aware of the business unit that allows them to do their work, then this means that the program manager does her job well. If on the other hand every GIS project starts from scratch and the only institutional memory is buried in the heads of those who did other GIS projects before, then the tool that constitutes GIS is clearly not used to its highest potential. This chapter aims to rectify this all-too-common situation by providing an analysis of best practices. Even in organizations that have an official GIS Program manager, this person more often than not has reached their position by seniority and learned by trial and error what works and what doesn't [2]. As mature as GIS is from a technical perspective [3], GIS Program management is still haphazard [4] and the best a GIS Program manager could do up to now is to talk to peers in a social network built over decades of professional experience [5].

The professionalization of GIS has made good progress [6]. GIS certificates, both academic and vendor-driven abound and several professional organizations have developed their own set of certifications for GIS technicians [7-10]; i.e., the bottom strung of a hierarchy of GIS professionals [11]. There is, or at least has not been, a corresponding body of knowledge for higher level GIS professionals or managers, which is surprising given that there are thousands of GIS departments in the United States alone. King County's (Seattle) GIS department, for instance, has 28 staff and spends over $5 million to support some 35 business units throughout the county [12]. Running such a unit could be seen as a public administration [13] or more generally a management science [14] task. But similar to GIScience being different from general information science [15], the body of knowledge in support of a GIS Program is different and needs to be codified. This necessity is underlined by the creation of the GIS Management Institute (GMI) that requires a scientific foundation for its accreditation of GIS Programs and the certification of GIS Program managers [16].

2   The Widening Gap between Bodies of Knowledge

There was a wave of interest in the fledgling GIScience literature on organizational and management aspects of GIS in the late 1990s [17-20] that has barely been kept alive in later years by vendor-sponsored monographs [21, 22]. But things have understandably since changed with respect to technology (from client-server to PC to web services) as well as the role of GIS in many organizations. The better academic departments are doing a good job teaching GIS project management [23] but there is only one school in the United States that offers a degree in GIS Management [24]. In spite of the flurry of publications in the 1990s, GIScience has not been acknowledged in the world of business schools [25].

At the same time, new standards [26 -28] have been widely adopted in the business community but are virtually unknown in the academic world. The PMI defines program management as "the application of knowledge, skills, tools, and techniques to a program to meet the program requirements and to obtain benefits and control not available by managing projects individually", [27, p. 6]. The scope of programs is hence beyond the sum of individual projects and includes training, operations and maintenance activities. All this applied to GIS Programs as well. Two dimensions are useful to keep in mind when there is confusion about the differences between projects and programs:

- Uncertainty; well-managed projects generally have a low level of uncertainty associated with them. This starts with project specification and improves as a project moves towards its goal. Programs, on the other hand do not start out with a well-defined scope and require continuous adjustment. In extreme cases, a successful project may still be abandoned because its program context has changed.

- Change management of projects is usually in form of fixes when the original outcomes seem to become unattainable. Program management, however, anticipates changes and aims to adapt the program to changing contexts.

The practice of GIS Programs would be categorized in management science as a portfolio, a higher level management structure that has temporal bounds and combines multiple programs to achieve an organization's strategic objectives [25]. In addition, portfolio projects do not need to be related to each other. Both of these characteristics (no temporal bounds and possible non-relatedness of the projects) are characteristic for GIS Programs. It follows that GIS Programs then combine the components of traditional programs and portfolios, namely: strategic planning, governance, benefits management, and stakeholder engagement. GIS Programs, like portfolios, manage recurring activities (producing values) as well as projectized activities that are aimed at increasing value production capability.

3 Contents of a GIS Program Management Body of Knowledge

3.1 Strategic Planning

Following Crosswell [29], the GIS Program roadmap has to fit with the larger organization strategy of the institution. This requires the identification of geographically oriented business processes to arrive at a GIS assessment and planning workflow. The program manager needs to determine internal and external influences to identify the benefits for stakeholders (see sub-sections beneath). That task itself is based on the recognition of assumptions, some SWOT analyses and feasibility studies. Fortunately, a number of county and state governments have published their GIS Strategic Plans [30-34], which form nice case study objects.

3.1.1 Program Benefits Management

Program benefits management aims at focusing stakeholders on the outcomes and benefits. The latter include internal improved financial performance and operational efficiencies as well as external customers (other business units) or intended beneficiaries such as a particular demographic of the general population. The challenge often lies in realizing that new or improved capabilities to consistently deliver and sustain program products, services, or capabilities are usually fast taken for granted and their continuing benefit is hard to quantify or monetarize. Some benefits such as access to building permit data show immediate results, while others such as improvement in school graduation rates may only become apparent when the program itself is completed. The program roadmap will help in managing expectations in this context.

3.1.2 Program Stakeholder Engagement

The importance of managing perceptions across stakeholder groups cannot be over-emphasized. A stakeholder map (see Figure 1) helps to keep oversight as to how tight the communication with each stakeholder (group) should be managed.

What are our key material issues?

#	Issue	#	Issue
1	Health and Safety	12	Customer satisfaction
2	Economic value	13	Employee development and engagement
3	Local air quality	14	Environmental compliance
4	Labor relations	15	Water use and recycling
5	Business integrity	16	Local supply chain engagement
6	Energy efficiency	17	Local employment
7	Material use efficiency	18	Waste water
8	Greenhouse gas emissions	19	Human rights
9	Use of recycled materials	20	Community involvement
10	Waste management	21	Environmental fines incurred
11	O₃ depleting emissions	22	Biodiversity

Our most material issues

Matrix — vertical axis: Current or potential impact (Critical, Major, Moderate, Minor); horizontal axis: Level of concern to stakeholders (Minor, Moderate, Major, Critical).

- Critical / Major concern: 4, 5, 6, 7
- Critical / Critical concern: 1, 2, 3
- Major / Moderate concern: 9, 10
- Major / Major concern: 8, 11, 12, 13, 14
- Moderate / Minor concern: 21
- Moderate / Moderate concern: 15, 17
- Moderate / Major concern: 16, 18, 19, 20
- Minor / Moderate concern: 22

Legend: ■ Safety   ■ Governance and commerce   ■ Environmental   ■ People and community

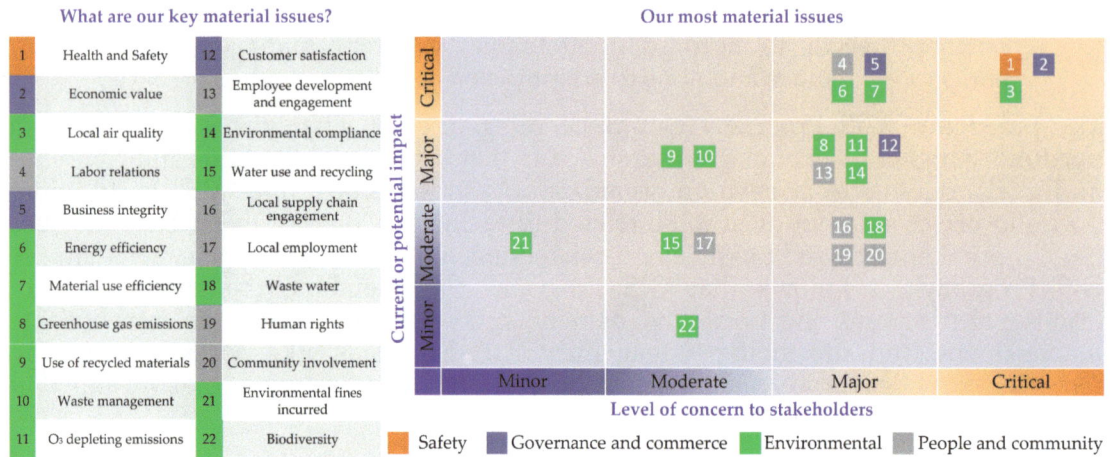

Figure 1: Stakeholder map (adopted from [34, p. 4])

Stakeholder engagement planning should include questions of organizational culture and acceptance of change, expectations of program benefits, degree of support or opposition to the program, and an estimation of the stakeholder's ability to influence the outcome of the GIS Program. The result of such work is a stakeholder engagement plan that should contain quantitative and qualitative measures of stakeholder engagement. Although it is discussed here as part of strategic planning, it should be noticed that stakeholder engagement planning like the strategic plan as a whole is a continuous effort and not limited to the beginning stages of a GIS Program.

3.2   Cost Benefit Evaluation

The purpose of a cost benefit evaluation is to get senior management support and secure funding. The business case for the GIS Program has to be developed in collaboration with key sponsors and stakeholders. Obermeyer [35] provided a general overview with examples for a range of benefits from GIS Programs across North America but until recently, the only methodological description was a very hands-on ten-step process developed for ESRI in 2008 [36], which was followed by individual studies reported on in the URISA Journal [12, 37]. A first detailed and systematic methodology is currently being developed and tested for a range of organizations at the University of Washington by Zerbe [38]. For smaller organizations, so-called cost-effectiveness analysis, balanced score card, total cost of ownership, or even basic payback period value-added approaches have been proposed [29, 39].

3.3   GIS Human Resources

One of the main differences between a GIS Project (even a big one) and a GIS Program is the issue of staff recruitment and hiring, which would usually be left to a personnel or human resource department. However, a GIS Program manager has to determine how to distribute workloads across full- and part-time positions, student interns, contract personnel, or using overtime of existing personnel. The Urban and Regional Information Systems Association (URISA) published a useful booklet about model GIS job descriptions [40] that illustrates the range of responsibilities, and a salary survey [41] that in addition to mere dollar figures also provides a wide range of tables that can be mined for how GIS tasks are distributed throughout different types of organizations. One of the unresolved issues of GIS human resources is the question of gender balance [42].

3.3.1 From Geospatial Technology Competency to Geospatial Management Competency

The US Department of Labor released in 2010 a nine-tiered geospatial technology competency model that specifies foundational, industry-wide, industry sector-specific, and finally occupation-specific competencies [43] (see Figure 2). It then contracted with URISA to develop a geospatial management competency model for the top tier of this pyramid [44]. It specifies 74 essential competencies and 18 competency areas that characterize the work of most successful managers in the geospatial industry. Its purpose is to guide individual professional development, to help people in move up or over in an organization or industry, to help educators and trainers develop curricula that address workforce needs, to inform development of interview protocols, as requirements for professional certification, and as criteria for academic program accreditation and articulation.

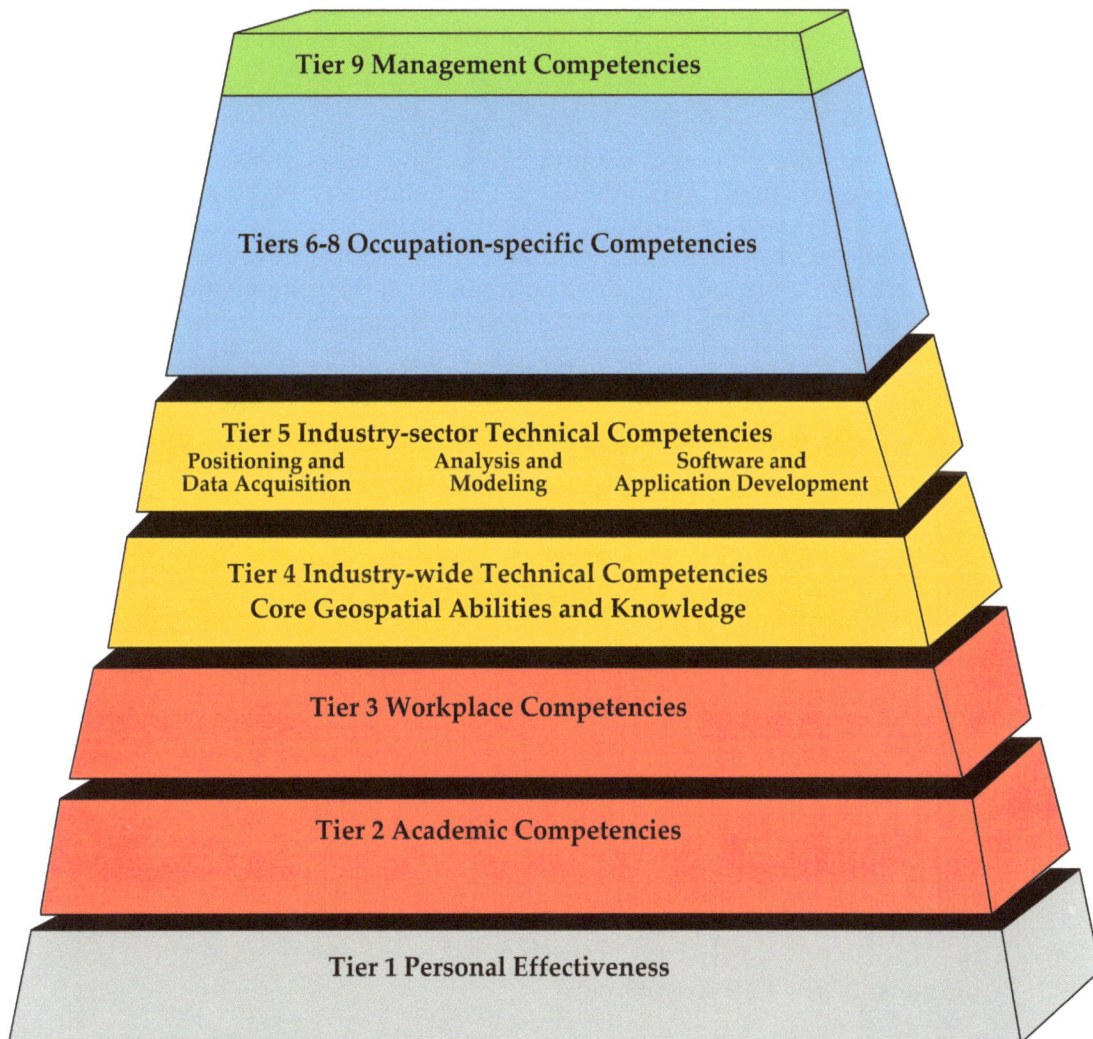

Figure 2: Geospatial competency model (adopted from [43, 44])

3.4   Financial Planning and Management

3.4.1   Costs

GIS Programs are often funded through line-items in the general fund—allocated through the organization's budgeting process. In addition to funds allocated through the normal budgeting process in an organization, there are often other funding sources such as special funds or capital funds (for road or utility improvements) that are managed separate from the general fund. Among program management one can distinguish traditional project costs from those that are more often seen as "fixed costs" such as system infrastructure, tech support, application development, or finance management. We are used to projects to have costs overruns. These will have to be buffered in the larger context of the GIS Program – something that puts GIS Program managers into a difficult position, where she has to defend herself in all directions. Flexibility gained from a wider range of staffing options (including the secondment of employees from other departments) goes a long way to create such buffers.

3.4.2   Outsourcing

An increasingly popular option for minimizing long term costs is the notion of outsourcing and contracting. Web services cover potentially more and more of the above mentioned fixed costs. In addition, needs assessment, field work, and many data maintenance tasks are now seen as areas that do not require in-house expertise. The difficult part here is that outsourcing does not relinquish the organization from its role to manage and oversee the work, and to take overall responsibility for it.

With increased reliance on outside vendors and contractors comes the issue of procurement. Traditionally the realm of a purchasing department, this is a prime example for where spatial is special, i.e., the expertise for running the complete workflow from the preparation of specifications and requests for information / qualifications / proposals / bids to review and contract preparation should lie within the GIS Program [29]. The need to incorporate legal counsel may cause this externalization of costs to become a rather drawn-out process. It is therefore the responsibility of the GIS Program manager to develop and maintain a good working relationship with the vendor/contractor.

3.5   The Technological Environment

3.5.1   Enterprise GIS

GIS Program management and enterprise GIS go hand in hand. An enterprise GIS without GIS Program management is unconceivable and the latter would be overkill if there is no wide adoption of GIS throughout the organization. The notion of an enterprise GIS assumes that multiple if not many business units are using GIS.

3.5.2   Components of a GIS Architecture

Although many businesses do not have a formal GIS architecture, enterprise GIS benefit immensely from an organized conceptual framework that enables the description and guides the construction and operation of complex GIS implementations. There is a large body of literature on architectural reference models and best practices [45, 46].

A solid architectural design is robust enough to cope with ever changing environments and demands. Examples for relatively recent demands that distinguish GIS architectures from general IT trends are: wireless data acquisition including real-time GPS/GNSS, "Open GIS" from desktop clients to web portals, web services and crowd-sourcing, coping with big data like LiDAR, CAD-GIS integration. Compared with most other business applications, GIS puts a much higher demand on the expertise and computational prowess of the IT infrastructure, which may in some instances cause the general IT department to be subsumed under the GIS Program.

Given the above mentioned demands, enterprise GIS tend to put a much higher strain on security, database administration, and user support than traditional IT departments are used to. Even the development of technical standards (in-house as well as outside all the way up to the International Standards Organization (ISO)) requires faster training and continuing education cycles.

3.5.3   Maintaining the In-house GIS Database

GIS projects are usually not expansive enough to warrant the development of guidelines for data quality. It is therefore at the GIS Program level, that organization-wide data quality specifications should be developed and enforced. The FGDC has developed a widely accepted base standard [47], which may, however, have to be expanded to fit the mission of the enterprise. It is in this context worthwhile to consult further standards developed by ISO [48] and the Open Geospatial Consortium.

The GIS Program manager is responsible for defining an enterprise-wide set of automated and manual checks both during (quality control) and after data editing (quality assurance). In some instances, this still involves data capture itself, but for most GIS programs, standardized procedures will have to be developed that ascertain that editing and analysis procedures are documented well enough to be reproducible.

3.6   GIS Program Governance

3.6.1   Reporting Structures and Responsibilities

Following directly from the previous section, a well-managed GIS Program has policies and practices for each of the categories listed in Table 1. These should be developed on a consensus basis and reviewed/revised on a regular basis.

• Personnel and professional development	• System administration and network security
• Standards compliance	• User support and help desk services
• Contract and financial management	• External communications
• Project coordination and management	• Data maintenance procedures and responsibilities
• Data/product access and sharing	

Table 1: Categories of GIS Program Policies (adopted from [29]).

3.6.2 Legal Issues

Except for health and financial institutions, few other IT managers have to deal as many legal concerns as the GIS Program manager. In the widest sense, these have to do with access to and distribution of geographic information. Legal authority for access to public records is granted in the United States by the federal freedom of information act [49] that are augmented by state laws and local regulations such as right-to-know laws and sunshine acts.

This is balanced by both security concerns and the threat of liability suits. A FGDC study [50] showed that security concerns are usually over-emphasized and that most of non-classified information is available through multiple pathways. Liability concerns are more difficult to deal with because the range of possible aggravations is so large. Reliability questions though are easiest to address by placing data into the public domain, which absolves authorities from almost any responsibility for inaccuracies [51] – but this contradicts another tenet of GIS Program management: to cover one's costs through revenues [52]. Interagency agreements for cost and data sharing carry their own rules and should be adhered to if for no other reason than that it would erode trust if partners do not act in sync.

With the transition from product to service delivery, the legal territory becomes ever more uncertain to the GIS manager because service providers usually exclude liability in case of service changes and traditional data backup procedures become obsolete.

4 GIS Capability Maturity Model (GISCMM)

The GIS Management Institute developed a tool to assess levels of capability and maturity of an organization's GIS operations [53]. The model was originally developed with a focus on local governments but is intended to be applicable to any enterprise GIS. The notion of a capability maturity model was originally developed by the Software Engineering Institute [54].

The capability maturity model is based on the characteristics of the organization's approach to individual defined processes. These processes are usually defined as:

Level 1 – Ad hoc (chaotic) processes-typically in reaction to a need to get something done.

Level 2 – Repeatable processes–typically based on recalling and repeating how the process was done the last time.

Level 3 – Defined process–the process is written down (documented) and serves to guide consistent performance within the organization.

Level 4 – Managed process–the documented process is measured when performed and the measurements are compiled for analysis. Changing system conditions are managed by adapting the defined process to meet the conditions.

Level 5 – Optimized processes–The defined and managed process is improved on an on-going basis by institutionalized process improvement planning and implementation. Optimization may be tied to quantified performance goals.

The National States Geographic Information Council (NSGIC) identified in 2010 seven categories for which GIS capability maturity should be measured: (1) people, (2) data, (3) processes, (4) policy, (5) strategy, (6) technology, and (7) legal [55]. Within these seven categories, the GMI chose to assess GIS organizations' maturity on a 7-point scale in 56 specific detailed characteristics based on their current implementation of each characteristic. The GIS Capability Maturity Model assumes two broad areas of GIS operational development: enabling capability and execution ability. Enabling capability can be thought of as the technology, data, resources, and related infrastructure to support typical enterprise GIS operations. Enabling capability includes GIS management and professional staff. However, the ability (execution capability) of the staff to utilize the enabling technology at its disposal is subject to a separate assessment as part of the model.

5   Conclusions

This chapter outlines a range of aspects in which the management of GIS projects and programs differ. The latter is a relatively undeveloped research area. Efforts to build a scientific foundation for program management practices just started with the development of a thorough return on investment study across a multitude of organization types [38]. Similarly, the data created by hundreds of organizations, who are as of 2015 conducting a GISCMM-based assessment will provide the foundation to build a generalizable body of knowledge for GIS Program management. Together with an analysis of best practices as identified, for example, through 35 years of peer review for the Exemplary Systems in Government Award [56], we are inching towards a theory of GIS Program Management

References

[1]   PETERS, P. Building a GIS. ESRI Press, Redlands, CA, 2008.

[2]   TOMLINSON, R. Thinking about GIS. ESRI Press, Redlands, CA, 2011.

[3]   ONSRUD, H. AND PINTO, J. Evaluating correlates of GIS adoption success and the decision process of GIS acquisition. URISA Journal, 5, 1 (1993), 18-39.

[4]   BABINSKI, G: URISA Develops the Geospatial Management Competency Model (GMCM) for USDOLETA. In Proceedings of WURISA GIS Conference 2012 (Tacoma, WA), http://www.waurisa.org/conferences/2012/presentations/05 Greg Babinski URISA Helps Develop the USDOL Geospatial Management Competency.pdf.

[5]   OBERMEYER, N. The maturation of a profession. Cartography and Geographic Information Science, 34, 2 (2007), 129-132, DOI: 10.1559/152304007781002280.

[6]   MCMASTER, R AND HARVEY, F. Geographic Information Science and Society. In Manual of Geospatial Science and Technology, J Bossler, Ed. CRC Press, Boca Raton, FL, 2010, ch 33, pp. 653-668.

[7]   WIKLE, T. An examination of job titles used for GIScience professionals. In Geospatial Technologies and Advancing Geographic Decision Making, D Albert, Ed. IGI Global, Hershey, PA, 2012, ch 6, pp. 66-81 DOI: 10.4018978-1-4666-0258-8.ch006.

[8]   JOHNSON, A. UCGIS Body of Knowledge, proposed and unanticipated benefits and possible future initiatives. In Proceedings seventh European GIS Education Seminar 2010 (Serres, Greece). http://eugises.eu/proceedings2008/johnson.pdf.

[9]   TRINDER, J. Competency standards, a measure of the quality of a workforce. Proceedings 37th ISPRS Congress, Commission VI, WG VI/5, http://www.isprs.org/proceedings/xxxvii/congress/6a_pdf/5_wg-vi-5/01.pdf.

[10]   PRAGER, S AND PLEWE, B. Assessment and evaluation of GIScience curriculum using the geographic information science and technology body of knowledge. Journal of Geography in Higher Education, 33, sup1 (2009), 46-69, DOI: 10.1080/03098260903034012.

[11]   LUKINBEAL, C AND MONK, J. Master's in Geographic Information Systems Programs in the United States: Professional Education in GIS and Geography. The Professional Geographer, 67, 2 (2015), pp. xxx, DOI: 10.1080/00330124.2014.983630.

[12]   BABINSKI, G. FUMIA, D. REYNOLDS, T, SINGH, P., SCOTT, T. AND ZERBE, R. An Analysis of Benefits from the Use of Geographic Information Systems by King County, Washington. 2012.

[13]   SHAFRITZ, J. Classics of Public Administration. Wadsworth Publishing, Boston, 2012.

[14]   DRUCKER, P. The Practice of Management. Harper Collins, 1954.

[15]   GOODCHILD, M. Twenty years of progress: GIScience in 2010. Journal of Spatial Information Science, 1 (2010), 3-20. doi:10.5311/JOSIS.2010.1.2.

[16]   BUTLER, A. URISA starts the task of reorganizing for the future. The GIS Professional, 252, 6-16.

[17]   CAMPBELL, H AND MASSER, I. GIS and Organizations. Taylor & Francis, London, 1995.

[18]   HUXHOLD, W. AND LEVINSOHN, A. Managing Geographic Information System Projects. Oxford University Press, New York, 1995.

[19]   FRANK, AU. Geographic information business in the next century. Proceedings of Third Joint European Conference on Geographical Information, JEC-GI'97, Vienna, Vol. 1, pp: 13-22IOS Press.

[20]   OBERMEYER, N AND PINTO, J. Managing Geographic Information Systems. Guilford Press, London, 2008.

[21]   THOMAS, C AND OSPINA, M. Measuring Up: The Business Case for GIS. Redlands: ESRI Press, 2004.

[22]   PETERS, D. System Design Strategies. ESRI Press, Redlands, CA, 2015. http://wiki.gis.com/wiki/index.php/System_Design_Strategies_Preface.

[23]   GIS Project Management. Course home page for GEOG 584 as part of their online MGIS Program, 2015. https://www.e-education.psu.edu/geog584/l1_p7.html.

[24]   SCOTT, M. Master of Science in GIS Management. Salisbury University, 2015, http://www.salisbury.edu/geography/msgism/docs/GIS_MS_Brochure_2011.pdf.

[25]   DOUGLAS, B. Achieving Business Success with GIS. John Wiley, 2008. DOI: 10.1002/9780470985595.

[26]   PMI. The standard for portfolio management. Program Management Institute, 2013.

[27] PMI. The standard for program management. Program Management Institute, 2013.

[28] PMI. A guide to the project management body of knowledge. Program Management Institute, 2013.

[29] CROSWELL, P. The GIS Management Handbook. Frankfort, KY: Kessey Dewitt Publications, 2009.

[30] WESTCHESTER COUNTY. Strategic Plan 2012. Department of Information Technology, Geographic Information Systems. http://giswww.westchestergov.com.

[31] APPLIED GEOGRAPHICS. State of New York Geographic Information System (GIS) Strategic Plan. NY State Office of Cyber Security and Critical Infrastructure Coordination, 2008.

[32] CITY OF ALEXANDRIA. Geographic Information Systems (GIS) Five-Year Strategic Plan 2013-2017. Department of Planning and Zoning, GIS Division, 2012.

[33] COUNTY OF LOS ANGELES. Enterprise Geographic Information Systems 2009 – 2012 Strategic Plan. Los Angeles Enterprise GIS, 2009

[34] APERAM. Sustainability Report 2013. Luxembourg. http://www.aperam.com/uploads/pdf/Sustainability/Aperam Sustainability Report 2013.pdf.

[35] OBERMEYER, N. Measuring the Benefits and Costs of GIS, In Geographical, Information Systems, Vol. 2, Management Issues and Applications, Abridged (M.F. Goodchild, P.A. Longley, D.J. Maguire, and D. W. Rhind (Eds.), pp. 255-264, John Wiley & Sons, 2005.

[36] MAGUIRE, D., KOUYOUMIJAN, V. And SMITH, R. The Business Benefits of GIS: An ROI Approach. Redlands: ESRI Press, 2008.

[37] JOFFE, B. Estimating GIS Return on Investment the Empirical Way. URISA Journal, 27, 1, pp. 2015.

[38] ZERBE, R. International GIS Return on Investment Study. URISA Journal, 27, 2, (in print).

[39] LONGLEY, P., GOODCHILD, M, MAGUIRE, D. AND RHIND, D. Geographic Information Systems and Science. John Wiley & Sons, 2005.

[40] BUTLER, A. Model GIS Job Descriptions. URISA, 2013.

[41] URISA. 2014 Salary Survey for IT/GIS Professionals. URISA, 2015.

[42] MAZUR, L. AND ALBRECHT, J. Women in GIS. The URISA Journal, 27, 2, (in print).

[43] DOLETA. Geospatial Technology Competency Model. US Department of Labor, Employment and Training Administration, 2010

[44] URISA. Geospatial Management Competency Model. URISA GIS Management Institute, 2012.

[45] FGDC. Geospatial Profile of the Federal Enterprise Architecture. 2009.

‌‌
‌‌‌‌‌‌

‌‌

‌‌

‌‌‌ Federal Geographic Data Committee, 2000.

[48] FGDC. ISO Metadata Resources. Federal Geographic Data Committee, 2012.

[49] US HOUSE OF REPRESENTATIVES. A Citizen's Guide on Using the Freedom of Information Act and the Privacy Act of 1974 to Request Government Records. United States House of Representatives, 2012.

[50] FGDC. Guidelines for Providing Appropriate Access to Geospatial Data in Response to Security Concerns. Federal Geographic Data Committee, 2005.

[51] ROSNAY, M AND JANSSEN, K. Legal and Institutional Challenges for Opening Data across Public Sectors: Towards Common Policy Solutions. Journal of Theoretical and Applied Electronic Commerce Research, 9, 3, (online). DOI: 10.4067/S0718-18762014000300002.

[52] CROSWELL, P. AND WERNHER, A. GIS Program Revenue Generation and Legal Issues in Public Sector Organizations. URISA, 2004.

[53] GIS Management Institute. Geospatial Capability Maturity Model. URISA GMI, 2013.

[54] PAULK, M, WEBER, C, CURTIS, B. AND CHRISSIS, M. The Capability Maturity Model: Guidelines for improving the software process. Addison-Wesley, 1995.

[55] NSGIC. Statewide Geospatial Maturity Assessment Model. National States Geographic Information Council, 2010.

[56] URISA. Exemplary Systems in Government Award. URISA, 2015. http://www.urisa.org/clientuploads/directory/Documents/ESIG/ESIG Award Winners.pdf

Prolegomena for an Ontology of Place

Andrea Ballatore

Center for Spatial Studies, Department of Geography, 1720 Ellison Hall, University of California, Santa Barbara, Santa Barbara, CA 93106-4060, USA

Abstract: The computational representation of place is one of the key research areas for the advancement of geographic information science (GIScience), bridging the gap between place-based human cognition and experience, and space-centered information systems. While many conceptual schemas, vocabularies and ontologies contain some notion of place, the concept is either left implicit or articulated in widely divergent ways. Because of its ubiquity, an ontological clarification of place seems overdue. Adopting the perspective of ontology engineering, and not that of philosophical Ontology, this article paves the way towards the formalization of a place ontology in two steps. First, it provides a critical survey of how this concept is currently represented from lightweight vocabularies to formal ontologies. Second, it presents a set of prolegomena for a place ontology that would overcome the limitations of current approaches. Acknowledging the cultural dependency of place, I argue that such an ontology should be seen as a module positioned between foundational and domain ontologies. This place ontology would provide (i) a conceptual tool to support the modeling of place in any domain, and (ii) a widely applicable ontology, whose deployment would increase the interoperability of datasets, particularly in the context of Linked Data.

Keywords: Place ontology, place semantics, geo-semantics, Linked Data, ontology engineering.

1 Introduction

Place occupies a pivotal role in human cognition, language, and knowledge representation. This highly polysemic and vague notion is constantly used to structure, ground, and connect other entities. Social and cultural processes create, shape and destroy places, objects move across places, transport and communication networks interconnect places, experiences and memories are situated in places. In this sense, places are not merely backgrounds or containers of processes, but they have been long recognized as entities with distinctive characteristics that deserve investigation [10]. Although it might be unwarranted to discern a 'placial turn,' recent trends in geography [3], GIScience [26], and philosophy [9], are reaffirming the centrality of place in human affairs, while acknowledging its elusiveness and multiple meanings. In fact, despite our intuitive grasp of its meaning in different contexts, place resists formalization and dwells uncomfortably in our information systems.

Focusing on the computational representation of place in information systems, remarkable ambiguity exists about its content and relations [12]. Widely different approaches to modeling place can be observed in existing knowledge bases and ontologies [6]. While spatial grounding, typically through spatial reference systems, enjoys a high degree of standardization, place is seen as too vague and culturally-dependent to provide a stable reference frame. In general, place is rarely given an explicit representation, and is modeled either as domain-specific tessellation (e.g., electoral districts, census tracts, and counties), or as toponyms linked to footprints, as in gazetteers. My contention is that this state of affairs is problematic, as it misses the potential of place as a connector between heterogeneous data spaces.

In this article, I critically survey the models of place that can be found in existing ontologies, ranging from lightweight, semantic networks, to more formal ontologies, focusing on the context of Linked Data. Recurring issues and ontological flaws in such cases are identified. Subsequently, I identify advantages and drawbacks to the development of a place ontology, arguing that such an ontology would help the modeling process of geographic information across domains. A successful place ontology should operate between the level of abstract space and the level of domain-specific, culturally defined concepts which vary widely across information communities, providing an intelligible layers between (ideally) stable geographic coordinates and culturally defined, elusive, context-dependent entities.

To find concrete applications, a place ontology should avoid the 'scope creep' problem by taking a quasi-foundational approach, and without venturing in domain-specific semantic fields. Prolegomena to such a place ontology are identified and discussed, as well as some counter-arguments, as a step preliminary to its formalization. To design a place ontology, fundamental questions need to be addressed: What is wrong with the representation of place (or lack thereof) in current data spaces? What is invariant in all entities that informally fall under the 'place' umbrella? What are the essential themes through which places are classified in different information communities? What are the relationships of place with relatively well-defined ontological categories such as 'spatial regions', and with GIScience core concepts, such as objects and fields? The remainder of this article tries to propose some answers.

2   Representing place in the Semantic Web

Central to human cognition and experience, notions of place emerges in various forms in online schemas, lightweight ontologies, and vocabularies in Semantic Web [6]. Linked Data is emerging as a prominent paradigm to structure, merge, and share geospatial data [17], and geography is a key element to ground and inter-connect entities. This section surveys how the concept is defined and formalized in existing linked datasets, starting from lightweight vocabularies, and then moving to formal ontologies.

2.1   Place in vocabularies and semantic networks

Schema.org. In this lightweight ontology, designed to annotate web pages with micro-formats, place is defined as "Entities that have a somewhat fixed, physical extension."[1] The concept takes a business-oriented view, stating that place has phone number and an address, as well as customer reviews. At the same time, place is subsumed by landforms and administrative areas, which indeed are not businesses – famously, *Mountain* has a fax number. *Place* has several sub-types, branching out to 197 concepts, including *AdministrativeArea*, *CivicStructure*, and *LandmarksOrHistorical-Buildings*. The ontology expresses containment through *containedIn*, and geographic grounding through property *geo*.

DBpedia. In this project, place is represented both as instance, and as a class. Place *qua* instance[2] corresponds to a Wikipedia page, describing place encyclopedically. By contrast, place *qua* class[3] is part of the DBPedia ontology, and is used to structure other concepts. This class, described as "immobile things or locations," is very central in the DBPedia ontology, and is used as a domain in more than 200 properties in other classes. The class is the range of about 200 properties, including informal spatial relations (*locatedInArea*), and obscure properties resulting from noise in the data such as *red ski piste number* and *president of the general council*.

Place has a hierarchy of 135 subclasses, ranging from very general and vague concepts (e.g., *NaturalPlace*) to very specific ones (e.g., *LunarCrater*). The top level of the hierarchy includes *WineRegion*, *ArchitecturalStructure*, *HistoricPlace*, *Monument*, *Mountain*, *MountainPass*, *NaturalPlace*, *PopulatedPlace*, *ProtectedArea*, *SiteOfSpecialScientificInterest*, *SkiArea*, *WorldHeritageSite*, *SportFacility*, *HotSpring*, *SkiResort*, and *Community*. Oddly, *Mountain* is not a subclass of *NaturalPlace*.

OpenStreetMap. This popular crowd-sourced cartographic project takes an administrative view of place, defining it as "populated settlements, including city, town, village, suburbs, neighborhoods and hamlets etc. and also unoccupied identifiable places ranging from very large (continents and oceans) down to very small features."[4]

The term is specialized to settlements using concepts from the British administrative context, including *place=city*, *place=town*, and *place=hamlet*. Points and polygons can be tagged as places. Because of its intrinsic ambiguity, the term is occasionally used to describe features that do not fit other terms, such islands (place=island) and seas (place=sea). The same term can be found in linked data projects OSM Semantic Network[5] and LinkedGeoData,[6] both based on OpenStreetMap [5].

GeoNames.   The GeoNames ontology[7] re-uses the place class from *schema.org* to model the feature classes at the core of the project. The Feature class subsumes place, and represents all features in the gazetteer, and has simple relations, including

---

[1] http://schema.org/Place – All URLs in this article were accessed in March 2015.

[2] http://dbpedia.org/resource/Place

[3] http://dbpedia.org/ontology/Place

[4] http://wiki.openstreetmap.org/wiki/Key:place

[5] http://spatial.ucd.ie/lod/osn/term/k:place

[6] http://linkedgeodata.org/ontology/Place

[7] http://www.geonames.org/ontology

located in, nearby features, neighbor features, children features, and parent feature. Features are grouped into Classes, and classified into 690 Codes, representing a wide variety of specific place types, such as logging camp and asphalt lake.

ConceptNet. In MIT's semantic network ConceptNet5, *place* is a node that is connected to other concepts through labeled edges such as *isA* and *relatedTo*. e.g., city → *isA* → place.[8] Unlike lightweight ontologies, place has relations related to human purpose (e.g., place → *UsedFor* → eat to meet friend). No formal semantics is defined for the spatial or non-spatial relations between place and its neighbors.

WordNet. Because of its polysemy, the term 'place' belongs to 16 different noun synsets and to 16 verb synsets in WordNet. Excluding the metaphorical/idiomatic meanings, the two noun meanings relevant to this discussion are defined as follows: (#1) "topographic point, place, spot (a point located with respect to surface features of some region) 'this is a nice place for a picnic'; 'a bright spot on a planet;' " This synset[9] has highly idiosyncratic hyponyms, such as *rendezvous*, *hiding place*, and *solitude*, i.e., a "solitary place." By contrast, the second synset is defined as: (#2) "place, property (any area set aside for a particular purpose) 'who owns this place?'; 'the president was concerned about the property across from the White House.' " Oddly, this synset has only four hyponyms, including *sanctuary*, and *hatchery*. Despite these limitations, WordNet can be used as a common ground to inter-link vocabularies [5].

Other lightweight ontologies. The *Places Ontology*[10] is a vocabulary containing 50 classes that describe natural features and man-made structures.   The vocabulary includes spatial relations *in, overlaps, bounded by*. Similarly, the BBC News ontology[11] contains a generic class place, used to described events reported in the stories, without formal semantics. Start-up Factual published a large vocabulary of place categories as part of their *Global Places* product.[12] This vocabulary contains about 460 categories, largely based on the US Yellow Pages. Drawing on WordNet, GeoNames, and DBpedia, the *PlaceVocabulary*[13] provides a vocabulary of 1,800 place types [4].

2.2   Place in formal ontologies

OSGB Buildings and Places ontology. This ontology was designed in 2008 the British Ordnance Survey to model cadastral data, described as "buildings and places that are topographically relevant, i.e., which are sufficiently important to be recognized and recorded by Ordnance Survey surveyors."[14] The OWL model contains 678 classes with 1,770 axioms, including mereological and topological relations, as well as specifications of activities and purposes. For example, the place subclass 'castle' has a part *Building*, has historic purpose *Defense*, and has a part *Defensive Wall*. Similarly, a 'cattery' is described as follows: "Every Cattery is a kind of Place. Every Cattery has purpose Housing of Cats. Every Cattery has part a Building that has purpose Housing of Cats."

---

[8] http://conceptnet5.media.mit.edu/web/c/en/place

[9] http://wordnet.rkbexplorer.com/id/synset-topographic point-noun-1

[10] http://purl.org/ontology/places

[11] http://www.bbc.co.uk/ontologies/news

[12] http://www.factual.com

[13] https://github.com/andrea-ballatore/PlaceVocabulary

[14] http://data.ordnancesurvey.co.uk/ontology

OpenCyc. In the OpenCyc project, the *Place*[15] concept is a synonym to point, site, and spot. The definition of the concept is more formal than any of the previous ontologies, and is summarized as follows: "A specialization of EnduringThing_Localized (q.v.). Each instance of Place is a spatial thing which has a relatively permanent location. Thus, in a given micro-theory, each Place is stationary with respect to the frame of reference of that micro-theory." This concept is a type of *enduring thing localized, site, spatial thing, thing that is not a perceptual agent, thing that is not someone, underspecified location.* In the project's documentation, the difference between place and locations is defined as follows:

> "An important specialization of EnduringThing_Localized is Place (q.v.). The salient distinction between places (instances of Place) and locations (instances of EnduringThing_Localized) is that places are assumed to have relatively permanent locations, whereas locations need not have permanent locations. Thus, from the perspective of someone standing on a beach, the crest of a breaking wave can be a location at which foaming is occurring (thus an EnduringThing_Localized), but it cannot be such a place (i.e., it cannot be an instance of Place)."[16]

OpenCyc is organized in micro-theories, and place is important to several of them, particularly to the definition of agency with respect to geo-political regions. In the knowledge base, geopolitical-entities can be viewed through two different micro-theories. In a *physical geography* micro-theory, geopolitical-entities are clearly distinguished from the regions they control. In these cases, the *TerritoryFn* function is used to demarcate the land mass (a geopolitical region) of a geopolitical entity. By contrast, in a *dualist geography* micro-theory, geopolitical entities are viewed as being both agents and land masses.

UMBEL Reference Concept Ontology. In this interoperability project, there is an elaborate attempt to model place.[17] Several concepts that subsume place are defined following OpenCyc micro-theories.

- *PopulatedPlace*: "A Place or area with clustered or scattered buildings and a permanent human population, including cities, settlements, towns, and villages. It does not include Locales."

- *Place_NonAgent*: "(Non-agent-like place) A collection of places which are not agent-like. Some things can be both places and exhibit agency; e.g., the City-OfMiamiFL is a region in Florida State, and it also can enter into agreements with other cities (see GeopoliticalEntity). Each instance of Place NonAgent is a Place that does NOT have any agency, e.g., LakeErie and OuterSpace."

- *GeographicPlace*: "(Site that is also a geographical thing) Point that is also a geographical thing, place that is also a geographical thing, spot that is also a geo- graphical thing."

- *HumanlyOccupiedSpatialObject*: "(Places occupied by humans) A specialization of InanimateObject. Each instance of HumanlyOccupiedSpatialObject is a place that humans occupy. Instances include both movable things, such as cars and

---

[15] http://sw.opencyc.org/concept/Mx4rvVjTtJwpEbGdrcN5Y29ycA

[16] http://sw.opencyc.org/concept/Mx4ro3lluGJHQdiVxrZReHS-jQ

[17] http://umbel.org/umbel/sc/Place

ships, and things having a more or less permanent location, such as houses or office buildings."

- *GeopoliticalEntity*: "A specialization of Organization and of LegalAgent and of GeographicalAgent; instances of this collection control Geographical-Regions. Each instance of GeopoliticalEntity includes a governing body, but is more than just that governing body."

- *GeographicalRegion*: "a tangible spatial region that includes some piece of the surface of a planet (usually PlanetEarth), and may be represented on a map of the planet."

A "super type" that aggregates many classes is Geopolitical,[18] defined as "Named places that have some informal or formal political (authorized) component. Important subcollections include Country, IndependentCountry, State Geopolitical, City, and Province." Through a geographic module, UMBEL is connected to the GeoNames ontology.[19]

DOLCE. While the DOLCE [11] foundational ontology has no direct representation of place, the CommonSenseMapping ontology, based on DOLCE, contains a rather sophisticated formalization of place and its related concepts [19, pp. 230-1].[20] This conceptualization hinges on the distinction between physical and non-physical places:

- *physical-place*: subclass of non-agentive-physical-object that subsumes all places.

- *geographical-object*: subclass of physical-place with geographic coordinates.

- *non-physical-place*: subclass of non-agentive-figure "for non-physical (i.e., socially- or cognitively-constructed) places." Non-physical places (e.g. Italy) are the hypostasis (i.e., figurative representation) of some physical-place.

- *geographical-place*: subclass of non-physical-place. It is a hypostasis of some geographical-object.

- *political-geographic-object*: subclass of geographical-place, "conventionally accepted by a community." The class has the meronomical property *geographic-part-of*.

- *country*: subclass of political-geographic-object.

Other formal ontologies. The Basic Formal Ontology (BFO)[21] distinguishes between an ontology for continuants that captures a state of affairs at a given time (SNAP), and an ontology for occurrents such as processes and events (SPAN). According the authors of BFO, place is a sub-class of a SNAP substantial entity. Places are a kind of site, but can also be geo-artifacts. For example, the term 'London' can refer to "London-as-site ('John lives in London') and London-as-geoartifact ('John admired London from the air')" [13, p. 164]. However, the distinction is not further clarified and formally expres-sed.

---

[18] http://umbel.org/umbel#Geopolitical

[19] http://techwiki.umbel.org/index.php/UMBEL - Annex J

[20] http://www.loa-cnr.it/ontologies/CommonSenseMapping#

[21] http://www.ifomis.org/bfo

In the General Formal Ontology (GFO),[22] developed by the Onto-Med Research Group, place is not specified. Its fundamental classes include *Spatial regions*, constructed on *Topoids*, i.e., connected compact regions of space with boundaries. The Suggested Upper Merged Ontology (SUMO)[23] purports to be a standardized foundational ontology, and includes a number of domain ontologies. In SUMO, place is spuriously formalized through classes *PlaceDescriptor*, *PlaceAddress*, *PlaceID*, *PlaceOf- Commerce*, and *PlaceOfWorship*.

3   Prolegomena for an ontology of place

The previous section surveyed the conceptualization of place in actual artifacts, from lightweight vocabularies to formal ontologies. Here, I argue that we need a new ontology of place to clarify the conceptual confusion that dominates the field. The goals of such an ontology are:

1. Provide an intermediate conceptual layer between foundational ontologies such as DOLCE and domain ontologies.

2. Allow the coherent articulation of multiple viewpoints on the same place.

3. Design a general tool to model places in different domains, aiming at a cross-cultural conceptualization.

4. Facilitate the integration of heterogeneous representations of place across academic disciplines, such as geography, economics, medicine, and history.

5. Model non-integrated aspects of place such as provenance, affordances, and social roles.

To frame my work towards these goals, I outline a minimal set of prolegomena, motivating reasons to construct such an ontology.

3.1   Why a place ontology?

Many counter-arguments can be formulated to deny the need for a place ontology. To date, simple models have been used to describe places in GISs. For example, gazetteers have traditionally relied on associations of the form <*place name, place type, geometry*>, where geometry is either a point or a polygon. While this approach is indeed sufficient in many contexts, it has several drawbacks: (i) it cannot express multiple viewpoints on the same place; (ii) it relies on a fixed typology of places, usually a taxonomy; (iii) it is not easy to integrate with other conceptualizations.

As shown in Section 2, a concept or a class called 'place' is present, in one form or another, in the vast majority of existing geographic vocabularies and ontologies. The many different ways used to model this concept suggest that each of these efforts rely on some implicit, commonsensical notion of place. The ubiquity and obscurity of the concept calls for an ontological work of clarification, ideally resulting in a usable conceptual modeling tool that would enable many communities to specify and share their places of interest.

---

[22] http://www.onto-med.de/ontologies/gfo

[23] http://www.ontologyportal.org

Other objections might come from the area of new generation, semantic gazetteers [16], and from the feature type and points of interest (POIs) ontologies, which are receiving attention in GIScience [14] and by the Open Geospatial Consortium (OGC).[24]

Similarly, microformats such as RDFa and Microdata aim at providing minimal mechanisms to specify places in unstructured web pages. The fundamental difference between my proposal and existing ontologies lies in the attempt of going beyond culture- and domain-specific places. While these approaches provide lists of culturally-bound place types, such as mountain, restaurant, and music store, we aim at identifying and formalizing fundamental aspects of place, supporting the design of place in domain ontologies.

One final objection might be the possibility of over-engineering place, adding an unwarranted layer of complexity in the model, without reaping tangible benefits. This objection is perhaps the most serious, and is certainly a major issue that hinders the adoption of foundational ontologies. To mitigate the risk of over-engineering, my approach aims at showing that simpler models of place have many implicit assumptions, which result in difficulties in the long run. To achieve this goal, the next sections outline the prolegomena for such a place ontology.

3.2 Place cognition and place engineering

A fundamental difference to grasp in relation to place research is the distinction between place cognition and place engineering. The former approach aims at understanding how humans understand and conceptualize place, using methodologies from cognitive science and psychology. In this framework, place is one of the key geographic concepts that has been targeted for clarification with respect to cognate concepts such as region, neighborhood, location, space, district and area [2]. In their linguistic analysis of the term 'place' in English, Bennett and Agarwal [7] identify four categories of place-related expressions: (i) count nouns (i.e., place types), (ii) locative property (e.g. 'in London,' 'on the hill,' 'by the sea-side'), (iii) place names (e.g. 'London,' 'England'), and (iv) definite descriptions (e.g. nominal expressions referring to places). The authors acknowledge that their attempt to formulate a logical theory of place clashed with the term's vagueness, polysemy, and variety of modes through which it is used in natural language.

Even in academic debates, unexamined notions of place are often used as a synonym to spatial or spatio-temporal region, relying on the commonsensical meaning of the term, making a precise definition difficult if not impossible. Geographers often refer to it as a spatial unit of analysis, as in case of demography or political science. From a philosophical perspective, Casati and Varzi's major mereotopological analysis [8] uses the term 'place' extensively, both as a noun and as a verb, carefully avoiding to define it. As fundamental assumptions about what place is and how it relates to cognate concepts, a complete formal theory of place seems a rather unlikely development.

My proposal, by contrast, falls within the area that can be defined place engineering, i.e., the modeling of the concept in computational systems to support its representation, processing, and retrieval. As well as the place vocabularies and ontologies discussed in Section 2, ontologies of place have attracted interest in the context of geographic information retrieval [15, 21, 1]. In many works, however, the term 'place ontology' is not used in sense intended in this paper, but refers to culturally-

---

[24] http://www.opengeospatial.org/projects/groups/poiswg

specific taxonomies of place types (e.g., city, town, etc.), without formalizing their ontological commitments. Assuming a skeptical position regarding the possibility of reaching a wide, transdisciplinary agreement on place, I believe that a place ontology should provide conceptual tools to help design places in domain ontologies, increasing their interoperability. In this sense, a place ontology should be inclusive, taking into account the multi-faceted representations of the concept across disciplines, and distilling their underlying commonalities.

3.3   Cultural and linguistic dependence of place

One of the reasons that make place difficult to formalize is its cultural and linguistic dependence. Entities that are commonly referred to as places are deeply embedded in a specific cultural context. Typically, place types present in the Anglo-American world are proposed as universal, such as in the case of *schema.org* and similar projects, which results in scope creep, i.e., the attempt to create all-encompassing, universal place types, which are hard to use outside the borders of the English-speaking world. Moreover, even within the same large national and linguistic contexts, different information communities can have radically different understandings of common-sensical terms.

Examples of these issues abound both in traditional, top-down ontologies and classifications devised by professional geographers and in crowd-sourced projects such as OpenStreetMap (OSM). Depending on the context, place types such as 'city,' 'park,' 'field,' and 'restaurant' can refer to very different concepts, and therefore should be modeled as part of domain ontologies. As Smith and Mark [24] pointed out, any of these categorizations rely on a "degree of human-contributed arbitrariness on a number of different levels, and it is in general marked by differences in the ways different languages and cultures structure or slice their worlds" (p. 312). The research program of ethnophysiography focuses precisely on these aspects for landforms [18].

Based on these considerations, a place ontology should avoid the explicit modeling of such domain-specific place concepts. I maintain that a place ontology should provide a foundational, shared platform to facilitate the modeling and integration of diverging conceptualizations of place, rather than forcing a standardization that appears politically oppressive and, incidentally, doomed to fail. A crucial element in this context is the possibility of expressing multiple views on a place, formalizing the provenance of a place concept, i.e., the information community that generated it. For this purpose, the PROV-O ontology can represent a promising starting point.[25]

3.4   Place in time

Much discussions about place hinge on the issue of the definition of its boundaries, which are often vague, mutable, and highly subjective. However, place is often modeled without taking into account its temporal dimension. New places are relentlessly created, while existing places are updated, re-defined, and some disappear as a result of human and natural disasters. Hence, in principle, a place ontology should be able to model the temporal dimension of place, to capture its changes in a coherent framework, as happens in historical gazetteers. The lack of place temporality results in considerable confusion. For example, 'Rome' as the capital of the Roman Empire and

---

[25] http://www.w3.org/TR/prov-o

'Rome' as the capital of the current Italian Republic are the same atemporal instance of a *City* in DBpedia, which renders it useless for reasoning purposes. Indeed, some applications (e.g., historical analysis) and some place types (e.g., businesses) need an explicit temporal dimension for places more than others. The Linking Open Descriptions of Events (LODE) ontology constitutes a promising model to handle the temporal dimension of place and its complex relationship with events [23].

3.5   Social roles of place

As geographers in the humanistic tradition point out, place originates from the attribution of human meanings to regions of physical space [25]. The representation of place in ontologies usually conflates the social and the physical dimension, e.g., a shopping mall *qua* set of trading activities and a shopping mall *qua* collection of buildings and infrastructure. A common problem, particularly visible in OSM, occurs when the same physical structure is devoted to different activities, and when the activities change. Modeling confusion arises, for instance, when a building originally designed and used as a hospital in Victorian times currently hosts private apartments, shops, and a hotel.

Clarifying the distinction between the physical structure and social roles of place might help the maintainability and re-usability of complex place-related data. To achieve this, physical and natural objects need to be associated with their social roles through appropriate relations, representing what patterns of social interaction occurs there. To tackle the complex nature of these relations, a starting point is offered by Masolo et al. [20], in their formal analysis of socially constructed entities and roles. Acknow-ledging the relational nature of place, specific anti-rigid roles can be fleshed out based on human geographic perspectives, e.g., power relations between physical space and agents, through property, ownership, and control relations.

3.6   Place and scale

The intuitive notion of place includes entities located at different scales, ranging from a room ('my bedroom') to continents ('Africa'). Scale, intended as phenomenon scale, influences the characteristics of place, constraining how they can be perceived, experienced, and conceptualized. An ecological view aims at modeling place through the lens of the influential theory of affordances by Gibson [22]. Place, in its combination of physical and social structures can enable ('afford') specific activities for human actors. While affordances are certainly a promising way to conceptualize part of human-scale places, such as venues, restaurants, parks, and barbers, they seem less useful for large- scale places that cannot be experienced in a holistic way.

Cities, seas and countries can indeed be depicted as wholes in aerial photographs and maps, but are experienced directly only in human-scale fragments, and their conceptualization can vary widely for different agents. As opposed to human-scale places, such entities cannot be characterized by a clearly defined, unmediated purposes and affordances. When comparing France and a restaurant as places, some common-alities emerge: they both have boundaries; it is possible to go to and leave them; they are social constructions; they have show stable patterns of interactions that distinguish them from other places. More importantly, they present many differences: a restaurant is presumably designed to afford food consumption, socialization, and so on, which can be observed directly in its physical structure; a country operates at a fundamentally different level, consisting in an aggregation a myriad of other directly observable heterogeneous places, and is promptly identified through administrative and political structures. It seems therefore appropriate to adopt specific approaches are needed to conceptualize large-scale places as opposed to small-scale ones.

3.7 Thematic structure of place

Given the variety of entities that are normally thought of as places, a place ontology should identify fundamental themes through which any place type can be conceptualized. These themes are located between the foundational level and domain ontologies with particular, culturally-bound place types. In existing place taxonomies and ontologies, these are the top level of the classification, with broad themes like healthcare, retail, transportation, and government. This is arguably the most difficult component of a place ontology to design and formalize.

Although complete cultural independence is indeed impossible, a set of broadly, trans-cultural themes would help design place in domain ontologies, facilitating their grouping and structuring. Cross-cultural linguistic analysis is needed in order to identify invariant themes in place conceptualizations across information communities. For instance, while domain ontologies need to represent restaurants in the US and in Italy with very different subclasses and properties, the underlying theme of food consumption and socialization is invariant and can be used to conceptualize and find connections between the two ontologies. Similarly, while address formats differ widely (e.g., ZIP codes in the US and Post Codes in the UK), the underlying theme is that of logistical reference systems.

4   Conclusions

While many academic disciplines, projects, and datasets rely on some notion of place, there is no consensus on what place is, and how to represent it in a computational model. Bridging the gap between spatial and platial perspectives constitutes one of the key areas of future research for GIScience [12]. This article contributes to the debate on place representation from two perspectives. First, I carried out a survey of existing place vocabularies and ontologies, outlining the need for common foundations to represent place across different domains and contexts. Second, I outlined several prolegomena for the construction of an ontology of place.

The purpose of this ontology is to provide an intermediate conceptual layer between foundational and domain ontologies, enabling the interoperability of representations of place across academic disciplines, such as geography, history, and the digital humanities. Such an ontology can operate at two levels. Its core ideas can guide ontology engineers and conceptual modelers to model place types in their domain ontologies. From a pragmatic perspective, possibly articulated in a lightweight version or as a design pattern, the place ontology might greatly support the production and integration of Linked Data, in which place is one of the main concepts used to interlink heterogeneous datasets.

Several challenges lie ahead of this project. As place and place types are culturally-bound, the identification of cross-cultural and cross-linguistic themes require much empirical work, and research is needed to identify meaningful themes. The risk of over-engineering always looms large on foundational ontologies. In this sense, the proposed place ontology needs to be grounded on several case studies, covering multiple domains. Existing place vocabularies, ontologies, and geographic datasets could be linked through the place ontology, showing the advantages of an conceptual foundation for a ubiquitous and yet elusive concept.

References

[1]   ABDELMOTY, A., SMART, P., AND JONES, C. Building place ontologies for the semantic web: issues and approaches. In *Proceedings of the 4th ACM Workshop on Geographical Information Retrieval* (2007), ACM, pp. 7–12.

[2]   AGARWAL, P. Contested Nature of Place: Knowledge Mapping for Resolving Ontological. In *Geographic Information Science*, M. Egenhofer, C. Freksa, and H. Miller, Eds. 2004, pp. 1–21.

[3]   AGNEW, J. A. Space and Place. In *Handbook of Geographical Knowledge*, J. Agnew and D. Livingstone, Eds. Sage Publications, London, 2011, ch. 29.

[4]   BALLATORE, A., AND ADAMS, B. Extracting Place Emotions from Travel Blogs. In *Proceedings of AGILE 2015*. 2015, pp. 1–5.

[5]   BALLATORE, A., BERTOLOTTO, M., AND WILSON, D. Linking geographic vocabularies through WordNet. *Annals of GIS* 20, 2 (2014), 73–84.

[6]   BALLATORE, A., WILSON, D., AND BERTOLOTTO, M. A Survey of Volunteered Open Geo-Knowledge Bases in the Semantic Web. In *Quality Issues in the Management of Web Information*, G. Pasi, G. Bordogna, and L. Jain, Eds., vol. 50 of Intelligent Systems Reference Library. Springer, 2013, pp. 93–120.

[7]   BENNETT, B., AND AGARWAL, P. Semantic categories underlying the meaning of 'place'. In *Spatial Information Theory*, S. Winter, M. Duckham, L. Kulik, and B. Kuipers, Eds., vol. 4736 of LNCS. Springer, Berlin, 2007, pp. 78–95.

[8]   CASATI, R., AND VARZI, A. C. *Parts and Places: The Structures of Spatial Representation*. MIT Press, Cambridge, MA, 1999.

[9]   CASEY, E. S. *The Fate of Place: A Philosophical History*. University of California Press, Berkeley, CA, 1997.

[10] CRESSWELL, T. *Place: A Short Introduction*. Short Introductions to Geography. John Wiley & Sons, Oxford, UK, 2004.

[11] GANGEMI, A., GUARINO, N., MASOLO, C., OLTRAMARI, A., AND SCHNEIDER, L. Sweetening ontologies with DOLCE. In *Knowledge Engineering and Knowledge Management: Ontologies and the Semantic Web*, V. R. Benjamins, Ed., vol. 2473 of LNCS. Springer, 2002, pp. 166–181.

[12] GOODCHILD, M. F. Formalizing place in geographic information systems. In *Communities, Neighborhoods, and Health*, L. Burton, S. Kemp, M. Leung, S. Matthews, and D. Takeuchi, Eds. Springer, Berlin, 2011, pp. 21–33.

[13] GRENON, P., AND SMITH, B. SNAP and SPAN: Towards dynamic spatial ontology. *Spatial cognition and computation* 1, March (2004), 69–103.

[14] JANOWICZ, K., SCHEIDER, S., PEHLE, T., AND HART, G. Geospatial Semantics and Linked Spatiotemporal Data – Past, Present, and Future. *Semantic Web* 3, 4 (2012), 321–332.

[15] JONES, C., ALANI, H., AND TUDHOPE, D. Geographical Information Retrieval with Ontologies of Place. In *Spatial Information Theory* (2001), vol. 2205 of LNCS, Springer, Berlin, pp. 322–335.

[16] KESSLER, C., JANOWICZ, K., AND BISHR, M. An agenda for the next generation gazetteer: Geographic information contribution and retrieval. In

Proceedings of the 17th ACM SIGSPATIAL International Conference on Advances in Geographic Information Systems (2009), ACM, pp. 91–100.

[17] KUHN, W., KAUPPINEN, T., AND JANOWICZ, K. Linked Data: A Paradigm Shift for Geographic Information Science. In *Geographic Information Science*, M. Duckham, E. Pebesma, K. Stewart, and A. U. Frank, Eds., vol. 8728 of LNCS. Springer, Berlin, 2014, pp. 173–186.

[18] MARK, D. M., TURK, A. G., AND STEA, D. Progress on Yindjibarndi Ethnophysiography. In *Spatial Information Theory*, S. Winter, M. Duckham, L. Kulik, and B. Kuipers, Eds., vol. 4736 of LNCS. Springer, Berlin, 2007, pp. 1–19.

[19] MASOLO, C., BORGO, S., GANGEMI, A., GUARINO, N., OLTRAMARI, A., AND HORROCKS, I. *WonderWeb: Ontology Infrastructure for the Semantic Web.* Tech. rep., 2001.

[20] MASOLO, C., VIEU, L., BOTTAZZI, E., AND CATENACCI, C. Social Roles and their Descriptions. In *9th International Conference on Principles of Knowledge Representation and Reasoning* (2004), pp. 267–277.

[21] SANTOS, D., AND CHAVES, M. The place of place in geographical IR. In *3rd Workshop on Geographic Information Retrieval, SIGIR* (2006), ACM, pp. 5–8.

[22] SCHEIDER, S., AND JANOWICZ, K. Place Reference Systems: A Constructive Activity Model of Reference to Places. *Applied Ontology* 9, 2 (2014), 97–127.

[23] SHAW, R., TRONCY, R., AND HARDMAN, L. LODE: Linking Open Descriptions of Events. In *The Semantic Web*, A. Gómez-Pérez, Y. Yu, and Y. Ding, Eds., vol. 5926 of LNCS. Springer, Berlin, 2009, pp. 153–167.

[24] SMITH, B., AND MARK, D. M. Ontology and geographic kinds. In *Proceedings of the 11th International Symposium of Spatial Data Handling* (Vancouver, 1998), T. K. Poiker and N. Chrisman, Eds., International Geographical Union, pp. 308–320.

[25] TUAN, Y.-F. *Space and place: The perspective of experience.* University of Minnesota Press, Minneapolis, MN, 1977.

[26] WINTER, S., KUHN, W., AND KRÜGER, A. Guest Editorial: Does Place have a Place in Geographic Information Science? *Spatial Cognition & Computation* 9 (2009), 171–173.

Copyright and Alternatives in Access to Scientific Information

James Campbell

School of Computing and Information Science and National Center for Geographic Information and Analysis, 5711 Boardman Hall, University of Maine, Orono, ME 04469-5711, USA

Abstract: As more and more spatially-referenced data are generated, as more and more papers are written based on those data, and as software programs are written to exploit that data, the issue of copyright becomes an increasingly important context within which Geographic Information Science practitioners work. Those who seek to find and use spatially-related information, and those who produce such information, are working within, and sometimes constrained by, copyright law. The tension between the limitations on open access to scientific information due to copyright, and the traditional mores of science that depend on open access, are more evident than ever in the digital age. A brief review of limiting trends in copyright in the United States over the past four decades shows that limitations of access to information have generated responses, including new alternatives to strict copyright. GIS practitioners, both as users and as generators of scientific information, are wise to be aware not only of copyright provisions but of alternatives that are becoming available to traditional copyright.

Keywords: Copyright, information access, open access, licenses, data access.

1 Introduction

As more and more spatially-referenced data are generated, as more and more papers are written based on those data, and as software programs are written to exploit that data, the issue of copyright becomes an increasingly important context within which Geographic Information Science practitioners work. In this paper, we look at the context of copyright as it exists today and its effect on access to scientific information and data, including spatially-referenced information.

This article examines the expansion of copyright and its effects on access to information over the past 40 years, reactions to that expansion, and some current efforts on the part of government, research funders, academic institutions, and some aspects of civic society to offer alternatives to traditional copyright in order to make scientific information more widely accessible on a free basis. The focus is primarily on US copyright law, with some mention of differing contexts in other jurisdictions, e.g., the European Union's *sui generis* regulations conferring protection of facts in some circumstances. However, with negotiations underway for new agreements such as the proposed Trans Pacific Partnership, the TransAtlantic Trade and Investment Partnership, and the Trade in Services Agreement that will have a major impact intellectual property rights, it is likely that there will be more rather than less conformity of copyright regimes internationally since copyright conformity is a major emphasis in what has been revealed to date through drafts of these secret negotiations. In this situation, the US context can be informative beyond its domestic borders.

2   The Enclosure of the Information Commons

In the United States, copyright is a socially granted right in the U.S. Constitution that establishes a "bargain" between creators and the larger society: "To promote the Progress of Science and useful Arts, by securing for limited Times to Authors and Inventors the exclusive Right to their respective Writings and Discoveries" (Article 1, Section 8). Creators get an "exclusive Right" to exploit the value of their work in economic terms for "limited Times," and society gets the benefit of having that work available for everyone to use and, after "limited Times," to build on directly.

For about the first 180 years of U.S. history, copyright law worked quite well to pursue this Constitutional goal. One reason for this general success was the law; another was the technology needed to violate copyright in any significant way. As Lawrence Lessig observes, in an atmosphere in which the technological burden is heavy, the legal burden may be light. [1]

In the U.S., historically, not all creators asserted copyright on their works. From 1800-1976, only about 25% of works were copyrighted. Copyright owners had to affirmatively renew their copyrights to extend the length of protection, and only about 3% chose to do so. This may be because about 97% of copyrighted works exhaust their commercial potential within five years. [2]

From 1976 on, however, there has been a sea change in copyright law, and a parallel change in the technological environment in which copyrighted materials are distributed. This confluence of changes in law and technology has led to a concern that the balance implicit in the copyright "bargain" has shifted, and that law and technology have now placed the rights of copyright owners far above those of users of copyrighted material, and of society as whole.

What has changed since 1976, and why is there such concern that this change adversely affects the information commons? For the purposes of this discussion, the "information commons" consists of any information that a potential user of that information does not have to obtain explicit prior permission to use. "Information," in this sense, encompasses creative as well as informative works expressed in any tangible medium, including digital media. It also includes data *per se*, including spatially-referenced data.

Information commons materials include any work in the public domains well as works that are under copyright but for which the copyright owners have given prior permission for use, usually under specific conditions. The conditions attached to Creative Commons licenses are examples of these "some rights reserved" conditions of use.

With this description of the information commons in place, we return to the question: What has changed since 1976, and why is there such concern that this change will adversely affect the information commons? To answer that question, we must briefly highlight recent key changes in law, in technology, and in the convergence of the two that give rise to concerns that the information commons is, in James Boyle's terminology, being "enclosed." [3] We will then look at responses to this perceived enclosure, with a focus on recent initiatives designed to make information available with minimal or no use restrictions.

2.1   Changes in Law and Technology

Three elements in U.S. copyright law have changed in recent decades: the necessity for claiming copyright; the term of copyright protection; and the role of government in protecting copyright in a digital environment. A fourth element, the scope of what copyright covers, is also under discussion in the U.S. We examine each element in turn.

2.2   The Claim of Copyright

Prior to 1978, those who wished to obtain copyright protection for a work had the affirmative obligation to register that work with the Registrar of Copyright and assert ownership in order to benefit from the protections available through copyright law. That requirement changed in the Copyright Act of 1976, which went into effect January 1, 1978. Since then, copyright exists the moment any original work is fixed in a tangible medium, whether registered with the Copyright Office or not. As a result, simply finding a copyright owner can now be a huge challenge.

In the year 1930, to take one example, over 10,000 books were published. In the year 2000, 176 of those titles were still in print. In 2013, according to the International Publishers Association, 304,912 books were published in the U.S. [4], and they have copyright protection for at least 70 more years. Yet, historically, almost 97% of published works exhaust their potential for economic return within five years. That may be why, when copyright extensions had to be affirmatively applied for, only 3% of copyrighted works applied for and had their copyright protection extended. [2] Others who wished to use those formerly copyrighted works were then free to do so with no restrictions, or in the case of the small percentage of copyrighted works whose copyright was extended, potential users could easily ascertain who owned the copyright, and for how long the period of protection ran.

Contrast this with the situation which a potential user of a work created since 1978 faces. A user who would like to build upon a certain work 50 years hence (or even 10 years hence) may have no way of knowing who the copyright owner is or how to contact that owner to ask permission. In such a scenario, it is unlikely that a potential user will risk using the copyrighted work without prior permission, and will simply decide not to use the work at all.

On the face of it, this may not seem like a cultural calamity: after all, the future user can simply create something entirely new. However, even a moment's reflection will point out the potential harm to the larger culture that this situation can cause. For example, suppose that the public domain had not been available to the Disney company. Would society have had any of the tremendously successful re-creations of Pinocchio, Aladdin, or dozens of other public domain stories in the film format that today's adults grew up with, or would today's children have access to animated versions of *The Velveteen Rabbit* and a host of other previously copyrighted works in the Rabbit Ears series?

Since the term of copyright in the U.S. is so long, and since it is no longer necessary to claim or register a copyright, the U.S. now faces a serious "orphan works" problem. Orphan works are works that are presumably under copyright but for which no copyright owner can be found to ask for permission to use a work.

The problem has become so acute that in 2005, Senators Hatch and Leahy requested that the Registrar of Copyrights study the problem, take testimony, and issue a report. The Registrar did so and the report she issued contained a number of recommendations as well as suggested language for legislation to amend the copyright law to deal with the problem of "orphan works." [5] While bills have been submitted in Congress to make the use of orphan works less risky for subsequent users who make good faith efforts to find a copyright owner but are unable to do so, none have made much progress and orphan works remain a serious limitation for those who wish to use or build on past works.

2.3   The Term of Copyright Protection

Congress first granted copyrighted works protection for a period of 14 years. For most of U.S. history, this term length, augmented by a possible extension of another 14 years if applied for, was the norm.

The period of copyright duration began to grow in the 20th century: the term of copyright was extended 11 times in 40 years culminating in the Sonny Bono Copyright Term Extension Act (CTEA) of 1997. The CTEA extended the term of copyright to an author's lifetime plus 70 years; or, for works in which copyright is held by a company, for 90 years from publication or 120 years from creation if the work was not published. For a rock musician or a young author or a student researcher who creates a work at age 20 and lives an average lifespan, the work would be under copyright protection for about 130 years under current U.S. law.

Not surprisingly, some have questioned whether a term of protection of 100+ years constitutes a grant of protection "for limited Times" or "promotes the Progress of Science and the useful Arts" as the Constitution directs. The CTEA extension of copyright protection, and its philosophical implications, have been challenged in court, and the courts have essentially deferred to Congress in deciding what the proper definition of "limited Times" may be (Eldred v. Ashcroft 2003). As it stands, therefore, the length of copyright protection in the U.S. is that contained in the Sonny Bono Copyright Term Extension Act.

2.4   The Role of Government in Protecting Copyright

Until recently, enforcement of copyright has been a civil matter in which a copyright owner who felt her rights had been violated would sue the alleged violator for damages and other, usually injunctive, relief. But in the digital age, this is changing, and changing fast.

In the past decade, the U.S. government has taken a much more active role in copyright enforcement, and in some cases has extended the legal definition of copyright violation to the criminal realm. The major piece of legislation in this effort has been the Digital Millennium Copyright Act (DMCA). The DMCA prohibits providing tools or even information that would enable circumventing any type of technological protection, usually referred to as DRM or "Digital Rights Management," devised by copyright owners to limit access to their digital works. Not only does the act allow anyone harmed by violation of the act's provisions to sue, it also makes willful violation for profit a felony.

In 2008, Congress passed the Prioritizing Resources and Organization for Intellectual Property Act (PRO-IP) of 2008 that, among other things, created a "Copyright Czar" in the Executive Branch, and dramatically increased penalties for copyright infringement.

Other government actions, while not specifically focused on copyright *per se*, have also had a significant impact on the overall health of the information commons. Governments allocate scarce public resources such as spectrum space in broadcasting. They also regulate competition through anti-trust and similar regulation. The past two decades in the U.S., and, in fact, throughout the world, has seen an unprecedented increase in the concentration of copyright ownership and in the ownership of channels of distribution for copyrighted works due in large part to changes in government regulations and/or policies.

The results have been dramatic. As of 2003 in the U.S., 80% of music for retail sale was distributed by only five companies, and 70% of the major radio markets were controlled by four companies. Of the 91 "major" televisions networks (including cable), 80% are owned by six companies, and 75% of prime time programming is owned by the networks. [6]

This concentration of ownership of copyrighted materials and of the channels to distribute those materials has significant repercussions on the information commons. Access to a large portion of culturally important copyrighted material now lies in the hands of a relatively few owners. Those owners are in a powerful quasi-monopolistic position to control use of that material through technologically enforced licensing provisions, provisions that often are at odds with traditional user rights such as fair use and first sale.

This situation is becoming more and more prevalent as more publications are being distributed in digital form. This is particularly noticeable in the world of academic journals where a decade long trend of consolidation has led to a half dozen large corporations controlling access to scholarly journals, and more and more journals being available in only digital format. Predictably, the price increase for scholarly publications taken as a whole have significantly exceeded the rate of inflation for over a decade at a time when library budgets have been generally decreasing. The result is more limited access to journals and scholarly works both on campus and off.

2.5   Scope of Copyright Protection

Under U.S. law, copyright protection can only be extended to works that exhibit some degree of originality. Simple facts or even the obvious arrangement of facts cannot be protected under U.S. copyright law. A simple alphabetical listing of place names, for example, or an alphabetical lists of names and telephone numbers does not reach the threshold of originality needed for copyright protection even though the bar for that originality is not high. In the words of Justice Sandra Day O'Connor, it requires but "a modicum of creativity." [7] Facts *per se* may be in the public domain in the U.S., but it does not take a great deal of "creativity" to make a collection of facts copyrightable.

In the area of geography and mapping, for instance, the geographic objects themselves are facts. How they are arranged in a map using various graphic symbols, colors, and other "nonfactual" modalities that offer a variety of ways to represent those facts, may qualify as original enough to merit copyright protection even if the facts themselves do not. Similarly, non-obvious categorization and arrangements of facts in tables or other database forms may also be original enough to merit protection.

Any public records generated by the federal government do not fall under copyright protection since in the United States the Copyright Act specifically excludes the federal government itself from claiming copyright in materials it produces. This includes everything from weather reports to court decisions to data on water purity to testimony before congressional committees. All material generated directly by federal government employees is in the public domain. Under the Freedom of Information Act, access to some federal government generated information may be limited by concerns for security or other political considerations but may not be limited because of copyright ownership by government.

Recently, there have been efforts that would have the effect of eroding components of the public domain in the U.S. The European Union now includes databases of facts as works that can gain protection, either through copyright or through a *sui generis* designation, and similar bills have been introduced in the U.S. Congress in recent years (e.g., HR 3261, HR 3872 in the 108th Congress, and others since). If bills of this type were to be enacted into law in the future, facts collected and arranged in even obvious ways could fall under copyright protection in the U.S.

This type of *sui generis* database protection scheme in the European Union has not, in the view of The Royal Society, been a good thing for science.

> Advances of technology and commercial forces have led to new IP [Intellectual Property] legislation and case law that unreasonably and unnecessarily restrict freedom to access and to use information. This restriction of the commons in the main IP areas of patents, copyright and database right has changed the balance of rights and hampers scientific endeavour. In the interests of society, that balance must be rectified. [8]

In the United States, there are two factors under copyright law that provide some utility to users of copyrighted materials in the face of the expansion of the scope of copyright: First Sale and Fair Use.

First Sale simply means that once a person purchases a lawful physical copy of a work, e.g., a book, an academic journal, a CD, or other copyrightable work, the copyright owner no longer exerts any control over that copy. The purchaser may loan the item, give it away, or even sell it since in none of those transactions is a copy of the work made. It is the First Sale doctrine that makes libraries and video rental stores possible in the U.S. As more and more sales of books and music become digital, however, licensing rather than selling is becoming more common, even for personal purchases, thus minimizing the effect of the First Sale doctrine since no sale technically took place. Some scholars are beginning to argue that many licenses actually should be considered as sales, e.g., those that allow unlimited use by the licensee. [9] Even the Registrar of Copyright has raised the question of whether a marketplace in which everything digital is licensed is the most desirable one for America's economic future. [10] These are, however, still only questions and courts to date have held that licenses trump First Sale rights.

Fair Use enables use of copyrighted materials for certain purposes without the copyright owner 's permission. The difficulty with Fair Use from the perspective of potential users is that Fair Use is a defense, not a right. A user may cite Fair Use as a defense if a copyright owner sues for violation of copyright. Although there is a four element test to help determine whether a particular use constitutes Fair Use, no one really knows if a use is a Fair Use until a judge's gavel falls. Lawrence Lessig once joked that "Your Fair Use right is your right to hire a lawyer." Nonetheless, Fair Use does provide some elasticity in an otherwise tightly bound U.S. copyright law.

2.6 Brief Summary of Changing Laws and Technology

Since the term of copyright is now so long, since DRM cannot be legally circumvented under the DMCA, and since the copyright holder can impose license conditions that restrict or remove traditional user First Sale rights under copyright law, and then enforce those license provisions through the use of DRM, Pamela Samuelson has suggested that DRM might more accurately be described as "digital restrictions management." [11]

And, indeed, that is the way that many view the current situation in copyright in the U.S.: as a situation in which law and technology have combined to radically alter the traditional balance between copyright owners and users of copyrighted materials in favor of copyright owners. Those who view the current copyright landscape in this way are reacting, and it is to the range and forms those reactions are taking that we now turn our attention.

3 Reactions to Enclosure of the Commons

As it became clear that the Sonny Bono Copyright Extension Act and the Digital Millennium Copyright Act were altering the copyright landscape in an unprecedented way in today's digital environment, those who found this landscape alteration undesirable or unacceptable began to respond. Responses took a variety of forms and approaches to addressing the problem of "enclosure." We classify the responses for the purposes of this review as:

- Legislate

- Litigate

- Legally re-interpret

- Create alternatives

We examine them in turn.

3.1 Legislate

In the U.S., no bills have been introduced in the Congress over the past decade designed to specifically counteract the automatic grant of copyright, or to shorten its statutory duration. There are however, examples of bills introduced to mitigate the effects of the CTEA in recent sessions of Congress, and to temper the effects of DRM technologies that copyright owners are increasingly using to control access to their digital products, technologies that are currently protected from circumvention under the DMCA.

While it is unlikely at this time that the periods of copyright protection codified into law through the Sonny Bono Copyright Term Extension Act will be reduced, given both World

Intellectual Property Organization treaty obligations and the tenor of Congress, some legislative initiatives have been brought forward that, had they been successful, would have ensured that only those works whose owners actually wish to utilize copyright over the full term provided in the CTEA would receive the full term of copyright protection.

Rep. Zoë Lofgren, for example, twice introduced The Public Domain Enhancement Act (108th and 109th Congresses). It would have required copyright owners who wish to continue to enjoy copyright protection to affirmatively assert their copyright after 50 years by paying a small registration fee of one dollar. Absent that assertion, copyright would expire after 50 years. While the bill attracted some co-sponsors, it went nowhere.

Another of the "enclosing" laws, the DMCA, has had a number of consequences that were not intended, according to testimony that led to passage of the act. Some businesses, for example, have attempted to use threats of suits or prosecution based on Sections 1201(a)(1), 1201(a)(2), and 1201(b) of the DMCA to stifle reporting of shortcomings in their products (e.g., HP and Microsoft). Others, such as SONY, have attempted to stifle competition, and Lexmark invoked the DMCA in suing and actually obtaining an injunction against Static Control Components, a company that sold aftermarket cartridges for Lexmark printers. That injunction stood for almost a year before being vacated in October of 2004 by the Sixth Circuit Court of Appeals, which later also ruled against Lexmark's DMCA violation claims. [12] The process took years to conclude and had a large impact on innovation and competition in the printer ink industry until it was resolved.

This example, others like it, and examples of the DMCA being applied against consumers in ways that do nothing to thwart large scale digital "piracy," which was Congress's avowed intent in passing the DMCA, alarmed some in Congress, and led to the introduction of bills that were intended to rectify some of the imbalances that the sponsors felt the DMCA has created in favor of copyright owners.

Rep. Zoë Lofgren, for example, twice introduced the BALANCE Act, which is designed to make legal in the digital realm what has been – and remains – a user's legal rights under copyright law in the paper realm. This proposed legislation, according to its sponsors, would have made traditional fair use and first sale rights available in the digital domain, and allowed a user who has lawfully obtained a copy of a digital work to defeat DRM restrictions that interfered with exercising those rights. The bill, in plain language, got nowhere in any Congressional session. In its absence, courts have continued to rule that any kind of copy made in the process of transfer, even if only one copy exists at the end of the process, is a violation of copyright. [13]

In short, in the U.S., no legislative initiatives to ameliorate the effects of changes in law and in technology as they affect access to information have had any success up to the beginning of the first session of the 114th Congress in 2015.

3.2   Litigate

While some were pursuing legislative remedies, others felt that recent changes in copyright law violated the spirit and letter of the U.S. Constitution. They mounted legal challenges to provisions of both the CTEA and to the Copyright Act of 1976, which made copyright protection automatic.

In Eldred v. Ashcroft, the lead plaintiff, Eric Eldred, made available on his web site, and in other fashions, works that had entered the public domain. Some of those works had their copyright terms extended retroactively by the CTEA. Eldred asserted he had standing in the case since his work and livelihood was directly impacted by the CTEA. He claimed in the suit that the CTEA was unconstitutional (1) because it violated the "limited Times" clause in the Constitution, and (2) because it constrained free speech.

The case went all the way to the Supreme Court, where it lost by a 7-2 vote. The majority found that the Constitution granted Congress the duty to determine what "limited Times" meant, and that the Court should defer to Congress's judgment. Justice Breyer, one of the dissenters, had long argued against the extension of copyright: "Taken as a whole, the evidence now available suggests that, although we should hesitate to abolish copyright protection, we should equally hesitate to extend or strengthen it." [14], and he continued that argument in his dissent.

On the free speech issue, the Court held that the act did not change the "traditional contour of copyright," and that any free speech concerns raised by the act could be dealt with through copyright's traditional established safeguards, e.g., Fair Use.

While those who sought to have the CTEA declared unconstitutional failed to achieve that goal, others felt that elements of the Supreme Court's Eldred decision strengthened the case for asserting that a combination of recent changes in copyright law did, in aggregate, affect the "traditional contour of copyright" for a certain class of works, and therefore that these laws essentially created a situation which required "further first amendment scrutiny."

That was the approach taken by plaintiffs in Kahle v. Ashcroft (original name: case as decided in 2007 is Kahle v. Gonzales). However, this suit gathered no traction and was dismissed by the Ninth Circuit, as was a similar case in the D.C. Circuit Court, Luck's Music v. Ashcroft.

A third suit addressed the extension of copyright term as well as first amendment issues from another perspective. It focuses on another "enclosing" copyright issue, that of restoring copyright protections for works, in this case foreign works, that had already entered the public domain. In the words of the original complaint:

> This is an action to challenge the constitutionality of Congress's attempt to remove and radically deplete the supply of literary and artistic works from the public domain...Congress's dramatic expansion of the term of copyright [in the CTEA] has been accompanied by an even more radical depletion of works from the public domain. On December 8, 1993, Congress amended the Copyright Act to recognize for the first time in the history of our copyright law a general provision that purports to "restore" copyrights – retroactively – in numerous works that heretofore had indisputably been in the public domain for failure to satisfy the requirements of the Copyright Act. [15]

Although this suit was not dismissed. The Tenth Circuit court held that, indeed, Congress's removal of works from the public domain that were already part of the public domain reached the Supreme Court's definition of changing the "traditional contour of copyright," and remanded the case to the district court for trial. The government, defendant in the trial, requested an *en banc* hearing by the entire 10th Circuit bench. That request was denied. In April, 2009, the District Court for the District of Colorado granted a motion for summary judgment in Golan v. Holder, accepting the change in the "traditional contour of copyright" argument. In the words of the plaintiff's attorneys: "It is the first time a court has held any part of the Copyright Act violates the First Amendment and the first time any court has placed specific constitutional limits on the government's ability to erode the public domain." [16] That decision was later reversed by the Tenth Circuit Court of Appeals. The plaintiffs appealed to the Supreme Court which affirmed the Tenth Circuit's decision and held that the government did not exceed its authority in removing the formally public domain works from the public domain

Like the legislative initiatives mentioned above, court challenges to extensions of copyright have universally failed. Prospects for relief through Congress or the courts, at the moment, do not seem bright.

3.3   Legally Re-Interpret

Underlying any legal statute concerning intellectual property, and thus copyright, is a set of assumptions about what "property" actually is. Laws such as the DMCA have emerged because the forms of property have changed in the digital age, while the conceptualization of the nature of property has not. Consumption, excludability, costs of replication, and other characteristics of physical property may not apply in the same way to intellectual property as they do to physical property, yet recent legislation and court decisions seem to assume they do.

In the last two decades, and particularly in the past decade, some scholars have argued that intellectual property and physical property such as land are not the same thing. Therefore, they argue, the set of assumptions underlying laws governing intellectual property in a digital environment should not be based on the analogy of physical property but rather on some other model more reflective of the nature of intellectual property itself. As Wesley Hohfeld has famously pointed out, intellectual property claims are claims between people [17], not, as earlier legal commentators described, claims of people on something inanimate but tangible such as land.

Why this upwelling of legal theory with respect to intellectual property now? Simply put, the need did not exist as urgently before.

Until 1976, using the model of physical property as the basis for copyright law worked reasonably well. "Excludability" had to be claimed through copyright registration, which only a minority of creators sought to assert, and that excludability was tempered by First Sale and Fair Use rights of users of the intellectual property. Economically, there were significant burdens encountered in large scale copyright violation. Any type of large scale violation of copyright required a significant investment, for example, in printing press equipment or video and film duplication equipment. In this environment, the analogy to physical property, despite the clear differences in intellectual property (e.g., it is non-rivalrous), worked well enough.

And then came digital and the Internet. The economic burdens of making perfect copies and distributing them widely almost completely disappeared. At the same time, the technology to enable creators to exclude potential users from the use of their works – supported by civil and criminal law – became widely available. Now the differences between physical property and intellectual property were thrown into sharp contrast, and legal and economic theorists such as Robert Heverly began to respond.

> We think of information as property; law and economic structures, we argue, make it so. But this should not be the end of our inquiry. If we believe information is property, we must ask: What kind of property is information?"[18]

Recent theorists have approached an answer to this question in a variety of ways. Heverly, for example, concludes that "information is not a private property regime: it is a semicommons" which, in his analysis, reflects the "dynamic relationship and interdependence of private and common property interests." P2P file sharing, for example, represents such an interdependence. On the one hand, P2P sharing of music may have a negative economic impact on a copyright owner by reducing some potential sales of a piece of music; on the other hand, the exposure and "word of mouth" available through P2P file sharing has a positive economic impact and increases sales and thus income for the same owner. [19]

In fact, some music companies are actually using P2P file sharing activity statistics to promote future "hit songs" to radio stations. They are doing this promotion through third parties in order not to dilute their claims of harm due to copyright infringement, since music companies are simultaneously suing those who distribute copyrighted music through P2P networks. Leaving aside the contradiction involved in these apparently conflicting activities, this example is precisely the type of interdependence that Heverly posits as a characteristic of a semicommons model of property.

Jacqueline Lipton asserts that there is nothing wrong with viewing information as property in the traditional sense, as long as property rights and obligations are viewed in a holistic manner. Problems arise when there is an imbalance in the rights and obligations of property owners: "the problem can be re-cast in terms of the 'absolutism' of information property rights…" [19] Lipton argues that even physical property rights are not absolute, and neither should information property rights be. Her point is that "where a government has created, or supported the creation of private rights in information, it should be prepared to create and support concurrent public duties."

Lipton shares a conclusion, if not the process of arriving at that conclusion, with Mark Lemley. He quotes with approval the view of the Supreme Court of Canada in Compo Co. Ltd. V. Blue Crest Music Inc.:

> copyright law is neither tort law nor property law in classification, but is statutory law. It neither cuts across existing rights in property or conduct nor falls in between rights and obligations heretofore existing in the common law. Copyright legislation simply creates rights and obligations upon the terms and in the circumstances set out in the statute. [20]

In short, Lemley argues that intellectual property is *sui generis* and needs to be envisioned as such when crafting legislation to define appropriate economic rights, characteristics, and obligations rather than to use terms of "inapposite economic analysis borrowed from the very different case of land."

All of these legal scholars find the root of the enclosure problem with respect to information to lie in the legal assumptions underlying the legislative and judicial analysis of the nature of intellectual property. They, as well as others [e.g., 15, 21, 22, 23, 24, 25, 26, 27, 28] propose alternative legal and economic analyses that, in their views, would go a long way toward reducing or eliminating at least some of the legal aspects of the enclosure of the information commons.

Fair Use has traditionally been the balancing mechanism in the copyright social contract. However, in the eyes of some scholars, the advent of works in digital form along with technological DRM protections have weighted that balance heavily on the side of rightsholders to the detriment of Fair Uses on the part of consumers.

> The more technology reflects only one set of interests, however, the more it departs from the law, which conceptualizes copyright as a balancing of interests, with the ultimate goal of fostering both creative expression and broad public availability of creative works. The result has been a perverse scenario nowhere commanded by the Copyright Act or the DMCA, in which technological measures have been allowed to override the fair use doctrine. [29]

This is not simply a theoretical problem, nor one confined to the United States. Lynne Brindley, CEO of the British Library stated in 2007 that:

> It seems to me, as CEO of the British Library and therefore representing the researcher in part, that the balance that is referred to here, between private rights and public domain, between free competition and monopoly rights - is not working; it is being undermined by a number of things from our perspective including:
>
> • A restrictive use of new technology (Digital Rights Management)
>
> • Poor or outmoded legislation (i.e. too complex, increasing durations and harmonising durations ever upward, etc)
>
> • The public interest aspects of copyright being undermined and made irrelevant by private contract. [30]

The issue has become widespread enough to involve the policy making bodies of some of the largest scholarly organizations in the world. For example, The Public Policy Council of the ACM in its "USACM Policy Recommendations on Digital Rights Management" recommended that:

> Because lawful use (including fair use) of copyrighted works is in the public's best interest, a person wishing to make lawful use of copyrighted material should not be prevented from doing so. As such, DRM systems should be mechanisms for reinforcing existing legal constraints on behavior (arising from copyright law or by reasonable contract), not as mechanisms for creating new legal constraints. Appropriate technical and/or legal safeguards should be in place to preserve lawful uses in cases where DRM systems cannot distinguish lawful uses from infringing uses. [31]

Not surprisingly, legal scholars have begun to re-think approaches to Fair Use in the digital age as well suggesting approaches that, in their views, would help to reestablish balance between rightsholders and users. [32] Armstrong, for example, proposes a regime of what he refers to as "Fair Circumvention" of DRM technologies. Reichman, Dinwoodie, and Samuelson propose a "Reverse Notice and Takedown Regime" under the DMCA in which those who would assert a claim to legally circumvent DRM for Fair Use purposes notify rightsholders they intended to take such circumvention steps, and rightsholders would have 14 days to object. [33] The details of these proposals are not the issue here. What is of import is the effort to reinterpret law to reflect the changes in the social contract that digital technologies have made possible.

Another stream of quasi-legal thought focuses not on definitions of intellectual property nor on the empirical economic, political, or legal validity of arguments in support of copyright extension. Rather these arguments assert that access to information is a right, based upon ethical principles as well as charters and statements of rights such as those authored by treaty organizations such as the Universal Declaration of Human Rights (Articles 19 and 27) as well as numerous non-governmental organizations such as the Library Bill of Rights of the American Library Association. Drawing on these and similar national and international declarations, some scholars, such as Kay Mathiesen, have argued that "the right to access is not merely a liberty right but also a welfare right. That is, individuals' information rights place duties on governments to provide access to information." [34]

At this point in time, these legal and moral speculations and theories remain speculations only and have to date had no real impact on access to information. However, they serve to provide a counterbalance, albeit a weak one at present, to the ongoing efforts of copyright owners to assert greater and greater control over copyrighted information in a culture that is increasingly digital.

3.4   Create Alternatives

In the absence of legislative or legal remedies, some have sought to leverage existing copyright law to realize goals of more open access that legislative proposals and law suits have not so far been able to accomplish.

This type of response encourages creators to forego some rights available under copyright law while retaining others. The desired effect is to widen the amount of material available in the information commons, if not in the public domain per se.

3.4.1   GNU General Public License.

There is ample precedent for this tactic. Free and Open source software has been released for over two decades under the GNU General Public License (GPL) or one of many "open source" variants. This class of licenses uses copyright law to license the use of copyrighted works under much less restrictive terms than exist under normal copyright conditions. So, for example, a work licensed under the GPL mandates that no charge can be made for the work itself (although charges for duplicating or distributing copies can be levied); that users are free to copy or modify the work as they see fit but that if any such modifications are made to the work, those modifications also must be made available under the same licensing terms as the original work. [35]

Creators use the GPL and its many derivatives and variants, such as the Berkeley Software Distribution (BSD) license, mostly in licensing free or open source software. However, similar licensing approaches can also apply to other types of copyrighted works such as text or music or photographs or motion pictures or datasets. The GNU Free Documentation License, for example, was the license underlying the text on Wikipedia for many years, one of the most popular sites on the World Wide Web, although Wikipedia has now brought its licensing terms into compliance with Creative Commons licenses.

3.4.2   Creative Commons.

Several of those who had been involved in some of the litigation summarized above decided that, while it was necessary to continue to challenge in court the validity of laws limiting access, something needed to be done at once to create alternatives to the closing off of the commons they felt was underway, and the Creative Commons was born.

The Creative Commons extends and broadens the "some rights reserved" approach of the GPL to licenses that creators can apply to a wide variety of creative works. The same digital technology that has made it possible for copyright owners to impose restrictive licenses on works in digital form also allows copyright owners to offer much less restrictive licenses for which users do not have to seek prior permission to use, as long as users adhere to the conditions set out in the license.

Typically, those conditions are much more liberal than those that obtain under copyright law *per se*. For example, Creative Commons offers a set of conditions that creators may choose to apply one or more of to their works to create a license.

Creative Commons takes whatever conditions the creator indicates she wishes to attach to her work, and creates a legal license that the creator attaches to the work. The license comes in three forms: human readable (a general description of the license terms in common language), lawyer readable (a legal language license), and machine readable. The creator indicates that the work is licensed under a Creative Commons license, and provides a link to the Creative Commons website where the specifics of the license are laid out for any potential user to view. As long as the user conforms to those conditions of use, there is no need to track down the copyright owner and obtain specific permission to use the work.

While these Creative Commons licenses do expand access to information in a commons spirit, the works are licensed under copyright and the licenses chosen draw their force and enforceability from copyright law. None of these licenses has yet had its validity fully tested in court in the U.S. although there are instances of courts in other countries upholding the validity of the Creative Commons licenses.

Some creators are uncomfortable with having their work under copyright for 70 years after their deaths. For these creators, the Creative Commons also offers a "Founder's Copyright" option. This option limits a creator's claim to copyright to 14 years, the original grant of copyright in the U.S., after which time the work enters the public domain. Creators may also choose to simply affirmatively donate their copyright to the public domain immediately, and Creative Commons provides a mechanism for doing that as well. U.S. law makes no specific provision for this type of dedication so the Creative Commons dedication is as close as a creator can come. Before 1976, a work entered the public domain unless copyright was registered. Now, as noted above, it is necessary to specifically disavow copyright ownership for a work to be considered in the public domain.

In the years since Creative Commons licenses have become available, creators have applied Creative Commons licenses to over a billion works as of December, 2015, and the rate of use has been growing steadily. While Creative Commons supporters do not pretend that this is more than a small percentage of created works on the Internet, they do assert that it is important to have a legal channel available for those who wish to contribute to the expansion of the information commons, even if not to the public domain itself.

Alternative licensing schemes such as those employed by Creative Commons or the Open Source software movement do create a mildly competing economic model to traditional markets in copyrighted material. Creators under these alternative licensing systems do not generally attempt to capture the entire value of their work but choose instead to reserve only some value for themselves. Some universities are incorporating Creative Commons licenses into their institutional structures. Stanford University, for example, no longer requires that theses and dissertations be microfilmed. Now they are simply made available electronically under Creative Commons licenses.

Open Access Publishing initiatives go even further and actually create an alternative model of academic publishing that competes directly in the market for academic scholarship.

3.4.3   Open Access Publishing.

Scientific progress depends on scientists having wide ranging access to scientific information. The same confluence of forces that has adversely affected the information commons in general has adversely affected the scientific commons, according to many in the scientific community, and to the communities of information professionals who serve them.

While there are over 24,000 scientific journals currently published by 2000+ publishers [36], fewer than half a dozen large publishers own or control the distribution of a large majority of those journals, including a majority of the intellectually most important ones. These publishers are in a quasi-monopolistic position and have been raising prices in excess of increases in the rate of inflation for two decades. During the past decade, publishers also have increasingly migrated their publications to digital form, in many cases abandoning paper publishing altogether.

Once their products are in digital form, publishers are in a position to impose technologically enforceable licensing controls, and most have done so. One result of this technologically enforceable quasi-monopolistic position is entirely predictable under capitalistic economic theory. Publishers, unfettered by competition, have bundled many titles into packages in a "take it or leave it" fashion, and have unilaterally set price points to maximize profits. The strategy has worked: the industry reported profit margins of 40% in the middle of the first decade of the 21st Century [37] and while profits may have declined somewhat since, they are still in very healthy double digit territory.

Academic publishers pay nothing for the articles they publish. Scholars who submit articles for publication are typically university faculty who are being paid to do research and for whom publication is part of the research process. Publishers pay nothing for the peer reviewers for the same reason. This "free labor," combined with an increasingly non-print distribution environment, reduces costs dramatically. When combined with a near monopolistic pricing ability, these advantages result in enviable profit margins.

They have also resulted in an increasing tide of customer resentment. Scholarly libraries have had to continually cut back on journal purchases and/or reduce monograph purchases in order to attempt to keep up with rising journal prices. In many libraries, journal purchases now make up two-thirds or more of acquisition costs, with only one third going for books and other materials.

Since scholars typically sign over copyright to publishers, some scholars have found themselves in the ironic position of not being able to legally provide copies of articles they have authored, and which they provided to publishers for free, to their students because their libraries can no longer afford to purchase the journals the articles were published in.

In this environment, libraries and librarians began to react, as did a host of non-governmental and professional organizations. One of the clearest statements of their view of the recent situation with respect to academic publishing is included in this description of SPARC:

> Scholarly Publishing and Academic Resources Coalition is an alliance of academic and research libraries and organization working to correct market dysfunctions in the scholarly publishing system...Its strategies expand competition and support open access to address the high and rising cost of scholarly journals, especially in science, technology, and medicines—a trend which inhibits the advancement of scholarship. [37]

SPARC, as well as many other organizations, encourages the development of open access journals, publications that make their articles available to the public at no cost to the user, and that typically allow the user to make copies in digital form, and often confer a wider set of usage rights. And those efforts have had some notable success.

The Directory of Open Access Journals (DOAJ) lists over 10,000 peer-reviewed open access journals containing nearly 1.2 million articles of which over 600,00 are searchable at the article level as of February of 2015. This is a small proportion of the articles published in scientific, technical, and medical journals each year, to say nothing of journals in other fields. Still, open access is becoming a serious, if still small, market force, and other forces are amplifying the impact of open access initiatives.

Funders, as well as government agencies, are beginning to take notice of the effect of limitations on access to information on scholarship and learning. In the U.S., the National Institutes of Health (NIH) require that all research results generated through NIH funding be made available to the public in an open access repository within a year of publication. Bills that would extend such mandates to other federal agencies have been introduced in both houses of several recent Congresses but none have to date passed. However, in the U.S., a provision in the Consolidated Appropriations Act of 2014 requires federal agencies in Labor, Health and Human Services, and Education with research budgets of over $100 million to provide public access within 12 months of publication in a peer-reviewed journal to research resulting from projects they fund.

Private funders are also promoting open access. The Welcome Trust, a major funder of research in the United Kingdom, has mandated that articles resulting from research it funds be placed in an open repository. Some research institutes, such as the The Howard Hughes Medical Institute, have made open access mandatory for research conducted by their employees. The Max Planck Institute in Germany is encouraging its many research employees to make their work open access as well. Faculty Senates and other policy setting bodies in educational institutions in this country and abroad including major institutions such as MIT, Harvard, and Stanford as well as over 30 other U.S. universities and colleges have voted to make open access mandatory for their faculty members.

There are many important obstacles for open access publishing to overcome to be a full- fledged market alternative to commercial academic publishing, including building sustainable economic models and changing the culture of academia to value open access and traditional publication credits equally when considering tenure and promotions. Nonetheless, open access scholarly publishing is already having an effect on the marketplace and, through market mechanisms, has already begun to expand the information commons.

4 Summary and Conclusions

There are tensions in the balance of copyright as established in the U.S. Constitution, and these tensions are even more obvious in the digital age. Access to data, research studies, academic papers, and other information in GIS, as in all scientific disciplines today, can be complicated. While copyright itself has evolved to be more restrictive in terms of access to information, there are offsetting though not yet completely countervailing forces pushing for less restrictive and more open access to information and data. GIS researchers, authors, and software writers are wise to understand copyright and alternatives to copyright. As researchers, such understanding can lead to more and better access to information needed for their work. As authors, such understanding can help authors to choose copyright options that best serve their purposes and make their work as widely known as possible.

References

[1]   Lessig, L. Building the Creative Commons.
      http://www.uwm.edu/Dept/SOIS/about/news/events/index.htm, 2004.

[2]   Lessig, L. Free Culture: How Big Media Uses Technology and the Law to Lock
      Down Culture and Control Creativity. Penguin Press, New York, 2004.

[3]   Boyle, J. The Second Enclosure Movement and the Construction of the Public
      Commons. Law and Contemporary Problems 66, 33 (2003), 33-75.

[4]   International Publishers Association. 2014. Annual Report 2013-2014. http://
      www.internationalpublishers.org/images/reports/2014/IPA-annual-report-
      2014.pdf, 2014.

[5]   Registrar of Copyrights. Report on Orphan Works. United States Copyright
      Office, Washington, 2006.

[6]   Lessig, L. 2003. The Future of Ideas and Code and Other Laws of Cyberspace.
      13th Annual Conference on Computers, Freedom & Privacy.
      http://www.cfp2003.org/cfp2003/ program.html, 2003.

[7]   Feist Publications, Inc. v. Rural Tel. Service Co., 499 U.S. 340 (1991).

[8]   The Royal Society. Keeping Science Open: the Effects of Intellectual Property
      Policy on the Conduct of Science.
      http://www.royalsoc.ac.uk/document.asp?tip=0&id=1374, 2003.

[9]   Asay, C. D."Kirtsaeng and the First-Sale Doctrine's Digital Problem," Stanford
      Law Review Online, volume 66,
      http://www.stanfordlawreview.org/online/kirtsaeng-and-first-sale-doctrines-
      digital-problem, 2013.

[10] Pallante, M. A. The Next Great Copyright Act. Columbia Journal of Law and the
      Arts. 36, 3 (2013), 315-344.

[11] Samuelson, P. DRM {and, or, vs.} the Law. Communications of the ACM. 46, 4
      (2003), 41-45.

[12] Lexmark International, Inc. v. Static Control Components, Inc., 387 F.3d 522 (6th
      Cir. 2004)

[13] Capitol Records, LLC v. ReDigi, Inc. 2013

[14] Breyer, S. The Uneasy Case for Copyright: A Study of Copyright in Books,
      Photocopies, and Computer Programs. Harvard Law Review. 84, 2 (1970), 281-
      351.

[15] Golan v. Ashcroft, now Golan v. Holder, 132 S. Ct. 873, 2012

[16] Falzone, A. URAA Held Unconstitutional.
      http://cyberlaw.stanford.edu/node/6149. 2009.

[17] Hohfeld, W. N. Fundamental Legal Conceptions As Applied in Judicial
      Reasoning. Yale University Press, New Haven, 1964 (copyright 1946).

[18] Heverly, R. A. The Information Semicommons. BTLJ. 18, (2003), 1127-1189.

[19] Lipton, J. Information Property: Rights and Responsibilities. Fla. L. Rev. 56, 1
      (2004), 140.

[20]   Lemley, M. Property, Intellectual Property, and Free Riding. Stanford Law and Economics Olin Working Paper No. 291, 2004.

[21]   McCarty, L. T. Ownership: A Case Study in the Representation of Legal Concepts. Artificial Intelligence and Law. 10, (2002), 1-3.

[22]   Lunney, G. S., Jr. Reexamining Copyright's Incentives-Access Paradigm. Vanderbilt Law Review. 49, (1996), 483-656.

[23]   Pessach, G. Reciprocal Share-Alike Exemptions in Copyright Law. Cardozo Law Review. 30, 3 (2008), 101-150.

[24]   Sohn, G. B. Six Steps to Digital Copyright Sanity: Reforming a Pre-vcr Law for a Youtube World. New Media and Marketplace of Ideas Conference, 2007.

[25]   Sprigman, C. Reform(aliz)ing Copyright. Stanford Law Review. 56, 2 (2004), 485-568.

[26]   Samuelson, P. Preliminary Thoughts on Copyright Reform. Utah Law Review. 2007, 3 (2007), 551-571.

[27]   Boldrin, M. and Levine, D. K. The Case Against Intellectual Property. American Economic Review Papers and Proceedings. 92 (2002), 209-212.

[28]   Parchomovsky, G. and Weiser, P. J. Beyond Fair Use. Cornell Law Review. 96, 1 (2010), 91-137.

[29]   Armstrong, T. K. Digital Rights Management and the Process of Fair Use. Harvard Journal of Law and Technology. 20, 1 (2006), 49-121.

[30]   Brindley, Lynne. Balance in IP "Not working". http://legacy.earlham.edu/~peters/fos/2007_12_02_fosblogarchive.html, 2007.

[31]   ACM US Public Policy Council. USACM Policy Recommendations on Digital Rights Management. ACM, 2006.

[32]   Armstrong, T. K. Fair Circumvention. Brooklyn Law Review. 74, 1 (2008), 1-50.

[33]   Reichman, J. H., Dinwoodie, G. B., and Samuelson, P. 2007. A Reverse Notice and Takedown Regime to Enable Public Interest Use of Technically Protected Copyrighted Works. Berkeley Technology Law Journal. 22 (2007), 981-1060.

[34]   Mathiesen, K. Access to Information as a Human Right. iConference 2009. http://ssrn.com/abstract=1264666, 2009.

[35]   St. Laurent, A. M. Understanding Open Source & Free Software Licensing. O'Reilly,Cambridge MA, 2004.

[36]   ÓhAnluain, D. 2004. Calls for Open Access Challenge Academic Journals. Online Journalism Review. http://www.ojr.org:80/ojr/stories/121004ohanluain, 2004.

[37]   Scholarly Publishing and Academic Resources Coalition (SPARC) 2006. What Is SPARC? http:/ /www.arl.org/sparc/ about/index.html, 2006.

From Observation to Prediction: The Trajectory of Movement Research in GIScience

Somayeh Dodge

Department of Geography and Environmental Studies University of Colorado, Colorado Springs, USA

Abstract: Movement is a key to understanding the underlying mechanisms of dynamic processes. Over the past two decades, the availability of an unprecedented amount of movement observations at fine spatial and temporal granularities has resulted in substantial advances in different areas of movement research in GIScience and other related disciplines. This article describes a continuum encapsulating essential elements of movement research. The study of movement involves development of concepts and methods to transform movement observations to knowledge of the behavior of moving phenomena under known conditions. This knowledge is then used to calibrate simulation models to predict movement and behavioral responses in varying environmental conditions. The article highlights significant achievements, existing gaps, and potential future directions of the trajectory of movement research across this continuum in GIScience.

Keywords: Movement analysis, movement, behavior, movement observations, environment, geographic context, trajectory analysis, movement research.

1 Introduction

Movement is essential to almost all organisms and spatiotemporal processes. Movement as "a *change* in the spatial location of the whole individual in time" [37, p.19052] results from complex states and behaviors of moving entities. Movement occurs in *space* and *time* across multiple scales and through an embedding *context* which influences how entities move. The importance of spatiotemporal aspect of movement has attracted a wide range of studies in Geographic Information Science (GIScience).

Movement research is important in many areas of science and technology, such as movement ecology, environmental studies, behavioral studies, epidemiology, and transportation, to name but a few [17]. Movement ecology aims at understanding local movement and global migration patterns of animals and their space utilization patterns [23, 13]. Trajectory analysis plays a key role in behavioral and social sciences, urban and transportation planning to study human mobility and activity pat- terns [21, 45, 39, 46]. Movement analysis is essential in public health and epidemiology to model disease spread in space and time, and estimate human exposure to pollution or infectious diseases [43, 20, 33]. The advent of inexpensive and ubiquitous positioning technologies has triggered a wealth of interdisciplinary research collaborations among developers of methods and domain experts. Demšar *et al.* [11] provides a comprehensive review of recent developments in movement analysis and visualization methodologies resulting from such collaborations between ecologists and experts from GIScience.

Over the past two decades, the study of movement has gained significant momentum in GIScience [28, 32, 29]. Although movement research crosses many disciplinary boundaries (e.g. movement ecology, behavioral studies, transportation, information science, human health), this article mainly focuses on the trajectory of movement research in *GIScience*. The main contribution of this article is the introduction of a new and overarching framework to illustrate the continuum of research that enables us to understand movement and its underlying processes. For each element, the article portrays the strengths and existing gaps in the current state of research, and provides some suggestions as where the research should be heading in the future. One of the key suggestions is that the field should be heading more towards the development of informed models to predict the future behavioral responses of spatiotemporal phenomena to environmental changes.

The remainder of this article is organized as follows: Section 2 introduces a continuum encapsulating the key elements of movement research. Section 3 describes the components of movement and their associations to one another. Section 4 discusses GIScience methods for *understanding movement*. Section 5 reviews *simulation and predictive models* for movement, which have received less attention in the past from the community. Section 6 summarizes the natural progression of movement research over the past twenty years, and discusses a proposal for future directions of the research and issues that need to be taken into considerations.

2 Movement Research Continuum

Figure 1 illustrates a continuum encapsulating fundamental areas of movement research, which are tightly linked to one another. Study of movement entails two inter-connected strands of research for (1) *understanding movement processes* (the right side of Figure 1); and (2) *modeling* behavior of moving phenomena and *prediction* of their responses to environmental changes (the left side of Figure 1). These two processes are tightly connected and feed into each other, often through a *validation* procedure on the basis of real *movement observations*.

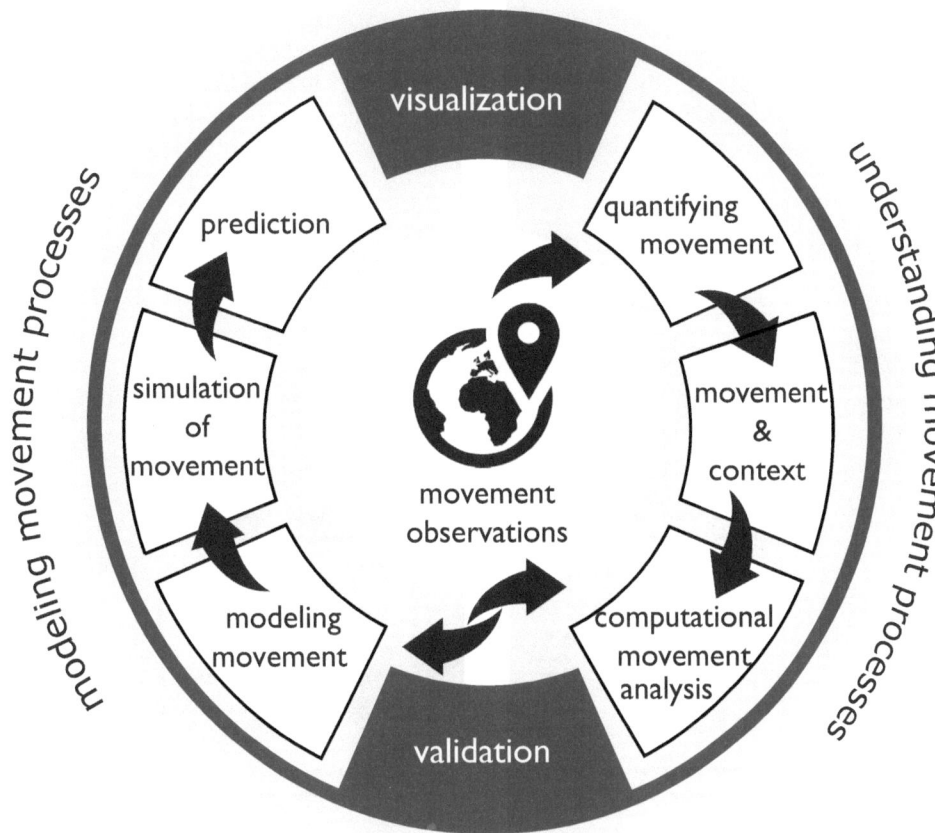

Figure 1: Movement research continuum

At its core, the continuum is supported by raw *movement observations*. Movement observations are often obtained through tracking real-world moving entities using satellite positioning, video tracking, or others sensor technologies (e.g. GPS, Argos, RFID tags, Geotags, Bluetooth). The continuum relies on *visualization* techniques for exploration of observations and communication of results, and on *validation* to ensure reliability of methods, models, and discovered patterns. Movement observations feed into analytical methods to *quantify movement* tracks, movement parameters and patterns, and their relationships to the *context* within which the movement is embedded. This information is transformed into knowledge of movement through "*computational movement analysis*" [29], (e.g. using movement pattern mining and machine learning). This facilitates the development of *movement models*, which can increase our understanding of the behavior of moving phenomena. The resulting knowledge are then used to *validate and calibrate models* to translate behavior of dynamic phenomena into *informed movement simulations*. Ultimately, the whole process feeds into the development of *predictive models* to capture behavioral responses and movement of dynamic phenomena through space and time and in varying environmental conditions. These models can be *parameterized* and *validated* using real *movement observations*.

In GIScience, the study of movement was initiated with quantifying trajectories, movement parameters and patterns through the development of computational

geometry and movement analysis approaches [25, 22, 32]. Movement research has
since progressed with the design of analytical and visualization methods to transform
raw observations to knowledge of the behavior of moving phenomena [35, 38, 11]. This
article provides a summary of the progress of movement research in GIScience along
this trajectory by highlighting significant achievements made over the past twenty
years on different elements of the continuum. For a comprehensive review of the state
of research, the readers are advised to refer to recent survey articles [32, 38, 29, 11].

3 Components of Movement

According to the movement ecology paradigm proposed by Nathan *et al.* [37],
movement consists of several components and different processes that connect these
components to one another. Figure 2 presents an adapted version of the movement
ecology paradigm with some modifications to account for a broader range of moving
phenomena applied to different domains of GIScience (e.g. behavioral studies,
environmental studies, ecological studies, transportation).

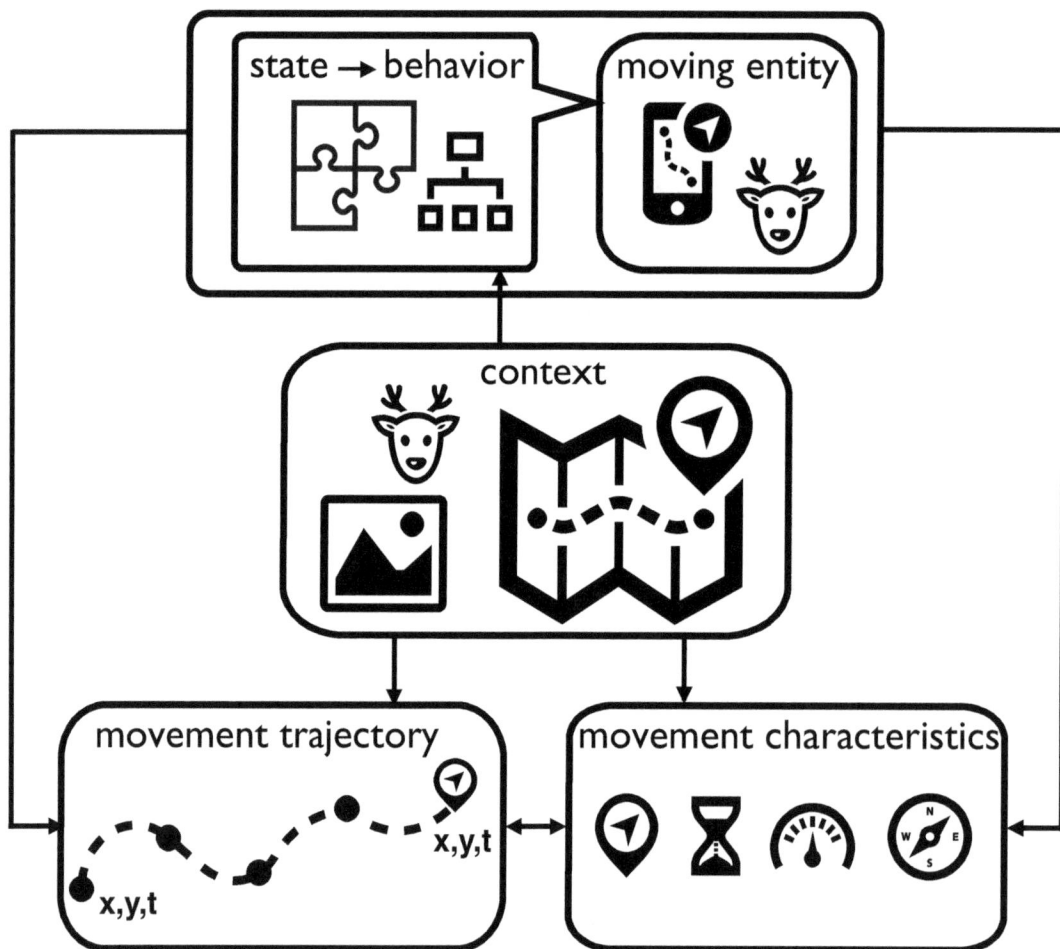

Figure 2: Components of movement

Movement is a process that occurs as a response to the *state* of a *moving entity* across
multiple *spatial* and *temporal* scales. Moving entities are individuals (e.g. vehicles,

humans, animals) or phenomena (e.g. hurricanes, wildfires, oil spills) whose position changes over time. The *state* of an entity either emerges from *intrinsic* properties of the individual (e.g. being hungry or readiness to move) or is influenced by the *context* (i.e. presence of a pray or predator for animals, daily schedule for humans, rise in sea surface temperature for development of hurricanes). The *context* includes influencing external factors such as the geography and physiography in which the movement takes place, environment and ambient attributes, transportation network, and presence of other moving agents in the vicinity. The entity's *state* leads to a *behavior* (e.g. hunting, patrolling, going to work, hurricane intensification). The *state* and resulting *behavior* determine the *characteristics* and *capacities* of movement (e.g. speeds, directions, accelerations, path sinuosity), which are highly influenced by *context*. Accordingly, the trajectory of a movement (i.e. a spatiotemporal path that is composed of a time-ordered sequence of coordinates) is driven by *behavior* and *context*. When more than one entity is involved in the process, their collective movements are driven by the interactions between the entities and their dynamics [19]. This collective behavior is also influenced by other contextual parameters in space and time.

4   Understanding Movement Processes

Movement observations are signals of real-world moving entities. These signals carry important information pertaining to *behavior* of these entities. To gain insights into movement processes it is necessary to develop methods to analyze these signals, identify *patterns* (i.e. regularities and structure) in movement datasets, and assess how they are influenced by their environment [12]. These insights then contribute to modeling, simulation, and ultimately prediction of movement (see Figure 1).

4.1   Quantifying Movement

The availability of fine resolution movement observations has facilitated GIScience with the development of effective methods to quantify the geometric properties of movement trajectories, their derivatives (e.g. speeds, acceleration, path sinuosity), and associated movement patterns [12]. These methods enable us to gain an understanding of the fundamental elements of movement and its patterns. This is indispensable as a basis for the development of computational and analytic techniques to extract knowledge from movement observations [17]. In many applications, studying *movement characteristics* of entities is more relevant than simply the geometry of their movement paths, as they convey the physical and biological notions of movement [16]. This information leads to insight into the semantics of trajectories, underlying mechanisms of movement, and the behavior of organisms.

4.2   Movement and Context

Movement is often driven by the characteristics of its embedding spatiotemporal *context*; the surrounding environment and the the nature of space (i.e. geographic and physiography) that the object is moving through. This includes external factors that influence a dynamic process at a specific time scale (moment or duration). Context can be characterized into different types such as networks (e.g. roads), obstacles (e.g. lakes, rivers), and landscapes, (e.g. land cover, vegetation, terrain), ambient attributes (e.g. weather conditions), and presence of other agents (e.g. interactions) [6]. These parameters can trigger a specific behavior (e.g. hunting, patrolling, walking, biking) and hence they can enable or limit movement as a consequence of that behavior. For instance, a tiger patrols a soft boundary of its home range more often than a boundary with rigorous terrain characteristics [2]. Therefore, movement observations alone cannot describe all mechanisms behind movement processes. In order to correctly identify patterns and their causes, and understand behaviors of moving phenomena it is essential to relate movement to its physical environment.

Context has been an important part of GIScience studies which have dealt with characterizing geospatial phenomena based on the geographic context of their neighboring space [44, 18, 8]. Thus far context has been considered as a static snapshot of the neighboring space and spatiotemporal context (i.e. context that changes over time) has received less attention. Although GIScience has been very successful in both quantification of movement and modeling geographic context, the link between *movement*, *behavior*, and *context* has largely been ignored. This also has been identified as a current limitation of GIScience studies on movement [30], and as an important aspect of the future agenda of movement research [38]. Recently, a few studies have tackled the quantification of such connections and interactions [4, 14, 6, 13, 36]. This area still requires a lot of attention in future studies to increase our understanding of the relationships between movement and its *spatiotemporal context*, and to learn how environment influences the *behavior* and accordingly drives movement processes.

4.3   Computational Movement Analysis

The term *computational movement analysis* was coined by P. Laube [29] and is defined as "computational techniques for capturing, processing, managing, structuring, and ultimately analyzing data describing movement phenomena". In GIScience, a large number of studies have pioneered innovative *computational movement analysis* approaches for quantitative assessment of movement trajectories and their similarities [7, 15], mining movement patterns [28], clustering analysis [26], segmentation and classification of trajectories [16], to name but a few. According to recent reviews on the progress of these methods in GIScience [22, 32], most advances in this area have taken place in data mining and machine learning techniques for the detection of movement patterns in moving individuals or groups. The proposed techniques aim at finding structures and associations in movement datasets, by seeking commonalities and arrangements in the geometric specifications of trajectories or in the variation of their movement parameters in space and time [15].

The above publications not only document the significant progress of computational movement analysis in GIScience over the past twenty years, they also highlight the fact that so far environmental factors and geographic context have largely been ignored in the development of methods as well as in analyses. Integrating context and characteristics of the neighboring space in computational movement analysis seems inevitable and a logical step forward for future studies.

4.4   Visualization of Movement

Visualization is a powerful tool in data science for data exploration and discovery of hidden patterns by giving structure to complex datasets through aggregations and cartographic processes. In movement research, visualization and animations enable collaboration among scientists of different domains to find common grounds to discuss movement observations, observe and interpret known patterns, discover unknown structures, and generate scientific hypotheses. Together with *validation*, *visualization* constitutes the backbone of the whole movement research continuum (Figure 1) because it communicates the outcomes of computational techniques, simulations, and predictive models in meaningful and effective ways by portraying the connections between movement and its context. Visualization can also support the validation process by facilitating the interpretation of results and providing real-time feedback for examining movement simulations.

Geographic visualization and visual analytic techniques developed to this date mainly provide a complex representation of spatiotemporal phenomena that is not intuitive [3]. These techniques are often based on the three dimensional Hägerstrand's space-time-cube representation [27, 10] or hierarchical structures of treemaps [40]. Although these static representations can be effective for a small number of trajectories, they are cognitively very complex, particularly, when a large number of long trajectories are involved. Animations have proven to be an efficient medium, specially when communicating movement to scientists of other disciplines [49]. GIScience community should seek to develop more effective ways of communicating patterns in movement datasets using simple, dynamic, and interactive visualization approaches. Context remains to be an inevitable and integral part of future movement visualization tools [31].

5   Modeling Movement Processes

In analyzing trajectories, the assumption is that entities move freely in a landscape and without constraints. This assumption ignores the *internal state* of moving individual (i.e. movement strategies and decisions) and its *behavior*, as well as how it interacts with its physical environment and other dynamic phenomena. It is therefore essential to develop effective modeling and simulation approaches that capture the complexity of movement and behavior of individuals as they relate to the environment in which they move, the other individual with whom they interact and their responses to varying environments [1].

5.1   Modeling and Simulation of Movement

Movement models are "simplified representation of real world" movement processes, which can be used "to explore, to understand better, or to predict" the behavior of such process [9]. These models are generated based on a set of assumptions on the *states* and *behaviors* of moving phenomena and their relationships with their embedding *context*.

In GIScience, the time geography approaches have provided a basis for modeling the space-time settings of movement (i.e. space-time path, prism, and station) mainly for human activity patterns by taking the uncertainty of observations into account [24, 34, 48, 42]. Approaches to date mainly consider movement capacities (i.e. max speed, time budget) when modeling the use of space. However, as mentioned earlier, these models need to be enriched with *contextual* parameters for a more realistic representation of movement processes. Thus far only a few studies have proposed such inclusive agent-based modeling of movement processes [2, 1, 5, 45]. This area still has room for growth in the future of GIScience research.

Traditionally, *simulation models* have been used to generate a set of artificial movement trajectories to test known scientific hypotheses about the behavior of movement processes. Future research should strengthen *simulation models for prediction* purposes based on quantitative analysis of *real movement observations*, and through an iterative *calibration* process.

5.2 Prediction

Our universe is dynamic and changing over time. Any change in the environment can have an impact on the behavior of organisms. Also peculiarities in the behavior of moving phenomena could give us cues about environmental changes. In order to predict future responses to changes and varying environmental conditions, it is critical to translate our understanding of movement processes (i.e. from the right side of the continuum in Figure 1) to inform and calibrate predictive models. As a natural progression of movement research in GIScience, we need to develop *predictive models* to assess *how movement processes are changing over time* and *how future environmental changes impact these processes*. Future simulation models should equip scientists with tools to assess how *changes* of any movement components (Figure 2) influence the susceptibility of the whole system over time. We now have available resources (i.e. valuable observations of real world movement processes and environmental information) and a solid foundation on which to generate effective and integrated simulation models enabling reliable prediction of movement and system outcomes/imbalances.

6 Discussion: Moving from Observations to Predictions

In the past, *direct observation* of moving individuals was the most frequently used approach to quantify movement [47]. Following the rapid growth in movement observations owing to tremendous advances in positioning technologies, analytical methods have enabled GIScientists to increase their *understanding of movement* of dynamic phenomena and their associated *behavior*. However, the investigation of the interactions between moving phenomena with one another and with the physical environment through is lacking. What is required is more research on *context-sensitive analytical techniques and simulation models*. The GIScience community has made significant contribution to the understanding of movement (i.e. transforming *movement observations* to knowledge of *behavior*). These approaches have yet to inform us about how movement is affected by changes in the environment or how behavioral changes influence movement (i.e. derive *movement* from *behavior* and *context*). Still, questions such as *to what extent movement observations convey information on the underlying behavior of moving phenomena? to what degree geographic and environmental contexts influence these behaviors? how susceptible are these behaviors to environmental changes? to what extent changes in the behavior of moving phenomena indicate changes in the environment?* remain unanswered.

In summary, GIScience has been successful in the past at extracting *patterns* and *structures* from *raw movement observations*. However, the community should strengthen its capacities to transform raw movement observations to behavior through informed models by incorporating contextual parameters and interactions with environment (i.e. the right side of the continuum in Figure 1). This knowledge should then inform simulation models in order to *predict* changes in movement in response to changes in environmental conditions (i.e. the left side of the continuum in Figure 1). En route to this goal, several important issues require careful considerations in future directions of movement studies in GIScience, which are summarized as follows:

Temporal scales and granularity of movement: Movement is often reduced to a series of spatial positions in most existing methods, with little attention paid to the temporal scales of movement and observation granularities. Geometric movement analysis techniques often disregard temporal information of trajectories (i.e. temporal resolution and frequencies). Future analytical techniques should take into account the temporal granularity of observations, temporal frequencies of movement patterns, and the sequential structure of trajectories [23, 30, 41].

Movement processes across scale: Movement processes form across different scales in space and time. In order to gain insights into hierarchical structures in movement processes, it is essential to explore movement patterns, their formation mechanisms, and their associations across a range of local to global scales [17, 30].

Movement uncertainty: Uncertainty is a fundamental and unavoidable issue in modeling, simulation, and prediction of movement. As noted in [9], "epistemic uncertainty", which includes "process errors, measurement errors, random individual and temporal effects, uncertainty about initial conditions", greatly affects models and resulting predictions. GIScience has been very successful in modeling measurement errors and making adjustments for locational errors and their propagations through the analysis [48, 42]. Future research should emphasize the effect of uncertainty on modeling and predictions of changes in movement processes.

Evaluation and calibration of models through observations and domain expert knowledge: Future studies should evaluate the strengths and shortcomings of GIScience computational approaches to movement research. Recent studies have shown that GIScience can benefit through interdisciplinary research collaborations [11]. Future movement research should embrace multidisciplinary collaborations to develop informed models by applying domain expert knowledge to effectively evaluate and calibrate models.

A number of important research gaps in computational movement analysis are summarized in [29]. These challenges include *handling big movement data*, *bridging the semantic gap* between low-level movement observations and extracted patterns and structures obtained from the analyses, *safeguarding individual's privacy* specifically in analyzing human mobility, and *generating smart mobile applications* through autonomous and decentralized spatial computing.

7 Conclusions

This article presented a *continuum of movement research* to summarize previous studies and future directions of movement research in GIScience. The continuum organizes movement research in two overarching sections: (1) *understanding of movement processes* and (2) *modeling movement processes*. This article discussed the main highlights of GIScience research across this continuum and suggested a proposal for future directions of movement studies. GIScience to date has made significant contribution to this area through the development of data-driven computational movement analysis techniques and time geography approaches to quantify movement and space use patterns. Still methods to investigate the connections between movement and its *context*, and *interactions* between moving individuals lags behind. The GIScience community should embrace interdisciplinary collaborations with domain experts (e.g. ecologists, health scientists, etc.) to advance its capacities by developing reliable methodologies which are grounded in thorough *knowledge* of the dynamic phenomena and parameterized through real *movement observations*. Movement research in GIScience should progress towards the development of *informed simulations and predictive models* to better understand the behavior of moving phenomena and assess their susceptibility to environmental changes. Issues such as working with *large and real-time* movement datasets, privacy issues, influence of *scale and granularity*, *uncertainty* in movement observations and models, *visualization* of dynamic phenomena remain as important technical and scientific challenges for further research.

Acknowledgements

The author wishes to thank Sean C. Ahearn (CUNY – Hunter College) for his valuable input and review of this paper, and Timothy F. Trainor (US Census Bureau), May Yuan (University of Oklahoma), and Stephan Winter (University of Melbourne) for their constructive feedback at the 2015 Vespucci Institute on Advancing Geographic Information Science: The Past and Next Twenty Years.

References

[1] AHEARN, S. C. and SMITH, J. L. D. Modeling the interaction between humans and animals in multiple use forests: a case study of *Panthera tigris*. In *GIS, Spatial Analysis, Modeling*, D. Maguire, M. Goodchild, and M. Batty, Eds., ch 18, pages 387–403. ESRI, Redlands, California, 2005.

[2] AHEARN, S. C. and SMITH, J. L. D, JOSHI, A. R., and DING, J. TIGMOD: an individual-based spatially explicit model for simulating tiger/human interaction in multiple use forests. *Ecological Modelling*, 140(1-2):81–97, 2001. doi:10.1016/S0304-3800(01)00258-7.

[3] ANDRIENKO, G., ANDRIENKO, N., BAK, P., KEIM, D., and WROBEL, S. Visual Analytics of Movement. Springer, 2013.

[4] ANDRIENKO, G., ANDRIENKO, N., and HEURICH, M. An event-based conceptual model for context-aware movement analysis. *International Journal of Geographical Information Science*, 25:1347–1370, 2011. doi:10.1080/13658816.2011.556120.

[5] BENNETT, D. A. and TANG, W. Modelling adaptive, spatially aware, and mobile agents: Elk migration in Yellowstone. *International Journal of Geographical Information Science*, 20(9):1039–1066, 2006. doi:10.1080/13658810600830806.

[6] BUCHIN, M., DODGE, S., and SPECKMANN, B. Similarity of trajectories taking into account geographic context. *Journal of Spatial Information Science*, 9(9):101–124, 2014. doi:10.5311/JOSIS.2014.9.179.

[7] BUCHIN, M., DRIEMEL, A., VAN KREVELD, M., and SACRISTÁN, V. An Algorithmic Framework for Segmenting Trajectories based on Spatio-temporal Criteria. In Proceedings of *the 18th SIGSPATIAL International Conference on Advances in Geographic Information Systems*, pages 202–211, New York, NY, USA, 2010. ACM. doi:10.1145/1869790.1869821.

[8] CLARKE, K. C. and GAYDOS, L. J. Loose-coupling a cellular automaton model and GIS: long-term urban growth prediction for San Francisco and Washington/Baltimore. *International Journal of Geographical Information Science*, 12(7):699–714, 1998. doi:10.1080/136588198241617.

[9] O'SULLIVAN, D., and PERRY, G. L. W. Spatial Simulation: Exploring Pattern and Process. Wiley-Blackwell, 2013.

[10] DEMŠAR, U. and VIRRANTAUS, K. Space–time density of trajectories: exploring spatio-temporal patterns in movement data. *International Journal of Geographical Information Science*, 24(10):1527–1542, 2010. doi:10.1080/13658816.2010.511223

[11] DEMŠAR, U., BUCHIN, K., CAGNACCI, F., SAFI, K., SPECKMANN, B., VAN DE WEGHE, N., WEISKOPF, D., and WEIBEL, R. Analysis and visualisation of movement: an inter- disciplinary review. *Movement Ecology*, 3(1), 2015. doi:10.1186/s40462-015-0032-y.

[12] DODGE, S. Exploring Movement Using Similarity Analysis. PhD thesis, University of Zurich, 2011.

[13] DODGE, S., BOHRER, G., BILDSTEIN, K., DAVIDSON, S. C., WEINZIERL, R., BECHARD, M. J., BARBER, D., KAYS, R., BRANDES, D., HAN, J., and WIKELSKI, M. Environmental drivers of variability in the movement ecology of turkey vultures (*cathartes aura*) in North and South America. *Philosophical Transactions of the Royal Society of London B: Biological Sciences*, 369(1643), 2014. doi:10.1098/rstb.2013.0195.

[14] DODGE, S., BOHRER, G., WEINZIERL, R., DAVIDSON, S. C., KAYS R., D., DOUGLAS, CRUZ, S., HAN, J., BRANDES, D., and WIKELSKI, M. The environmental-data automated track annotation (Env-DATA) system: linking animal tracks with environmental data. *Movement Ecology*, 1(1):3, 2013. doi:10.1186/2051-3933-1-3.

[15] DODGE, S., LAUBE, P., and WEIBEL, R. Movement Similarity Assessment Using Sym- bolic Representation of Trajectories. *International Journal of Geographic Information Science*, 26(9):1563–1588, 2012. doi:10.1080/13658816.2011.630003.

[16] DODGE, S., WEIBEL, R., and FOROOTAN, E. Revealing the Physics of Movement: Comparing the Similarity of Movement Characteristics of Different Types of Moving Objects. *Computers, Environment and Urban Systems*, 33(6):419–434, Nov. 2009. doi:10.1016/j.compenvurbsys.2009.07.008.

[17] DODGE, S., WEIBEL, R., and LAUTENSCHÜTZ, A.-K. Towards a Taxonomy of Movement Patterns. *Information Visualization*, 7(3-4):240–252, Aug. 2008. doi: 10.1057/palgrave.ivs.9500182

[18] DOUGLAS, D. H. Least-cost path in GIS using an accumulated cost surface and slopelines. *Cartographica: The International Journal for Geographic Information and Geovisualization*, 31(3):37–51, 1994.

[19] GALTON, A. Dynamic Collectives and their Collective Dynamics. In *Spatial Information Theory*, Lecture Notes in Computer Science, vol. 3693, pages 300–315. Springer, 2005.

[20] GLASGOW, M. L., RUDRA, C. B., YOO, E.-H., DEMIRBAS, M., MERRIMAN, J., NAYAK, P., CRABTREE-IDE, C., SZPIRO, A. A., RUDRA, A., WACTAWSKI-WENDE, J., and MU, L. Using smartphones to collect time–activity data for long-term personal-level air pollution exposure assessment. *Journal of Exposure Science and Environmental Epidemiology*, 2014. doi:10.1038/jes.2014.78.

[21] GONZÁLEZ, M. C., HIDALGO, C. A., and BARABÁSI, A.-L. Understanding individual human mobility patterns. *Nature*, 453(7196):779–82, June 2008.

[22] GUDMUNDSSON, J., LAUBE, P., and WOLLE, T. Computational Movement Analysis. In *Springer Handbook of Geographic Information*, W. Kresse and D. M. Danko, Eds., ch 22, pages 725–741. Springer, Berlin-Heidelberg, Berlin, 2012.

[23] HOLYOAK, M., CASAGRANDI, R., NATHAN, R., REVILLA, E., and SPIEGEL, O. Trends and Missing Parts in the Study of Movement Ecology. *Proceedings of the National Academy of Sciences of the United States of America*, 105(49):19060–5, Dec. 2008. doi:10.1073/pnas.0800483105.

[24] HORNSBY, K. and EGENHOFER, M. Modeling Moving Objects over Multiple Granularities. *Annals of Mathematics and Artificial Intelligence*, 36(1):177–194, 2002.

[25] IMFELD, S. Time, Point and Space- Towards a Better Analysis of Wildlife Data in GIS. PhD thesis, University of Zurich, 2000.

[26] KISILEVICH, S., MANSMANN, F., NANNI, M., and RINZIVILLO, S. Spatio-temporal clustering. Springer, 2010.

[27] KRAAK, M.-J. The space-time cube revisited from a geovisualization perspective. In *Proceedings of the 21st International Cartographic Conference*, pages 1988–1996, 2003.

[28] LAUBE, P. Progress in Movement Pattern Analysis. In *Behaviour Monitoring and Interpretation - Ambient Assisted Living*, B. Gottfried and H. K. Aghajan, Eds., pages 43–71, IOS Press BV, 2009.

[29] LAUBE, P. Computational Movement Analysis. Springer Briefs in Computer Science. Springer International Publishing, 1st edition, 2014.

[30] LAUBE, P. and PURVES, R. How fast is a cow? Cross-scale analysis of movement data. *Transactions in GIS*, 15(3):401–418, 2011. doi:10.1111/j.1467-9671.2011.01256.x.

[31] LAUTENSCHÜTZ, A.-K. Assessing the relevance of context for visualizations of movement trajectories. PhD thesis, University of Zurich, 2011.

[32] LONG, J. A. and NELSON, T. A. A review of quantitative methods for movement data. *International Journal of Geographical Information Science*, 27(2):292–318, 2013. doi:10.1080/13658816.2012.682578.

[33] LU, Y. and FANG, T. Examining Personal Air Pollution Exposure, Intake, and Health Danger Zone Using Time Geography and 3D Geovisualization. *ISPRS International Journal of Geo-Information*, 4(1):32–46, 2015. doi:10.3390/ijgi4010032.

[34] MILLER, H. J. A Measurement Theory for Time Geography. *Geographical Analysis*, 4(2):63–45, Jan. 2005. doi:10.1111/j.1538-4632.2005.00575.x.

[35] MILLER, H. J. and HAN, J. Geographic Data Mining and Knowledge Discovery. Taylor & Francis Group, second edition, 2009.

[36] MILLER, J. A. Towards a better understanding of dynamic interaction metrics for wildlife: a null model approach. *Transactions in GIS*, 19(3):342–361, 2015. doi:10.1111/tgis.12149

[37] NATHAN, R., GETZ, W. M., REVILLA, E., HOLYOAK, M., KADMON, R., SALTZ, D., and SMOUSE, P. E. A Movement Ecology Paradigm for Unifying

Organismal Movement Research. *Proceedings of the National Academy of Sciences of the United States of America*, 105(49):19052–9, 2008. doi:10.1073/pnas.0800375105.

[38]   PURVES, R. S., LAUBE, P., BUCHIN, M., and SPECKMANN, B. Moving beyond the point: An agenda for research in movement analysis with real data. *Computers, Environment and Urban Systems*, 47(0):1– 4, 2014.

[39]   SANG, S., OKELLY, M., and KWAN, M.-P. Examining Commuting Patterns: Results from a Journey-to-work Model Disaggregated by Gender and Occupation. *Urban Studies*, 48(5):891–909, 2011. doi:10.1177/0042098010368576.

[40]   SLINGSBY, A., DYKES, J., and WOOD, J. Using treemaps for variable selection in spatio-temporal visualisation. *Information Visualization*, 7(3-4):210–224, 2008. doi:10.1057/palgrave.ivs.9500185

[41]   SOLEYMANI, A., CACHAT, J., ROBINSON, K., DODGE, S., KALUEFF, A., and WEIBEL, R. Integrating cross-scale analysis in the spatial and temporal domains for classification of behavioral movement. *Journal of Spatial Information Science*, 8(8):1–25, 2014. doi:10.5311/JOSIS.2014.8.162

[42]   SONG, Y., and MILLER, H. J. Simulating visit probability distributions within planar space-time prisms. *International Journal of Geographical Information Science*, 28(1):104–125, Jan. 2014. doi: 10.1080/13658816.2013.830308.

[43]   THEOPHILIDES, C. N., AHEARN, S. C., BINKOWSKI, E. S., PAUL, W. S., and GIBBS, K. First evidence of West Nile virus amplification and relationship to human infections. *International Journal of Geographical Information Science*, 20(1):103–115, 2006. doi: 10.1080/13658810500286968.

[44]   TOMLIN, C. D. Cartographic Modelling, 1991.

[45]   TORRENS, P. M., NARA, A., LI, X., ZHU, H., GRIFFIN W. A., and BROWN, S. B. An extensible simulation environment and movement metrics for testing walking behavior in agent-based models. *Computers, Environment and Urban Systems*, 36(1):1–17, 2012. doi:10.1016/j.compenvurbsys.2011.07.005.

[46]   TRIBBY, C. P., MILLER, H. J., BROW, B. B., WERNER, C. M., SMITH, K. R. Assessing built environment walkability using activity-space summary measures. *Journal of Transportation and Land Use*, 9(1):1–21, 2016.

[47]   TURCHIN, P. Quantitative Analysis of Movement: Measuring and Modeling Population Redistribution in Animals and Plants. vol. 1. Sinauer Associates, Sunderland, MA, USA,1998.

[48]   WINTER, S., and YIN, Z.-C. The elements of probabilistic time geography. *GeoInformatica*, 15(3):417–434, Apr. 2010. doi:10.1007/s10707-010-0108-1.

[49]   XAVIER, G., and DODGE, S. An Exploratory Visualization Tool for Mapping the Relationships between Animal Movement and the Environment. In *Proceedings of the 2nd ACM SIGSPATIAL International Workshop on Interacting with Maps*, pages 36–42, 2014. doi:10.1145/2677068.2677071.

Beyond Homeomorphic Deformations: Neighborhoods of Topological Changes

Matthew P. Dube

School of Computing and Information Science, University of Maine, Orono, Maine 04469, USA

Abstract: The past 20 years has seen the vast growth of the field of qualitative spatial reasoning. While qualitative formalisms have been developed to identify topologically similar binary relations from the point-of-view of the 9-intersection, one of the most important pieces of the spatial reasoning puzzle is in that of the conceptual neighborhood graph. Conceptual neighborhood graphs remain restricted to homeomorphic deformations of regions. In this paper, topological changes to the structure of an object are considered, such as that of hole formation and separation generation. This paper lays the groundwork for neighborhoods of non-homeomorphic deformations, a necessity in a sensor world.

Keywords: Topological spatial reasoning, topological changes, conceptual neighbourhood graph, complex regions, spatial queries

1 Introduction

Qualitative spatial reasoning is a topic that developed dramatically over the last 20 years. Dominated by sound formalisms for qualitative spatial relations, in particular binary topological relations [16][31], it has expanded into automated abstract inferences without a need for exact geometric representations, including reasoning about spatial similarities. The majority of such approaches assume changes in the objects' locations and shapes, yet they rely on the preservation of the objects' topological structure. For instance, in such reasoning, regions may change their sites or footprints, but they otherwise remain holed or hole-free, separated or separation-free. This paper lays the foundation for non-homeomorphic deformations between objects, a necessity in a world driven by sensor technologies. In other words, how do topological structure changes change object relations?

Within a single object, a topological change represents simply a transformation of that single object in one of many ways [23][30]: *topology preserving changes*, such as the changes exhibited by a receding or advancing glacier, *hole forming changes*, such as the creation of an oxbow lake or a loss of coverage within a sensor network, *separation forming changes*, such as a natural disaster dividing an ecosystem or the historical acquisition of territory such as Seward's Folly, *hole removing changes*, such as sea level rise, *separation removing changes*, such as countries declaring independence from a colonial power or the reunification of Germany, or any combination of such changes.

Relation changes occur between a pair of objects [15][19] or between a collection of objects [2][25][26] when the topological or mereotopological interactions between the objects change vis à vis some formalism such as the 9-intersection [17], the 9^+-intersection [24], or the region connection calculus [31]. These changes ultimately reflect the similarity between distinct topological states. Such changes have been modelled through the *conceptual neighborhood graph* [19]. A simple example of a relation change is the movement of the moon's shadow across the Earth during a solar eclipse relative to political boundaries. As the Earth rotates "beneath" the shadow, the moon's shadow moves relative to the objects on the Earth, potentially changing basic topological relations on its surface.

Spatial query languages are reliant upon the conceptual neighborhood graph in a key operation: nearest neighbor matching. In such instances where the particular result cannot be found in the database, a nearest neighbor match is declared when the distance within the conceptual neighborhood graph is minimized [12]. To effectively execute such a match requires knowledge not just of topology preserving changes (or combinations thereof) [11], but also requires knowledge of what happens when a dynamic object is allowed to change its topological structure. While Liu and Schneider [30] have attempted to explain how to convert from one topological structure to another through a state transition graph, the impact upon the relations themselves has not been studied past the level of their determination as a possibility for complex regions [27][33].

In this paper, the study of conceptual neighbors is moved from the realm of topology preserving changes to the realm of topology modifying changes using the approach of *typed relations*. While researchers have considered type-independent conceptual neighborhood graphs [4], conceptual neighborhood graphs within simple types [11][14][15][20], or even context-based conceptual neighborhood graphs [5], complex relations have not been studied through the approach of typed relations other than the environments holed region to simple region [18] and holed region to holed region [37], but even in those cases, the neighborhoods are based on topology preserving deformations.

The remainder of this paper is structured as follows. In Section 2, the basics of topological structure changes within an object are presented. In Section 3, the basics of topological relation changes between objects are presented. In Section 4, the impact of *first order topology modifying changes* is addressed, identifying the transition from simple regions to such object types as holed region, self-merging region, separated region, and self-splitting region, and the corresponding effect upon the relation to a second simple region. In Section 5, the impact of *second order topology modifying changes* is addressed, resulting in regions with multiple holes, multiple separations, and regions with a hole and a separation together, and the corresponding effect upon the relation. Section 6 considers if second order topology modifying changes are closed, namely that the execution of yet another operation upon the relations of that type results in additional connections in the neighborhood. Section 7 provides conclusions and calls for future study.

2 Topological Changes to a Single Object

Regions often undergo changes. In this section, we consider the topological changes that can occur to a single region. The remainder of this paper is based off of the definitions of Liu and Schneider [30] for (1) an empty region, *ER*, (2) a simple region, *SR*, (3) a single-holed region, *SHR*, (4) a multi-holed region, *MHR*, (5) separated regions or multi-regions, *MR*, and (6) holed and separated regions, *HSR*.

Empty regions are artefacts of creating the first object in a space. From a sensor perspective, this affordance is critical. Empty regions also serve the purpose of destroying the last object in a space.

Simple regions are the most studied of all topological instances. They serve as the foundation for the 9-intersection [17] and the compound object model [13], built off of stacking multiple simple regions together to construct arbitrarily complex objects.

Single holed regions have been studied extensively, including Egenhofer and Vasardani [18], Vasardani and Egenhofer, [37], and Huo *et al.* [22]. In the context of this paper, we will consider only proper holes, holes specifically contained by their host object. Holes can also be formed from a *covers* context at finitely many points [7]. Multiple holed regions have not been as extensively studied, but have been constructed using the compound object model [13] and identified as possibilities within the 9-intersection by both Li [27] and Schneider and Behr [33].

Multi-regions serve as the complement of holed regions. As such, using the concept of dual [8][28], reasoning on holed regions can serve as a representation that sufficiently addresses multi-regions by exchanging interior and exterior at a fraction of the mathematical and computational cost.

Holed and separated regions have been previously given the name *complex regions* by Liu and Schneider [30]. Since simple and complex are cognitively opposite terms as antonyms, the name in this case has been replaced, allowing holed regions and separated regions to be considered as complex regions as well.

On top of identifying the basic types of complex regions, it is important to address the particular topological changes that can be endured by a complex region. Liu and Schneider [30] and Jiang and Worboys [23] identify a set of 11 transformations that can topologically occur to an object: *topology preserve, region appear, region disappear, hole form, hole fill, region split, region merge, region self-touch, ring half-split, hole split,* and *hole merge*. These operations each (with the exception of *topology preserve*) fundamentally alter the structure of the object. The result of some operations (e.g., *region split* and *region appear*) produces objects of similar types, but the context of their occurrence changes drastically. If one were to use an approach such as that by Tryfona and Egenhofer [36], such a difference would be immediately manifest in the representation.

3 Topological Relations and Conceptual Neighborhood Graphs

While the focus of topological spatial reasoning work with sensor reasoning systems has been centered on the detection of self-topological changes, spatial relations focus on the relations between objects. In this section, a short review of the foundational work within this field is discussed.

Topological relations between pairs of objects have been studied predominantly through a pair of formalisms that have found great traction in the literature: the intersection models (the 4-intersection [16], the 9-intersection [17], and the 9^+-intersection [24]) and the region connection calculus [31]. Each formalism bases its relations on topological or mereotopological concepts such as set intersection and point connectivity. For simple regions, both formalisms produce the same relations in $\mathbb{R}^2$ [17][31] and in $\mathbb{S}^2$ [14][28]. Composition of these relations has been a fruitful pursuit as well [9][10][14][29][32], providing the opportunity to extrapolate information not explicitly stored within a spatial database.

Topological relations have proven a valuable contribution to spatial reasoning through query mechanisms [3][6][12]. Topological relations have also led to the construction of arbitrarily complex regions [7][13] and to understandings of n-ary relations [25][26]. Furthermore, topological relations have been used to generalize objects, deriving relations with other objects along the way [36], and also as a mechanism for modelling topological changes [21].

An important extension to spatial reasoning relative to topological relations is that of the *conceptual neighborhood graph* [19]. Originally developed for temporal intervals [1], the conceptual neighborhood graph has been extended into the spatial domain through relating the original definitions of Freksa [19] to such regional applications as *anisotropic scaling* (Figure 1), *isotropic scaling, translation,* and *rotation* [15][20]. More recently, conceptual neighborhoods have been grouped into a family structure [11], lending toward modifications of conceptual neighborhoods based on purpose. While Liu and Schneider [30] have created a network diagram that explores what types of complex regions can be constructed by non-topological deformations, the approach has not been extended to the acquisition of conceptual neighborhoods upon the identified complex region-region relations of Schneider and Behr [33] and Li [27] (Figure 2), of which the A-neighborhood in Figure 1 is an aggregated subset.

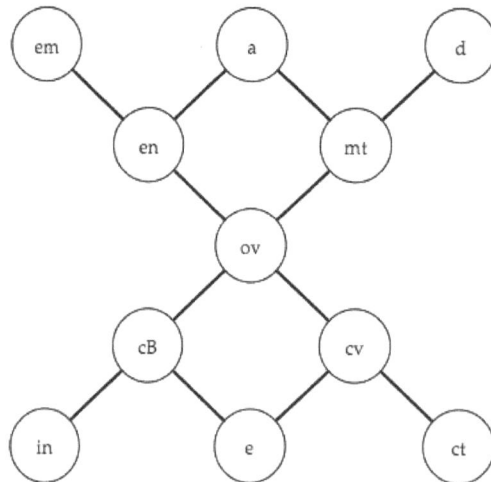

Figure 1: A-neighborhood graph of the spherical relations, demonstrating connections under anisotropic scaling [14].

$$\begin{pmatrix}1&0&0\\0&1&0\\0&0&1\end{pmatrix}\ \begin{pmatrix}0&0&1\\0&0&1\\1&1&1\end{pmatrix}\ \begin{pmatrix}1&0&0\\1&0&0\\1&1&1\end{pmatrix}\ \begin{pmatrix}1&1&1\\0&0&1\\0&0&1\end{pmatrix}\ \begin{pmatrix}1&1&1\\1&0&0\\1&0&0\end{pmatrix}\ \begin{pmatrix}0&0&1\\0&1&1\\1&1&1\end{pmatrix}\ \begin{pmatrix}0&0&1\\0&1&0\\1&1&1\end{pmatrix}$$
$$e\qquad d\qquad in\qquad ct\qquad em\qquad mt\qquad mt1$$

$$\begin{pmatrix}0&0&1\\0&1&1\\1&0&1\end{pmatrix}\ \begin{pmatrix}0&0&1\\0&1&0\\1&0&1\end{pmatrix}\ \begin{pmatrix}1&0&0\\1&1&0\\1&1&1\end{pmatrix}\ \begin{pmatrix}1&0&0\\0&1&0\\1&1&1\end{pmatrix}\ \begin{pmatrix}1&0&0\\1&1&0\\1&0&1\end{pmatrix}\ \begin{pmatrix}1&0&0\\0&1&0\\1&0&1\end{pmatrix}\ \begin{pmatrix}1&1&1\\0&1&1\\0&0&1\end{pmatrix}$$
$$mt2\qquad mt3\qquad cB\qquad cB1\qquad cB2\qquad cB3\qquad cv$$

$$\begin{pmatrix}1&1&1\\0&1&0\\0&0&1\end{pmatrix}\ \begin{pmatrix}1&0&1\\0&1&1\\0&0&1\end{pmatrix}\ \begin{pmatrix}1&0&1\\0&1&0\\0&0&1\end{pmatrix}\ \begin{pmatrix}1&1&1\\1&1&0\\1&0&0\end{pmatrix}\ \begin{pmatrix}1&1&1\\0&1&0\\1&0&0\end{pmatrix}\ \begin{pmatrix}1&0&1\\1&1&0\\1&0&0\end{pmatrix}\ \begin{pmatrix}1&0&1\\0&1&0\\1&0&0\end{pmatrix}$$
$$cv1\qquad cv2\qquad cv3\qquad en\qquad en1\qquad en2\qquad en3$$

$$\begin{pmatrix}0&0&1\\0&1&0\\1&0&0\end{pmatrix}\ \begin{pmatrix}1&1&1\\1&1&1\\1&1&1\end{pmatrix}\ \begin{pmatrix}1&0&1\\1&1&1\\1&1&1\end{pmatrix}\ \begin{pmatrix}1&1&1\\0&1&1\\1&1&1\end{pmatrix}\ \begin{pmatrix}1&1&1\\0&1&0\\1&1&1\end{pmatrix}\ \begin{pmatrix}1&1&1\\1&1&1\\1&0&1\end{pmatrix}\ \begin{pmatrix}1&1&1\\1&1&0\\1&1&1\end{pmatrix}$$
$$a\qquad ov\qquad ov1\qquad ov2\qquad ov3\qquad ov4\qquad ov5$$

$$\begin{pmatrix}1&0&1\\1&1&1\\1&0&1\end{pmatrix}\ \begin{pmatrix}1&0&1\\1&1&0\\1&1&1\end{pmatrix}\ \begin{pmatrix}1&0&1\\0&1&1\\1&1&1\end{pmatrix}\ \begin{pmatrix}1&1&1\\0&1&1\\1&0&1\end{pmatrix}\ \begin{pmatrix}1&1&1\\0&1&0\\1&1&1\end{pmatrix}\ \begin{pmatrix}1&1&1\\1&1&0\\1&0&1\end{pmatrix}\ \begin{pmatrix}1&1&1\\1&0&1\\1&0&1\end{pmatrix}$$
$$ov6\qquad ov7\qquad ov8\qquad ov9\qquad ov10\qquad ov11\qquad ov12$$

$$\begin{pmatrix}1&1&1\\1&0&0\\1&1&1\end{pmatrix}\ \begin{pmatrix}1&1&1\\0&0&1\\1&1&1\end{pmatrix}\ \begin{pmatrix}1&0&1\\1&0&1\\1&1&1\end{pmatrix}\ \begin{pmatrix}1&0&1\\1&1&0\\1&0&1\end{pmatrix}\ \begin{pmatrix}1&0&1\\0&1&1\\1&0&1\end{pmatrix}\ \begin{pmatrix}1&0&1\\0&1&0\\1&1&1\end{pmatrix}\ \begin{pmatrix}1&1&1\\0&1&0\\1&0&1\end{pmatrix}$$
$$ov13\qquad ov14\qquad ov15\qquad ov16\qquad ov17\qquad ov18\qquad ov19$$

$$\begin{pmatrix}1&0&1\\0&1&0\\1&0&1\end{pmatrix}$$
$$ov20$$

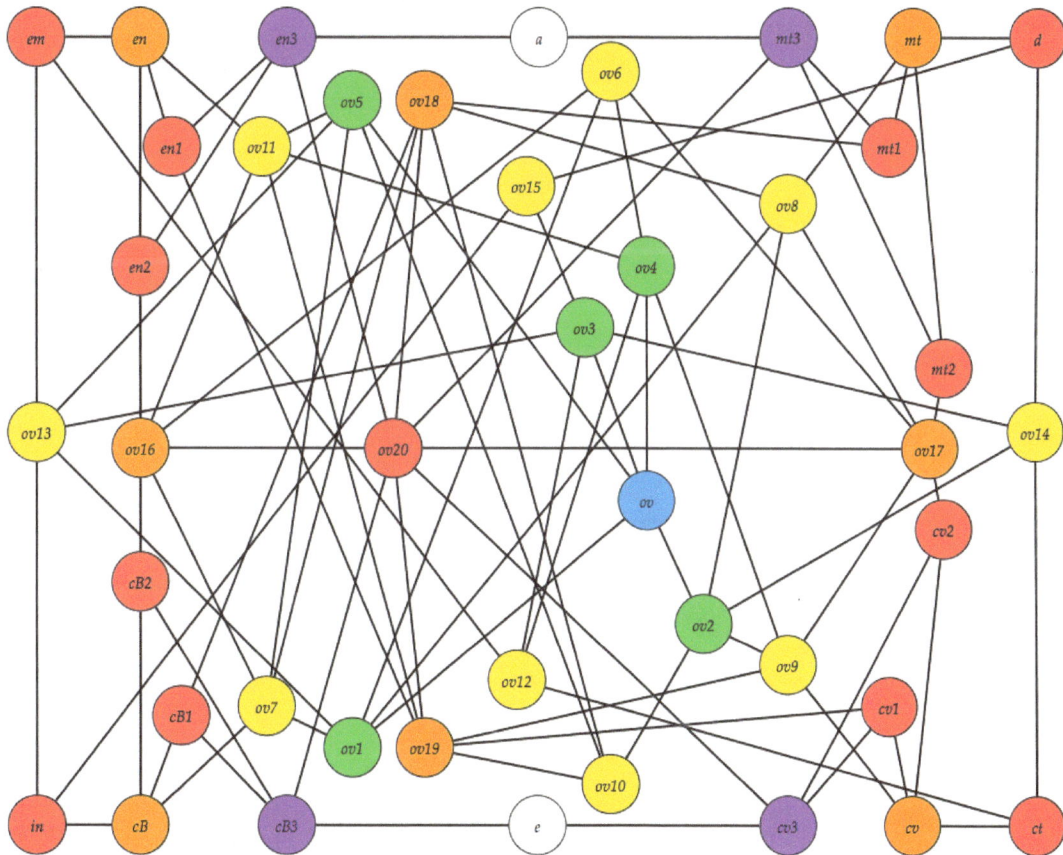

Figure 2: Shortest topological distance neighbors as measured by the 9-intersection matrix [4]. Same color nodes have same matrix cardinality.

Conceptual neighborhood graphs have also led to the development of properties that lead to more efficient computation of spatial relations and their conceptual neighbors. While the concept of a converse relation comes directly from relation algebras [35], exchanging figure for ground [34], complementation is a property that has important structural ramifications topologically. Duntsch [8] and Li and Li [28] refer to this property as *duality*. Simply put, dual relations have boundaries in the same locations, but exchange interior for exterior. A left dual exchanges the interior and exterior of the figure object; the right dual exchanges the interior and exterior of the ground object; the double dual exchanges both.

4   Neighborhoods from First-Order Non-Homeomorphic Deformations

For the duration of this paper, we consider the deformation of a region type from Section 2 and relate such an object to a simple region, either as the figure object or as the ground object [34]. Using the left-dual operation [28] and the converse relation, each presented deformation neighborhood is extended to an additional three that are fundamentally related to it (e.g., SHR rel SR is related by converse to SR rel SHR, by left dual to MR rel SR, and by left dual and converse to SR rel MR). We consider two types of topological deformations in this section, each of which result in the same net set of matrices: *cutting a hole in one object* (Section 4.1) and *forming a hole through self-intersection* (Section 4.2). Figure 3 demonstrates that these two operations without historical context lead to an identical output. These are transformations that might occur over time. A hole may be (at least visually) cut into an ocean by the ascension of volcanoes like the Hawai'ian Islands. Similarly, a region may double-back and touch itself, such as through erosion of a retaining wall through tidal or wind forces.

Figure 3: (a) Cutting a hole from an object, and (b) self-intersection of an object, both resulting in the same output: a ring.

Relations in this context refer to the output matrix from the 9-intersection. Many different topological constructions can share the same 9-intersection matrix. The work in this paper merely addresses the matrix transfer, the computational heart of topological queries [3].

4.1   Conversion from Simple Region to Single Holed Region

Egenhofer and Vasardani [18] defined a set of 23 relations between a region with a hole and a simple region within $\mathbb{R}^2$, a set of relations that extends to 37 relations within $\mathbb{S}^2$ [24]. These relations, however, map back to a total of 13 9-intersection matrices. Which of these 9-intersection matrices result from carving a hole in a simple region? The answer to this question is attainable through *inside* ; X, representing the relation between the hole and X (Figure 4). As such, the largest possible number of matrices that may result from a particular region having a hole carved within it is the cardinality of the composition.

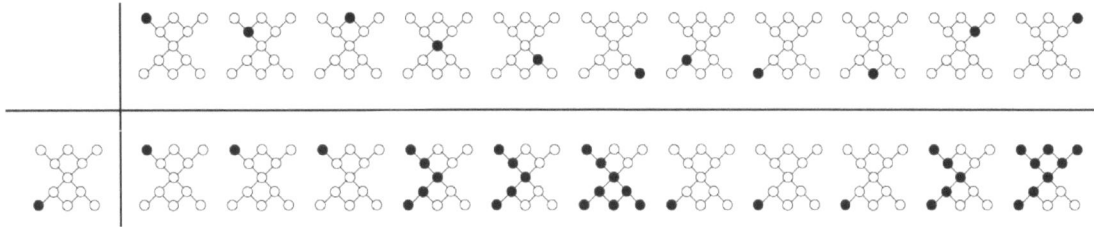

Figure 4: Composition of *inside* with each simple region-region relation, following the structure presented in Figure 1 [14].

A hole can be placed in any of eleven ways (representing each of the topological relations), given that it is present within the composition in Figure 4. Each relation leads to a specific transformation to an individual matrix of a simple region-region relation, as prescribed in Figure 5. The resulting matrix can be computed by taking the input simple region matrix (i.e., *disjoint*, *meet*, etc.) and applying the transformation from Figure 5. Entries listed as 0 or 1 must become that value. Entries listed as * keep their previous value. These transformations are defined by which components of B serve as the host, and which components of A are affected by the creation of a hole. These transitions are universal for the domain of simple regions.

Hole Relation	Effect			Hole Relation	Effect			Hole Relation	Effect		
	*	*	1		*	*	*		1	0	0
d	*	*	1	mt	*	1	1	a	1	1	0
	*	*	1		*	*	1		1	0	1
	1	*	*		*	*	*		0	0	1
in	1	*	*	cB	1	1	*	e	0	1	1
	1	*	*		1	*	*		1	0	1
	0	0	1		1	1	1		0	0	1
ct	0	0	1	ov	1	1	1	cv	0	1	1
	1	1	1		1	1	1		1	1	1
	1	0	0						1	0	0
em	1	0	0					en	1	1	0
	1	1	1						1	1	1

Figure 5: Effects upon the original matrix of a hole with the given relation.

Applying each of the transformations to the relevant matrices, the set of matrices identified when applying a hole in the given fashion are presented in Figure 6, the set of connections possible between a simple-region region relation and a holed region-simple region relation.

Using the converse property, the left dual property, and reversing the directions of connections, this set of transformations produces the neighborhoods for not just SHR to SR, but also SR-SHR, MR-SR, SR-MR, and the corresponding removal of the holes and separations created. To apply the converse and left dual properties, the particular operation is applied to both the original relation as well as each of the connections. Of the 38 relations (removing the special relations resulting from the Wada property [37]), 27 are involved in one of these eight neighborhoods, each involving a set of 15 relations. Under aggregation for unutilized relations in Figure 2, each relation's outputs form a connected set of the shortest-matrix difference neighborhood graph (ov7, ov8, ov9, and ov11 omitted).

e	*cB2*	*in*	*in*	***ov***	*ov*
d	*d*	*cB*	*cB*	***em***	*in, cB, cB2, ov, ov4, ov12, em, en*
mt	*mt*	*ct*	*d, mt, mt2, ov, ov4, ov12, cv, ct*	***en***	*ov, ov4, en*
a	*mt2*	*cv*	*ov, ov4, cv*		

Figure 6: Resulting matrices after hole creation.

4.2   Converting a Simple Region to a Ring through Self-Intersection

Unlike the creation of holes or separations, where there are specific effects tied to changes in the relation, the formation of a ring within a simple region does not follow such a systematic pattern. The formation of a ring is the culmination of an A-neighborhood transformation [14], namely an anisotropic scaling. As such, if an object can be deformed while maintaining the same relation to within a small distance of the self-merge, then the new matrix can be attained. Since a ring is the topological equivalent of hole with no recollection of history, the same 13 matrices must be the result of this operation, however the linkages between instances are different. In this case, we perform a graphic demonstration of the transformations available (Figure 7).

While holes and ring formations end in the same set of relations, the legacy of how the hole arose within the object changes the structure of the transition substantially. None of the relations result in the same set of relations under both procedures. This assertion is a testament to hole creation making an object smaller whereas ring formation makes an object larger and creates a hole in the process.

From the process of ring formation, we also derive the neighborhoods for region splitting (left dual), the converse of both ring formation and region splitting, ring splitting (inverse of ring formation), and region merging (inverse of region splitting), both from the reversal of the linkage directions.

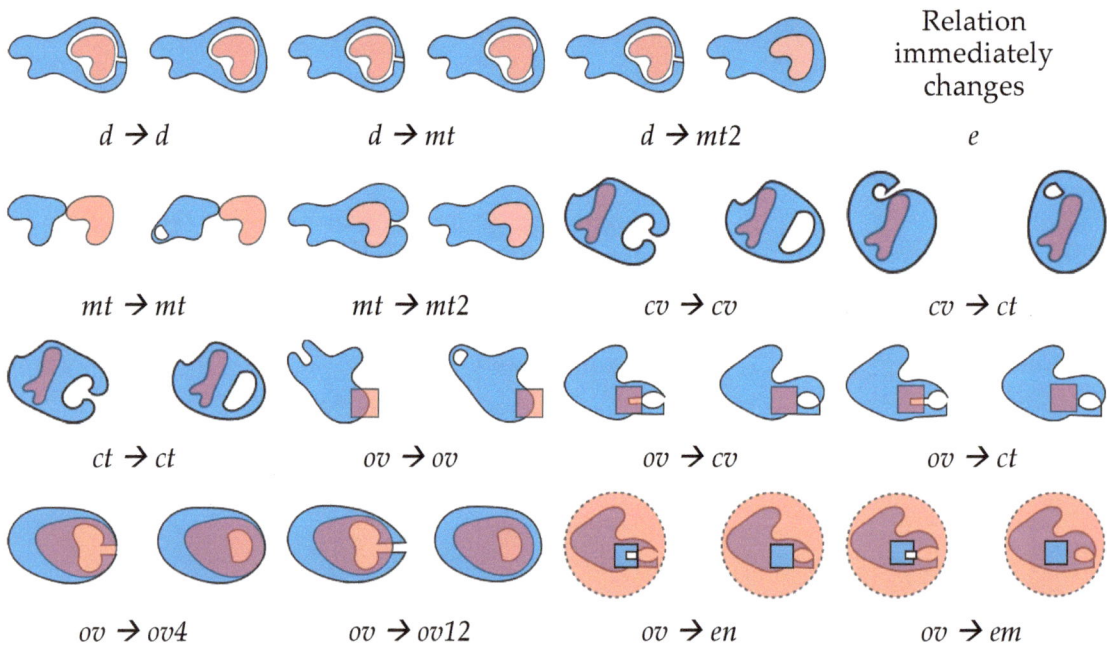

Relation immediately changes

$d \rightarrow d$ $d \rightarrow mt$ $d \rightarrow mt2$ e

$mt \rightarrow mt$ $mt \rightarrow mt2$ $cv \rightarrow cv$ $cv \rightarrow ct$

$ct \rightarrow ct$ $ov \rightarrow ov$ $ov \rightarrow cv$ $ov \rightarrow ct$

$ov \rightarrow ov4$ $ov \rightarrow ov12$ $ov \rightarrow en$ $ov \rightarrow em$

Figure 7. Neighborhood connections from the formation of a ring via a self-merge. Relations *in*, *cB*, *a*, *em*, and *en* can be attained through right dual properties.

As also seen in Figure 6, the changes under ring formation also form connected sets after aggregation of non-used relations *ov7, ov8, ov9,* and *ov11*.

5   Neighborhoods for Second-Order Non-Homeomorphic Deformations

Section 4 considered the transitions that resulted from making a single change to a simple region. In this section, we consider deformations upon these deformations, what we term second order non-topological deformations. Second order non-topological deformations lead to such object types as MHR, MSR, and CR. At the level of second order deformations, a hole and a ring are the same basis, and similarly a separation and a split are the same basis. The operations themselves, however, are not equivalent as previously demonstrated. We will only consider second order deformations as occurring to a previously deformed region, not to a simple region opposite a previously deformed region. This application is saved for future work. Similarly, we will only consider second order deformations formed under the insertion of a hole, the creation of a separation, or the splitting of a hole.

5.1   Adding Extra Holes (or Adding Extra Separations)

Like for simple disks, the insertion of a hole with a particular relation to B will have the same effects as it did in Figure 5. As such, to accomplish the mapping, we must determine which matrices can have an additional hole inserted in a particular topological relation to B. Simply put, a hole can be placed in A wherever A's components will allow it relative to B (Figure 8), having always an impact on A's interior, but in some cases having further impacts.

Applying the transformations in Figure 5 to the relations from Figure 8 produces the viable matrices that arising from the insertion of a second hole into A for a SHR – SR relation. These relations are shown in Figure 9. While additional relations are connected to one another, the set of relations is closed under hole formation solely and under separation generation solely. This closure property suggests that under one type of complexity, only a small set of matrices are available. While the type of complexity can be exchanged, the small set of matrices is equivalent in size and only differs by the converse property or the dual properties.

The connections established in Figure 9 can be converted in much the same way as single holed relations were converted to single separations and their converses. Using this powerful transformation produces the relation between simple regions and multiple-holed regions, n-separations to simple regions ($n > 2$), and its converse. Like their predecessors, these connections are again closed under neighborhood aggregation over relations *ov7, ov8, ov9,* and *ov11*.

Hole Relation	Conditions	Satisfactory Candidates
d	D1: $A^o \cap B^- = \neg\emptyset$	$d, mt, mt2, ov, ov4, ov12, en, em, cv, ct$
mt	M1: $A^o \cap B^- = \neg\emptyset \wedge$ M2: $A^o \cap \partial B = \neg\emptyset$	$ov, ov4, ov12, en, em, cv, ct$
ov	O1: $A^o \cap B^- = \neg\emptyset \wedge$ O2: $A^o \cap \partial B = \neg\emptyset \wedge$ O3: $A^o \cap B^o = \neg\emptyset$	$ov, ov4, ov12, en, em, cv, ct$
cB	B1: $A^o \cap B^o = \neg\emptyset \wedge$ B2: $A^o \cap \partial B = \neg\emptyset$	$ov, ov4, ov12, en, em, cv, ct$
in	I1: $A^o \cap B^- = \neg\emptyset$	$ov, ov4, ov12, en, em, cv, ct, cB, cB2, in$
ct	C1: $A^o \cap B^- = \neg\emptyset \wedge$ C2: $A^o \cap \partial B = \neg\emptyset \wedge$ C3: $A^o \cap B^o = \neg\emptyset \wedge$ C4: $\partial A \cap B^o = \emptyset \wedge$ C5: $A^- \cap B^o = \emptyset \wedge$ C6: $\partial A \cap \partial B = \emptyset$	ct
cv	same as *contains*	ct
e	same as *contains*	ct
em	E1: $A^o \cap B^- = \neg\emptyset \wedge$ E2: $A^o \cap \partial B = \neg\emptyset \wedge$ E3: $A^o \cap B^o = \neg\emptyset \wedge$ E4: $\partial A \cap B^- = \emptyset \wedge$ E5: $A^- \cap B^- = \emptyset \wedge$ E6: $\partial A \cap \partial B = \emptyset$	em
en	same as *embrace*	em
a	same as *embrace*	em

Figure 8. Rules that allow a hole to be placed with relation x to B. Eligible holed relations in the rightmost column.

d	d		$ov12$	$ov, ov4, ov12$	en	$ov, ov4, en$
$mt2$	$mt2$		$cB2$	$cB2$	$ov4$	$ov, ov4$
mt	mt		cB	cB	cv	$ov, ov4, cv$
em	$ov, ov4, ov12, em, en, in, cB, cB2$		in	in	ct	$ct, cv, ov, ov4, ov12, d, mt, mt2$
			ov	ov		

Figure 9: Resulting matrices after the creation of a second hole within A.

5.2   Holed and Separated Regions from either Holed or Separated Regions

The addition of a separated region to a holed region (and vice versa) represent the transformation to what we have termed HSRs. These relations are referred to by Liu and Schneider [30] as *complex regions*. While a holed and separated region is the same as a separated and holed regions, the origin relations are not the same. As such, we must demonstrate the transfer for both sets, but under left dual, the second set is given.

The addition of a separated region is governed ultimately by the composition *disjoint ; rel* (Figure 10). The context where the object is inserted within the hole is covered by the exchange of the classified exterior. Using the left dual of Figure 5 provides the necessary changes to apply to each holed matrix, applied in Figure 11.

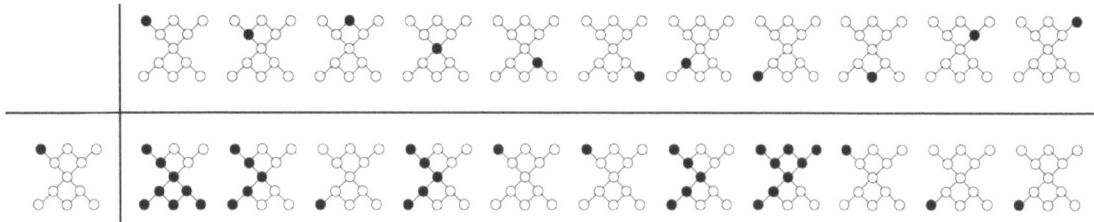

Figure 10. *disjoint ; rel* for each of the relations on the sphere [14].

ov12	*ov12*	*em*	*em*	*ov4*	*ov4*
mt2	*mt2, ov6*	*en*	*en*	*cB2*	*cB2, ov6*
mt	*mt, ov, ov1*	*ct*	*ct*	*cB*	*cB, ov, ov1*
		cv	*cv*		
d	*d, mt, ov, cv, cv2, ov1, ov15, ct*	*ov*	*ov*	*in*	*in, cB, en, en2, ov, ov1, ov15, em*

Figure 11. Results of applying separation transformations to the holed relation matrices.

Figure 11 represents the relations that are derivable from holed relations by adding a separation, but that transformation is not the only transformation that results in a holed and separated region. We could also just as easily have started with a separated region. These relations can be demonstrated by using the left dual transformation of Figure 11, shown in Figure 12. As is not a surprise, the two sets of output relations are identical, but connected to different relations. Furthermore, like exhibited for first order deformations, this set again forms connected sets under aggregation, identifying the set *ov16*, *ov17*, *ov18*, and *ov19* as necessary omissions.

ov15	*ov15*	*in*	*in*	*ov1*	*ov1*
cv2	*cv2, ov6*	*cB*	*cB*	*en2*	*en2, ov6*
cv	*cv, ov, ov4*	*d*	*d*	*en*	*en, ov, ov4*
		mt	*mt*		
ct	*ct, cv, d, mt, mt2, ov, ov4, ov12*	*ov*	*ov*	*em*	*em, en, in, cB, cB2, ov, ov4, ov12*

Figure 12. Results of applying hole transformations to the separated relation matrices under the left dual property.

5.3   Dividing a Hole

The division of a hole into two separate components, each co-located with the original hole requires the conversion of part of the exterior to boundary and interior, and some of the boundary to interior. Intuitively speaking, this is the same concept as the creation of a ring, therefore the division of a hole constitutes not only hole division, but also ring formation in the presence of a hole, and the splitting of a separation.

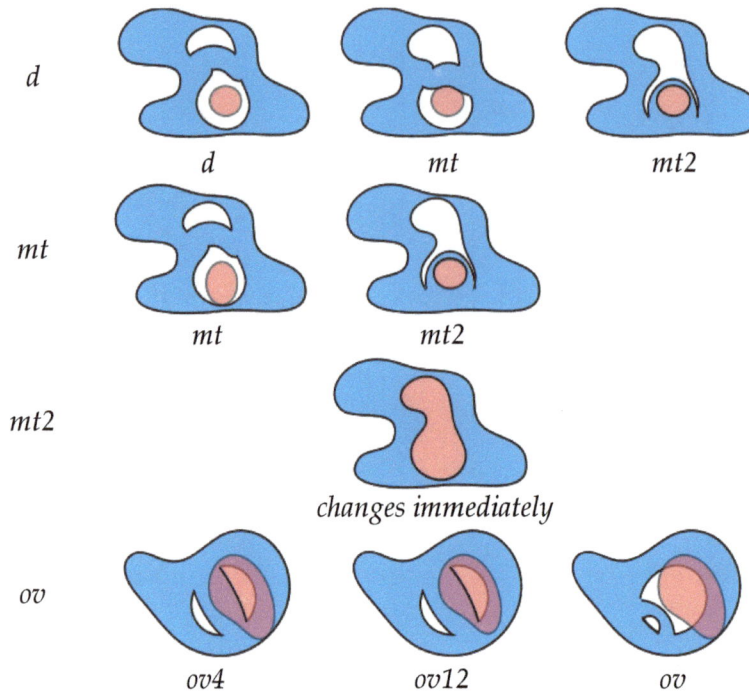

Figure 13. Hole splitting changes to *d*, *mt*, *mt2*, and *ov*.

Of the 37 compositional placements of a hole on the sphere, 27 placements place the hole immediately in a position where any division of the hole will not change the matrix at all. The additional ten compositional placements are subject to analysis. Matrices *ov4*, *ov12*, *em*, *en*, *cv*, and *ct* are thus unaffected by hole division. The remainder: *d*, *mt2*, *mt*, *ov*, *in*, *cB2*, and *cB* are subject to modification. Of these, knowledge of *d* provides knowledge of *in*, and similarly *mt2* and *cB2* have commonality, as do *mt* and *cB*. We will focus on the four matrices *d*, *mt*, *mt2*, and *ov* as their constructions are planar (Figure 13), with the others inferable by duality.

6 Conclusions and Future Work

In this paper, we have considered the types of topological changes that occur to regions in $\mathbb{R}^2$ and $\mathbb{S}^2$. While previous work has left the pursuit of these changes at this level or at a detection level, this paper has gone a step further, organizing the results of these changes into the structure of conceptual neighborhood graphs at the resultant matrix level. This work is particularly important in modelling the transfer between neighborhood graphs underneath different types of relations. The work presented here shows the link that occurs from one graph to the other at the moment that the topological structure of the object is altered, the non-homeomorphic step.

Throughout this paper, we have seen many important properties about spatial regions that are of note. The first is that particular deformations of objects are related to other deformations of objects through the use of the left dual (in the case of deformations of *A*) or right dual (in the case of deformations of *B*). While relations such as adding a hole and removing a hole are synonymous with one another (simply by reversing directions within the conceptual neighborhood graph), deformations such as adding a separation (and correspondingly removing a separation) are related to these operations. Using the left dual and the converse operations, knowledge of the matrices that result from adding a hole to A can be used to create removal of a hole, addition of a separation, removal of a separation (all in A), and by converse can be used to create the same deformations within the object B. On top of these deformations, deformations such as ring formation, object splitting, ring splitting, and object merging are all related to one another in a similar manner. This paper used these fundamental properties to streamline the process of full identification.

Another interesting insight with regard to hole formation and ring formation is that the two deformations result in the same output set of matrices (as each forms a hole in the end), but the manner in which the corresponding simple region relations are connected to these output relations in either case is not equivalent. This assertion is not a large surprise, but is rather important to note. The history and context of hole formation is very important in this light. Similarly, a region that divides is different contextually than a region that spawns a separation. These differences are the result of two concepts: A-neighborhood deformations that lead to rings or splits, and secondly, the semantics of ring formation versus hole formation. Ring formation is in addition to the object (a composition with *covers*), whereas hole formation is a composition with *inside*. Both relations (part of a larger converse family under generalization) lead to vastly different inferences, and thus vastly different connections to simple region parents. For second order deformations and beyond, the historical legacy of hole formation or ring formation is inconsequential as the output structures are identical.

After considering the deformations in this paper, 29 of the 38 matrices proposed by Li [27] (excluding the Wada property) have been accounted for within a conceptual neighborhood graph setting. The other nine matrices thus are the result of the combination of holes and separations in both A and B, a set of deformations not accounted for in this paper. To complete the process of this work requires the study of the relation between complex objects A and B, not just the relation between a single complex object and a simple region. These missing relations are *ov3*, *ov7*, *ov8*, *ov9*, *ov11*, *ov16*, *ov17*, *ov18*, and *ov19*. The Wada relations are *ov20*, *mt3*, *en3*, *cB3*, and *cv3*. Furthermore, under aggregation of these 14 relations, the conceptual neighbors from the particular non-homeomorphic changes are all neighbors within the shortest-distance neighborhood graph, the suggested prototype for neighborhood graphs [4].

Apart from the additional construction of neighborhood graphs is the insight that the type of relation matters in deformation neighborhoods. If an object is a simple region and a separation is added to it, a set of 13 matrices result. Similarly, if an object is a holed region and a separation is added to the holed region, a set of 16 matrices result. Type thus is instrumental in understanding the qualitative possibilities that deformation provides. This knowledge is critically important for the advancement of spatial information systems in a world where complexity is becoming evermore the normal expectation. Since underlying formalisms for query models in geographic information systems are mostly topological in nature [3], types of regions that can share a 9-intersection matrix represent a fundamental need for addressing the type to better equip nearest-neighbor matching procedures. A sensor world makes us slave to such a phenomenon, but the world itself has always operated in this manner. Moving beyond homeomorphism is the next step to a more advanced world of spatial intelligence systems that can respond to the needs of a dynamic information world.

From a practical perspective, these deformations are imperative to understand our dynamic world. One need only conceive of structures that might be weakened or strengthened by holes or separations in a measurement (such as heat's expanding and contractive effects on metals) to see that systems in the future could see dramatic impact from non-homeomorphic changes. These changes are just as important as the simpler changes of Freksa [19] and Egenhofer and Al-Taha [15], but are much harder to fully comprehend and formally define relative to existing topological formalisms. While the 9^+-intersection can manage the interactions after the fact or in a static environment [24], it is ill equipped to model the change in a dynamic fashion.

Acknowledgments

The author wishes to gratefully acknowledge his advisor Max J. Egenhofer for support and guidance through the process of effective dissemination. The author also gratefully acknowledges support under a Michael J. Eckardt Dissertation Fellowship from the University of Maine under the Maine Economic Investment Fund.

References

[1]   ALLEN, J. Maintaining knowledge about temporal intervals. Communications of the ACM 26,11 (1983): 832-843.

[2]   BRUNS, T., AND EGENHOFER, M. Similarity of Spatial Scenes. In Seventh International Symposium on Spatial Data Handling (Delft, The Netherlands, 1996), Springer-Verlag, pp. 31-42.

[3]   CLEMENTINI, E., SHARMA, J., AND EGENHOFER, M. Modelling topological spatial relations: strategies for query processing. Computer Graphics 18,6 (1994): 815-822.

[4]   DUBE, M. An embedding graph for 9-intersection topological spatial relations. Masters Thesis, University of Maine (2009).

[5]   DUBE, M., AND EGENHOFER, M. Establishing similarity across multi-granular topological-relation ontologies. In Quality of Context (Stuttgart, Germany, 2009), Springer, pp. 98-108.

[6]   DUBE, M., AND EGENHOFER, M. Surrounds in partitions. In Proceedings of the 22nd ACM SIGSPATIAL International Conference on Advances in Geographic Information Systems (Dallas, TX, USA, 2014), ACM Press, pp. 133-142.

[7]   DUBE, M., EGENHOFER, M., LEWIS, J., STEPHEN, S., AND PLUMMER, M. Canton regions: a model for complex objects in geographic partitions. In Conference on Spatial Information Theory (Santa Fe, NM, USA, 2015), Springer, pp. 309-330.

[8]   DUNTSCH, I. A tutorial on relation algebras and their applications in spatial reasoning. At Conference on Spatial Information Theory (1999): pp. 25-29.

[9]   DUNTSCH, I., WANG, H., AND MCCLOSKEY, S. A relation-algebraic approach to the region connection calculus. Theoretical Computer Science 255,1 (2001): 63-83.

[10]   EGENHOFER, M. Deriving the composition of binary topological relations. Journal of Visual Languages and Computing 5,2 (1994): 133-149.

[11]   EGENHOFER, M. The family of conceptual neighborhood graphs for region-region relations. In Geographic Information Science (Zurich, Switzerland, 2010), Springer, pp. 42-55.

[12] EGENHOFER, M. Query processing in spatial-query-by-sketch. Journal of Visual Languages and Computing 8,4 (1997): 403-424.

[13] EGENHOFER, M. A reference system for topological relations between compound spatial objects. In Advances in Conceptual Modeling – Challenging Perspectives (2009), Springer, pp. 307-316.

[14] EGENHOFER, M. Spherical topological relations. Journal on Data Semantics III 2 (2005): 25-49.

[15] EGENHOFER, M., AND AL-TAHA, K. Reasoning about gradual changes of topological relationships. In Theories and Methods of Spatio-Temporal Reasoning in Geographic Space (Pisa, Italy, 1992), Springer, pp. 196-219.

[16] EGENHOFER, M., AND FRANSOZA, R. Point-set topological spatial relations. International Journal of Geographical Information Science 5, 2 (1991), 161–174.

[17] EGENHOFER, M., AND HERRING, J. A mathematical framework for the definition of topological relationships. In Fourth International Symposium on Spatial Data Handling (Zurich, Switzerland, 1990), Springer, pp. 803-813.

[18] EGENHOFER, M., AND VASARDANI, M. Spatial reasoning with a hole. In Conference on Spatial Information Theory (Melbourne, Australia, 2007), Springer, pp. 303-320.

[19] FREKSA, C. Temporal reasoning based on semi-intervals. Artificial Intelligence 54,1 (1992): 199-227.

[20] GOODAY, J., AND COHN, A. Conceptual neighbourhoods in spatial and temporal reasoning. In European Conference on Artificial Intelligence (Amsterdam, The Netherlands, 1994).

[21] HORNSBY, K., AND EGENHOFER, M. Identity-based change: a foundation for spatio-temporal knowledge representation. International Journal of Geographical Information Science 14,3 (2000): 207-224.

[22] HUO, L., OUYANG, J., AND LIU, D. A Model for Representing Topological Relations between Regions with Holes. In 1st IEEE International Conference onInformation Science and Engineering (Nanjing, China, 2009), IEEE, pp. 1147-1150.

[23] JIANG, J., AND WORBOYS, M. Event-based topology for dynamic planar objects. International Journal of Geographical Information Science 23,1 (2009): 33-60.

[24] KURATA, Y. The 9+-intersection: a universal framework for modelling topological relations. In Geographic Information Science (Park City, UT, USA, 2009), Springer, 181-198.

[25] LEWIS, J., DUBE, M., AND EGENHOFER, M. The Topology of Spatial Scenes in $\mathbb{R}^2$. In Conference on Spatial Information Theory (Scarborough, United Kingdom, 2013), Springer, pp. 495-515.

[26] LEWIS, J., AND EGENHOFER, M. Oriented regions for linearly conceptualized features. In Geographic Information Science (Vienna, Austria, 2014), Springer, 333-348.

[27] LI, S. A complete classification of topological relations using the 9-intersection method. International Journal of Geographical Information Science 20,6 (2006): 589-610.

[28] LI, S. AND LI, Y. On the complemented disk algebra. The Journal of Logic and Algebraic Programming 66,2 (2006): 195-211.

[29] LI, S. AND YING, M. Region connection calculus: its models and composition table. Artificial Intelligence 145,1 (2003): 121-146.

[30] LIU, AND SCHNEIDER, M. Tracking continuous topological changes of complex moving objects. In Proceedings of the 2011 ACM Symposium on Applied Computing (Taichung, Taiwan, 2011), ACM Press, pp. 833-838.

[31] RANDELL, D., CUI, Z., AND COHN, A. A spatial logic based on regions and connection. In Knowledge Representation 92 (Cambridge, MA, USA, 1992), Morgan Kauffmann, pp. 165-176.

[32] RENZ, J., AND NEBEL, B. On the complexity of qualitative spatial reasoning: a maximal tractable fragment of the region connection calculus. Artificial Intelligence 108,1 (1999): 69-123.

[33] SCHNEIDER, M., AND BEHR, T. Topological relationships between complex spatial objects. ACM Transactions on Database Systems 31,1 (2006): 39-81.

[34] TALMY, L. Cognitive semantics: an overview. In Handbook of Semantics: An International Handbook of Natural Language Meaning (2011), pp. 622-642

[35] TRYFONA, N., AND EGENHOFER, M. Consistency among parts and aggregates: a computational model. Transactions in GIS 1,3 (1996): 189-206.

[36] VASARDANI, M., AND EGENHOFER, M. Single-holed regions: their relations and their inferences. In Geographic Information Science (Park City, UT, USA, 2008), Springer, pp. 337-353.

[37] YONEYAMA, K. Theory of continuous sets of points. Tohoku Mathematical Journal 11, 12 (1917): 43-158.

Mapping Practices in a Digital World

Benjamin D. Hennig

School of Geography and the Environment, University of Oxford, Oxford, OX1 3QY, United Kingdom

Abstract: Current GIS and mapping techniques are highly technologically driven. With advances in the capabilities especially of online mapping platforms but also advanced geovisualization applications for considerably enhancing digital maps, the map has turned into an advanced digital product that goes far beyond the capabilities of a printed paper map. However, digital mapping practices often remain a mere technical challenge while the wider implications of this digital turn for cartographic practice are less discussed. What is needed is a new approach to rethinking cartographic principles in the digital era.

Keywords: Neocartography, digital mapping, computer cartography, cartographic principles, GIS, online, internet.

1   Introduction

The advent of digital technology and the internet has led to the question being asked of how maps can be visualised beyond the traditional paper map. GIS-derived maps make great use of digital technology in the process of their creation, and their great potential to get new perspectives on the world using highly advanced techniques can only be exploited because of the most recent advances in digital technology. Therefore, the question remains whether digital technology beyond its analytical power may also be able to provide new means of cartographic practice to show maps in the digital world.

Changing technologies have a considerable impact on cartography. Several technological revolutions marked important steps in the practice and process of creating maps. Mechanical, optical and photo-chemical technologies changed the way maps were produced. Then, the discovery of electronic capabilities made a new dimension in map production accessible: Not only were most of the design techniques transferred to digital platforms, but also the possibility to deal with huge amounts of data that can hardly be analysed by a single person enables cartographers to find new ways of handling data for cartographic visualisation [32].

This paper puts the issue of cartographical principles into the main focus and discusses in this context what role cartography can play in the digital world and the internet age about thirty years after digital technology has become widely used in cartographic practice with personal computers having become much more affordable in the 1980s [23]. This discussion is framed by a reflection on current digital mapping techniques. Based upon that, exemplary suggestions for directions of cartographic research and practice are made that take the implications of digital and web technology into account. This is also illustrated on some simple examples that link cartographic principles and their technical realisation.

The following remarks are not intended to give a complete overview of developments in digital mapping (see [9] for an extensive compilation of relevant works in the field). The main emphasis is put on the aspect of cartographic principles to demonstrate and propose future perspectives for digital mapping beyond what is currently done.

2 Digital Mapping Techniques

2.1 Geospatial analysis and geovisualization

Geospatial analysis has become a standard operation in data processing. It is not only a necessity given the huge amount of data which many geospatial sciences are working with, but also a result of growing data availability and increasing computing power. The pivotal element in this process often is the geographic information system (GIS), which brings data together and allows performing a large number of geospatial analyses. Many new techniques find their way into GIS applications fairly quickly. Programming interfaces allow a highly specialized customization of these applications and the integration of particular algorithms and techniques in the process of geospatial analysis.

The main purpose of using GIS software is the execution of spatial analysis and the integration of various geospatial-related data. Mapping and cartography are subordinate elements in these applications. Although maps can be designed using a set of design options, these capabilities are rudimentary. This is a weak point of using GIS for geospatial analysis while at the same time aiming for good cartographic practice or looking for innovative visual mapping approaches. Map results derived from GIS software often lack that design component that is essential to convey a message or tell a story with a map beyond the sole purpose of putting data on a map display [21].

Drawing visually appealing maps starts with the way in which data is analysed and how results from this spatial analysis come out of that process. This process of spatial and statistical data processing is essential for the mapping results, but the outcome of the techniques is only a first step that results in a rough draft that needs particular cartographic treatment before it can be seen as a more understandable and as such also more meaningful cartographic representation of the processed data. Visualisation concepts are thus as essential as the underlying methodologies themselves, which makes cartographic concepts so valuable and their outcome a key component of geographic visualisation.

The emergence of geovisualization as a sub-discipline of the so-called GIScience is a result of advances in the field. The debate about whether GIScience can be seen as a scientific discipline for itself or *only* as a powerful technology of scientific visualisation is ongoing [4]. Most important in this rapidly evolving field is that digital methods of advanced data analysis and data visualisation play a crucial role in the understanding of ever growing amounts of data. New techniques are not only different ways of looking at data, but are central elements in the process of understanding geographic information. Here, geovisualization connects to the very fundamental elements of cartographic research, and with others may lead to the assumption that cartographic practice is part of scientific research as well (for instance part of a communication science [28]).

I do not want to argue for or against the perception of cartography and GIScience as scientific disciplines, although I see them as an integral part of geographical methods. As such research on new geovisualizations (cartographic or else) is part of the scientific advance in geographical science. Anyway, the spectrum of GIS- and cartography- related research is too broad to be categorised in one discipline only or to be linked to only one discipline. As a matter of course all these advances could not be made without a solid geographic background in mind.

As pointed out by many before me, GIS is not the magic black box that produces meaningful results of geospatial analysis and creates stunning images [12, 29, 33]. It is the user who influences that process considerably and needs the knowledge about the methods and the science behind the data. The only problem is that often there is a gap between those who are capable of advancing technology and those who are capable of advancing science.

With the recent trends and advances in geovisualization, visualising geospatial data has left the domain of cartography, and maps or map-related visuals have become only one option to show geographical information. The line between digital cartography and data visualisation has vanished. Visual designers as well as geographical information science researchers see maps as one of many ways to make sense of data and information. Despite the boom in data visualisation in the digital world, advances in cartographic visualisation in academic geography remain limited. Kessler & Slocum [21] make the disconcerting finding of an overall low quality of map design in an analysis of thematic maps in two major geographical academic journals. They argue that geography as a core discipline of mapping should embrace map design as a vital component of geographic education, and that good practice of mapping needs to be actively promoted and easy to perform. Digital technology can be one part of that process that reduces the barriers to create better maps with new and easier to use tools that do not require the advanced skills that are needed to perform more complex geospatial analysis.

2.2   Mapping tools

There are growing numbers of tools for digital mapping and geovisualization outside GIS environments that do not require the corresponding technical knowledge about the use of geodata and GIS techniques. The range of tools is widespread and contains different degrees of complexity and specialisation of currently available visualisation environments. Many other resources exist, and the developments and advances in this field are very dynamic.

Other digital mapping tools include specialised but easy to use resources that solve specific cartographic tasks. The examples shown in Figure 1 demonstrate the range of tools and resources that have become available with digital technology. These are targeted at users who produce maps in the common map design environments, such as Adobe InDesign. All applications have basic cartographic principles built into their functionality that supports inexperienced users to make the right design choices in creating maps. GIS software fails to provide a similarly simple assistance, which then results in the often bad mapping practice of the *Modern Dark Ages* of map design [10].

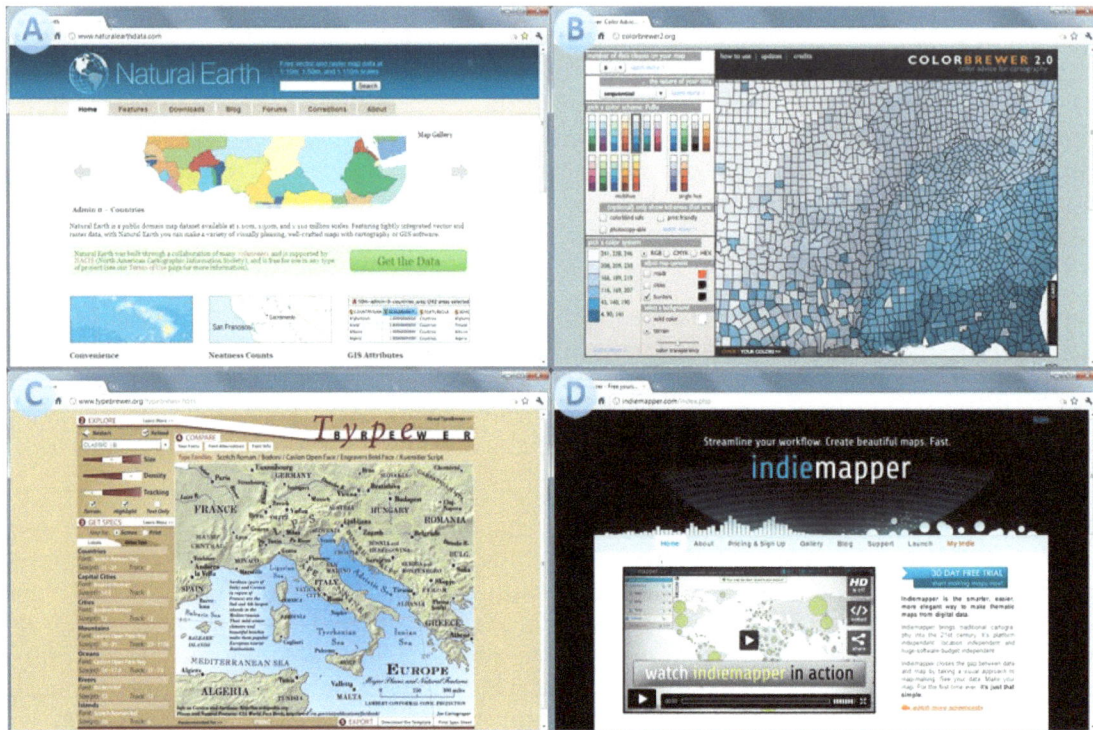

Figure 1: Digital cartography in the internet. A: *Natural Earth* geodata repository (http://www.naturalearthdata.com), B: *Colorbrewer* map colour guide (http://colorbrewer2.org), C: *Typebrewer* map typography guide (http://www.typebrewer.org), D: *Indiemapper* online cartography application (http://www.indiemapper.com)

The importance of the development of such mapping applications with digital technology should not be underestimated in its value for cartographic practice. Not only can better mapping practices be promoted with these tools, but they can also help to encourage the academic use of cartographic visualisations to make scientific work and results from academic research visible and understandable. Cartographic methods are also an important element of communicating geographical science.

Advances and new concepts in geographic visualisation require approaches different from easy to use mapping tools. Here, the investigation of new ways of data analysis and new ways of visualisation are essential, and can only be carried out in specialised computer environments. GIS software is one main part of these tools, but other applications with different capabilities can be used for digital mapping and data visualisation, such as the statistics software *R* or the visualisation programming environment *Processing* to name only two of many non-commercial applications that have become popular in this field in the last years.

3 The Role of Maps in Digital Publishing

The recent advances in digital mapping demonstrate how digital technology has become a standard element in the process of creating maps in manifold ways. This applies to the traditional cartographic practices that are nowadays often performed using graphic design software such as Macromedia Freehand or Adobe Illustrator. Here, principles of map design are generally transferred to the digital world, and basic cartographic principles are used as in the non-digital process of creating a map. In this context, digital technology mainly has the role of reducing the manual work and simplifying and automating the work stages.

Digital technology has also become a routine element in analysing and generating scientific raw data for a map or a geovisualisation, which is then finalised in the design software and dedicated mapping tools, or which is further visualised in new visualisation environments such as Processing. The degree of expertise that is needed to create maps is slowly declining. New tools are becoming available that allow map making following basic cartographic principles also for less experienced users. Advanced cartographic works, however, remain part of the work for trained experts. Computers play a crucial role in the task of analysing and visualising data in novel ways or using new approaches, which require expert knowledge to be realised. Many mapping techniques were impossible to realise without present-day computing power. The digital turn in cartography thus has not led to a simplification of the process of making maps, but has enabled new dimensions of data analysis and new ways to visualise that data.

Often the result of using digital technology in the mapping process remains some form of paper map, which still is seen as the ultimate final product of the cartographic visualisation process. Even if the final map remains a digital entity that is only used on a computer screen, it is treated as being a paper map, and the screen only resembles the paper. This is a widespread phenomenon in digital media. Digital equivalents of analogue products are often oriented in their appearance to the real world, resulting in the creation of effects that resemble a physical product. A paramount example of this is the visual page turning effect in digital books on portable computers and tablets.

Publishers are struggling with adapting to new media concepts that embrace the capabilities of advancing digital technology, which at present can be described as an experimental phase of creating innovative new concepts for media on digital devices. One key problem is to find new applications that enhance the usability or add value to digital media. Current attempts of that often fail because they do not add significant value [5, 11,15].

What is described here is a general issue that affects the publishing scene more than it perhaps affects cartography as a discipline. Nevertheless, it reveals a gap in cartographic research ever since digital technology arrived in the discipline: While cartographic practice was translated into digital techniques, and geospatial analysis was introduced to the spectrum of (geo)scientific methods [26] – arguably resulting in the creation of GIScience as a discipline between geosciences, cartography and informatics – the map as a publishing product itself has changed little.

Mobile mapping applications and GPS-technology are part of geospatial research that does not focus on the map itself or on visualisation problems. Here basic mapping principles have been conducted by pragmatic and technology-led decisions, which have often been initially set by technology companies rather than geovisualisation research. Most research in this field currently focuses on advancing database structures and queries, and analytical algorithms that better connect the increasing amount of geospatial information [3]. Geovisualisation in these digital map products has only become more relevant with advancing display capabilities that include more complex information, with the aim to improve the visualisations towards a more realistic appearance (rather than alternative concepts of visualising complex data). Despite being in the centre of the visualisation of the information shown in mobile mapping applications, the map itself as a cartographic element plays a subordinate role, while major efforts are put into the analytical capabilities [22, 25, 26].

Online maps and cartographic geovisualisations in the internet move maps away from their static character towards interactive and versatile multimedia products. Maps in the internet are widely used and appear in diverse forms.

The development of GoogleMaps and OpenStreetMap both date back to the years 2004/05. GoogleMaps quickly gained high user numbers, which was further encouraged by the implementation of interfaces to allow the integration into external websites and the combination with external datasets. OpenStreetMap took longer to attract a wider perception, because the initial phase included the compilation of a geodatabase, which GoogleMaps could acquire from commercial providers of geodata. Meanwhile, there is no significant difference in data quality for many parts of the world, and in some regions OpenStreetMap even provides more data than GoogleMaps [2, 31, 36].

The direction of these services is largely driven by technological advances that Google implements in its platform(s). Google increasingly adds functionalities that aim to make an online replica of the world. The recent additions of live traffic information and similar services appear to help the Google mapping platform remain successful in the digital world, significantly influencing the way online maps are created and consumed. OpenStreetMap follows a different direction that is not driven by monetary considerations. It is more open to user input and therefore relies on individual projects that push the technical progress ahead. The increasing implementation of OpenStreetMap in scientific applications may turn OpenStreetMap into a non- commercial alternative to integrating scientific data in dynamic and interactive mapping environments [36].

The web interfaces of GoogleMaps and OpenStreetMap are very similar in terms of cartographic capabilities. Some basic cartographic principles, such as different levels of detail at changing scales, colour schemes for the major geographic features and other elements are well integrated in these platforms. Advantages of the digital world include the large degree of interactivity using simple navigation tools to zoom in and out, and pan the map inside the display window. In terms of usability, these mapping services are major improvements to earlier online mapping attempts in the late 1990s and the first years of the 21st century, which were in very experimental stages of development with sluggish interfaces. These examples hardly exist anymore, not least because of the possibility to integrate GoogleMaps, OpenStreetMap, and other web mapping services into self-made map projects.

Further advanced cartographic elements or new cartographic practices are less prevalent so far. The user adaption of maps based on online mapping services remains very limited to adding new layers onto the basemaps, and depicting basic geometric elements such as lines or points in form of the infamous (but customisable) pushpins to depict locations. Cartographic design for this additional information lies in the hand of the user who creates map mashups, but is nevertheless limited to what general digital mapping tools provide.

Digital map design principles are extensively discussed in cartographic literature (see e.g. [1, 16, 17, 18, 19, 35]). Topics focus on specific design guidelines for digital technology and the investigation of cartographic principles in relation to the specific technological configurations. Issues such as screen typography, colour rendition, and map navigation tools to simplify the user interaction are among the well discussed issues that solve some of the key problems in transferring existing cartographic practice to the (not so) new digital environments [19]. Problematic remains their implementation in some of the most commonly used and mainly technology-driven web mapping services. More open projects such as OpenStreetMap are more progressive in this regard, also because their ties with academic research and GIScience are much closer and the prime interest is not commercial.

Digital mapping in the online world shows a divided picture. Online maps are largely based on digital mapping services that serve as a fundament for the actual mapping and provide the main framework for controlling and visualising the topic of interest. Improvements that benefit from digital technology include considerable technical advances of the underlying geographical databases, and the improved capabilities to interact with maps by moving them around, changing scales, showing dynamic changes in animated form, or interactively selecting the relevant information. These are capabilities that mark clear advances over static (and therefore printed) maps. On the other hand, the standards upon which these digital interfaces and usability are based are largely set by commercially driven decisions to extend the capabilities of digital mapping platforms, rather than well-considered choices on the best practices and most elegant forms of visualisation. Online maps still resemble to a great degree paper maps, with a little bit more interactivity, but otherwise with all the concepts of the analogue world translated into the digital world – sometimes better, sometimes worse, just like good and bad maps in the offline world.

Online maps are currently a major focus of the developments in digital mapping, and the underlying more technically oriented GIS-related areas of research in this field are major subjects of methodological advances in this field (see e.g. [1, 23, 25]). Work on more cartography-oriented practices of digital mapping and new approaches that focus on maps as a publishing product (e.g. [17, 34]) are less common fields of cartographic research.

4   Creating Maps using Web Technology

4.1   The advent of digital technology in mapping

The examples of the use of maps in contemporary digital platforms demonstrate how using computer technology considerably enhances the value of maps. Cartographic practice is an indispensable foundation for these new technologies. Principles of cartography and mapping techniques are the underlying common ground of these innovations, and the emergence of the field of geovisualisation finds its manifestation in these new digital mapping platforms [24, 25]. Although taken for granted in most industrialised societies – as is the internet in general – these techniques have only become available a decade ago, many of which we use today are even much younger.

Before that, digital mapping was generally more focused on experimenting with the multimedia capabilities of the first multitasking operating systems. First maps as digital media products were developed for a small group of people and not the wider public. Home computers only became a standard configuration in many households and in education in the 1990s, but did not immediately become a primary source for media consumption [23].

The first digital mapping products in the 1990s were often complementary to existing publications, such as an additional CD-ROM that accompanied textbooks, or similar extras for printed atlases [8, 32]. The main aim was an additional incentive for buying, or multimedia products were targeted at people exploring the new technologies. These early digital mapping products were less the inevitable move of map products away from paper form to digital, but rather an early explorative phase of a wider trend to create multimedia content for the new media devices that started to occupy the mass markets.

Media consumption on digital devices has accelerated in recent years [6, 30]. Digital media has not yet replaced traditional publishing. Books, newspapers, magazines and their likes still outnumber their equivalents on digital devices. But their profits are falling sharply, while digital content has started to be a major source for consuming news and other content, including maps and map-like visualisations.

It may not be a daring assumption that the majority of maps nowadays are consumed in digital form. Satnav systems (replacing paper maps), location based services on mobile phones (replacing maps in guidebooks, and guidebooks themselves), online route planners (replacing the road atlas), and many other of these examples introduced before are these new digital maps that people consume. Content created by the *new mapmakers* (who often have no cartographic training) published online is widely consumed solely online. If their likes are used in analogue media, they often have a digital origin, which is where the majority of their audience has accessed them (not least because of their more widespread and immediate availability).

What is needed to enhance the value of digitally published maps are new ways of visualising and presenting them. New forms of map presentation in the digital world need to make optimum use of technical capabilities, and new approaches should be as unconstrained as possible to create a map that can be consumed regardless of the specific nature of the digital platform or device on which the map is accessed. Cartographers produced analogue maps so that the final product can be printed in a book, in a magazine, on a poster, and in many other similar ways. Traditional cartographic practices are suitable for all these ways of publishing, because their analogue nature does not allow much innovation in this regard. The same products can be used in digital media, but that remains an incomplete map product that makes best use of digital technology. The maps published in the Worldmapper project for example face similar problems and demonstrate this dilemma. The maps on the project's website (www.worldmapper.org) are produced with very recent technological advances using state of the art GIS methods, but the end product is a static map that works on screen as it does on printed paper. The website itself makes some use of digital technology by providing additional material and allows accessing all relevant data, but the maps that stand in the centre of the project remain static.

What is needed apart from the technological advances is a standardisation of rules for digital cartographic practice that go beyond the mere translation of existing principles. The principles for digital mapping need to be extended by new, very basic concepts of designing and creating digital maps. The development of new principles obviously has to be oriented on technical capabilities, but should not be driven by them and has to be formulated outside the specific ways of technical realisation. Just as there are principles defined for the creation of map elements, symbols, colours, without explaining how these are implemented using pen and paper or using a design software, there should be new principles defined for digital maps that become part of the toolbox for digital cartographers.

Cartographic practices for digital publishing platforms must be examined and defined in a way that they can be realised in different ways and using different tools and applications, therefore must not be restricted to the capabilities of a specific software or hardware platform. They should be independently applicable and make use of the new capabilities of digital devices.

Cartographic textbooks try to consider the most recent trends by adding sections about web mapping and virtual environments (e.g. [4, 26]). Often these are already out-dated at the time of print, and quickly need to be adjusted if not rewritten. HTML5 and the recent more serious attempts to monetise digital publishing products may change this, which is why for cartography it could prove valuable to look into these technologies to provide innovative concepts for publishing maps in the digital world.

4.2   Examples of digital mapping with HTML5 and jQuery

To demonstrate in a very basic manner how HTML5 in combination with an extension by JavaScript libraries can improve digital maps and help to define new principles for digital cartography, I looked at some basic applications that can be used to enhance the digital presentation of the gridded cartograms from my own geospatial research [14]. These two examples are clearly technology-driven realisations of what is possible (and commonly used) in online mapping, but the actual aspect of translating these two examples into some more general principles are the key points that are relevant. The realisation of such principles will always require an adequate technical solution, while the underlying principles could be defined much more general than it is being done at the moment.

All concepts developed in this section can be applied to a basic HTML5 project that works online as well as offline and is not restricted to be used as an internet website, but as a digital map product that can be integrated in other forms of digital publishing. Looking back at my own research on cartograms [14], creating an animation to demonstrate the transition between a conventional map and a cartogram or two versions of a cartogram is time consuming and can be highly technical. An alternative concept would be the interactive presentation of the original and the transformed state of the map where the map reader can use an interactive slider element to switch between the two maps. This can also be a useful way to compare two different states presented in a map. A functionality that overlays two maps and lets the map reader interactively switch between them is an interactive image slider (Figure 2).

The slider is a simple example of how the basic design capabilities of the jQuery library [20] can be exploited for digital map displays. The resulting digital map has a substantial added value that embraces digital technology. Rather than simply showing two maps opposing each other, the map reader can explore the two maps, and unlike in similar examples from GoogleMaps mashups, the full implementation here is realised on the local computer system only using the HTML document in conjunction with the JavaScript library and the actual map files. The gridded cartograms can therefore be shown with different layers in comparison or different information, or in comparison to a conventional map projection to highlight the areas where the map changes most.

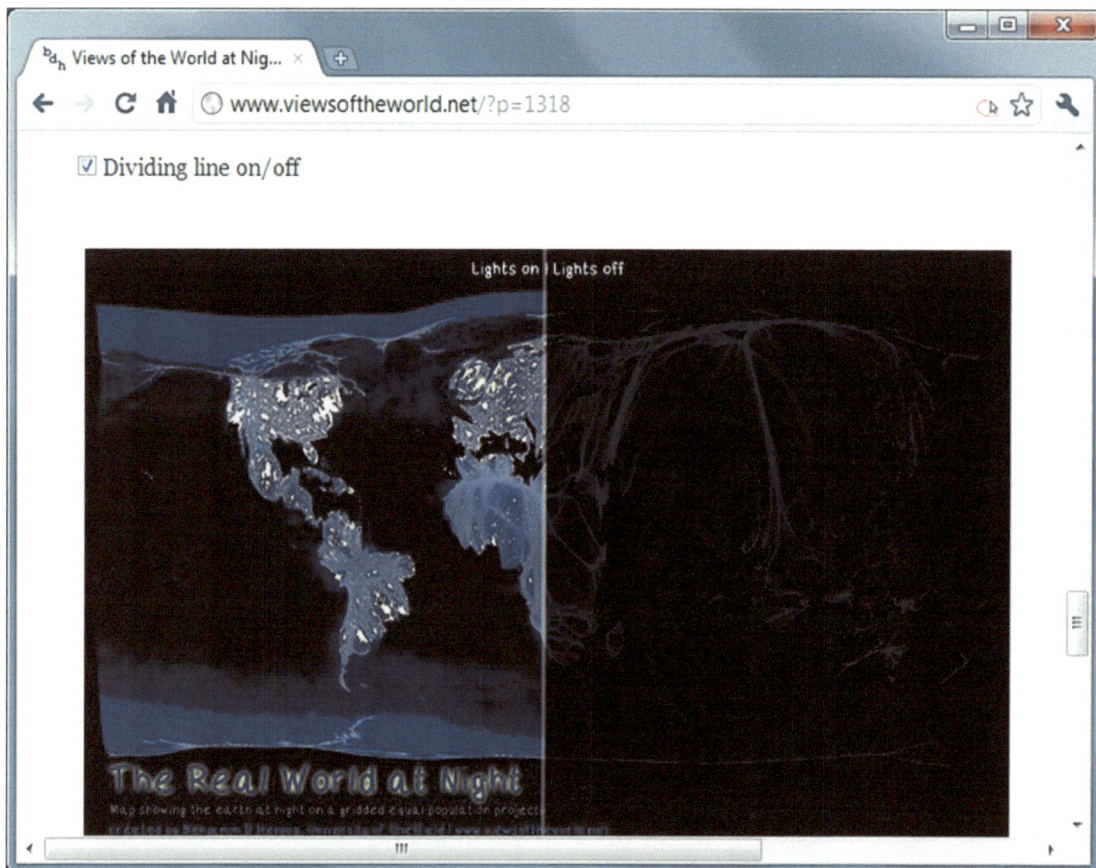

Figure 2: Interactive slider on a gridded population cartogram. The dividing line can be moved to the left and right to switch interactively between the two maps.

A different implementation is the integration of a virtual magnifier that does not only magnify the areas in the map, but can use a second map file for the enlarged view in the magnifying view, so that two different maps with different levels of detail can be prepared to give a less complex overview and highlight details in the magnified view. The implementation of such a concept can be achieved with the *Zoomy* plugin that connects to the jQuery library [20].

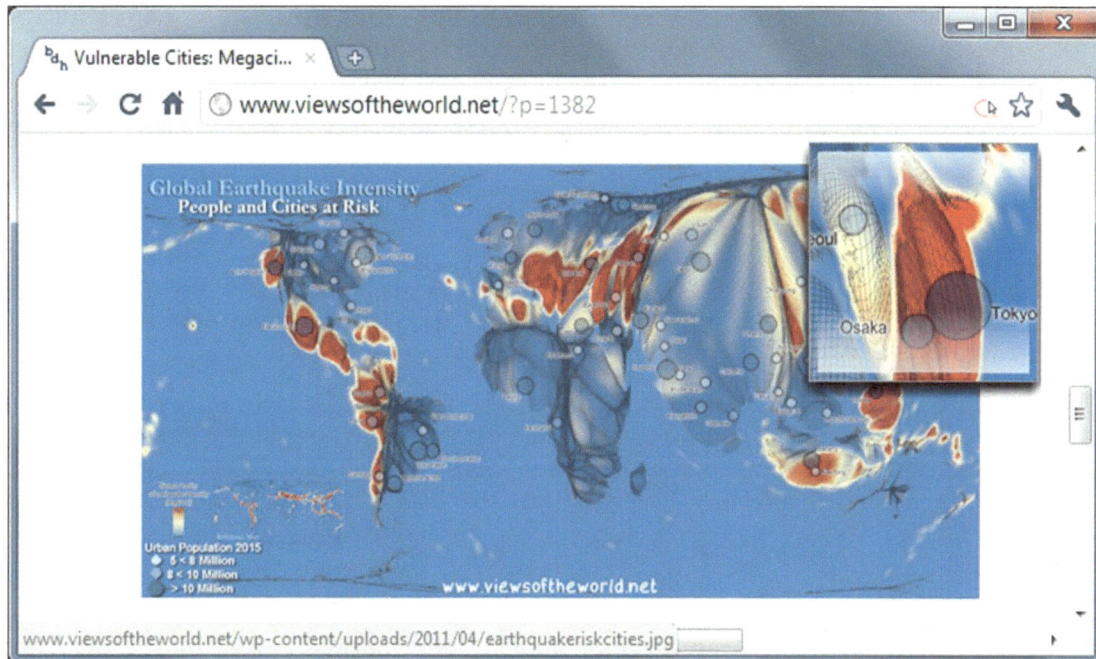

Figure 3: Interactive magnifier on a gridded population cartogram. The magnifier in the top right corner can be used to interactively enlarge sections of the map.

This example is a view of an earthquake risk map shown on a gridded population cartogram [13] which displays additional information about the largest cities of the world in the enlarged view of the magnifier. It can be interactively investigated by moving the mouse over the map. The complex appearance of the gridded cartograms can be made more understandable by allowing the map reader to investigate the map with different levels of information and in an interactive way, where the initial view does not contain too complex information, but the additional information can then be accessed in an intuitive and easily accessible way making more advantage of the possibilities of a digital mapping environment as compared to a printed map.

5   Discussion: New principles for digital cartography

This paper investigated current digital mapping practices and their implications for cartographic practice. Mapping techniques are highly technology driven, and ongoing advances in the capabilities especially of online mapping platforms but also advanced geovisualisation applications have considerably enhanced digital maps. Digital map products have entered multifaceted aspects of people's lives, and the map has turned into an advanced digital product that goes far beyond the capabilities of a printed paper map.

The advances made in this field do not only move digital mapping into an area where digital cartographers need to be highly skilled, but also lead to welcoming trends in the development of tools and applications that allow less experienced users to create maps based on good cartographic practice. This is a promising development to improve the overall quality of maps that even in academic geographical publications showed a decline in their cartographic quality [21]. The advances in digital mapping may help to encourage better mapping practices for the less experienced users, while research in cartography and geovisualization continues to discover new forms of geospatial data analysis and visualization.

While technological advances are generally necessary and important, the focus of cartographic research should, at the same time, be turned on the development of new digital design principles. Currently existing rules define technical settings for map representations on the screen (such as image resolutions, color spaces, symbol sizes) and even have the potential print output of screen maps in mind in these guidelines [7]. Design principles that focus on maps specifically created for the digital world and that make more use of digital capabilities, in contrast exist only to a small degree.

The simple examples using HTML5 and JavaScript technology are very basic illustrations of improved functionalities and of the type design principles that need to be developed for online mapping, while the focus here has to move away from the mere technical aspects of the issue towards a more general conceptualization how digital map content can be displayed.

This will be even more relevant with digital publishing becoming slowly a mainstream way of publishing content, and digital media becoming increasingly a main part of media consumption. Books, newspapers and magazines are increasingly consumed on digital devices (the online book retailer Amazon announced in May 2011 that the number of e- books sold in April have for the first time exceeded the number of printed books sold [27]), and also scientific journals are moved to the online world. The concepts of creating maps as a (static) printed product should therefore be extended by new map elements that allow novel ways of presenting maps digitally and might even make some map principles for printed maps obsolete in the digital world.

Digital publishing can be seen as a chance for maps to evolve, and for cartographic research to actively contribute to this process by examining new techniques and translating them into general principles for good cartographic design in digital publishing. It is necessary to move design principles from isolated applications into overall solutions that work across the different digital platforms. The implementation of corresponding techniques can then follow. The technical realization and its description is necessary to test and understand the underlying principles, but the resulting map elements can be turned into more generalized digital mapping practices that do not require an extensive technical documentation of how they can be realized.

The technical examples outlined before are very simple examples of such digital mapping principles. Further cartographic work should also focus on how their specific realization is achieved best: The use of a slider as an element in digital maps that show two different states of the map (or compare a map and a satellite image) and the use of a magnifier element to show additional information are the underlying principles of these technically outlined examples. They are as useful elements for an improved digital presentation of the gridded cartograms as the realisation of animations, but they may also prove useful and valuable for maps other than cartograms.

The important principles that need to be considered in the implementation of the elements (how are such maps created, etc.) need to be further investigated, and the final result of such very traditional cartographic research should result in a new set of digital cartographic design principles that extend and possibly also replace some of the existing cartographic rules developed for printed maps.

Existing cartographic principles describe for example how symbols are created and which rules should be followed in their creation, as outlined very basically in a handbook by the British Cartographic Society [7]. The statements about digital maps (or screen maps, as they are called there) focus on the limitations of digital technology, rather than constituting a set of new tools for maps created for the digital world. A structured analysis of specific advantages of digital devices, and a new set of rules could change the way in which digital maps are produced and help to bring cartographic principles into the world of digital mapping (Figure 4), while reducing the risk to create technical instructions for specific digital map applications that become outdated faster than they can be established in cartographic practice.

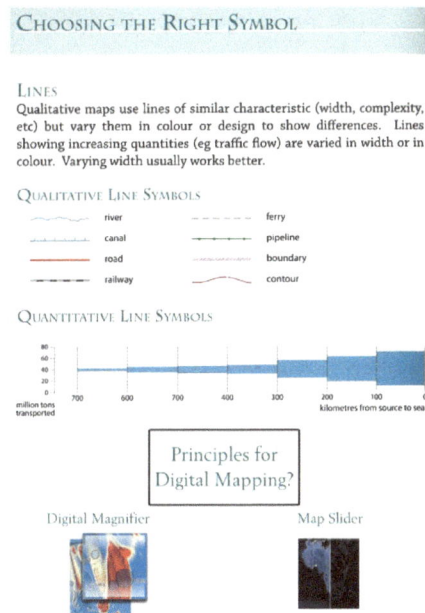

Figure 4: Good cartographic practice today ~ …and tomorrow? (modified from [7])

Promoting good digital cartographic practice can also include the capabilities of very specific map services like GoogleMaps and similar products, by investigating how the elements implemented here can be valuable additions for digital maps. The option to zoom in and out and change the level of detail in the cartographic information could similarly be translated into basic principles without the need to produce a technical documentation of the specific realisation. There are many different technical ways to implement such functionality, so that the description of these new approaches to cartographic practice can and should be much less dependent on specific technical implementations that change so quickly.

6 Conclusion

Digital technology has made the process of map making and geographic visualisation easier and more complex at the same time. New tools and applications have a great potential to lower the obstacles for inexperienced users to create better maps, and can also encourage the general use of cartographic visualisations to illustrate geographical research. New digital developments and web applications are promising steps towards a better use of cartographic practice that previously required a solid theoretical and technical background in specialised mapping environments.

Digital technology has also extended our capabilities to visualise large amounts of data by digital processing methods. For achieving that, a number of new tools and applications have emerged in the last years. They specialise in the different tasks of statistical analysis and visualisation, which allows more and more advanced geovisualisation concepts and new forms of working with data outside the domain of informatics and pure computer sciences.

The perspective of new concepts being integrated into common mapping tools for normal users is an essential part in the process of new visualisation techniques and should always be an objective for new techniques. This allows the broader acceptance and wider use by non-experts, while specialised visualisation algorithms that remain not (or badly) integrated in common mapping tools, will less likely succeed as successful geovisualisation concepts despite their promising capabilities.

Digital technology has also changed the way we consume maps, which so far is often neglected in the development of digital mapping applications. Therefore, it may also be essential to extend cartographic practice into the digital domain and to look at new ways of presenting maps in digital environments.

Creating new cartographic principles and hence novel rules can be a major challenge to move digital mapping from an innovative but highly technical and very fragmented entity towards an integral part of cartographic practices, and move digital mapping (not opposed to but still in contrast to GIS or GIScience) towards being part of a cartography for the 21st century.

Acknowledgments

Part of this research was made possible by the generous funding provided by the Leverhulme Trust.

References

[1]   ASCHE, H. AND HERRMANN, C. Web.Mapping 2. Heidelberg: Wichmann, 2003.

[2]   BENNETT, J. OpenStreetMap. Birmingham, Packt Publishing, 2010.

[3]   BERNARD, L., J. FITZKE AND WAGNER, R. Geodateninfrastruktur. Grundlagen und Anwendungen. Heidelberg, Wichmann, 2004.

[4]   CARTWRIGHT, W. Advancing global cartography and GIScience. The Cartographic Journal, 48 2 (2011), 81-85.

[5]   CHAPMAN, N. AND CHAPMAN, J. Digital multimedia. Edinburgh: Wiley, 2009.

[6]   COULDRY, N. AND MCCARTHY, A. Mediaspace: place, scale and culture in a media age. Abringdon, Routledge, 2004.

[7]   DARKES, G. AND SPENCE M. Cartography - an introduction. London, The British Cartographic Society, 2008.

[8]   DENT, B. D. Cartography: thematic map design. Boston: William C Brown, 1999.

[9]   DODGE, M., R. KITCHIN AND PERKINS, C. The map reader. Chichester: Wiley-Blackwell, 2011.

[10] FRIENDLY, M. A brief history of data visualisation. In Handbook of data visualisation, C. Chen, W. Härdle and Unwin, A., Eds. Berlin / Heidelberg: Springer, 2008, pp. 15-56.

[11] GRAHAM, G. AND SMART A. The regional-newspaper industry supply chain and the internet. Supply Chain Management, 15 3 (2010), 196-206.

[12] GUERIN, S. M. Peeking into the black box: some art and science to visualizing agent-based models. In Proceedings of the 36th conference on Winter simulation (Orlando, FL, 2004).

[13]   HENNIG, B. D. Gridded cartograms as a method for visualising earthquake risk at the global scale. Journal of Maps, 10 2 (2014), 186-194.

[14] HENNIG, B.D. Rediscovering the World: Map Transformations of Human and Physical Space. Heidelberg / New York / Dordrecht / London, Springer, 2013.

[15] HIRST, M. News 2.0: Can journalism survive the internet? Sydney: Allen & Unwin, 2011.

[16] JENNY, B. Geometric distortion of schematic network maps. Bulletin of the Society of Cartographers SoC, 40 (2006), 15-18.

[17] JENNY, B., H. JENNY AND RÄBER, S. 2008. Map design for the internet. In International perspectives on maps and the internet, ed. M. P. Peterson, 31-48. Berlin/Heidelberg/New York: Springer, 2008.

[18] JENNY, B., T. PATTERSON AND L. HURNI, L. Flex projector: interactive software for designing world map projections. Cartographic Perspectives, 59 (2008), 12-27.

[19] JENNY, H., A. NEUMANN, B. JENNY AND HURNI, L. A WYSIWYG interface for user-friendly access to geospatial data collections. In Preservation in Digital Cartography, ed. M. Jobst, 221-238. Berlin / Heidelberg / New York, Springer, 2010.

[20] JQUERY PROJECT jQuery API. http://docs.jquery.com/Main_Page (last accessed 2015-03-01).

[21] KESSLER, F. C. AND SLOCUM, T. A. Analysis of thematic maps published in two geographical journals in the twentieth century. Annals of the Association of American Geographers, 101 2 (2011), 292-317.

[22] KIM, B. AND JEONG, S. A comparison of algorithms for origin-destination matrix generation on real road networks and an approximation approach. Computers and Industrial Engineering, 1 56 (2009), 70-76.

[23] KORDUAN, P. AND ZEHNER M. L. Geoinformation im Internet: Technologien zur Nutzung raumbezogener Informationen im WWW. Heidelberg, Wichmann, 2008.

[24] KRAAK, M.-J. From geovisualisation toward geovisual analytics. The Cartographic Journal, 45 3 (2008), 163-164.

[25]   KRAAK, M. J. AND ORMELING, F. Cartography: visualisation of geospatial data. Boston, MA, Pearson Education, 2010.

[26]   LONGLEY, P. A., M. F. GOODCHILD, D. J. MAGUIRE AND D. W. RHIND, D. W. Geographic information systems and science. New York, NY: John Wiley & Sons, 2011.

[27]   MILLER, C. C. AND BOSMAN, J. E-books outsell print books at Amazon. http://www.nytimes.com/2011/05/20/technology/20amazon.html?_r=1AN Ds cp=2ANDsq=amazonANDst=cse (last accessed 2015-03-01).

[28]   MORRISON, J. L. The science of cartography and its essential processes. International Yearbook of Cartography, 16 (1976), 84-97.

[29]   POORE, B. S. The open black box: the role of the end-user in GIS integration. The Canadian Geographer, 47 1 (2003), 62-74.

[30]   POSTER, M. Consumption and digital commodities in the everyday. Cultural Studies, 18 2 (2004), 409-423.

[31]   RAMM, F., J. TOPF AND CHILTON, S. OpenStreetMap: using and enhancing the free map of the world. Cambridge, UIT, 2010.

[32]   ROBINSON, A. H., J. L. MORRISON, P. C. MUEHRCKE, A. J. KIMERLING AND GUPTILL, S. C. Elements of cartography. New York, NY, Wiley & Sons, 1995.

[33]   SCHUURMAN, N. The ghost in the machine: spatial data, information and knowledge in GIS. Canadian Geographer, 47 1 (2003), 1-4.

[34]   SWIENTY, O. Attention-guiding geovisualisation. A cognitive approach of designing relevant geographic information. PhD thesis. München, Technische Universität, 2008.

[35]   TURNER, A. J. Introduction to Neogeography. Sebastopol, CA, O'Reilly Media, 2006.

[36]   ZIPF, A. OpenStreetMap - Datenqualität und Potentiale der Nutzung mit OpenGIS Diensten in 2D und 3D. In GIS-Report 2010/11, B. Harzer, Ed. Karlsruhe, Bernhard Harzer Verlag, 2010, pp. 33-58.

Map Related Experiments Using Oculus Rift: Can low cost VR technology provide sufficient realism?

Steffen Pøhner Henriksen and Terje Midtbø

Norwegian University of Science and Technology, Trondheim, Norway

Abstract: In the last years a new kind of virtual reality equipment has emerged. Low cost head mounted displays (HMD) like "Oculus Rift DK1" are intentionally made for the gaming industry. However, the technology opens for a much wider range of use. If the recreation of the real world is adequate it might be possible to explore human experience and behavior in a spatial environment more efficiently. This paper looks closer into different aspects with using Oculus Rift for experiments where map navigation is in focus. Limitations in the present version of the actual device are discussed and general challenges when using virtual reality is studied in an experiment. This includes simulator sickness and the user's experiences of presence in the virtual world. This study concludes that interactions with the device during the user's motions still need improvements to make the equipment adequate for map related experiments.

Keywords: Virtual reality, Oculus Rift, map navigation, presence in VR

1 Introduction

Even before the computers were able to handle digital models, mechanical equipment was constructed in order to recreate the impression of the real world [3, 20]. However, when we are talking about VR today it is about software and digital models handled by special input and output equipment connected to a computer. Output devices are responsible for presentation of the virtual environment to the user. There are several types of output devices, from Binocular Omni Orientation Monitor (BOOM) [4] to more advanced Computer Assisted Virtual Environment (CAVE) outfit (virtual reality room) and Head-Mounted Displays (HMDs) [6, 7]. The selection of input devices is even more diverse. Of course we have general input devices as mouse and joystick, however wireless game controllers, sometimes equipped with motion sensors (for example Nintendo Wii) or followed by camera sensor (for example Playstation Move), may be more applicable. Finally, we have input devices that are developed for VR like wired gloves, built in motion sensors in HMDs and walking interfaces as Virtuix Omni [3, 20, 33]. Several of these input devises may also include haptic output to the user. New and low cost virtual reality devices have showed promising performance compared to more advanced equipment used in virtual reality research some years ago [35]. Virtual reality used together with geospatial data is able to give a realistic virtual environment. In research activities can all variables in the virtual world be controlled and a detailed registration of the behaviour of the test subjects may be available for studies. Hence, it is our prediction that we will see an increased use of virtual reality devises for map related research in the future. In this work we have explored peoples experience when finding their ways through a virtual environment by the use of maps. Various orientations of the map were tested during the experiment.

The ultimate goal of virtual reality is to give the opportunity to step into a virtual world which feels as real as our own. This is called presence. Presence is the key to directly transfer results gathered in the virtual world to real world scenarios. Presence in virtual reality refers to the subjective experience of being in the virtual world and having the feeling that it is real, while you are actually situated in another place [34]. [2] phrase the definition of presence as ``a cognitive state which occurs when the brain processes and makes sense of the myriad of stimulus information impinging upon the human sensory systems". In this paper answers in a questionnaire is indicating the level of presence for the participants in the experiment.

In the experiment related to this paper human subjects were moving inside a "spatial environment". It has been shown that spatial abilities measured with the SBSOD questionnaire correlates with the performance in wayfinding tasks [11, 28]. Hence, it is possible that people showing good spatial abilities might perform better when navigating in the virtual environment.

Many people experience simulator sickness, similar to motion sickness, when using VR equipment [14, 22, 27]. The degree of simulator sickness varies from person to person, and some may not feel any discomfort. The symptoms induced are often grouped into nausea, oculomotor, discomfort and disorientation [22] and include general discomfort, apathy, drowsiness, headache, disorientation, fatigue, pallor, sweating, salvation, stomach awareness, nausea and vomiting [18].

Kennedy and Fowlkes [15] state that simulator sickness is polysymptomatic and may best be described as a syndrome. The cause of simulator sickness is hard to isolate, and many factors come to play as described by [18], but the mismatch between the vestibular system and the visual system is a major factor according to [13].

How familiar the participants are with computer games can also affect the end result and metrics, as virtual reality applications can resemble computer games. The movement system used to control the virtual world in this paper is a gamepad. This may add to the feel of playing a computer game, and give those familiar with such equipment an advantage. The relationship between performance in the virtual environment and how often the participants play computer games is hence studied. This paper strives to answer these questions:

1. Which problems are prominent when using Oculus Rift for studying the map orientation performance?

2. Can we learn something about how factors as simulator sickness, good spatial abilities or videogame experience influence on map related experiments by the use of Oculus Rift?

2 Oculus Rift

Hardware for high quality experience within VR has, until a few years ago, been quite expensive to acquire [20]. Typical users have been the military and research projects. However, this has changed recently. A company called ``Oculus VR, Inc." [23] changed this in 2012 with the release of ``Oculus Rift Development Kit, version 1" (Oculus Rift DK 1) after a successful crowd-funding project at the kickstarter.com web site [17]. Oculus Rift DK1 was used in the experiments described in this paper. This version of the virtual reality experience from ``Oculus VR, Inc." is not intended to be a product for the end consumer. It is merely a preview of what is to come, and gives developers hands-on experience on developing VR content and to improve the technology.

Figure 1: Use of Oculus Rift Development Kit, version 1.

The device resembles ski goggles (Figure 1). A head mounted display (HMD) is attached to the head with straps and connected to a control unit. Stereoscopic 3D is achieved by rendering the scene from the left eye and the right eye in the left portion and right portion of the screen, respectively. A wide field of view is important for immersion and to give the feeling of being in the scene rendered. This is achieved by displaying the image on the screen in a distorted fashion, but is warped back to natural viewing by two lenses in front of the eyes.

Information from the gyroscope, magnetometer and accelerometer in the device is gathered in the control unit at a sampling rate of up to 1000Hz. This can be utilized by developers through a USB-cable connecting the Oculus Rift and the developer's computer. Information about rotation can be observed in three degrees of freedom; yaw, pitch and roll. The key specifications Oculus Rift is listed in Table 1 [1].

Display	Tracker
Display area: 7 inches	Up to 1000Hz in sampling rate
Resolution: 1280x800 in total, 640x800 per eye.	Gyroscope: three-axis
Fixed lens distance: 64mm	Magnetometer: three-axis
LCD Panel: 60Hz	Accelerometer: three-axis

Table 1: Specifications for Oculus Rift Development Kit, version 1.

The orientation of the equipment is fixed by combining the data from the sensors. The API for Oculus Rift can also use yaw-pitch-roll as illustrated in Figure 2. The gyroscope measures relative orientation while the magnetometer improves the yaw by using the Earth's magnetic field. The accelerometer improves the pitch and roll. The SDK documentation [1] provides a more thorough explanation of the different sensors.

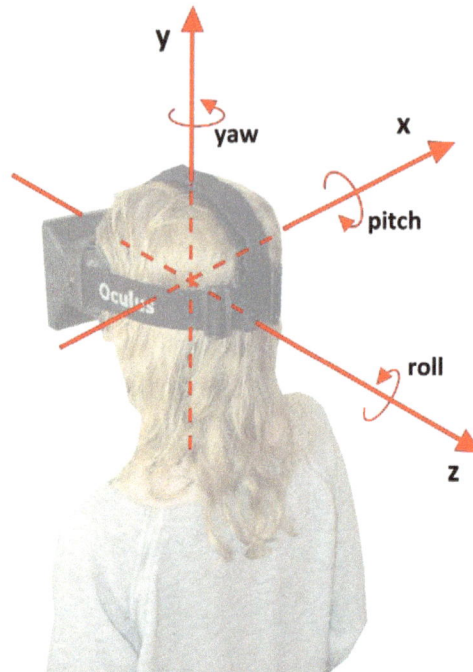

Figure 2: Orientation of Oculus Rift.

The Oculus Rift DK1 is a step on the way to a virtual reality experience of immersion and presence. There are many challenges to be solved before the technology is good enough to give a realistic feeling of presence and can allow us to step into a virtual world without questioning. Current challenges for achieving presence in the equipment used [5, 10] are described below.

2.1   Display Resolution

An important aspect of immersion is the field of view. For the viewer to feel immersed in the virtual world both the peripheral vision as well as the center of vision need to be stimulated. [25] points at the trade-off between resolution of the display and the field of view. The display used in the Oculus Rift DK1 was developed for other applications where the view distance is substantially longer. The display in Oculus Rift DK1 has a resolution of 1280 x 800 pixels, which translates to 640 x 800 per eye [1]. This might seem adequate, but the short viewing distance and enlarged view makes the grid between the pixels visible.

2.2   Optics

The display used in the Oculus Rift DK1 is a regular LCD display. Stereoscopic 3D vision is achieved by rendering the scene for the left eye on the left side of the display and for the right eye on the right. The image is actually displayed in a distorted fashion, and corrected through two lenses. This is done to improve the field of view of the device. The lenses used are critical for a realistic experience. In the DK1 each lens consists of a single lens element. A more elaborate setup with several lens elements is needed for perfect optical quality.

The Oculus Rift DK1 comes with three sets of lenses. These lenses can correct eye sight to a certain degree. One lens assumes perfect vision, but the other to can correct near sight and far sight, respectively.

2.3 Persistence

Persistence is the time each pixel remains lit on the head mounted display. In the real world the information we see through our eyes is always correct. When viewing a display, the frame does not update at an infinite speed. Between each frame update the previous frame is still present before the next one is presented. In this time in between frames, information which is not updated is shown. This often leads to motion sickness as we try to interpret the wrong information [24]. More specifically, a visual system called vestibulo-ocular reflex (VOR), responsible to stabilize the visual impression on the retina during head movement, are affected [9]. The effect is experienced as a motion blur when the user moves its head. Motion blur is also present when objects are moving relative to the user.

One solution to this problem is to use a low persistence display such as OLED. This display does not wait for the next image to be ready before switching to a new colour of the pixel, but can turn off the pixels between frames. In this way no incorrect information is sent to the brain, and the experience is more comfortable.

2.4 Latency

A computer display simulates motion by displaying images in series. How often this image updates affects how smooth we experience the motion. A display conveying a virtual reality needs a fast refresh rate for realistic animations. The Oculus Rift DK1 uses a 60Hz display. This may not be enough for a perfect realistic experience. In addition, we need computer hardware capable of rendering frames to match the display refresh rate. As the refresh rate increases, the number of pixels needed to be rendered per second rises. When the level of detail in the scene is expected to be higher, the requirements of powerful computer graphics hardware are even tougher.

``Motion-to-last-photon'' latency is a common term in VR terminology. It describes the time it takes for the photons from the display to hit your retina after a movement was made. Keeping this latency low is the key to immersion and the experience of being present in a virtual world. If the latency is too large the human perceptual system will tell us that we are looking at rendered images not reality. One important factor affecting the latency is tracking the movement of the equipment. To minimize the latency a prediction paradigm is established. Developers use the sensors to record information of a previous point in time, and use software algorithms to predict where the next movement is going to be.

2.5 Positional Tracking

A VR system needs a tracking system. The tracking system detects the user's point of view for updating the display. The system needs to respond to the user's action quickly for a realistic experience. Oculus Rift DK1 tracks head movement in three degrees of freedom and update sensory information at a rate up to 1000 Hz [1]. Yaw, pitch and roll are registered and made available for the application. The tracking is also predicted in software to further speed up the process. All in all is this sampling rate sufficient for a satisfying experience as the bottleneck in the system lies elsewhere. However, the human head moves in space as well, not just turns. We crouch, lean forward and move our heads slightly back and forth, side to side when experiencing our world. The computer needs to know where and how the body moves to accurately model these viewers motion. This is done by an external tracking system. Several techniques are used for tracking such as electromagnetic tracking, acoustic tracking, mechanical tracking and optical tracking [21]. The most popular tracking system is by the use of external tracking cameras.

In June 2014 Oculus Rift Development Kit, version 2 was released. This new version brings many improvements to the first prototype. It includes positional tracking with a tracking camera, a low persistence 7 inch 75Hz OLED display to prevent simulator sickness as well as a better display resolution (960 x 1080 pixels per eye).

3   Methodology

To evaluate the use of Oculus Rift for map related experiment we made a virtual environment where participants were supposed to navigate in two different mazes (Figure 3). By using a map in the virtual world they were supposed to find their way to different locations in the maze. Each location was marked by a figure in the map. The time used from start to the final location in the maze was measured. Both north-up and head-up maps was presented in turns for the participants in the experiment. The participants used a ``Logitech RumblePad 2'' gamepad to move in the virtual environment. All controls on the RumblePad were disabled in the setting files of UDK, except the left analogue stick. Details about the wayfinding experiment are reported in [12]. The participants were supposed to visit different figures in the maze in a given order. Figure 4 shows one of the mazes together with a heat map based on their movements in the maze. Order of the waypoints was: heart – globe – H.

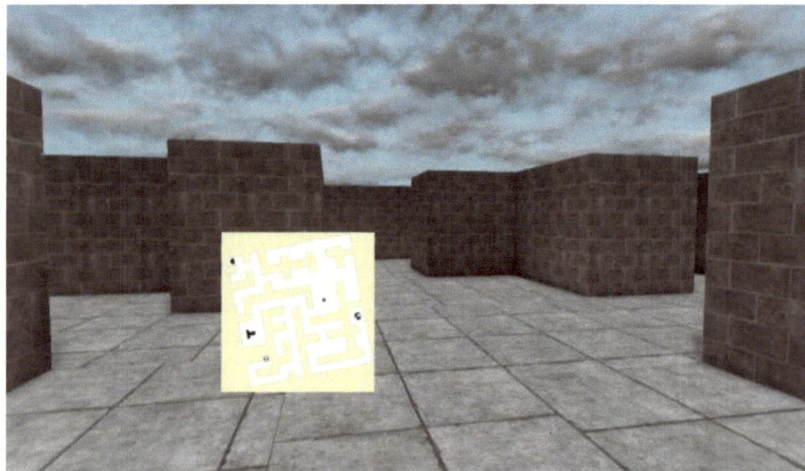

Figure 3: Screenshot of the virtual environment in the experiment.

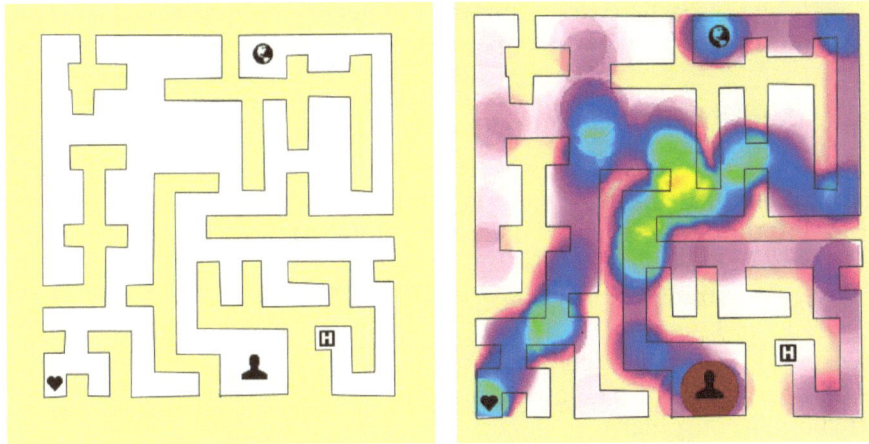

Figure 4: Map of one of the mazes and a heat map of where the participants moved.

3.1 Simulator Sickness

The Simulator Sickness Questionnaire (SSQ) [16] is a frequently used questionnaire for measuring simulator sickness. It differentiates between motion sickness and simulator sickness, and measures the degree of nausea, oculomotor and disorientation. The questionnaire consists of 16 statements which the candidate must address with ``none'', ``slight'', ``moderate'' or ``severe''. The questionnaire used in this paper was a Norwegian translation of the Simulator Sickness Questionnaire [16].

Each participant got a Simulator Sickness score (SS score) based on their answers in the web form. If he or she answered ``none'' that will result in a score of 0, ``slight'' equals 1, ``moderate'' 2 and finally ``severe'' 3. The questionnaire gives an indication of experienced nausea, oculomotor and disorientation as well as a combined score. A higher SS score indicates that the subject was affected more than a subject with a low SS score.

3.2 Presence

An important aspect to how virtual reality can be used to study map orientation is presence. Presence is `` the subjective experience of being in one place or environment, even when one is physically in another'' [34]. To investigate how people navigate with maps in the real world, the virtual test ground needs to be as real as possible to the participants.

The degree of presence was measured using the questionnaire by [29]. Using questionnaires to measure presence has been questioned. [31] found no significant difference when subjects answered the questionnaire after being in a virtual world and being in a real test area. These questionnaires are to be interpreted with caution. As the virtual world in this paper was not created specifically with realism in mind, the answers given will be interpreted merely as an indication.

The questionnaire is translated to Norwegian, and adapted to the specific environment. The term ``computer generated world'' was therefore substituted with ``the maze''. The original questionnaire uses a scale from 1 to 7 to answer all questions. Three of the answers in our version could only be answered by writing sentences, and not by using the scale as in the original. This was done to get a more detailed picture of the degree of presence felt by the participants. It made it easier for the participants to convey their experience, although the results are harder to measure objectively.

3.3 Spatial Abilities

The spatial abilities of a person are known to affect how easily mental rotation is done [8], and navigating with north-up maps require mental rotation as explained in the introduction. Individual differences in spatial ability can be measured by psychometric tests or self-report measures. Psychometric tests include mental rotation of different shapes and solving small navigational problems [32]. However, self-report measures have been found to be sufficient [11]. In this paper a translated version of the Santa Barbara Sense of Direction Scale (SBSOD) [11] was used to measure individual differences in spatial ability. The questionnaire was translated to Norwegian and made available through a computer.

One statement was added to the standard SBSOD. Studies have shown a correlation between spatial abilities, gender and how familiar the test subject is to computer games [19, 26]. Since the movements in the virtual environment in the experiment were done with a game controller, it may favour subjects that are familiar with this kind of equipment. The statement ``I often play video games" was added to study this correlation further, and to judge whether computer game experience and/or spatial abilities affected the result.

3.4 Experiment

For the experiment it is important to use adequate computer equipment in order to make the Oculus Rift perform at a maximum refresh rate of 60Hz. In our experiment a computer including an Intel i7-3720QM @ 2,6Ghz processor, 16 GB of memory and a NVIDA Quadro K4000M 12GB GDDR5 solved this issue.

27 subjects (5 females and 22 men) participated in the experiment. The youngest was 17 and the oldest 70 years old. However, 4 of the females and 18 of the men were between 20 and 28 years. The experiment went as follows:

1. The participant was introduced to the study and its purpose. He or she was informed of the tasks to be solved and in which order.

2. The risk of simulator sickness was conveyed and the SBSOD questionnaire was answered.

3. The head-mounted display, gamepad and test area was adjusted to fit the participant and validated as the participant experienced a simple virtual environment. The movement pattern using the gamepad was shown and learned before proceeding.

4. The time was measured when the participant completed two mazes run-through each, one using a north-up map and by a head-up map. The run-through was aborted if a participant was affected by strong discomfort.

5. The simulator sickness questionnaire was answered.

6. The presence questionnaire was answered.

During the experiment most participants managed to stand in the range of the wires connecting the head-mounted display to the computer. However, there were times were participants needed correction because they moved away from the starting position. They started walking in the real world when using the gamepad. This interrupted the trial and it felt unnatural for the participants to be moved in the real world when the virtual world did not reflect this movement. It would have been beneficial to have used a wireless system. Then the corrections would have been fewer and the participants could have moved with fewer impediments.

4 Evaluation and results

4.1 Statistical tests

The information gathered through questionnaires and trials have resulted in five sets of data. We want to see if there exists a statistical relationship between these. The existence or absence of correlation, or dependence, between factors can give valuable information to further discussion. It is important to remember that correlation does not imply causation.

All the maze runs are collected into one table. Each maze has information about what maze was used, which map that was used, the SBSOD score for the participant as well as Simulator Sickness score, and whether the participant is familiar with video games or not. By using Minitab 17, a Pearson product-moment correlation coefficient is calculated along with a Student-t test to test for significance. The Pearson correlation coefficient is a value between -1 to +1, where -1 is total negative correlation, 0 denotes no correlation and 1 defines total positive correlation. The significance level for the Student-t test is set to 0.05.

	Total time	Maze	Map	SBSOD	Videogames
Maze (p-value)	-0.375 0.010				
Map (p-value)	-0.092 0.544	0.044 0.773			
SBSOD (p-value)	-0.120 0.428	-0.075 0.622	0.204 0.174		
Videogames (p-value)	-0.129 0.411	-0.091 0.560	0.011 0.944	0.199 0.200	
SS score (p-value)	-0.174 0.249	-0.003 0.986	0.047 0.759	0.150 0.321	-0.221 0.154

Table 2: Correlation between total time, maze, map, SBSOD, videogames and simulator sickness.

The results of the correlation calculation are presented in Table 2. By studying the p-values we find one significant relationship. The p-value is lower than 0.05 and we reject the null hypothesis which says that there is no correlation, and accept the alternative hypothesis which says there is correlation. Total time and the type of Maze are correlated with a significant coefficient of -0.375. This indicates that the second maze is less complicated, and is completed faster by the participants. This is no surprise since there is one less waypoint in the second maze. Furthermore, we see no significant correlation between the other factors.

4.2   Simulator sickness

Two of 27 participants aborted the trial due to a feeling of discomfort. The Simulator Sickness Questionnaire shows large individual differences. The average score was 31.2 with a standard deviation of 31.45. The scores range from 0 as the lowest score to 130.9 for the highest. Several participants said they were affected by light simulator sickness after the first maze, but reported that they felt better after the second maze.

4.3   Presence

Both quantifiable data and text was collected from the presence questionnaire. The mazes were not designed to be perfectly realistic. Few landmarks and details are in the mazes, which are basically just walls and a floor. However, the questionnaire can give hints to how the virtual environment was experienced by the participants.

One question was to be answered using a scale from 1 to 7. It sounded ``Please rate your sense of being in the virtual environment, on a scale of 1 to 7, where 7 represents your normal experience of being in a place". The average result was 4.88 with an estimate of the standard deviation of 1.34.

Two questions were to be answered with only two choices. 20 of 27 answered that when they think back to the experience, they remember the virtual environment as a place they have visited rather than a series of images. 25 of 27 answered that they had the strongest sense of being in the maze rather than somewhere else.

The text answers seem to be diverse. Some people experience the virtual environment as very real, others are aware of the simulation during the whole trial. When answering the question: ``to what extent were there times during the experience when the virtual environment was the reality" some commented the poor graphical quality, others said that the movement in the virtual environment felt unnatural and broke presence. Most experienced the visual impression as real, but factors such as sound and haptics reminded them of where they really were. It was often mentioned that it always felt like a computer game, and that the gamepad used for movement contributed to this feeling. Eight participants answered with phrases similar to ``it felt real all the time".

The answers to the question ``How often did you think to yourself that you were actually in the virtual environment?" was polarized. 17 answered that they were aware of being in a virtual environment through the whole trial. At the same time 8 of the participants answered the opposite; that they were not aware of being in a virtual environment.

As shown the results from the presence questionnaire are quite diverse, and it is hard to see a common trend. How realistic the virtual environment used in the trials is quite different from person to a person, and there were no signs that this depended on the personal characteristics like sex or age.

5   Discussion

During the trial a gamepad was used as input device. This may have clouded the end result since those who were familiar with the gamepad used less time to move around corners. Participants with the slowest times did often got stuck when turning corners, and needed to back up and turn before walking forward and around the corner. A more natural way of moving in the virtual world would have been preferred. By adding positional tracking, the subjects could have moved more freely and natural. These tracking systems often have a limited range and subjects can only move within a radius of a few meters. This can be improved by increasing the speed of movement in the virtual world. In this way the subject can explore large virtual environments, but remain in a small place [30]. Another option is an omni-directional treadmill like the Virtuix Omni [33]. The Omni lets the user move in all directions, by using special shoes which slide down from a curved floor while you are held in place with a harness.

No significant correlation was found based on the total time and SBSOD score registered in the trials, although this was expected. It is possible that factors not considered in this paper are affecting the end result, and hide the expected result.

Two of 27 participants aborted the trial due to strong discomfort. An average Simulator Sickness score of 32.00, and just two scores of 0, indicate that simulator sickness is an important factor to consider. Most participants experienced some degree of discomfort. But the correlation of SS score and total time shows no relationship between the performance in the mazes and the level of simulator sickness experienced. The movement system may be an important factor in inducing simulator sickness. Some participants reported that the mismatch between the movement experienced in the virtual environment and the real world made them dizzy and disoriented. This mismatch may have felt unnatural as the vestibular system sensed no motion but the visual system did. All actions done in the real world which is not reflected in the virtual world, particularly related to movement, might induce simulator sickness.

If results collected using virtual environments are to be directly transferable to the real world, then the virtual world needs to feel real, and participants in trials needs to feel presence. To achieve this, the experiment must be designed specifically with VR in mind from the beginning, and include all sensory inputs. As both VR content frameworks are getting better, and the hardware is improving, it is expected that presence will be easier to achieve. On a scale from 1 to 7 the participants in our experiment gave an average score of 4.88 for the virtual world to be real. Furthermore, no participant gave a score indicating that the virtual world felt as real as reality. A minimalistic approach to details in the virtual environment may have contributed to this, as well as the movement system. Nevertheless, the hardware needs to be improved to achieve presence. Still, the results were not black and white. As with all results presented in this paper those regarding presence also show great individual differences. Some participants said it felt real all the time, while others thought of it as a computer game. The map was displayed to the user in a way that may have impacted presence. The map was placed floating in the air on the left side of their field of view. A more natural path would have been displaying it as a real map when looking down. The map could have been held by hands, mimicking how the participant would hold a real map. This would require extensive developing and was not prioritized in the time frame available for this paper.

6 Conclusions and further work

Map related experiments in virtual reality depend on a realistic representation of the virtual world. Likewise, it is crucial that all motions are apprehended as it is anticipated and that interaction with the equipment is natural for the user. Oculus Rift has still some challenges with respect to this. The motion system was reported as unnatural, and made the feeling of being in the virtual environment more like a videogame. The presence questionnaires showed great individual differences. Oculus Rift DK2 meets some of these challenges by introducing a display with better resolution, a better response time as well as lower persistence.

During the experiment two participants aborted the trials due to a high level of discomfort. The Simulator Sickness Questionnaire revealed that most participants felt symptoms, but the severity varied. No correlation between simulator sickness and performance was found and concluding from this that the Oculus Rift Dk1 is suitable for trails as those conducted in this paper. Nevertheless, the movement system was questioned by participants and may have been a source to the induced simulator sickness.

Through multiple questionnaires the spatial abilities, familiarity with computer games,

the level of simulator sickness and feeling of presence were registered among the participants. These factors, along with the total time, which map that was used, and in which maze the trail was conducted, were included in a correlation analysis. The correlation analysis showed no significant correlation between the factors other than the total time and which maze used.

All results collected in this paper show large variation and individual differences. Since peoples experience of VR is very different from person to person it is very difficult to extract clear answers from an experiment that engaged a relative small group of participants. Some find it very realistic while others do not share the same feelings. The degree of simulator sickness also varied greatly as with the total time registered in the mazes.

References

[1]   ANTONOV, M., MITCHELL, N., REISSE, A., COOPER, L., LA VALLE, S. AND KATSEV, M. 2013. *SDK Overview, SDK Version 0.2.5*. Oculus VR.

[2]   BARFIELD, W., ZELTZER, D., SHERIDAN, T. AND SLATER, M. 1995. Presence and performance within virtual environments. *Virtual environments and advanced interface design*. (1995), 473–513.

[3]   BOAS, Y. 2013. Overview of Virtual Reality Technologies. *Interactive Multimedia Conference*, Southhampton, January 8th 2013.

[4]   BOLAS, M.T. 1994. Human factors in the design of an immersive display. *Computer Graphics and Applications, IEEE*. 14, 1 (1994), 55–59.

[5]   BURDEA, G. AND COIFFET, P. 2003. Virtual reality technology. *Presence: Teleoperators and virtual environments*. 12, 6 (2003), 663–664.

[6]   CRUZ-NEIRA, C. 1993. Virtual reality overview. *SIGGRAPH'93* (1993).

[7]   CRUZ-NEIRA, C., SANDIN, D.J., DEFANTI, T.A., KENYON, R.V. AND HART, J.C. 1992. The CAVE: Audio Visual Experience Automatic Virtual Environment. *Commun. ACM*. 35, 6 (Jun. 1992), 64–72.

[8]   DARKEN, R.P. AND CEVIK, H. 1999. Map usage in virtual environments: Orientation issues. *Virtual Reality, 1999. Proceedings., IEEE* (1999), 133–140.

[9]   VAN DER STEEN, J. 2009. Vestibulo-Ocular Reflex (VOR). *Encyclopedia of Neuroscience*. Springer. 4224–4228.

[10] DURLACH, N.I., MAVOR, A.S. 1994. *Virtual reality: scientific and technological challenges*. National Academies Press. ISBN: 978-0-309-05135-4

[11] HEGARTY, M., RICHARDSON, A.E., MONTELLO, D.R., LOVELACE, K. AND SUBBIAH, I. 2002. Development of a self-report measure of environmental spatial ability. *Intelligence*. 30, 5 (2002), 425–447.

[12] HENRIKSEN, S.P. AND MIDTBØ, T. 2015. Investigation of map orientation by the use of low cost virtual reality equipment. *Lecture notes in Geoinformation and Cartography: Cartography – Maps Connecting the World*. Eds: C.R.Sluter, C.B.M.Cruz and P.M.L.de Menez. 27th International Cartographic Conference 2015.pp:75-88. Available at: http://link.springer.com/book/10.1007/978-3-319-17738-0

[13] HETTINGER, L.J., BERBAUM, K.S., KENNEDY, R.S., DUNLAP, W.P. AND NOLAN, M.D. 1990. Vection and simulator sickness. *Military Psychology*. 2, 3 (1990), 171.

[14] KENNEDY, R., LILIENTHAL, M., BERBAUM, K., BALTZLEY, D. AND MCCAULEY, M. 1989. Simulator sickness in US Navy flight simulators. *Aviation, Space, and Environmental Medicine*. 60, 1 (1989), 10–16.

[15] KENNEDY, R.S. AND FOWLKES, J.E. 1992. Simulator sickness is polygenic and polysymptomatic: Implications for research. *The International Journal of Aviation Psychology*. 2, 1 (1992), 23–38.

[16] KENNEDY, R.S., LANE, N.E., BERBAUM, K.S. AND LILIENTHAL, M.G. 1993. Simulator sickness questionnaire: An enhanced method for quantifying simulator sickness. *The international journal of aviation psychology*. 3, 3 (1993), 203–220.

[17] KICKSTARTER: *https://www.kickstarter.com/*. Accessed: 2014-05-12.

[18] KOLASINSKI, E.M. 1995. *Simulator Sickness in Virtual Environments*. DTIC Document. Technical Report 1027. U.S. Army Research Institute.

[19] LISI, R.D. AND CAMMARANO, D.M. 1996. Computer experience and gender differences in undergraduate mental rotation performance. *Computers in Human Behavior*. 12, 3 (1996), 351 – 361.

[20] MAZURYK, T. AND GERVAUTZ, M. 1996. *Virtual Reality - History, Applications, Technology and Future*. Institute of Computer Graphics and Algorithms, Vienna University of Technology.

[21] MEYER, K., APPLEWHITE, H.L. AND BIOCCA, F.A. 1992. A survey of position trackers. *Presence: Teleoperators and Virtual Environments (ISSN 1054-7460), vol. 1, no. 2, p. 173-200.* (1992), 173–200.

[22] MOURANT, R.R. AND THATTACHERRY, T.R. 2000. Simulator sickness in a virtual environments driving simulator. *Proceedings of the Human Factors and Ergonomics Society Annual Meeting* (2000), 534–537.

[23] OCULUS RIFT: *http://www.oculusvr.com?>*. Accessed: 2014-05-12.

[24] PELI, E. 1995. Real vision & virtual reality. *Optics and Photonics News*. 6, 7 (1995), 28.

[25] PIANTANIDA, T.P., BOMAN, D.K., LARIMER, J.O., GILLE, J. AND REED, C. 1992. Studies of the field-of-view/resolution tradeoff in virtual-reality systems. *SPIE/IS&T 1992 Symposium on Electronic Imaging: Science and Technology* (1992),448–456.

[26] QUAISER-POHL, C., GEISER, C. AND LEHMANN, W. 2006. The relationship between computer-game preference, gender, and mental-rotation ability. *Personality and Individual Differences*. 40, 3 (2006), 609 – 619.

[27] REGAN, C. 1995. An investigation into nausea and other side-effects of head-coupled immersive virtual reality. *Virtual Reality*. 1, 1 (1995), 17–31.

[28] SKUNDERGARD, K., KIRSH, D. AND DAHLBÄCK, N. 2012. Maps in the Head and Maps in the Hand. *CogSci 2012* (2012), 2339–2344.

[29] SLATER, M., USOH, M. AND STEED, A. 1994. Depth of presence in virtual environments. *Presence*. 3, 2 (1994), 130–144.

[30] STEINICKE, F., BRUDER, G., JERALD, J., FRENZ, H. AND LAPPE, M. 2010. Estimation of detection thresholds for redirected walking techniques. *Visualization and Computer Graphics, IEEE Transactions on*. 16, 1 (2010), 17–27.

[31] USOH, M., CATENA, E., ARMAN, S. AND SLATER, M. 2000. Using presence questionnaires in reality. *Presence: Teleoperators and Virtual Environments*. 9, 5 (2000), 497–503.

[32] VANDENBERG, S.G. AND KUSE, A.R. 1978. Mental rotations, a group test of three-dimensional spatial visualization. *Perceptual and motor skills*. 47, 2 (1978), 599–604.

[33] VIRTUIX OMNI: 2013. *http://www.virtuix.com/*. Accessed: 2014-05-12. [34]

[34] WITMER, B.G. AND SINGER, M.J. 1998. Measuring presence in virtual environments: A presence questionnaire. *Presence: Teleoperators and virtual environments*. 7, 3 (1998), 225–240.

[35] YOUNG, M.K., GAYLOR, G.B., ANDRUS, S.M. AND BODENHEIMER, B. 2014. A Comparison of Two Cost-differentiated Virtual Reality Systems for Perception and Action Tasks. *Proceedings of the ACM Symposium on Applied Perception* (New York, NY, USA, 2014), 83–90.

Enriching Top-down Geo-ontologies Using Bottom-up Knowledge Mined from Linked Data

Yingjie Hu and Krzysztof Janowicz

STKO Lab, Department of Geography, University of California Santa Barbara, Santa Barbara, CA 93106, USA

Abstract: Geo-ontologies provide formal specifications of geographic concepts, and can be embedded into geographic information systems to support automatic reasoning. Traditionally, geo-ontologies are developed through a top-down approach in which a group of experts collaboratively decide about the formalization. While such an approach captures valuable expert knowledge, the resulting geo-ontologies could be biased, miss certain useful properties, or may not reflect existing data needs. The fast evolving Linked Open Data (LOD) cloud offers a large amount of structured data contributed by authoritative agencies, companies, and the general public. With the diverse perspectives and the structured data organization, the LOD cloud contains knowledge which could be used to enrich top-down geo-ontologies. This paper proposes a workflow to mine bottom-up geographic knowledge from the LOD cloud. We describe each step of this workflow, and conduct an experiment using a dataset from the LOD cloud to learn a geographic concept *port city*. We perform an evaluation and show that the workflow can extract useful knowledge for enriching top-down geo-ontologies.

Keywords: geo-ontology, ontology engineering, concept learning, Linked Data, Semantic Web, semantics, DBpedia.

1 Introduction

Geo-ontologies provide formal specifications of geographic concepts, and have been discussed in a variety of GIScience studies. As concept mediators, geo-ontologies can enhance the semantic interoperability among heterogeneous data and distributed systems. For example, Fonseca et al. (2002) proposed an architecture which used ontologies as an essential component to integrate different geographic information (GI) systems [7]. In the domain of environmental monitoring, Pundt and Bishr (2002) developed an ontology to facilitate the sharing of data collected from different field survey activities [20]. Kuhn (2005) proposed *semantic reference systems* which employed ontological specifications to ground and map geographic information in different systems

[15]. Geo-ontologies have also been used to improve geographic information retrieval. Jones et al. (2001) combined the semantic relatedness calculated from place ontologies with the traditional Euclidean distance to rank the relevance between the candidate results and the input queries [14]. Li et al. (2011) employed the SWEET ontology to expand the input query with semantically relevant terminologies, thereby enhancing the capability of the traditional keyword-based search [18]. In previous work, we demonstrated how semantic search can be implemented on top of Esri's ArcGIS Online [11]. Capturing expert knowledge, geo-ontologies have also been applied to multiple decision making scenarios. Existing use cases include ontology-driven spatial decision support [17] as well as geodesign [16]. For next generation GI systems, geo-ontologies may play an even more important role by enabling GI systems to automatically recognize geographic entities from data and recommend suitable spatial analysis tools.

Designing good geo-ontologies, however, is not an easy task. Traditionally, a top-down approach has been used, in which a group of experts collaboratively specify the terms and relations of the target ontology. Such an approach has many merits. It captures the valuable domain knowledge from experts, which sometimes can only be acquired after years of experience in the specific field. In addition, the terms assigned by experts are often concise and meaningful since such terms generally have to undergo the deliberations and discussions of multiple professionals. While possessing these merits, the developed geo-ontologies may nevertheless be biased towards the knowledge of the participating experts, may miss some properties which could be useful for understanding the specific geographic concept, and many not well reflect particular datasets or future use cases.

Progress in Semantic Web technologies [6] fostered the fast evolution of the Linked Open Data (LOD) cloud [2]. From 2007 to 2014, the LOD cloud has grown from its initial 12 datasets to more than 570 datasets with billions of triples (see Figure1). These rich amount of data are contributed by authoritative agencies (e.g., the U.S. Census and data.gov.uk), the industry, and also the general public. Examples of such user-contributed datasets include DBpedia and LinkedGeoData, which are the Linked Data versions of Wikipedia and OpenStreetMap respectively [1, 25]. Data instances in the LOD cloud are structured using the Resource Description Framework (RDF). This structured

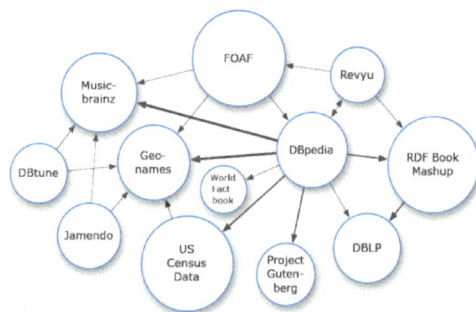

(a) The LOD cloud in 2007.   (b) The LOD cloud in 2014.

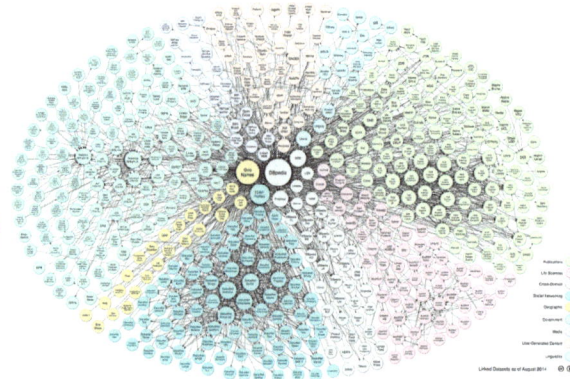

Figure 1: Evolution of the Linked Open Data cloud from 2007 to 2014 [22].

organization distinguishes LOD datasets from other unstructured user-contributed content such as most social media data.The LOD cloud presents a valuable resource from which bottom-up knowledge could be mined to enrich the top-down geo-ontologies. The value of the Linked Data cloud can be seen in two ways. First, with many different data contributors, datasets on the LOD cloud reflect the diverse perspectives of people towards the same concepts and entities, and therefore can be exploited to enrich the knowledge from the limited number of participating experts. Second, the structured data enable knowledge to be extracted in a structured manner (e.g., in the form of properties and property-values) which is often desired for an already formalized top-down geo-ontology. However, mining knowledge from the LOD cloud demands suitable methods, since improper approaches (e.g., using a natural language processing method based on a *bag of words* model) may simply break the links among data instances and convert the structured data back to an unstructured form.

This paper is an effort towards extracting bottom-up knowledge from the LOD cloud. **The contributions of this work are as follows:**

- We develop a workflow that mines knowledge about geographic concepts from the structured Linked Data.

- We demonstrate the use of the workflow by applying it to a sample dataset from DBpedia and an example top-down geo-ontology.

- We design a preliminary experiment to evaluate the extracted bottom-up geographic knowledge.

The remainder of this paper is organized as follows. Section 2 reviews related work on geo-ontology engineering, and provides some background on Linked Data and DBpedia. Section 3 presents the workflow for extracting geographic knowledge from Linked Data. In section 4, we employ the proposed workflow to mine knowledge from DBpedia, and perform a preliminary evaluation on the extracted knowledge. Finally, section 5 summarizes our work and discusses future directions.

2   Related work

The value of geo-ontologies has long been recognized by the GIScience community, and the history can be traced back to a NCGIA specialist meeting in 1998 [19]. Unlike the ontology discussed in philosophy, geo-ontologies are closer to those in computer science, which are designed to help machines turn data into sharable knowledge [4, 9]. Different from ontologies in other domains (e.g., bioinformatics), geo-ontologies focus on achieving better understanding of the geographic world and facilitating the implementation of conceptually sound GI systems [23]. Since the 1998 meeting, a lot of studies have been devoted to developing geo-ontologies. Smith and Mark (2001) investigated the conceptualization of non-expert subjects on geospatial phenomenon, and derived an ontology of geographical categories [24]. Frank (2003) designed a 5-tier ontology for spatio-temporal databases which starts from the observations in the physical world and completes at the knowledge of cognitive agents [8].

Scheider et al. (2009) developed a formalization for grounding geo-ontologies in the physical environment [21]. Focusing on geographic information constructs, Couclelis (2010) developed a hierarchical framework with the user intentionality on one end and the existence of information on the other [5]. Janowicz (2012) proposed an observation-driven ontology engineering framework which aims at deriving ontological primitives from observation data [12]. The work at hand has been influenced by these previous studies. However, we focus on extracting bottom-up geographic knowledge from Linked Data to enrich top-down geo-ontologies, which has been rarely examined so far.

The growth of the LOD cloud brings a large amount of structured spatiotemporal data, and is changing the ways of publishing, searching, and sharing geographic information [13]. The term *Linked Data* has two folds of meanings that are often used interchangeably. On the one hand, it refers to a set of principles recommended by W3C for publishing data on the Semantic Web. On the other hand, it represents the data which are structured and published following these principles. Among the many datasets on the LOD cloud, DBpedia is a central hub, which provides information about more than 4.5 million entities (many of which are geographic places) [3]. The content of DBpedia originates from Wikipedia, and each Wikipedia article has a corresponding DBpedia page. As a result, DBpedia inherits many great features of Wikipedia. For example, Wikipedia articles are contributed by over 25, 272, 000 users (http://en.wikipe dia.org/wiki/Wikipedia:Statistics, retrieved in May 2015), and accordingly, DBpedia data obtain the diverse perspectives from the large number of people. Meanwhile, a lot of data on Wikipedia have their original sources from authoritative agencies. For example, by examining the Wikipedia page of *San Francisco*, one can find that the data about the city's land and water areas come from the U.S. Census, while the elevation data are from the U.S. Geological Survey. Unsurprisingly, DBpedia also inherits these valuable authoritative data. Since new contents are being constantly added to Wikipedia, DBpedia updates its data regularly to synchronize with Wikipedia.

Categorization systems are frequently used by datasets on the LOD cloud to group similar instances. In contrast to LOD datasets that employ pre-defined categorization schemata, Wikipedia allows voluntary contributors to create customized categories and to classify entities into these categories. For example, there exists a category called *Port cities and towns of the United States Pacific coast* (see http://en.wikipedia.org/wiki/Category:Port_cities_and_towns_of_the_United_ St ates_Pacific_ coast) which contains cities, such as *San Francisco* and *Los Angeles*. According to Wikipedia, the intention of these categories is to *"group together pages on similar subjects"*. To some degree, the categorization result is similar to the data that Smith and Mark (2001) collected in [24]. In their experiment, non-expert human subjects were asked to give examples for geographic categories, whereas Wikipedia invites users to perform categorization tasks on the Web. DBpedia inherits these customized categories and the classification results from Wikipedia. In this work, we make use of the data instances under specific geographic categories to discover the properties which differentiate the instances that are in a category from those that are not.

3 Workflow

The objective of the proposed workflow is to extract geographic knowledge from Linked Data in a bottom-up manner. Specifically, we aim at discovering the knowledge which may be missing or biased in top-down geo-ontologies. The top-down geo-ontologies discussed in this paper are not the top-level ontologies in existing literature, which provide abstract and domain-independent terms, such as *endurant* and *perdurant*. Instead, these top-down geo-ontologies model concrete geographic concepts (e.g., *lake* and *university town*), and are micro-ontologies which serve as building blocks in specific applications [13]. Figure 2 shows an overview of the designed workflow.

The workflow starts from the *Linked Datasets* at the lower-left corner of the figure. Based on the categorization system, the workflow first selects a *Target category* that corresponds to the geographic concept modelled by the top-down geo-ontology. Meanwhile, both *positive instances* and *negative instances* are selected according to the category. Positive instances are the entities which are classified by users as belonging to the target category, whereas negative instances are those that do not belong to the category. For example, if the target category is *university town*, then positive instances are the towns which have been classified into this category, while negative instances are those which are not considered as *university town*. Selecting suitable positive and negative instances are important since they will be used as the input for the next three-stage process to learn the target category.

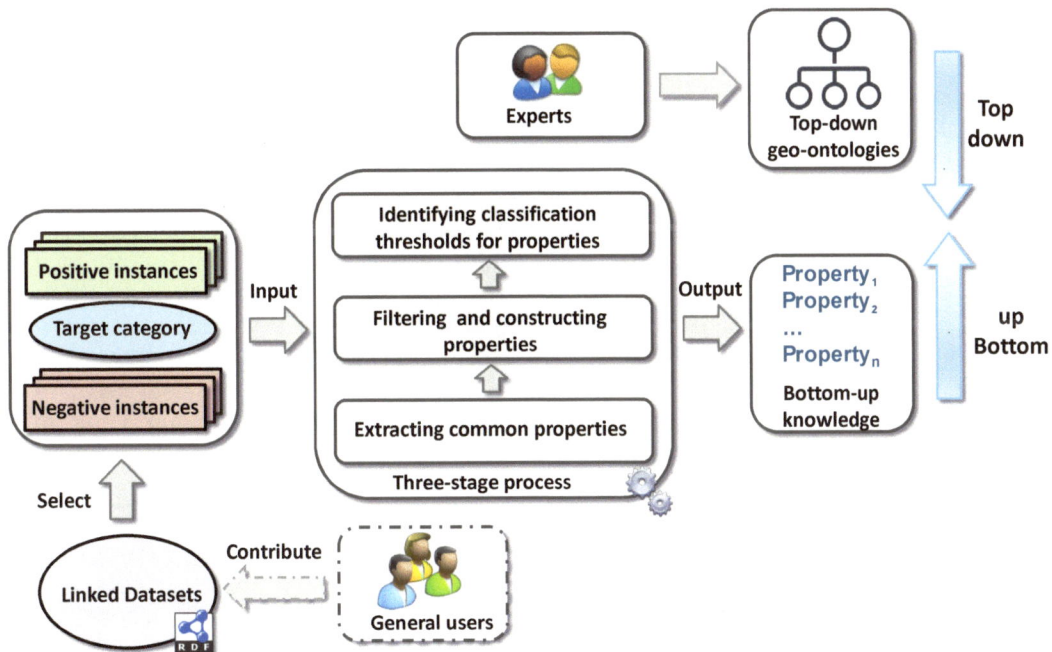

Figure 2: An overview of the workflow. The dotted lines of the *General users* box and the *Contribute* arrow represent that some Linked Datasets are not contributed by general users).

The first stage extracts common properties among the input instances. It examines all the properties that each instance has, and answers two questions: 1) what are the property-value pairs that only exist in the *majority* of the positive instances? 2) what are the properties that are shared by both the positive and negative instances? Answering the first question can help discover the properties whose existence indicates a strong membership between a geographic instance and the target category. For example, an examination of the instances in the category of *university town* may reveal that the property-value pair (i.e., a *predicate* and *object* pair) *hasUniversity.University* is shared among the majority of the positive instances while not in most of the negative instances. Such a result indicates that this property-value pair is a strong indication for an instance to be considered as a *university town*. The term *majority* should be determined based on the requirements of specific applications. For example, if the goal is to learn a category that is compatible to a few outliers, then a value of 95% could be used as the *majority* threshold, and it means the properties are shared by at least 95% of the positive instances and by no more than 5% of the negative instances. Answering the second question can help find the candidate properties whose value ranges can be potentially used to distinguish a geographic concept. For example, to learn the concept *big city* in the mind of the general public, a property *population* may be shared by both positive and negative instances. While this property is not unique to positive instances, its value can still be used to differentiate the target category (e.g., a *big city* might have *population* > 1, 000, 000 based on the user-contributed data).

The second stage filters out certain irrelevant properties and constructs new properties which might be useful for understanding the target concept. This stage is a supervised process and requires manual intervention. The reason that this filtering is necessary is because the LOD cloud is a big knowledge base that is not merely for one specific application: the information available on the LOD cloud is much richer than what is typically needed for an application. Thus, instead of directly picking and using the data, applications should be selective in terms of what data are relevant and what are not. When it comes to learning knowledge about a specific geographic concept, some properties may not be considered as relevant. For example, in DBpedia, a geographic place is often linked to the celebrities who were born there through the property *isHometownOf*. Such a property can be useful in understanding the relations between people and places, and in fact, we have utilized these relations from DBpedia to improve place name disambiguation in a previous study [10]. However, this property may not be relevant if the concept we want to learn is *university town*. One may wonder why this property filtering is not put into the first stage to pre-process the data. This is due to the manual work it requires: removing the irrelevant properties after the common ones have been identified can save a lot of human effort. In addition, new properties can be constructed based on the existing ones. For example, if both *total area* and *total population* about a city are available in the data, one can construct a new property *population density*, which may become very valuable information in identifying some geographic concepts, such as *populous city*.

The third stage examines the properties that are the output from the second stage. This stage also answers two questions for each examined property: 1) whether this property can be used to differentiate positive and negative instances? 2) if yes, what is a suitable threshold for this property to separate data instances? Before the more detailed method is presented, let us first consider two example properties (see Figure 3). Intuitively, the property in Figure 3(a) can be used to differentiate positive and negative instances, whereas the property in Figure 3(b) cannot since its instances are mixed together.

(a) A property with a clear cut.   (b) A property with mixed instances.

Figure 3: Two example properties. Green circles are positive instances and red circles are negative ones. The horizontal arrow indicates the increasing direction of the property value.

In order to find the properties similar to Figure 3(a), we use a method based on entropy and information gain. Entropy is a metric which quantifies the randomness of information [6], which can be calculated using equation 3.1.

$$entropy(X) = -\sum_{i=\{pos,neg\}} P(x_i) \log P(x_i) \qquad (3.1)$$

where $entropy(X)$ represents the entropy of the dataset X, x_{pos} represents the positive instances in X, and x_{neg} represents the negative instances. $P(x_i)$ is the empirical proportion of either positive or negative instances in the dataset, which can be calculated, for example, by $x_{pos}/(x_{pos} + x_{neg})$ for positive instances.

Information gain (IG) is the entropy difference before and after an action has been performed on the data. It can be calculated using equation 3.2.

$$IG = entropy_b(X) - entropy_a(X) \qquad (3.2)$$

where IG represents the information gain, $entropy_b(X)$ is the entropy before applying the action (i.e., regular segmentation in this work), and $entropy_a(X)$ is the entropy after the action.

Our method integrates entropy, IG, and regular segmentation to examine the properties output from the second stage. For each property, we segment the data instances evenly into multiple groups, and calculate the information gain by subtracting the entropies before and after the segmentation. We perform this process iteratively with an increasing number of segmentations. The rationale behind this method is that for the properties that have a clear cut, their information gain will increase quickly and reach a plateau with the increasing number of segmentations, since most of the segmented groups will contain only one type of instances; on the contrary, for the properties that have mixed instances, their information gain will not show such a rapid increase, since larger number of segmentations still cannot separate the positive and negative instances. Figure 4 illustrates this process by applying an increasing number of segmentations to the two example properties shown in Figure 3.

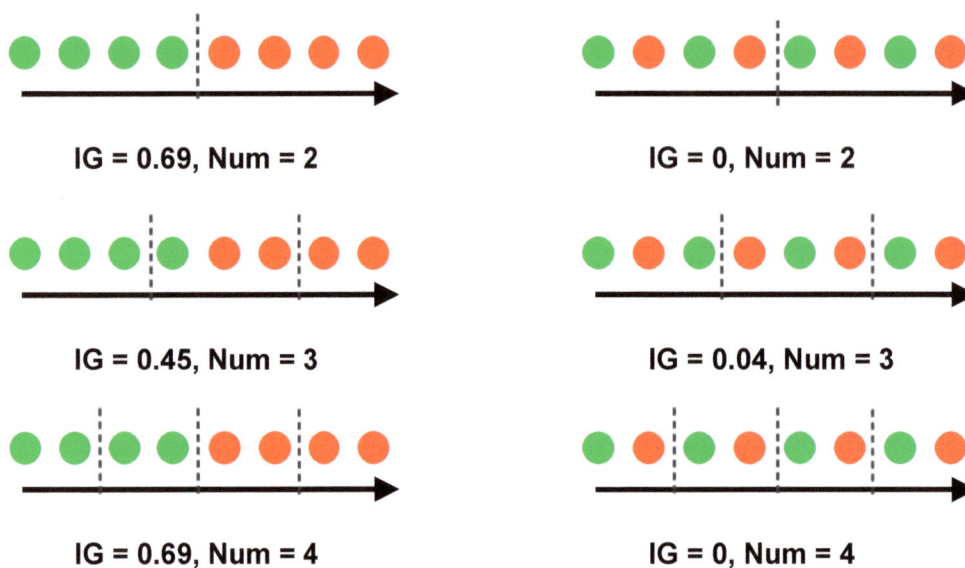

(a) A property with a clear cut.   (b) A property with mixed instances.

Figure 4: Information gains with different numbers of segmentation.

It can be seen that the property in Figure 4(a) quickly reaches its highest IG value (in this example, the IG reaches the highest value of 0.69 when the number of segmentation is 2). Although there are fluctuations, the IG will become stable when the segmentation number further increases. In contrast, the IG value of the property in Figure 4(b) only increases slowly with fluctuations. Both properties will reach their highest IG values, when the number of segmentations becomes extremely high, in which each separated group contains only one single instance. By plotting out the relation between IG and the number of segmentations, we can visually identify those properties which quickly reach their plateaus. Examples of such plots will be shown in the following section 4. After these properties have been identified, their suitable value ranges can be extracted by aggregating the values of the major positive instances. Similarly, a majority threshold, such as 95%, could be used to make the learned concept compatible to a few outliers.

4   Experiment

This section describes an initial experiment which uses the proposed workflow to learn the geographic concept *port city* from the DBpedia data.

4.1   Experimental data and geo-ontology

A top-down geo-ontology constructed to model this concept can be in the form of Figure 5. In this ontology, a *port city* inherits from a super and more general class *city*, and it has a *port* and is close to a *water body*. These are some intuitive properties that make a *city* as a *port city*.

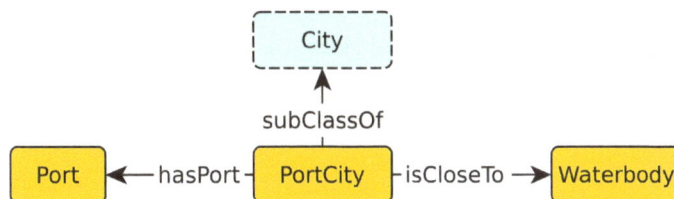

Figure 5: A simplified example top-down geo-ontology for *port city*. The light blue rectangle represents the super class defined in an existing geo-ontology, and the yellow rectangles represent the classes defined in this ontology.

To learn bottom-up geographic knowledge about this concept, we can follow the presented workflow. First, a *target category* needs to be identified. In this experiment, two categories from DBpedia have been used, which are *Port cities and towns of the United States Atlantic coast* and *Port cities and towns of the United States Pacific coast*. The cities belonging to these two categories are combined into one set as the positive instances. In total, 49 positive cities have been identified, and all of their properties have been retrieved from DBpedia. It is worth noting that these 49 cities do not cover all port cities in the U.S., and some cities, such as *New Orleans*, can be well considered as port cities. However, these 49 cities have been explicitly classified by Wikipedia users as port cities, and therefore have been used as the training data. For negative instances, since DBpedia does not provide the data on which cities are not port cities, 29 inland U.S. cities have been randomly selected. Figure 6 shows the geographic distribution of the selected cities. As can be seen, the port cities used in this experiment are distributed along the east and west coasts, while the non-port cities are located inside the U.S. continent.

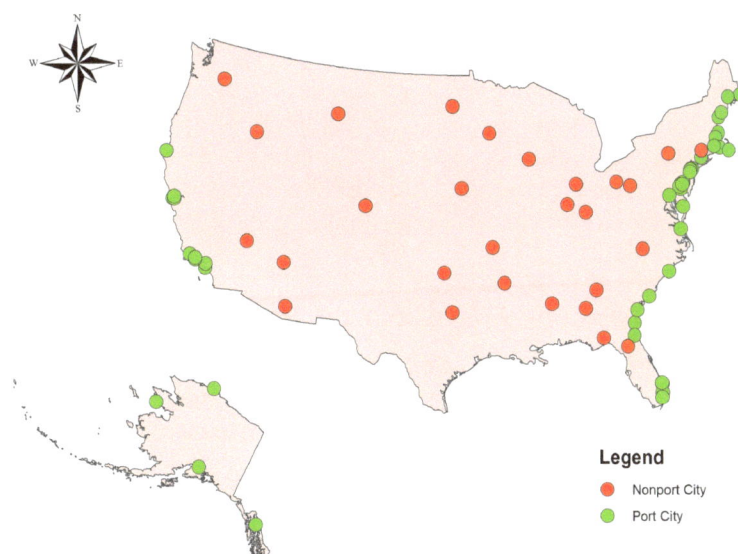

Figure 6: Geographic distribution of the port and non-port cities. Green circles are positive instances and red circles are negative instances.

4.2   Experimental procedure

Extracting common properties. A 95% threshold has been used to extract the common properties. The extraction process takes two steps. First, we examine all data to identify the properties that are shared by both positive and negative instances. The identified properties are shown in Table 1. As can be seen, many properties provide useful information about the cities, such as their populations, land areas, related roads, companies, and other information. In the second step, the same 95% threshold has been applied to extract the distinctive properties shared by positive instances. In addition to the properties shown in Table 1, one more property-value pair was extracted, which is *is dbpedia-owl:homeport of*. This result is consistent with what has been defined in the top-down geo-ontology: a *PortCity* should have a *Port*, and accordingly should be the *homeport* of something, such as a ship. This consistence demonstrates that the properties developed in a top-down approach can be confirmed by the bottom-up knowledge extracted from the data.

dbpedia-owl:areaTotal	is dbpedia-owl:city of
is dbpedia-owl:premierePlace of	dbpedia-owl:leaderName
is dbpedia-owl:routeStart of	dbpedia-owl:foundingDate
is dbpedia-owl:location of	dbpedia-owl:leaderTitle
dbpedia-owl:areaLand	is dbpedia-owl:builder of
dbpedia-owl:isPartOf	is dbpedia-owl:locationCity of
is dbpedia-owl:assembly of	dbpedia-owl:type
is dbpedia-owl:headquarter of	is dbpedia-owl:foundationPlace of
dbpedia-owl:routeEnd	is dbpedia-owl:region of
dbpedia-owl:owner	is dbpedia-owl:residence of
is dbpedia-owl:nearestCity of	is dbpedia-owl:broadcastArea of
dbpedia-owl:abstract	is dbpedia-owl:populationPlace of
dbpedia-owl:populationTotal	is dbpedia-owl:broadcastArea of
is dbpedia-owl:deathPlace of	dbpedia-owl:timeZone
is dbpedia-owl:routeJunction of	dbpedia-owl:locatedInArea
dbpedia-owl:utcOffset	is dbpedia-owl:hometown of
dbpedia-owl:areaWater	is dbpedia-owl:restingPlace of
is dbpedia-owl:birthPlace of	dbpedia-owl:elevation
geo:lng geo:lat	dbpedia-owl:postalCode
dbpedia-owl:areaCode	

Table 1: Properties shared by 95% of both the positive and negative instances.

Filtering out irrelevant properties and constructing new properties. This stage removes the irrelevant properties and constructs new ones for learning the concept *port city*. The irrelevant properties have been classified into the following categories:

- Linking to persons related to the place, e.g., *is residence of, is deathPlace of, is home- Town of, is restingPlace of, is birthPlace of, ...*

- Linking to organizations at the place, e.g., *is city of, is location of, is headquarter of, is foundationPlace of, is broadcastArea of, ...*

- Linking to roads and highways, e.g., *is routeStart of, is routeEnd of, ...*

- Linking to political or administrative information, e.g., *leaderName, leaderTitle, postCode, areaCode, ...*

After filtering out these irrelevant properties, the rest are summarized in Table 2. Although only 5 properties remain, they all convey important geographic information about the places. In addition to the 5 properties, one new property, *waterLandPercentage*, has been constructed which is calculated by *areaWater/areaTotal*. This new property is added since it can be directly relevant to the concept of *port city*. These properties will be tested in the next stage to see if they can be used to differentiate the positive and negative instances.

dbpedia-owl:areaTotal	dbpedia-owl:areaLand	dbpedia-owl:areaWater
dbpedia-owl:populationTotal	dbpedia-owl:elevation	waterLandPercentage

Table 2: Properties output from the second stage.

Identifying classification thresholds for properties. Regular segmentation, entropy, and information gain have been applied to the 6 properties in Table 2. Figure 7 shows the plotted results with the number of segmentations on the x axis, and the values of IG on the y axis. As can be seen, with the increase of the segmentation number, the information gains of different properties increase in different manners. For some properties, such as the *elevation* (Figure 7(e)) and the *waterLandPercentage* (Figure 7(f))), their information gains increase rapidly and reach the plateau soon. These are the properties which can effectively separate positive and negative instances. The other 4 properties, in contrast, show slow increases and constant fluctuations with different segmentations. This result indicates that these properties have mixed positive and negative instances, and therefore are not suitable for learning the concept *port city*.

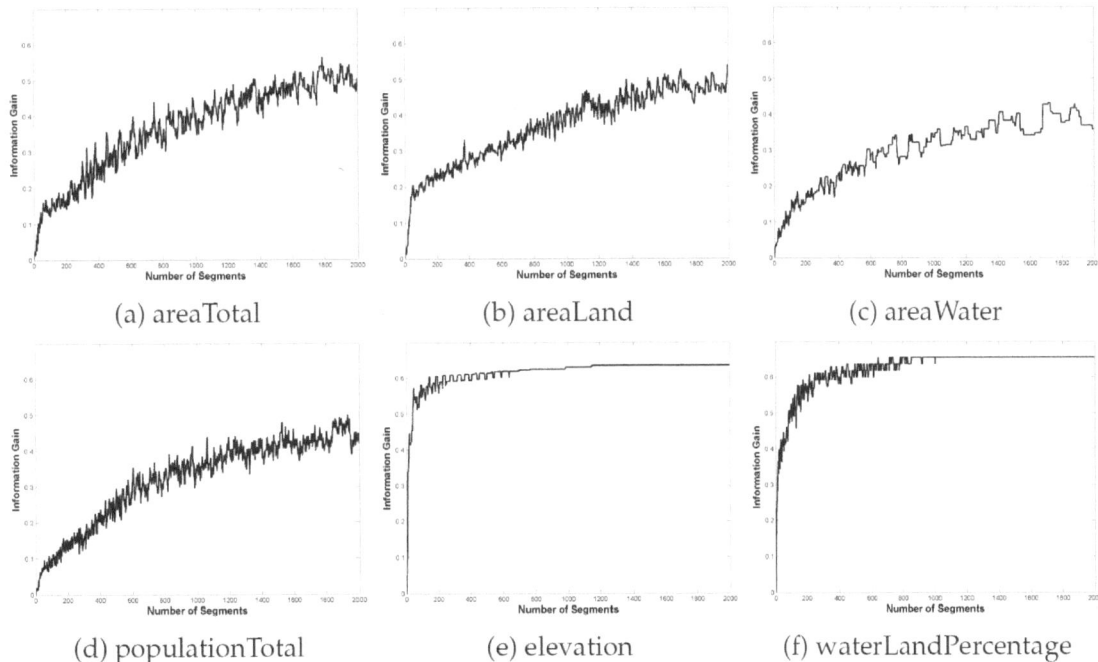

(a) areaTotal   (b) areaLand   (c) areaWater

(d) populationTotal   (e) elevation   (f) waterLandPercentage

Figure 7: Plots of information gain and segmentation numbers for different properties.

For the two identified properties, *elevation* and *waterLandPercentage*, the values of 95% of the positive instances are aggregated, and the obtained threshold results are listed as below (the unit of elevation is *meter*).

$$elevation < 49.36 \qquad (4.1)$$

$$waterLandPercentage > 11.79\% \qquad (4.2)$$

The extracted knowledge about *port city* is reasonable: generally, a port city is located at places where the average elevation is not too high and which have quite an amount of water within the city boundary. However, such knowledge could be missed during a top-down ontology development process.

4.3   An evaluation of the extracted knowledge

To evaluate the quality of the learned geographic knowledge, an unseen DBpedia dataset has been used. This dataset contains 21 German cities which have been classified by Wikipedia users into the category *port cities* in *Germany*, as well as 17 cities randomly selected from the inland of Germany as the negative instances. The geographic distribution of the positive and negative instances in this testing dataset is shown in Figure 8.

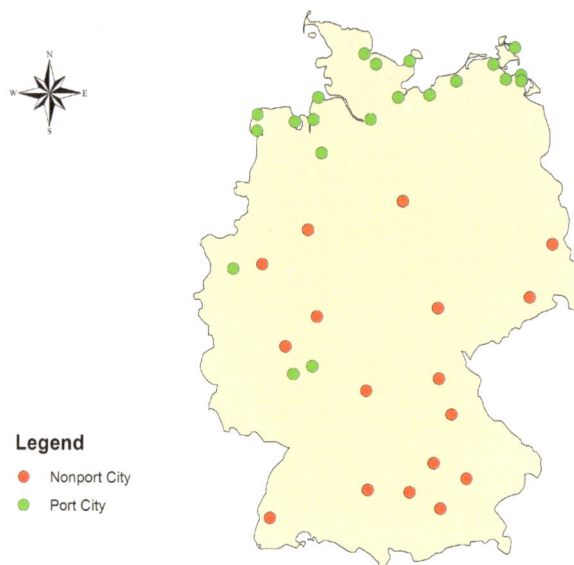

Figure 8: Geographic distribution of the positive and negative instances in the testing dataset (green circles are positive instances and red circles are negative ones).

It can be seen that two of these positive port cities, namely *Frankfurt* and *Mainz*, lie in the inland of the country. These two cities are along the *Main* river, and have been considered as *river port* cities (in contrast to the other *seaport* cities). This observation can help ontology developers rethink and complement the target concept (e.g., a *port city* could have a seaport, a river port, or an airport).

The two pieces of mined knowledge in equations 4.1 and 4.2 are examined using the metric of *accuracy* from information retrieval, which is defined in equation 4.3.

$$accuracy = (TP + TN)/(P + N) \qquad (4.3)$$

where *TP* represents *true positive* which are the number of positive instances that are also considered as positive by the extracted knowledge. For example, if a port city (positive instance) has an average *elevation* lower than 49.36 meters as learned from our experiment, then this instance will be counted into *TP*. Similarly, *TN* represents *true negative* which are the number of negative instances that are also considered as negative based on the extracted knowledge. For example, if a non-port city (negative instance) has a *waterLandPerventage* lower than 11.79% (thus, it is correctly considered as a non-port city), then this instance will be counted into *TN*. *P* and *N* are the total numbers of positive and negative instances in the testing dataset. The metric *accuracy* measures the consistency between the extracted knowledge and the unseen testing instances.

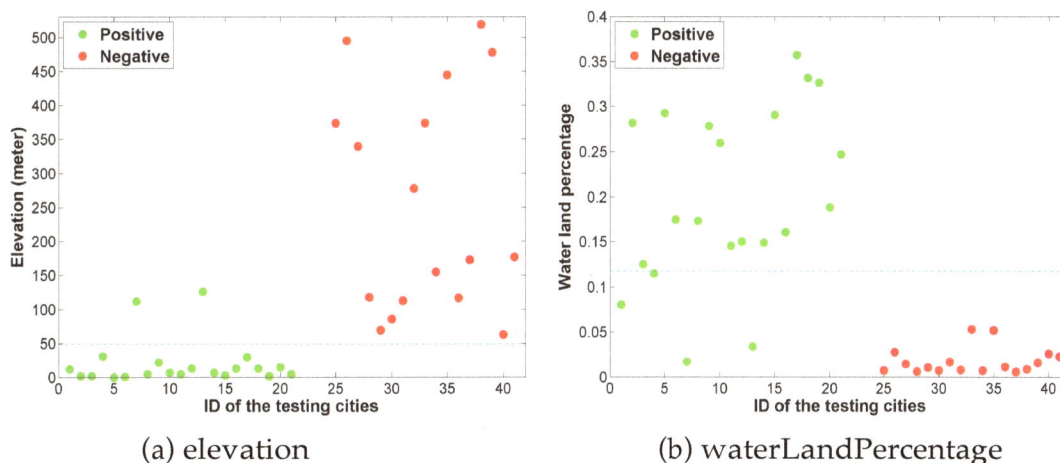

(a) elevation (b) waterLandPercentage

Figure 9: Evaluation of the testing cities in Germany based on the two extracted properties. Green circles are positive instances, and red circles are negative ones. The dotted line represents the reference value based on the extracted knowledge.

The knowledge about *elevation* is first evaluated against the testing data (see Figure 9(a)), and the following result is acquired: $TP/P: 19/21, TN/N: 17/17$, *accuracy*: 94.74%. It can be seen that the geographic knowledge learned about *elevation* is highly consistent with the testing data. The two cities which are classified incorrectly are the two inland river port cities.

When it comes to evaluating the knowledge on *waterLandPercentage*, there exists a challenge: the *Germany* cities in the testing DBpedia dataset do not have the property of *areaWater* which is necessary in this experiment to calculate the *waterLandPercentage*. Such a situation can be attributed to the varied data availability in different countries. In order to test this extracted knowledge, we make use of the geographic data from OpenStreetMap. The administrative boundaries and the water-related areas (including *bay*, *river*, *lake*, and *reservoir*) have been downloaded for each of the testing cities. We sum up the water areas and the administrative areas respectively, and then calculate the water land percentages by dividing the former with the latter. The calculated values are plotted out in Figure 9(b). By applying the knowledge *waterLandPercentage* > 11.79% to the testing cities, we obtain the following result: $TP/P: 17/21, TN/N: 17/17$, *accuracy* : 89.47%.

5 Conclusions and future work

Geo-ontologies can play an even more important role in developing the next generation intelligent GIS by enabling the systems to automatically recognize geographic concepts from data and recommend suitable tools. While a top-down approach has often been used to develop geo-ontologies, such an approach may be biased towards the knowledge of the participants or miss some useful properties. The fast growth of the Linked Open Data cloud provides a valuable resource for deriving knowledge in a bottom-up manner. Such knowledge can then be used to enrich and complement the top-down geo-ontologies. This paper presents early results about a workflow for mining bottom-up geographic knowledge from Linked Data. Based on both positive and negative instances of a target concept, the workflow identifies the common properties, filters irrelevant information, and extracts suitable thresholds. An initial experiment has been conducted, in which the workflow has been used to extract knowledge about a geographic concept *port city* from a DBpedia dataset. We evaluate the extracted knowledge using an unseen dataset, and the evaluation result shows a good consistency between the learned knowledge and the testing cities. While DBpedia has been used as the data source in the experiment, the proposed workflow can also be applied to other LOD datasets.

The performance of the proposed workflow depends on the availability and quality of the training data which contain the target category, the positive instances, and the negative ones. While we obtained our data from the Wikipedia categorization system in this work, other approaches could also be used. For example, traditional human participant experiments could be employed to elicit the typical instances of a target category. The derived instance memberships can then be embedded into the presented workflow, and combined with the LOD datasets to mine bottom-up knowledge. Alternatively, one can create the target category on Wikipedia, encourage online users to classify instances based on this category, and then harvest the data. While the latter approach might require less human effort and thus better scale up, traditional human participant tests provide more information about the background of the participants (e.g., age and gender), and therefore can provide a more representative data sample.

The presented research can also be extended in several directions. First, our experiment so far has examined the applicability of the proposed workflow using one geographic concept. While fair performance has been observed, it is still necessary to investigate some additional concepts to understand the merits and limitations of the proposed workflow more thoroughly. Such investigation could also help quantify the degree of improvement that our workflow can bring to existing top-down geo-ontologies. Second, the evaluation experiment indicates that the *port cities* in the U.S. are similar to the *port cities* in Germany in terms of their elevations and water land percentages. This result is intriguing since some geographic concepts (e.g., *mountain* and *hill*) may be conceptualized differently in different countries. Thus, it would also be interesting to examine which concepts are more regionally sensitive and which others are more stable across different geographic areas.

References

[1]   AUER, S., BIZER, C., KOBILAROV, G., LEHMANN, J., CYGANIAK, R., AND IVES, Z. DBpedia: A nucleus for a web of open data. In *The semantic web*. Springer, 2007, pp. 722–735.

[2]   BIZER, C., HEATH, T., AND BERNERS-LEE, T. Linked data - the story so far. *International Journal on Semantic Web and Information Systems 5*, 3 (2009), 1–22.

[3]   BIZER, C., LEHMANN, J., KOBILAROV, G., AUER, S., BECKER, C., CYGANIAK, R., AND HELLMANN, S. Dbpedia-a crystallization point for the web of data. *Web Semantics: science, services and agents on the world wide web 7*, 3 (2009), 154–165.

[4]   COUCLELIS, H. Ontology, epistemology, teleology: triangulating geographic in- formation science. In *Research trends in geographic information science*. Springer, 2009, pp. 3–15.

[5]   COUCLELIS, H. Ontologies of geographic information. *International Journal of Geographical Information Science 24*, 12 (2010), 1785–1809.

[6]   FLACH, P. *Machine learning: the art and science of algorithms that make sense of data*. Cambridge University Press, 2012.

[7]   FONSECA, F. T., EGENHOFER, M. J., AGOURIS, P., AND CÂMARA, G. Using ontologies for integrated geographic information systems. *Transactions in GIS 6*, 3 (2002), 231–257.

[8]   FRANK, A. U. *Ontology for spatio-temporal databases*. Springer, 2003.

[9]   GUARINO, N. *Formal ontology in information systems: Proceedings of the first international conference (FOIS'98), June 6-8, Trento, Italy*, vol. 46. IOS press, 1998.

[10] HU, Y., JANOWICZ, K., AND PRASAD, S. Improving Wikipedia-based place name disambiguation in short texts using structured data from DBpedia. In *Proceedings of the 8th workshop on geographic information retrieval* (2014), ACM New York, NY, pp. 1–8.

[11] HU, Y., JANOWICZ, K., PRASAD, S., AND GAO, S. Enabling semantic search and knowledge discovery for arcgis online: A linked-data-driven approach. In *AGILE 2015*. Springer, 2015, pp. 107–124.

[12] JANOWICZ, K. Observation-driven geo-ontology engineering. *Transactions in GIS 16*, 3 (2012), 351–374.

[13] JANOWICZ, K., SCHEIDER, S., PEHLE, T., AND HART, G. Geospatial semantics and linked spatiotemporal data–past, present, and future. *Semantic Web 3*, 4 (2012), 321–332.

[14] JONES, C. B., ALANI, H., AND TUDHOPE, D. Geographical information retrieval with ontologies of place. In *Spatial information theory* (2001), Springer, pp. 322–335.

[15] KUHN, W. Geospatial semantics: why, of what, and how?   In *Journal on Data Semantics III*. Springer, 2005, pp. 1–24.

[16] LI, N., ERVIN, S., FLAXMAN, M., GOODCHILD, M., AND STEINITZ, C. Design and application of an ontology for geodesign. *Revue internationale de géomatique, 22* (2012), 145–168.

[17] LI, N., RASKIN, R., GOODCHILD, M., AND JANOWICZ, K. An ontology-driven framework and web portal for spatial decision support. *Transactions in GIS 16*, 3 (2012), 313–329.

[18] LI, W., YANG, C., NEBERT, D., RASKIN, R., HOUSER, P., WU, H., AND LI, Z. Semantic-based web service discovery and chaining for building an arctic spatial data infrastructure. *Computers & Geosciences 37*, 11 (2011), 1752–1762.

[19] PEUQUET, D., SMITH, B., AND BROGAARD, B. O. The ontology of fields. Tech. rep., National Center for Geographic Information and Analysis, 1998.

[20] PUNDT, H., AND BISHR, Y. Domain ontologies for data sharing–an example from environmental monitoring using field GIS. *Computers & Geosciences 28*, 1 (2002), 95–102.

[21] SCHEIDER, S., JANOWICZ, K., AND KUHN, W. Grounding geographic categories in the meaningful environment. In *Spatial Information Theory*. Springer, 2009, pp. 69–87.

[22] SCHMACHTENBERG, M., BIZER, C., JENTZSCH, A., AND CYGANIAK, R. Linking open data cloud diagram, http://lod-cloud.net/, 2014.

[23] SMITH, B., AND MARK, D. M. Ontology and geographic kinds. In *Proceedings of the Tenth International Symposium on Spatial Data Handling*, T. Poiker and N. Chris- man, Eds. Simon Fraser University, 1998, pp. 308–320.

[24] SMITH, B., AND MARK, D. M. Geographical categories: an ontological investigation. *International journal of geographical information science 15*, 7 (2001), 591–612.

[25] STADLER, C., LEHMANN, J., HÖFFNER, K., AND AUER, S. LinkedGeoData: A core for a web of spatial open data. *Semantic Web 3*, 4 (2012), 333–354.

Analysis of Dynamic Radiation Level Changes Using Surface Networks

Myeong-Hun Jeong[1], Shaowen Wang[1], and Clair J. Sullivan[2]

1 CyberGIS Center for Advanced Digital and Spatial Studies, CyberInfrastructure and Geospatial Information Laboratory, Department of Geography and Geographic Information Science, National Center for Supercomputing Applications, University of Illinois at Urbana-Champaign, Champaign, IL, 61820, USA
2 Department of Nuclear, Plasma, and Radiological Engineering, University of Illinois at Urbana-Champaign, Champaign, IL, 61820, USA

Abstract: The Fukushima nuclear accident reminds us of severe risk of radioactive substances. Citizen scientists voluntarily collect and share radiation data using geo-tagged sensors for radiation preparedness. However, radiation levels are affected by a number of factors including for example weather conditions, naturally occurring radioactive materials (NORM), and large marble structures. It is therefore difficult to determine whether a higher radiation level comes from a normal variation in background or not. This research analyzes the radiation changes using surface networks that can be used to characterize complex surfaces. A new algorithm has been developed to identify salient peaks and their hills by merging insignificant peaks recursively. Salient peaks and their hills are converted into graphs. The structural similarities of graphs were compared over time. The radiation measurements in the city of Koriyama, Japan were analyzed as a case study. The results demonstrated that structural analysis of dynamic radiation levels revealed stable changes, while numeric analysis of radiation levels presented statistically significant differences. This method is able to detect radiation level changes irrespective of background variations.

Keywords: Surface networks, structural similarities, graph indices, radiation levels.

1 Introduction

Radiation levels have been a subject of major debate after a nuclear disaster – Fukushima Daiichi accident – released substantial contamination into our environments. Citizen scientists, as it came to be known, started gathering and sharing environmental radiation levels using mobile detectors (e.g., Geiger counters) across the world due to awareness of health effects. In particular, the non-profit organization such as Safecast has been building a radiation sensor network from crowd-sourced data. Its data points have been over 25 million at the end of 2014 [1].

While an immense number of radiation sensors quantify the levels of radiation in our environment, it is difficult to understand accurate radiation levels due to background variations [29, 18]. For example, some regions have naturally occurring radioactive materials (NORM); weather such as precipitation causes the increase of background levels, or background levels have a tendency to increase as a result of the presence of large marble structures. It is challenging to predict whether the amplitude of the count rate is due to the possible release of radioactive materials or not.

However, looking beyond direct background effects on radiation levels, this paper investigates how the structure of regions of higher count rates have changed as time varies. We assume if radioactive materials are continually stable, the structure of the regions of higher count rates would have similar patterns, irrespective of background fluctuations. In this paper, the regions of higher count rates are represented by surface networks, consisting of critical points (peaks, pits, and passes) and critical lines (ridges and channels) [24, 25]. We particularly focus on salient peaks and their hills such as catchments areas. Salient peaks are connected by edges. Such a graph between subsequent time steps has been analyzed and compared using graph structural analysis techniques [26]. The structural analysis can provide dynamic radiation level changes without knowing accurate background variations.

In the reminder, the following section starts by discussing the previous computations of surface networks and structural similarity measurements between surface networks. Section 3 describes the data processing for parsing and filtering radiation data set. Section 4 provides a surface network algorithm presented in this study. In addition, this section provides the information about analysis methods. Section 5 presents evaluations of structural analysis. The results confirm the effectiveness of the approach, discussed in Section 6. Finally, the conclusions and future works are drawn in Section 7.

2 Background

This paper utilizes spatial reasoning for identifying radiation level changes. The radiation level changes may be identified by using cluster analysis from a group of radiation measurements. However, it is difficult to separate radiation measurements appropriately because radiation levels are floating at even the same location due to background effects.

In this paper, radiation measurements are converted to raster maps. The radiation scalar fields (i.e., raster maps) are characterized by surface networks. The regions of higher count rates are represented as peaks and their hills on the surface network. The structural similarity of surface networks is compared in order to infer radiation level changes.

Surface networks originate from the work of [6, 17], which do not describe the Earth's surface as hills and valley, but also propose relations between the number of peaks, pits, and passes. In a later, Morse theory uses differential topology generally to define surface networks [19]. Morse theory pertains to the relationship between the shape of the space and functions on defined on the space. If the derivative of a height function $z = f(x, y)$

equals to zero at a point (x_0, y_0), this point (x_0, y_0) is called a critical point, if and only if the determinant of the Hessian matrix $\begin{pmatrix} f_{xx}(x_0,y_0) & f_{xy}(x_0,y_0) \\ f_{yx}(x_0,y_0) & f_{yy}(x_0,y_0) \end{pmatrix}$ is not zero, where $f_{xx}, f_{xy}, f_{yx}, f_{yy}$ are partial derivatives of the height function, z [16].

There are broadly two approaches to construct surface networks from continuous surfaces to discrete data structures: explicit and implicit cell complexes.

Explicit cell complexes can be regarded as triangulations. The critical points are extracted from the triangular mesh by comparing values with adjacent points [30] or piecewise linear functions [10, 8]. Illicit cell complexes make use of a grid such as raster-based DEMs [23, 35]. We use a grid configuration of each radiation measurements (i.e., a raster map). In particular, we focus on the detection of peaks and their hills because our purpose is to identify regions of higher count rates. The hills of peaks are called as Morse complexes [8]. One example for using Morse complex is to analyze and track burning structures [3].

Based on a raster map, there are several ways to identify critical points. [23] use local comparisons between eight direct neighbors. Local comparisons are known to identify spurious critical points due to continuity constraints [27]. [34, 35] uses biquadratic interpolation as well as geomorphological parameters, which help to remove spurious critical points. However, geomorphological parameters (e.g., slope and curvature) cannot guarantee that all peaks are identified due to the violation of geomorphological parameters' constraints, although geomorphological approach is good at removing spurious critical points. The regions of higher does rates are important in our application. In such context, this paper presents a new algorithm for identifying salient critical points (i.e., peaks) in a radiation scalar field using prominence (i.e., the relative height difference between adjacent peaks) and horizontal distance (i.e., distance between adjacent peaks). Our approach recursively removes insignificant peaks.

In terms of measuring similarity between surface networks, there is very few research on the structural analysis of surface networks. One example is to calculate structural similarity index for the analysis of urban population surfaces [21]. In the first step, identified surface networks are generalized by removing peaks that have the minimum difference in height with associated passes. Critical points are then sorted based on the height. Sorted critical points are continually deleted until there is only one peak left. During this process, structural similarity index is given if two surface networks are isomorphic. However, this approach is ill-suited to our problem in the sense that background fluctuations lead to different radioactive levels in spite of the same count rates in reality.

Another approach is to use graph theoretic indices (e.g., density or connectivity) to analyze the surface and its changes over time [12]. However, graph theoretic indices are not enough to characterize radiation level changes because network connectivity can be different without significant radiation level changes. None of approaches encountered are directly applicable to our problems. Therefore we adapt graph similarity measurement techniques for quantifying the similarity of surface networks. There are a broad range of applications in graph similarity scoring and matching techniques: chemical structures [14, 32], social media [5, 20], web searching [2, 9] or medical diagnostics [28].

In summary, this paper provides a new algorithm to identify salient peaks among spurious peaks. In addition, the structural similarity of surface and its changes are measured using graph similarity scoring and measuring techniques. We demonstrate that this approach can provide global radiation level changes without accurate background measurements.

3 Data processing

Based on our previous literature review, we will now proceed with data processing for the analysis of radiation level changes. We acquired experimental radiation data set from Safecast in February 2015. The data size is over 26 million records and over 3 GB as a csv file format.

The experimental area was selected in Japan because citizen scientists have been gathering substantial numbers of radiation measurements across Japan. Our experimental region is the city of Koriyama that is 82km away from Fukushima Daiichi nuclear power station (i.e., WGS84 bounds are 140.32564, 37.36191, 140.40993, 37.43678). We gathered all measurements each month in 2013. Thus, there are twelve data set for the city of Koriyama.

In order to analyze a large volume of data, we exploited Apache Pig and Hadoop. The former is a programming language designed to ease the development of distributed applications for analyzing large volumes of data. The later can be thought of distributed computing framework designed for processing large distributed data [22]. By using Pig and Hadoop, we can derive experimental data set with ease and speed.

Finally, all measurements per month are converted into raster maps using Empirical Bayesian Kriging (EBK). EBK is well known to have smaller prediction uncertainty and the ability to filter out measurement errors [15]. These interpolation maps have been used as the cornerstone for identifying surface networks as well as analysing radiation level changes.

4 Surface networks

In this section, we explore a new algorithm to identify peaks and their hills in a radiation scalar field. Further, the analysis methods are presented: how well surface networks reflect the radiation measurements; numerical summaries of surface networks' structure; and structural similarity of surface and its changes over time.

4.1 Identification of peaks and hills

In order to explain an algorithm, it is necessary to mention basic definitions related with critical points.

In brief, a peak, pk is defined as a cell that all neighbors of pk have a lower value than pk. The ascent vector, av of an each cell is defined as the unique directed edge from that cell to its one-hop neighbor with the highest value of all neighbors. Prominence, $prom$ is described as relative height difference between adjacent peaks. These basic definitions have been already defined by previous works [30, 13, 7]. In addition, we can add another definition such as a horizontal distance, hd between adjacent peaks. Prominence and horizontal distance are mainly used to remove spurious peaks in our algorithm. Figure 1 illustrates prominence and horizontal distance.

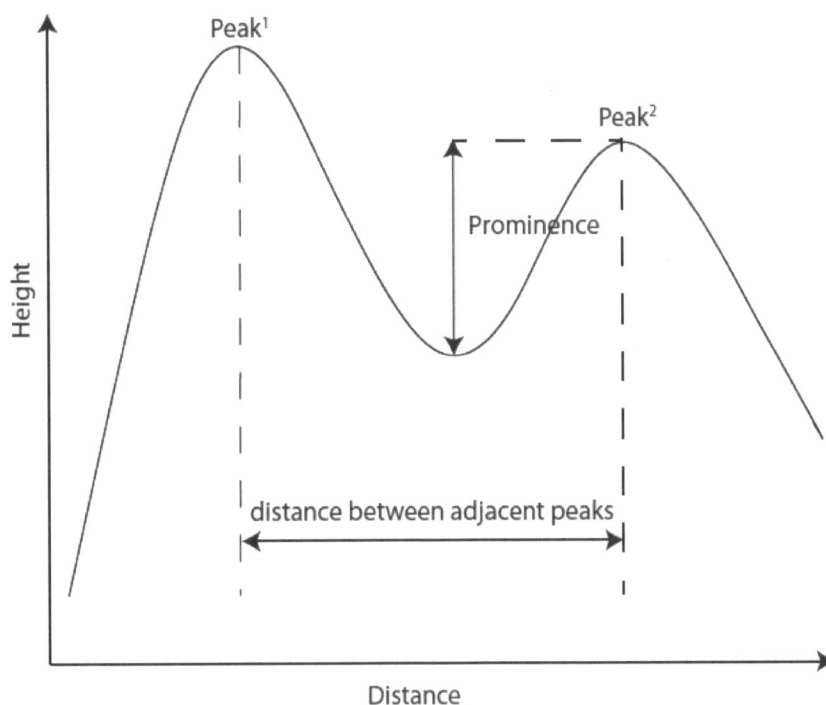

Figure 1: Prominence and horizontal distance between $Peak^1$ and $Peak^2$. This figure is adapted from [7].

Based on definitions mentioned above, the algorithm proceeds as follows:

• Each cell decides its ascent vector by comparing values with direct eight neighbors (Algorithm 1, line 7). If a cell has the highest value among neighbors, this cell becomes a peak (Algorithm 1, line 4)

• Each peak broadcasts top-down sweep messages to neighbors. Each cell updates its peak identifier, *pkid* based on its *av*'s peak identifier (Algorithm 1, line 9). During this process, if there are neighbors that have a different peak identifier, this cell becomes a channel (i.e., the direction of ascent vectors are divided at channels into different peaks).

• Peaks are recursively merged using prominence and horizontal distance (Algorithm 1, line 11).

• All cells' peak identifier will be updated and reconciled if a cell has a disappeared peak identifier (Algorithm 1, line 17).

Algorithm 1 Identifying peaks and their hills

1: Input: Raster-based radiation grid, *prom*: user defined prominence threshold, *hd*: user defined horizontal distance threshold
2: Local variables: an ascent vector, *av*, initialized empty; a peak id, *pkid*, initialized empty
Step I
  3: Comparing radiation values with direct 8 neighbors
  4:   if a cell has the highest value among neighbors **then**
  5:     this cell becomes a local peak (*pk*)   *--local comparisons between direct 8 neighbors*
  6:   **else**
  7:     **set** *av* := one of neighbors' peak identifier that has the highest value
Step II
  8: Top-down sweep from local peaks
  9:   **set** *pkid* := *av*'s peak identifier
Step III
 10: Remove insignificant peaks   *--Considering all identified peaks*
 11:   if peaks are adjacent to each other **then**   *--There are channels between two peaks*
 12:     if relative height < *prom* **then**
 13:       if horizontal distance < 1.5 × IQR and horizontal distance < *hd* **then**
 14:         **set** *pkid* := adjacent peak's identifier   *--If there are no more two adjacent peaks, we use a default horizontal distance*
Step IV
 15: Merge peaks and hills
 16:   if an insignificant peak identifier is merged into a new peak identifier **then**
 17:     **set** *pkid* := new peak's identifier   *--Update a peak identifier if a cell has an disappeared peak identifier*

In particular, step III can remove spurious peaks. There are two steps. First, if the relative height between adjacent peaks meets a threshold prominence, a peak that has a lower height will be merged into another peak. Thus, we can generalize the surface networks if a radiation difference is negligible. This is a similar approach of Wolf pruning [33] in terms of simplifying surface networks using relative height. Next, each peak has usually several adjacent peaks. When we repeat the merge process, we consider the distance between adjacent peaks because spatially near measurements are more related. If a horizontal distance between adjacent peaks is far away compared with other adjacent peaks (i.e., horizontal distance > 1.5× interquartile ranges (IQR)), the algorithm does not merge adjacent two peaks. The interquartile ranges can be calculated with distances from other adjacent peaks. If there are only two peaks such as a very smooth field, we can use a user defined threshold distance.

Figure 2 presents how the initial identified peaks are merged into salient peaks. 317 peaks are initially identified in Figure 2a. The number of peaks is then reduced to 73 in Figure 2b. In addition, Top 5 representative peaks are highlighted using bigger triangle symbols in Figure 2b. These peaks and hills are main interest in our radiation level analysis (see Section 5).

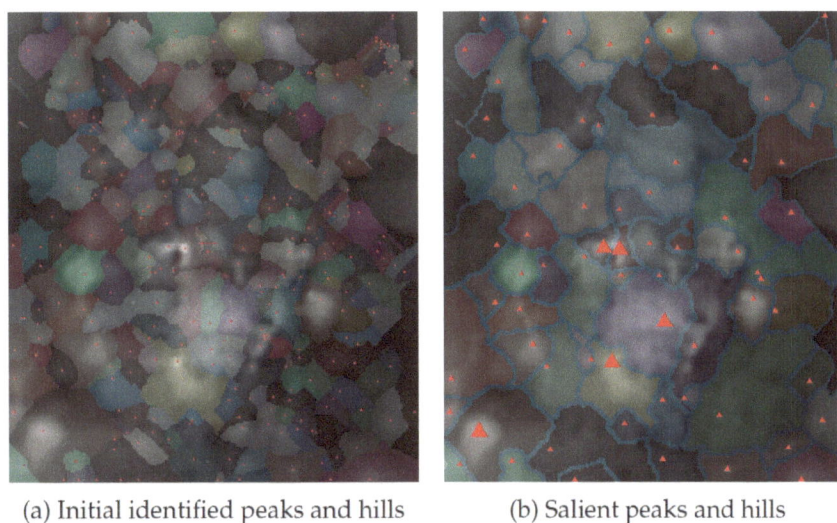

(a) Initial identified peaks and hills   (b) Salient peaks and hills

Figure 2: Identification of salient peaks and hills at Koriyama in May 2013

4.2 Analysis techniques

Three analysis methods are exploited in this paper: feature-based parameters for analyzing the correlation between identified surface networks and radiation measurements; graph indices; and graph structural similarity for comparing surface networks over time.

First, identified surface networks were measured using feature-based parameters. There are a couple of feature-based parameters, including the absolute peak height, the peak area, the peak volume, the peak curvature in sliding direction, or the peak density per unit area. These feature parameters have been used to understand the surface functional performance in nanotechnology [11, 31]. We will use the absolute peak height to measure the relationship between feature-based parameters and the numeric calculations of radiation measurements. If the radiation measurements are reflected in the identified surface networks, the feature-based parameters correlate well with the radiation measurements.

Next, surface networks were distilled based on graph theory. Graph indices can provide succinct numerical summaries of the network structure [12]. Graph density and connectedness are used to describe the network structure in this paper. In brief, the density refers to the number of observed edges over the number of possible ones. The connectedness indicates whether there exists an undirected path from a node u to a node v in a graph [26]. If both values equal to one, the regions of high count rates are densely clustered.

Lastly, we can analyze the surface network and its changes over time using structural similarities. The basic idea is to establish a matching between the edges of one graph and the edges of another using density [4]. The structural correlation can be derived from structural comparison measures. For example, if the structural correlation = 1, the graphs are isomorphic. We use the SNA R package to calculate structural correlation. This package provides a wide range of graph analytic functionalities [5].

Analysis methods mentioned above were experimentally conducted and tested in the following section.

5   Results

The following section started by investigating the numerical analysis of the raw radiation measurements. The algorithm described in the previous section was evaluated with the relationship between feature-based parameters and numerical analysis of radiation measurements. In order to measure radiation level changes, the structural variations of surface networks over time were analyzed with graph indices and structural similarity correlations.

5.1   Numerical data analysis

Figure 3 presents the spread of radiation measurements. It is clear that there was a significance difference for each measurement. This visual impression was confirmed using statistical analysis, which is to find whether there is a statistically significant difference in radiation levels between each month.

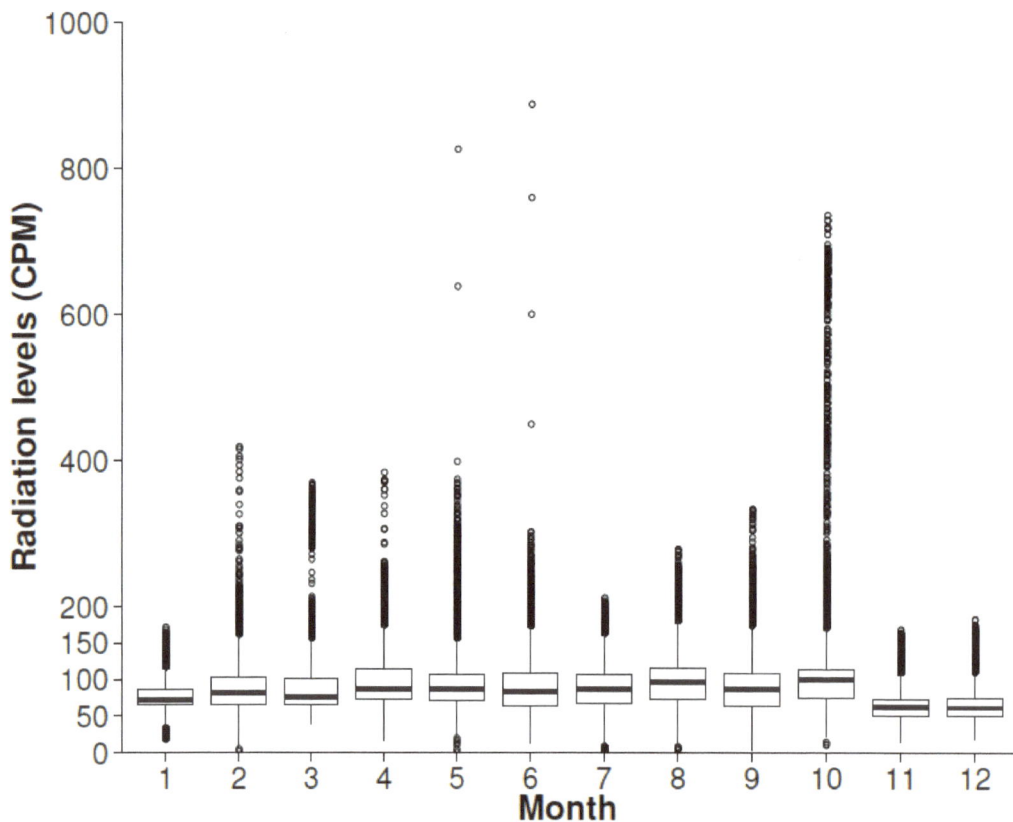

(a) The city of Koriyama, Japan in 2013

Figure 3: Boxplot of radiation levels split by month: 7 measurements over 1000 cpm were removed from the figure.

As you may expect, the data violated the normal distribution assumption (F (11, 510299) = 1048.5, p < 0.05). Robust alternative one-way ANOVA test (i.e., Kruskal-Wallis test) was used for non-normal distributions. There was a statistically significant difference between each month (H (11) = 48220.16, p = 2.2e − 16). We conducted a follow-up analysis such as pairwise comparisons using Wilcoxon rank sum test to present which dependent variables (i.e., month) show a significant difference.

There were no significant differences between February and June, and February and September (p > 0.05), while presenting significant differences on other cases.

However, it is difficult to mention that there were significant differences in radiation levels in the city of Koriyama in 2013. These significant differences may be due to background variations such as precipitations. Further, there is not enough information to quantify background effects on the radiation levels, which makes it difficult to understand the real changes of radiation levels. Therefore, the following sections investigate the dynamic radiation levels using spatial structures of surface networks.

5.2   Feature-based parameter analysis

Feature-based parameters can provide information about how identified surface networks reflect the original radiation measurements. The feature-based parameters (i.e., the average of absolute height) were calculated from the top 5 representative peaks in Table 1.

Table 1: Results for the mean of radiation measurements and the average of absolute height of top 5 representative peaks per month in 2013 (The unit is cpm).

	1	2	3	4	5	6	7	8	9	10	11	12
Mean	77.23	91.75	91.53	100.9	93.31	88	88.31	96.32	87.55	102.9	64.15	66.38
Height	149.71	166.70	156.42	163.88	178.21	159.26	145.19	172.93	158.04	215.55	134.97	149.58

The correlation between the average of absolute height and the mean of radiation measurements was analyzed using Pearson's correlation coefficients, r. The null hypothesis is that there is a no correlation between feature-based parameters and the mean of radiation measurements. The result indicated that the average of absolute height was significantly related to the increase of the radiation levels, $r = 0.74$, $p = 0.004$. In terms of effect sizes, the correlation coefficient, r is greater than 0.5. It can be interpreted as a large effect. Therefore, the radiation levels are appropriately reflected in the surface networks.

5.3   Structural indices analysis of surface networks

Surface networks are naturally a graph. The regions of higher count rates are of interest in our application. These regions can be represented by peaks and their hills. Since the regions with very high radiation levels are meaningful, we only consider the top 5 representative peaks. These salient peaks are extracted to form an undirected graph. For example, in Figure 2b, the top 5 representative peaks are converted into an undirected graph by connecting adjacent peaks in Figure 4a. This graph is also represented as an adjacency matrix in Figure 4b. This adjacency matrix can be used as the basis for graph indices and similarity analysis.

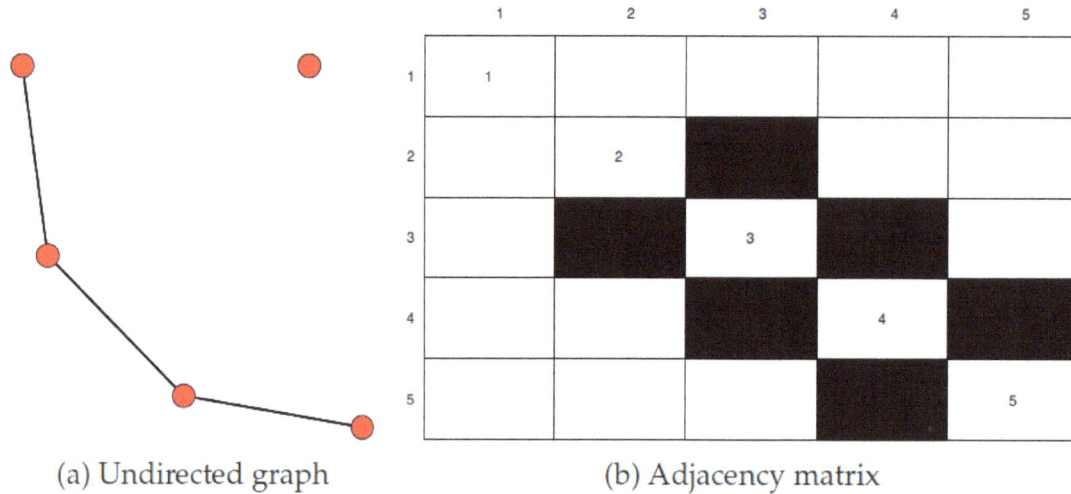

(a) Undirected graph   (b) Adjacency matrix

Figure 4: Undirected graph and its adjacency matrix for the top 5 salient peaks in Figure 2b.

Surface networks in every month were converted into undirected graphs. These graphs were analyzed with graph indices and connectedness measurements in Figure 5a.

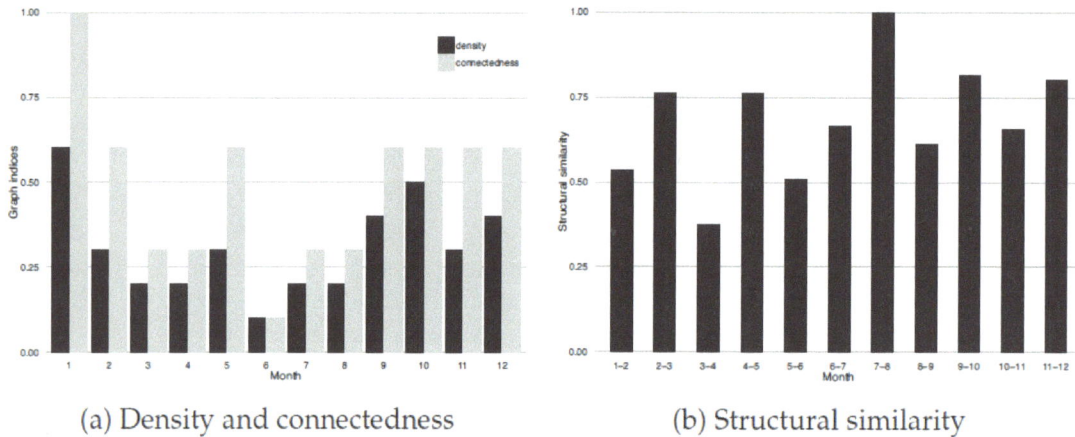

(a) Density and connectedness   (b) Structural similarity

Figure 5: Graph indices and structural similarities

If you look at the density, most values of density were lower values, which indicated a sparsely connected graph. Further, the value of connectedness indicated there was an isolated node (i.e., a peak and its hill) except January. However, these graph indices are not related with radiation level changes. In other words, as the mean of radiation levels increase, the graph indices are not correlated. We can just quantitatively summarize the structure of a graph per month. Thus, the following section compared the structure similarity of graphs associated with the mean of radiation levels.

5.4   Structural similarity analysis of surface networks

An important alternative to graph indices is a direct comparison of edges sets between two graphs. The structural correlations between two graphs were calculated for measuring structural similarity.

Results for the structural correlations over time are represented in Figure 5b. For example, the first bar indicates the structural correlation between January and February, 0.54.

Overall, the structural similarities were fairly correlated except between March and April. These results are a total contrast to the numeric analysis in Section 5.1. Even though there is no information about accurate background effects, it is available to infer how radiation levels have changed using structural similarities of surface networks.

6   Discussion

Our numerical analysis of radiation measurements demonstrated that there were statistically significant differences between each month in terms of radiation levels. However, it is difficult to understand whether this difference comes from radioactive materials release or background fluctuations.

In terms of the feature based parameters analysis, the identified surface networks well reflected the radiation measurements. The correlation coefficient, r between the average of absolute height and the mean of radiation measurements was greater 0.7. This can be regarded as large effect size. Further, this feature-based parameter was significantly correlated to the radiation measurements ($p < 0.05$). However, the computational analysis of the algorithm proposed was not conducted in this research because this paper focused on the analysis of radiation level changes.

When it comes to structural indices analysis, we can quantitatively summarize the structure of radiation levels per month. Using structural indices, it can be inferred whether the regions of higher count rates are highly clustered or separated per month. However, it is difficult to determine radiation level changes using graph indices.

The last evaluation criterion was the structural similarity analysis. The structural correlations presented that there were fair correlations for the radiation level changes over time. This result confirmed that the variations of radiation levels were attributed to background fluctuations rather than radioactive contamination. However, the structural similarities were not exactly the same each month. Some parts of salient regions had been changed per month. This work should be incorporated into research on principal component analysis such as precipitation, or wind. In addition, the structural similarity just provides the correlation coefficient. It is difficult to infer what kinds of topological events occur between subsequent time steps. Tree morphism and Homology algorithm could be exploited to detect qualitative topological events of radiation level changes.

7   Conclusions

This paper has demonstrated how radiation level changes can be identified using the structural similarities of surface networks. The structural similarities over time provide fair correlations for the radiation level changes, even though the numerical analysis indicates there are statistically significant differences for radiation levels.

The approach presented in this paper has taken a key step in addressing background effects in radioactive engineering. This research is part of a larger project to detect the illicit movement of nuclear materials with big data. The structural analysis can be used efficiently to monitor illicit nuclear materials, irrespective of background fluctuations.

Acknowledgments

This work was supported in part by the U.S. National Science Foundation (grant numbers: 0846655, 1047916, and 1443080) and the Defense Advanced Research Projects Agency (grant number: N66001-14-1-4043). The views, opinions, and findings contained in this article are those of the authors and should not be interpreted as representing the official views or policies, either expressed or implied, of the National Science Foundation, the Defense Advanced Research Projects Agency or the Department of Defense.

References

[1] Safecast. http://blog.safecast.org. [Online; accessed 04-March-2015].

[2] BLONDEL, V. D., GAJARDO, A., HEYMANS, M., SENELLART, P., AND VAN DOOREN, P. A measure of similarity between graph vertices: Applications to synonym extraction and web searching. *SIAM review 46*, 4 (2004), 647–666.

[3] BREMER, P., WEBER, G., PASCUCCI, V., DAY, M., AND BELL, J. Analyzing and tracking burning structures in lean premixed hydrogen flames. *IEEE Transactions on Visualization and Computer Graphics 16*, 2 (2010), 248–260.

[4] BUTTS, C., AND CARLEY, K. Multivariate methods for interstructural analysis. Casos working paper, Carnegie Mellon University., 2001.

[5] BUTTS, C. T. Social network analysis with sna. *Journal of Statistical Software 24*, 6 (2008), 1–51.

[6] CAYLEY, A. On contour and slope lines. *Philosophical Magazine Series 4 18*, 120 (1859), 264–268.

[7] CHAUDHRY, O. Z., AND MACKANESS, W. A. Creating mountains out of mole hills: Automatic identification of hills and ranges using morphometric analysis. *Transactions in GIS 12*, 5 (2008), 567–589.

[8] DANOVARO, E., DE FLORIANI, L., PAPALEO, L., AND VITALI, M. A multi-resolution representation for terrain morphology. In *Geographic Information Science*, M. Raubal, H. Miller, A. Frank, and M. Goodchild, Eds., vol. 4197 of *Lecture Notes in Computer Science*. Springer, Berlin Heidelberg, 2006, pp. 33–46.

[9] DEHMER, M., STREIB, F. E., MEHLER, A., KILIAN, J., AND MÜHLHÄUSER,
     M. Application of a similarity measure for graphs to web-based
     document structures. In *International Conference on Data Analysis ICA* (2005).

[10] EDELSBRUNNER, H., HARER, J., AND ZOMORODIAN, A. Hierarchical Morse
     Smale complexes for piecewise linear 2 manifolds. *Discrete and Computational
     Geometry 30* (2003), 87–107.

[11] HAO, Q., BIANCHI, D., KAESTNER, M., AND REITHMEIER, E. Feature based
     characterization of worn surfaces for a sliding test. Tribology International 43, 5
     (2010), 1186–1192.

[12] HU, Y., MILLER, H. J., AND LI, X. Detecting and analyzing mobility
     hotspots using surface networks. *Transactions in GIS 18*, 6 (2014), 911–935.

[13] JEONG, M.-H., DUCKHAM, M., MILLER, H., KEALY, A., AND PEISKER, A.
     Decentralized and coordinate-free computation of critical points and
     surface networks in a discretized scalar field. *International Journal of Geographical
     Information Science 28*, 1 (2014), 1–21.

[14] KAZIUS, J., NIJSSEN, S., KOK, J., BÄCK, T., AND IJZERMAN, A. P.
     Substructure mining using elaborate chemical representation. *Journal of
     Chemical Information and Modeling 46*, 2 (2006), 597–605.

[15] KRIVORUCHKO, K. *Spatial statistical data analysis for GIS users*. Esri Press
     Redlands, CA, USA, 2011.

[16] MATSUMOTO, Y. *An Introduction to Morse Theory*, vol. 208. American
     Mathematical Society, USA, 2002.

[17] MAXWELL, J. C. On hills and dales. *Philosophical Magazine Series 4 40* (1870),
     421–427.

[18] MERCIER, J.-F., TRACY, B., D'AMOURS, R., CHAGNON, F., HOFFMAN, I., KOR
     -PACH, E., JOHNSON, S., AND UNGAR, R. Increased environmental
     gamma-ray dose rate during precipitation: A strong correlation with
     contributing air mass. *Journal of environmental radioactivity 100*, 7 (2009), 527–
     533.

[19] MILNOR, J. *Morse Theory*. Princeton University Press, 1969.

[20] MURATA, T., AND MORIYASU, S. Link prediction of social networks based
     on weighted proximity measures. In *IEEE/WIC/ACM international conference
     on Web Intelligence* (2007), IEEE, pp. 85–88.

[21] OKABE, A., AND MASUYAMA, A. A method for measuring structural
     similarity among activity surfaces and its application to the analysis of
     urban population surfaces in japan. In *Topological Data Structures for Surfaces:
     An Introduction for Geographical Information Science* (2004), S. Rana, Ed., Willey, pp.
     103–120.

[22] PASUPULETI, P. *Pig Design Patterns*. Packt Publishing Ltd, 2014.

[23] PEUCKER, T. K., AND DOUGLAS, D. H. Detection of surface-specific points
     by local parallel processing of discrete terrain elevation data. *Computer
     Graphics and image processing 4*, 4 (1975), 375–387.

[24] PFALTZ, J. L. Surface networks. *Geographical Analysis 8*, 1 (1976), 77–93.

[25] RANA, S. *Topological Data Structures for Surfaces*. John Wiley & Sons, Ltd., Chichester, UK, 2004.

[26] SAMATOVA, N. F., HENDRIX, W., JENKINS, J., PADMANABHAN, K., AND CHAKRABORTY, A. *Practical Graph Mining with R*. CRC Press, 2013.

[27] SCHNEIDER, B., AND WOOD, J. Construction of metric surface networks from raster-based dems. In *Topological Data Structures for Surfaces: An Introduction for Geographical Information Science*, S. Rana, Ed. Willey, 2004, pp. 53–70.

[28] SHARMA, H., ALEKSEYCHUK, A., LESKOVSKY, P., HELLWICH, O., ANAND, R., ZERBE, N., AND HUFNAGL, P. Determining similarity in histological images using graph-theoretic description and matching methods for content-based image retrieval in medical diagnostics. *Diagn Pathol 7* (2012), 134.

[29] SULLIVAN, C. J. Nuclear forensics driven by geographic information systems and big data analytics. In *Proc. the Institute for Nuclear Materials Management on Information Analysis Technologies, Techniques and Methods for Safeguards, Nonproliferation and Arms Control Verification Workshop* (2014), pp. 273–286.

[30] TAKAHASHI, S., IKEDA, T., SHINAGAWA, Y., KUNII, T. L., AND UEDA, M. Algorithms for extracting correct critical points and constructing topological graphs from discrete geographical elevation data. *Computer Graphics Forum 14*, 3 (1995), 181–192.

[31] TIAN, Y., WANG, J., PENG, Z., AND JIANG, X. A new approach to numerical characterisation of wear particle surfaces in three-dimensions for wear study. *Wear 282* (2012), 59–68.

[32] WALE, N., WATSON, I. A., AND KARYPIS, G. Comparison of descriptor spaces for chemical compound retrieval and classification. *Knowledge and Information Systems 14*, 3 (2008), 347–375.

[33] WOLF, G. W. Knowledge diffusion from Giscience to other fields: The example of the usage of weighted surface networks in nanotechnology. *International Journal of Geographical Information Science 28*, 7 (2014), 1401–1424.

[34] WOOD, J. *The geomorphological characterisation of digital elevation models*. PhD thesis, University of Leicester, 1996.

[35] WOOD, J. Modelling the continuity of surface form using digital elevation models. In *Proc. 8th international Symposium on Spatial Data Handling* (1998), IGU Commission of GIS New York, pp. 725–736.

Spatial Scene Representation: A Survey and Categorization

Joshua A. Lewis

School of Computing and Information Science, 5711 Boardman Hall, University of Maine, Orono, ME 04469-5711, USA

Abstract: In modeling a geographic reality, one identifies the participating objects and captures the relations that exist between them. This process results in the creation of a spatial scene. Spatial scenes can take on many forms: the chosen embedding space has implications on which types of objects one represents and the set of possible relations between them. Further restricting the set of represented objects to suit a specific need provides additional focus; considering just points, lines, regions, or a combination of objects are some of the many possibilities. Furthermore, the types of relations captured are often the centerpiece of any qualitative depiction: does one care only about intersections, does sequence matter, or dimension? This survey seeks to categorize some of the ways in which a spatial scene can be captured, and provides a perspective where research can be seen in the wider context of choices one makes.

Keywords: Spatial reasoning, points, lines, regions, complex objects, holes, separations, spatial scenes.

1 Introduction

There are many models for representing spatial scenes. A spatial scene is a collection of objects and their spatial arrangement [5, 32, 35, 37]. Models of spatial scene representation will be considered with respect to the embedding space, the objects represented, and the topological relations between those objects. While domain specific surveys illustrate a wide range of theories concerning qualitative topological representation [6, 11, 12, 27], this work aims to illustrate the process of constructing or selecting a topological model, touching on the implications of choices encountered along the way. In such a fashion the body of work represented herein can be seen within a larger context, spanning the last two decades of thought on such issues, beyond simply grouping research into singular categories.

For instance, a model may work within a specific embedding space, or it might be modified by this choice. The objects modeled may vary, based on this decision, or based on the outcomes desired by the researcher. The topological relations described then fall into a number of different research areas within the topological setting, such as relations based on connection, direction, or orientation. Thus the combined choices of embedding, objects represented, types of relations all work to define the conceptual space in which we work and invent. To this end, the survey touches on these elements in succession, motivating each with specific work in order to illustrate the representation of spatial scenes in a broad context. Section 2 explores different choices of embedding space, Section 3 handles various constructions for objects, and Section 4 showcases the relations between sets of objects. Section 5 concludes this work.

2   Embedding Space

For most depictions of geographic reality an embedding in the Euclidian Plane, $\mathbb{R}^2$, suffices. However, this is not always the case if 3D objects are being represented, for instance. The choice of embedding space matters as it can affect the types of objects that can be represented. A region or a volume cannot be described in a 1-dimensional embedding, but lines can take on additional configurations when represented in two or more dimensions. Even when a model supports multiple embedding spaces there are often consequences. As an example, a model known as the 9-intersection allows eight region-region relations in $\mathbb{R}^2$, but allows three additional relations when the sphere is considered as the embedding space [17] (Figure 1).

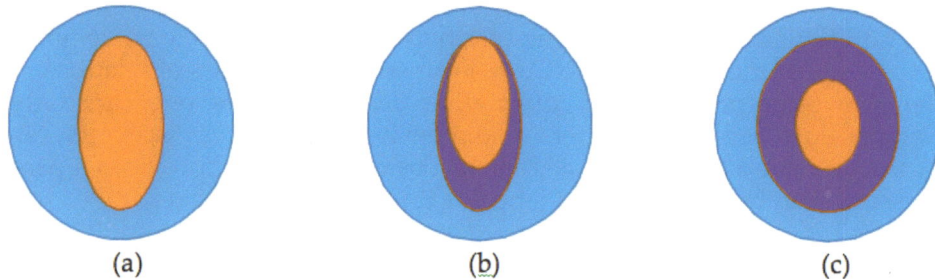

Figure 1: Topological relations only applicable on the sphere, but not in $\mathbb{R}^2$: (a) *attach*, (b) *entwined*, (c) *embrace* on the sphere.

Similarly, the standard region-region relations are also a subset of what can be represented in the integer plane, $\mathbb{Z}^2$, giving 15 relations [23]. An integer-based embedding is also unique in that adjacency relations can be defined through a 4-neighborhood (vertically and horizontally adjacent points) or an 8-neighborhood (additionally, diagonally adjacent points) in the plane, resulting in three additional relations.

While everyday experience has given us familiarity with three-dimensional and

two-dimensional representations, and perhaps even representations of objects on the surface of a sphere, the interrelation between embedding space and the types of object we can construct are not always immediately apparent. For instance, when reasoning with a holed region on the surface of a sphere which division of the exterior space is the hole, and which surrounds the object (Figure 2)?

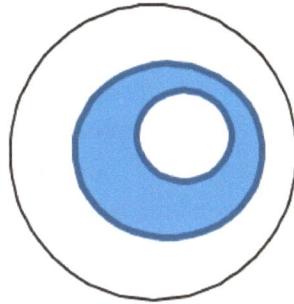

Figure 2: A holed object on a sphere where the position of the hole is ambiguous.

Furthermore, a simple line may pass for a spatial object in $\mathbb{R}^2$, but when considered in $\mathbb{R}^1$ a line can be used as an interval to represent the duration of events [3]. Thus a spatial object takes on a temporal representation. Thus the choice of embedding space can be seen to drastically impact a qualitative representation of space.

3 Types of Object

The most common objects represented are points, lines, and regions. In geographic space the choice of object may represent different levels of abstraction, such as depicting a town as a point or a region, with certain elements preserved or removed, depending on scale and interest [4, 34, 40, 43]. This can change based on what needs to be represented for a given purpose; different views may necessitate interpreting a traditionally linear approach through the use of regions, for example [32]. Therefore, it is important to understand not only the relations that exist between various objects, but first how they are constructed. Many have described not only this process for simple objects, but also the construction of additional objects, such as those with holes or other complexities.

3.1 Simple Objects

Generally, spatial entities such as points and regions are described in terms of sets under general (point-set) topology. While the most basic definitions fall outside of the scope of this paper, a basic text should provide an acceptable overview [1]. It is using such an approach that the basic relations between simple regions in $\mathbb{R}^2$ can be expressed [20]. In this setting Egenhofer and Franzosa describe a spatial region through the following definitions involving the concepts of interior (A^o), boundary (∂A), and closure ($\bar{A}$), for some object A:

Definition 2.1.1 Let X be a connected topological space. A spatial region in X is a non-empty proper subset A of X satisfying (1) A^o is connected and (2) $A = \overline{A^o}$.

Proposition 2.1.2 If A is a spatial region in X then $\partial A \neq \emptyset$.

Under this specification a region is a set of points defined by the closure of a connected interior. Later approaches would also incorporate the exterior ($^-$) which is the set difference between X and A, A's compliment [21]. By considering the intersection between interior, boundary, and exterior sets for a pair of regions it is possible to generate a set of base relations (Figure 3). The framework for this approach is called the 9-intersection [21], and expands upon the similar 4-intersection [20, 24] which omits the five exterior components.

$$R(A,B) = \begin{pmatrix} A^o \cap B^o & A^o \cap \partial B & A^o \cap B^- \\ \partial A \cap B^o & \partial A \cap \partial B & \partial A \cap B^- \\ A^- \cap B^o & A^- \cap \partial B & A^- \cap B^- \end{pmatrix} \tag{1}$$

Each intersection is recorded as either empty ($\emptyset$ 0) or nonempty ($\neg\emptyset$ 1) based on the configuration of the objects being described. Though there are 512 possible matrices (2^9), only eight correspond to the base relations between two regions in $\mathbb{R}^2$.

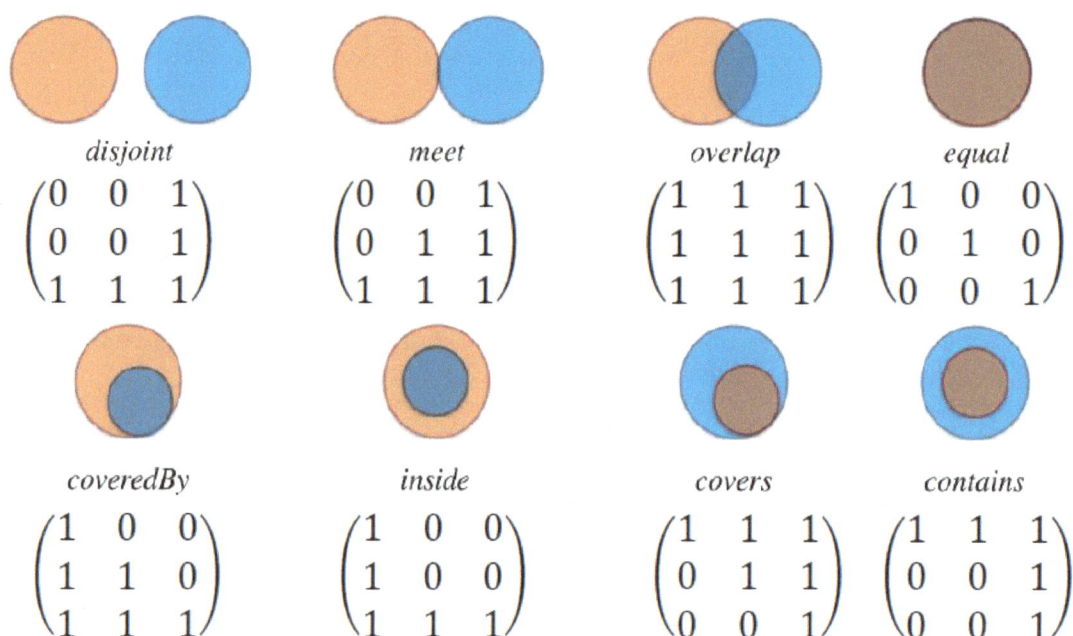

$$\text{disjoint}\quad \begin{pmatrix} 0 & 0 & 1 \\ 0 & 0 & 1 \\ 1 & 1 & 1 \end{pmatrix} \qquad \text{meet}\quad \begin{pmatrix} 0 & 0 & 1 \\ 0 & 1 & 1 \\ 1 & 1 & 1 \end{pmatrix} \qquad \text{overlap}\quad \begin{pmatrix} 1 & 1 & 1 \\ 1 & 1 & 1 \\ 1 & 1 & 1 \end{pmatrix} \qquad \text{equal}\quad \begin{pmatrix} 1 & 0 & 0 \\ 0 & 1 & 0 \\ 0 & 0 & 1 \end{pmatrix}$$

$$\text{coveredBy}\quad \begin{pmatrix} 1 & 0 & 0 \\ 1 & 1 & 0 \\ 1 & 1 & 1 \end{pmatrix} \qquad \text{inside}\quad \begin{pmatrix} 1 & 0 & 0 \\ 1 & 0 & 0 \\ 1 & 1 & 1 \end{pmatrix} \qquad \text{covers}\quad \begin{pmatrix} 1 & 1 & 1 \\ 0 & 1 & 1 \\ 0 & 0 & 1 \end{pmatrix} \qquad \text{contains}\quad \begin{pmatrix} 1 & 1 & 1 \\ 0 & 0 & 1 \\ 0 & 0 & 1 \end{pmatrix}$$

Figure 3: The eight region-region relations and their matrices as described by the 9-intersection [20]

As an addition to general topology, algebraic topology [2, 42] allows for the creation of objects by gluing together cells of varying dimension, allowing more complex constructions. Egenhofer and Herring [21] describe the construction of points, lines, regions, and more complex objects in $\mathbb{R}^2$ through the use of 0-cells (vertices), 1- cells (a segment connecting two 0-cells) and 2-cells (an area, represented by closed, non-intersecting 1-cells). A cell complex is taken to be an aggregate of cells. In such a manner a point is described simply as a 0-cell, a line as a connected sequence of 1-complexes that neither cross nor loop with two disconnected boundaries, and a region is represented as a 2-complex with a connected interior, boundary, and exterior. Such an approach necessarily shares many similarities with graph-based representations of space. Using this method, 33 relations have been identified between lines, 23 additional relations with complex lines, and 19 relations between a region and a line [21].

The Region Connection Calculus (RCC), however, handles the definition of regions in a different fashion [38] than either of these methods. RCC is introduced as an alternative to point-based constructions, considering regions as objects unto themselves, instead of derived objects. The definition of a *region* is also more nuanced, with an RCC-region being of arbitrary dimension, as long as all regions within a scene are of similar dimension. A pair of regions is considered connected if their closures share a common point, as the regions themselves do not consist of points. RCC can capture the same eight base relations between regions (albeit with a different naming convention), but cannot capture points or lines.

Beyond points, lines, and regions, another set of simple objects and their relations requires three dimensions. Utilizing a 3-dimensional embedding one also gains access to objects such as simple volumes, and surfaces [28, 47]. These objects, along with the various constructions of points, lines, and regions can also lead to the construction of more complex spatial entities.

3.2   Complex Objects

The simple regions are but a small subset of the possibilities that may apply in $\mathbb{R}^2$. Regions with holes and regions with separations are additional categories of object worth considering. As with the simple objects, point-set topology, algebraic topology, and alternative methods like RCC provide unique means to generate complex objects.

The simplest method to construct holed regions or regions with separations is through point-set topology alone: one must utilize the set difference operation for holes [32, 44, 45] and the union operation for separations [14, 32, 41]. Additional approaches consider a hole to be an independent or composite object [7, 38, 46]. Reasoning with holed regions has been covered extensively, with 23 relations existing between a region and a holed region [45], and 152 relations between two holed regions [44].

RCC can also accommodate regions with holes or separations, and its extensions cover additional features, such as concavities [8]. Additional, nuanced holed and separated configurations are shown (Figure 4):

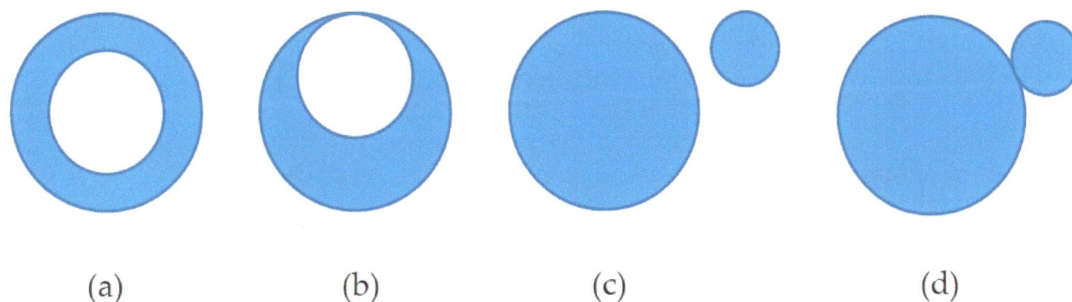

(a)	(b)	(c)	(d)

Figure 4: Four complex objects: (a) a region with a hole, (b) a region with a fringed hole, (c) a region with a separation, and (d) a region with a weak separation.

3.3   Mixed Objects

It is also possible to produce objects of mixed type, such as instances where a single object is constructed from a line and a region, for example. These relations expand on the previously defined objects, and the result is a significant number of additional configurations, for instance, using a point-set methodology to generate a set of spiked regions created by the union of a region and a simple line [14]. Alternatively, Clementini and Di Felice expand beyond the point-set method to include additional features such as lines with self-intersections [8]. Schneider and Behr provide an extensive accounting of relations that exist between the complex objects they define, which may contain separations, holes, and cycles [41]. There are, for instance, 33 relations between such complex regions, 82 relations between complex lines, and 43 relations between a complex region and a complex line. Relations between groups of points are also considered. These complex objects are specialized, including lines with bifurcations, regions with handles and spikes, cyclic lines, disconnected points, and other configurations.

4 Sets of Objects

After choosing an embedding space and which objects to represent, the specificity of the chosen representation needs to be considered. So far a small number of models capturing binary sets of relations have been explored. Deriving the topological relations between a pair of spatial objects based on intersection is the foundation of models such as the 4-intersection and the 9-intersection. In such model the content of intersections is recorded as either empty or nonempty. This property is topologically invariant. The resulting matrix defines a unique relation between two objects, such as *meet* or *disjoint*. However, there are alternative models that rely on different invariant properties, such as connectedness. An exemplar of an approach utilizing connectivity is RCC.

It is possible to not only expand on these models (and others like them) to incorporate extra features into a representation (such as dimension), but it is also possible to use existing knowledge and relations to reason about additional relations. One can also choose to represent all possible relations between spatial entities in concert, without relying on strictly defined relations between sets of objects.

4.1 Binary Relations

Often objects within a scene are related through a set of binary relations. This representation is the most common, and is the category representing both the 9-intersection and RCC. The eight region-region relations [21, 38], or the 19 region-line relations are examples of this [22]. It has been shown that these theories can handle the representation of complex objects of differing construction, although scenes that are designed to handle specific features and complexities may fare better.

The 9^+-intersection is such an approach [29]. While the 9-intersection utilizes a 3x3 matrix, the 9^+ method allows multiple separations for the boundary, interior, or exterior of the spatial object—each cell of the matrix can be further subdivided. The below matrix (Eqn. 2) divides the boundary of a directed line (DLine) object D into two components, a head (∂_1) and a tail (∂_2).

$$R(D,R) = \begin{pmatrix} D^o \cap R^o & D^o \cap \partial R & D^o \cap R^- \\ \begin{bmatrix} \partial_1 D \cap R^o \\ \partial_2 D \cap R^o \end{bmatrix} & \begin{bmatrix} \partial_1 D \cap \partial R \\ \partial_2 D \cap \partial R \end{bmatrix} & \begin{bmatrix} \partial_1 D \cap R^- \\ \partial_2 D \cap R^- \end{bmatrix} \\ D^- \cap R^o & D^- \cap \partial R & D^- \cap R^- \end{pmatrix} \tag{2}$$

Using this method, Kurata expanded the existing framework of binary spatial relation and represent the relations for DLine-Region relations in $\mathbb{R}^3$, as well as DLine-Line and Region-HoledRegions in numerous of embedding spaces, displaying the descriptive power of this extension. Similar work has led to the development of relations between additional directed line segments utilizing a modified 9-intersection [28, 30].

Another fine-grained approach allows for an advanced expression of an *overlap* relation between two objects (Eqn. 3), where:

x is the number of connected components of $A \cap B$,
a is the number of connected compoenents of $A \setminus B$,
b is the number of connected componenets of $B \setminus A$, and
o is the number of connected components of $(A \cup B)^o$.

$$[A,B] = \begin{pmatrix} x & a \\ b & o \end{pmatrix} \tag{3}$$

Using a specialized *overlap matrix* (Eqn. 3), it is possible to take a single topological relation (overlap, loosely) and distinguish 23 simple variations [26]. This approach allows one to determine the similarity between different overlap configurations. The expression of similarity in the topological setting is important and leads to the distinction between the coarse topological relations we have encountered such as the eight region-region relations, and detailed topological relations, which also may consider sequence, dimension, type of intersection, crossing direction, boundedness, and the compliment relationship [16, 19].

Specifying the dimension of an intersection, for instance, can bring the representation of a scene closer to the reality that it purports to represent. While a specification for overlap has been investigated already, consider two overlap scenes that need intersection dimension to distinguish them (Figures 5a and 5b).

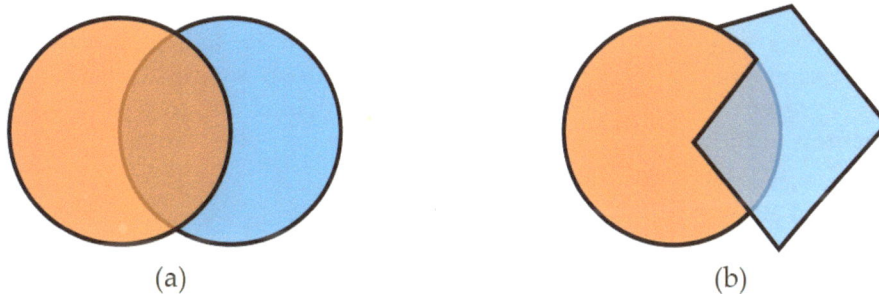

(a)   (b)

Figure 5: Two overlapping objects: (a) a simple 0-dimensional overlap and (b) an overlap with a 1-dimensional component.

Both scenes have been described as overlap, but they clearly have additional distinctions, such as a 1-dimensional crossing versus a 0-dimensional crossing. Egenhofer and Franzosa investigated the content invariant of the 4-intersection in an attempt to more fully represent the relations between two objects [19]. The resulting theory requires not only dimension, but also intersection sequence, intersection type (touching or crossing), and the relationship with the compliment. This determines whether or not a boundary component is bounded by a partition of the exterior.

The sequence is also of particular interest; in any setting that records more than a course representing of a scene, allowing a pair of objects to exhibit multiple intersections, it is possible to place them in sequence. This allows for distinctions such as (touch, cross, cross), and (cross, touch, cross), for instance. Without an associated ordering additional scene specification will still result in ambiguity.

4.2   Similarity, Composition, and Simplification

Such detailed relations are but one means of comparing the similarity between different scenes of spatial objects. The need for similarity assessment when handling spatial data arises from the complexity and quantity of relations being stored [36]. Another method of representing the similarity between binary topological relations is through a conceptual neighborhood graph [5, 10, 18, 22, 24]. By comparing the matrices for each relation in a 9-intersection setting it is possible to determine the conceptual distance between them. The matrices for *meet* and *disjoint* (Fig. 1) only vary in the content of their boundary-boundary intersection, so they are conceptually close, for instance.

When two topological relations are known, and those relations share an object in common, it is possible to infer an additional relation. For instance, if A equals B, and B overlaps C, one infers that A also overlaps C. The systematic reasoning behind this is known as composition and can be expressed in terms of inference rules about point sets [15]. The composition table for region-region relations contains 64 entries, and through this composition it is possible that two region-region relations yield a unique result (27 entries), a mixed result (34 entries), or the universal relation (3 entries). In the case of the universal relation no information is gained through the composition, but in all other instances composition allows some degree of information to be derived for additional relations without the explicit representation of those relation. Composition is also useful when considering the relation between a part of a compound object, such as the hole in a holed region, and another object in the scene [25].

Both approaches, neighborhood and composition, can be leveraged to simplify the process of reasoning over sets to topological relations by relaxing the constraints needed to represent a given relation [15, 39] and can also be used to bridge topological representations of different granularity [13].

4.3   Detailed Scene Representation

An even more detailed methodology can allow the construction of spatial scenes that relate an arbitrary number of objects in concert or is able to express an arbitrary amount of complexity between two objects. These complex scenes may make use of simple or complex objects within some predefined embedding space.

Other recent examples involving dimension, touching/crossing, and sequence include the o-notation and its extension, the i-notation. Both approaches were specifically designed to accommodate an arbitrary number of regions and intersections [32, 33]. A scene in *o-notation* is described in terms of the individual intersections each object participates in. Each intersection is represented by a string, and strings are recorded in sequence by walking around each object in a clockwise traversal (Eqn. 4).

$$\partial A_{comp}: o_S(dim, T, C) \tag{4}$$

For an *o-notation* string ∂A_{comp} represents the boundary component of a region A. S is the collection of regions the boundary component is currently outside of, *dim* is the qualitative length of the intersection (0 or 1), T is the collection of region boundaries subject to a touch relation in the specified intersection, and C is the collection of region boundaries subject to a cross relation.

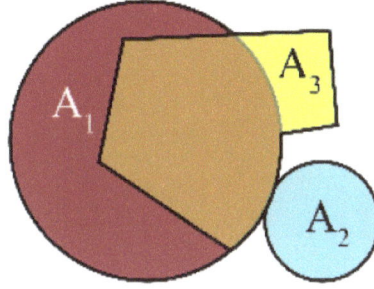

Figure 6: An example scene featuring 3 regions.

The notation for Figure 6 results in three *o-notation* strings (Eqs. 5-7) in order to completely represent the depicted scene.

$$\partial A_1 : o_{\{A_2,A_3\}}(0,\emptyset,A_3)o_{\{A_2\}}(1,\emptyset,A_3)o_{\{A_2\}}(0,A_2,A_3)o_{\{A_2\}}(1,\emptyset,A_3) \tag{5}$$

$$\partial A_2 : o_{\{A_1,A_3\}}(0,\{A_1,A_3\},\emptyset) \tag{6}$$

$$\partial A_3 : o_{\{A_1,A_2\}}(1,\emptyset,A_1)o_{\{A_1,A_2\}}(0,A_2,A_1)o_{\{A_1,A_2\}}(1,\emptyset,A_1)o_{\{A_2\}}(0,\emptyset,A_1) \tag{7}$$

The *o-notation* and *i-notation* are further empowered by their ability to discern holes and separations within an object, and created by an ensemble of objects, through the use of the *topological hull*. The *hull* operation reduces separated objects into their path connected components, and fills holes within objects so they can be identified through set difference. It is also possible to ascertain whether an ensemble of objects surround another object, using this method (Figure 7).

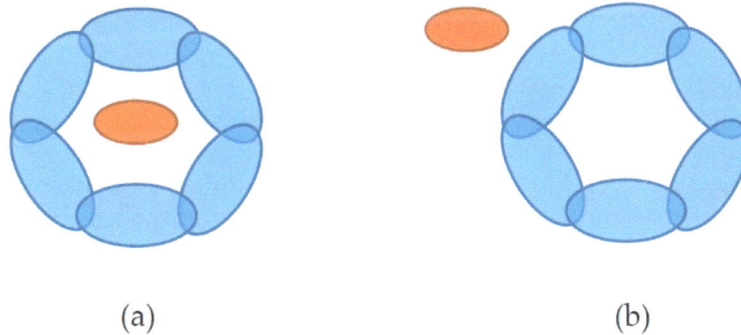

(a)   (b)

Figure 7: Two scenes where (a) a region is surrounded by an ensemble and (b) where a region is outside of an ensemble.

An alternative approach, utilizing a graph structure instead of strings of relations, is MapTree [46]. MapTree utilizes combinatorial maps to build a model of space based on nodes and edges in order to partition space and develop a containment hierarchy (Figure 8).

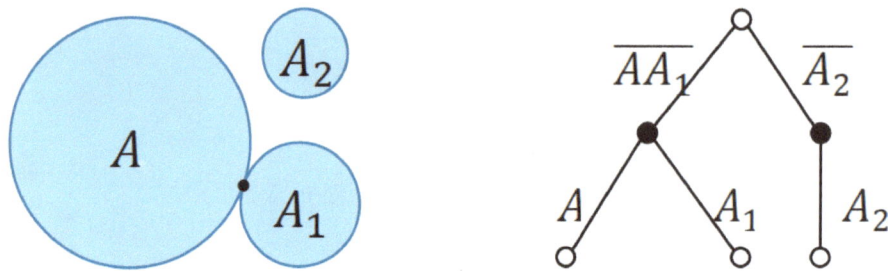

Figure 8: A Complex scene modeled with MapTree [46].

MapTree is able to represent complex objects, such as those with separations (Fig. 8), as well as holed objects, and scenes containing an arbitrary number of objects, but does not distinguish objects individually. These methods and those like them go beyond the traditional approach of representing a scene through an arbitrary number of binary relations, allowing a representation potentially much closer to the true form of the objects being described.

5   Conclusions

Ultimately there are many models and methods for describing spatial scenes, and many more problems awaiting novel solutions. This work seeks to provide a small snapshot of the variability present in topological modeling, focusing on the impact of various representation choices rather than a deep representation of the spatial domain. Even with the restricted to set of models represented it is possible to identify many competing interpretations. The selection of embedding space, the objects of interest, the set of described relations, and the number of objects being represented all impact the choices we make when reasoning about a scene and determining which model is the correct fit for the problem at hand.

The advancement of theories involving the representation of more than two objects [32, 33, 46] can lead to new and interesting developments. However, the added detail that may be captured in such a scene is often at odds with more familiar (and simpler) semantics, such as "this meets that", which makes natural language descriptions a more difficult target. Additionally, capturing the similarity between two scenes of complex objects, or even modeling how such a scene might transition from one possible state to the next, provide interesting research challenges going forward that build on the rich theories and tools developed over the past several decades.

Acknowledgments

This work was partially supported by NSF Grants IIS-1016740 (PI: Max Egenhofer).

References

[1]   Adams, C., Franzosa, R. *Introduction to Topology: Pure and Applied*. Pearson Prentice Hall (2008).

[2]   Alexandroff, P. *Elementary Concepts of Topology*. Dover Publications (New York, 1961).

[3]   Allen, J. F. Maintaining Knowledge about Temporal Intervals. *Communications of the ACM, 26*(11), (1983), 832-843.

[4]   Barkowsky, T., Latecki, L., Richter, K. Schematizing Maps: Simplification of Geographic Shape by Discrete Curve Evolution. In: Freksa, C., Brauer, W., Habel, C., Wender, K. (eds.) Spatial Cognition II, (2000), 41–53.

[5]   Bruns, T. and Egenhofer, M. Similarity of Spatial Scenes. *Seventh International Symposium on Spatial Data Handling.* Delft, The Netherlands (1996) pp. 31-42.

[6]   Chen, J., Cohn, A. G., Liu, D., Wang, S., Ouyang, J., and Yu, Q. A Survey of Qualitative Spatial Representations. *The Knowledge Engineering Review, 30,* (2015), pp. 106-136.

[7]   Clementini, E., Di Felice, P., and Califano, G. Composite Regions in Topological Queries. *Information Systems* 20(7), (1995), 579-594.

[8]   Clementini, E. and Di Felice, P. A Model for Representing Topological Relationships Between Complex Geometric Features in Spatial Databases. *Information Sciences* 90(1-4), 121-136 (1996)

[9]   Cohn, A. G. A Hierarchical Representation of Qualitative Shape Based on Connection and Convexity. In *Spatial Information Theory A Theoretical Basis for GIS,* Springer Berlin Heidelberg. (1995) pp. 311-326.

[10]   Cohn, A., Bennett, B., Gooday, J., Gotts, N. Qualitative Spatial Representation and Reasoning with the Region Connection Calculus. *GeoInformatica* 1(3), (1997) 275-316.

[11]   Cohn, A., Hazarika, S.: Qualitative Spatial Representation and Reasoning: An Overview. Fundamenta Informaticae 46(1-2), (2001) 2-32.

[12]   Cohn, A., Renz, J.: Qualitative Spatial Representation and Reasoning. In: van Hermelen, F., Lifschitz, V., Porter, B. (Eds.) *Handbook of Knowledge Representation,* pp. 551-596 (2008)

[13]   Dube, M. P., and Egenhofer, M. J. Establishing similarity across multi-granular topological–relation ontologies. In *Quality of Context,* Springer Berlin Heidelberg, (2009) pp. 98-108).

[14]   Egenhofer, M. A Reference System for Topological Relations between Compound Spatial Objects. In: Heuser, C., Pernul, G. (Eds.) *Advances in Conceptual Modeling — Challenging Perspectives,* ER 2009 Workshops, Lecture Notes in Computer Science Vol. 5833, (2009) pp. 307-316.

[15]   Egenhofer, M. J. Deriving the Composition of Binary Topological Relations. *Journal of Visual Languages and Computing, 5*(2), (1994) 133-149.

[16]   Egenhofer, M. J. Query Processing in Spatial-Query-by-Sketch. *Journal of Visual Languages and Computing, 8*(4), (1997) 403-424.

[17]   Egenhofer, M. J. Spherical Topological Relations. *Journal on Data Semantics III,* (2005) pp. 25-49.

[18]   Egenhofer, M. J., and Al-Taha, K. K. Reasoning about Gradual Changes of Topological Relationships. In *Theories and methods of spatio-temporal reasoning in geographic space,* Springer Berlin Heidelberg. *(1992)* pp. 196-219.

[19] Egenhofer, M. J. and Franzosa, R. D. On the Equivalence of Topological Relations. International Journal of Geographical Information Systems 9(2), (1995) 133–152.

[20] Egenhofer, M., Franzosa, R.: Point-Set Topological Spatial Relations. International Journal of Geographical Information Systems 5(2), (1991) 161-174.

[21] Egenhofer, M. J. and Herring, J. Categorizing Binary Topological Relationships between Regions, Lines and Points in Geographic Database. Technical report, University of Maine (1991).

[22] Egenhofer, M. J., and Mark, D. M. Modelling Conceptual Neighbourhoods of Topological Line-Region Relations. *International journal of geographical information systems*, 9(5), (1995) 555-565.

[23] Egenhofer, M. J. and Sharma, J. Topological Relations Between Regions in R2 and Z2. In *Proceedings of the Advances in Spatial Databases*, Third International Symposium, SSD'93, Singapore, June 23–25. Lecture Notes in Computer Science 692, Springer (1993) 316–336.

[24] Egenhofer, M. J., Sharma, J., and Mark, D. M. A critical Comparison of the 4-intersection and 9-intersection Models for Spatial Relations: Formal Analysis. In *AUTOCARTO*). McMaster R. and Amrstrong M. (eds.), Minneapolis, MN, (1993) pp. 1-11.

[25] Egenhofer, M. J. and Vasardani, M. Spatial Reasoning with a Hole. In *Proceedings of the Spatial Information Theory*, 8th International Conference, COSIT 2007, Melbourne, Australia, September 19–23. Lecture Notes in Computer Science 4736, Springer, (2007) pp.303–320.

[26] Galton, A. Modes of Overlap. *Journal of Visual Languages and Computing* 9(1), (1998) pp.61-79.

[27] Galton, A. Spatial and Temporal Knowledge Representation. Earth Science Informatics 2(3), (2009) 169-187.

[28] Kurata, Y. From three-dimensional topological relations to contact relations. In *Developments in 3D Geo-Information Sciences*. Springer Berlin Heidelberg (2010) pp. 123-142.

[29] Kurata, Y.: The 9+-Intersection: A Universal Framework for Modeling Topological Relations. In: Cova, T., Miller, H., Beard, K., Frank, A., Goodchild, M. (eds.) *Geographic Information Science*. Park City, UT, LNCS 5266, Springer (2008) 181-198.

[30] Kurata, Y., Egenhofer, M.: The Arrow Semantic Interpreter. Spatial Cognition and Computing 8, 4, (2008) 306–332.

[31] Kurata, Y., Egenhofer, M.: The Head-Body-Tail Intersection for Spatial Relations Between Directed Line Segments. In: Raubal, M., Miller, H., Frank, A., Goodchild, M. (eds.) Geographic Information Science, Münster, Germany, LNCS 4197, (2006) 269–286.

[32] Lewis, J., Dube, M., Egenhofer, M. The Topology of Spatial Scenes in R^2. In: Tenbrink, T., Stell, J., Galton, A., Wood, Z. (eds.) Spatial Information Theory COSIT '13, Scarborough, UK, LNCS 8116, (2013) 495-515.

[33] Lewis, J. A., and Egenhofer, M. J. Oriented regions for linearly conceptualized features. In *Geographic Information Science*, Springer Berlin Heidelberg (2014) pp. 333-348.

[34] Morehouse, S.: GIS-Based Map Compilation and Generalization. In: Müller, J. C., Lagrange, J., Weibel, R. (eds.) GIS and Generalization: Methodology and Practice. Taylor&Francis, Bristol, PA (1995) pp. 21–30.

[35] Nedas, K. A., Egenhofer, M. J. Spatial-Scene Similarity Queries.*Transactions in GIS*, *12*(6), (2008) 661-681.

[36] Nedas, K. A., Egenhofer, M. J.. Spatial similarity queries with logical operators. In *Advances in Spatial and Temporal Databases,* Springer Berlin Heidelberg (2003) pp.430-448.

[37] Papadimitriou, C. H., Suciu, D., Vianu, V. Topological Queries in Spatial Databases. In *Proceedings of the fifteenth ACM SIGACT-SIGMOD-SIGART symposium on Principles of database systems, ACM* (1996) pp. 81-92.

[38] Randell, D., Cui, Z., Cohn, A.: A Spatial Logic Based on Regions and Connection. In: Third International Conference on Knowledge Representation and Reasoning, (1992) pp. 165-176.

[39] Rodríguez, M. A., Egenhofer, M. J., Blaser, A. D. Query Pre-Processing of Topological Constraints: Comparing a Composition-Based with Neighborhood-Based Approach. In *Advances in Spatial and Temporal Databases,* Springer Berlin Heidelberg (2003) pp. 362-379.

[40] Ruas, A., Lagrange, J.: Data and Knowledge Modelling for Generalization. In: Müller, J., Lagrange, J., Weibel, R. (eds.) GIS and Generalization: Methodology and Practice. Taylor&Francis, Bristol, PA, (1995) pp. 73–90.

[41] Schneider, M., Behr, T. Topological Relationships between Complex Spatial Objects. ACM Transactions on Database Systems 31(1), (2006) 39-81.

[42] Spanier, E. *Algebraic Topology* (McGraw-Hill Book Company, New York, 1966).

[43] Timpf, S., Volta, G., Pollock D., Egenhofer, M. A Conceptual Model of Wayfinding Using Multiple Levels of Abstraction. In: Frank A., Campari, I., Formentini, U. (eds.) Theories and Methods of Spatio-Temporal Reasoning in Geographic Space, Pisa, Italy, LNCS 639, (1992) 348–367.

[44] Vasardani, M. Egenhofer, M. J. Comparing Relations with a Multi-Holed Region. In Proceedings of the Spatial Information Theory, 9th International Conference, COSIT 2009, Aber Wrac'h, France, September 21–25. Lecture Notes in Computer Science 5756, Springer (2009) 159–176.

[45] Vasardani, M. Egenhofer, M. J. Single-Holed Regions: Their Relations and Inferences. In *Proceedings of the Geographic Information Science*, 5th International Conference, GIScience 2008, Park City, UT, USA, September 23–26. Lecture Notes in Computer Science 5266, Springer (2008) 337–353.

[46] Worboys, M. The Maptree: A Fine-Grained Formal Representation of Space. In: Xiao, N., Kwan, M., Goodchild, M., Shekhar, S. (eds.) *Geographic Information Science*. Columbus, OH, LNCS 7478, (2012) pp. 298-310

[47] Zlatanova, S. On 3D topological relationships. In *Database and Expert Systems Applications,* IEEE (2000), pp. 913-919.

Linked Landmark Data:
Toward the Automatic Detection of
Landmarks on the Web of Data

Teriitutea Quesnot

Center for Research in Geomatics, Laval University, 1055 Avenue du Séminaire,
Pavillon Louis-Jacques Casault, Quebec City, QC G1V 0A6, Canada

Abstract: Providing relevant landmark-based route instructions remains a decisive challenge in the field of spatial cognitive engineering. Firsts automatic landmark detection systems emerged in the early 2000's and relied on a heavy desktop architecture. Landmarks were usually detected through a Geographic Information System connected to a database that contained points of interest (POIs) potentially useful for navigation. This approach was not suitable for a web deployment, let alone a cloud computing one. The advent of Web 2.0 and Volunteered Geographic Information allowed researchers to move beyond the boundary of POIs. Place-based information shared by social web users constitutes a local geographic knowledge that is now accessible through APIs. However, it is important to keep in mind that landmarkness is a relative characteristic *per se*. Its measure primarily depends on the configuration of the environment, the surrounding objects, the context of navigation, and the traveler's spatial knowledge. Yet, taking those parameters into account by relying on isolated databases remains quite complex. In this way, I explain through this chapter the main reasons why I am convinced that the slow-growing sphere of linked data is worth exploring to overcome this gap.

Keywords: Landmarks, linked data, open data, RDF, wayfinding, web of data.

1 Introduction

Location-based services (LBS) became commonplace in everyday life. Among these services, navigational aid systems are constantly used by mobile device users. For instance, the Google Maps application gathered 54% of smartphone users in 2013 (against 44% for Facebook) [1]. This growing consumption and production of spatial data is an opportunity now taken to understand urban dynamics and to improve the management of the next generation of cities; commonly named *Smart Cities*. Specifically, the *smart mobility*, which is one of the main characteristics of a smart city, is defined by the three following aspects: the accessibility of urban places and services, the presence of sustainable transport systems, and the availability of relevant (spatial) information for communication systems [2].

In this context, *mobility* is not only a matter of transportation. Helping people to better *read* the environment and to quickly reach a destination is a major concern. To address this need, navigational aid systems should ideally be compatible with human spatial communication and reasoning. In order to match as accurately as possible with users' mental maps, navigation systems should include landmarks inside traditional street name-based instructions. Indeed, research that investigated the role of landmarks found that their inclusion inside route instructions helps people to better memorize itineraries and orient themselves [3].

Those findings were highlighted in the early 2000's but one can notice that current web mapping platforms (e.g. Google Maps) do not provide such information in their verbal instructions. Actually, designing a system that automatically identifies relevant landmarks (i.e. ALDS) is harder than it looks. I will support this statement in the following section through a brief state of art about the concept of landmark. Furthermore, landmarks are necessarily extracted from *data*. To my knowledge, all the solutions proposed for the automatic detection of landmarks rely on the exploitation of data extracted from isolated databases. This approach implies several limits that I summarize in the third section. Since the measure of the landmarkness needs to establish *links* between data, I do argue that research in the area of ALDS should address the potential of *linked data*. I notably propose a first approach for identifying landmarks through the web of data in the final section.

2   Landmarks Within the Field of GIScience

2.1   A Brief History of Landmarks

In his work on the *imageability* of the city in the early sixties, Lynch clearly formalized the concept of *landmark* [4]. According to him, a landmark is a feature that is sufficiently prominent to be memorized by individuals and recalled when necessary. Specifically, it is a *visual marker* that gives global orientation information to travelers. In 1975, Siegel and White proposed a theory of the acquisition of human spatial knowledge called *Landmark-Route-Survey* [5]. Their *sequential* theory suggests that landmarks constitute the core of human spatial knowledge. In this way, landmark knowledge appears before the route and survey knowledge in the spatial learning process.

In the same vein, Golledge proposed his theory of *anchor points*. He suggests that landmarks are hierarchically structured according to three levels [6]. The first one embraces primary landmarks, which are highly familiar places such as homes and workplaces. The second level includes often-visited venues like marketplaces, whereas the third one gathers rarely practiced places (e.g. a venue visited during vacations). Research conducted between the 80's and 90's focused on the concept of *points of reference* and the evaluation of cognitive distances. In the late 90's, Lovelace et al. categorized landmarks according to their *locations* [7]. More precisely, the authors proposed four types of landmarks: (i) *on-route points*, which unlike (ii) *off-route points*, are used by travelers to ensure the route control, (iii) *choice points*, which unlike (iv) *potential choice points*, are located around an intersection where a turn is scheduled in the itinerary.

Finally, Sorrows and Hirtle proposed a typology of landmarks based on three categories [8]. According to them, the characteristics of a landmark are essentially *visual, structural,* and *cognitive*. Visual landmarks are similar to Lynch's landmarks. They are visually remarkable and highly visible from a long distance. Structural landmarks are associated with advantageous positions such as the intersection of major streets. Finally, cognitive landmarks (sometimes described as *semantic* landmarks) are outstanding because of their historical and cultural significance or their atypical function (e.g. a monument surrounded by offices). Such landmarks are particularly meaningful for travelers (i.e. subjective landmarks). Raubal and Winter adapted Sorrows and Hirtle's landmark typology when they formalized the first model of landmarkness applied to the facades of buildings [9].

2.2 Major Findings Around Landmark Saliencies

The measure of visual salience is crucial since visually prominent objects generally grab our attention. In fact, people tend to *unintentionally* pick-up and store distinctive useful objects while traveling [10]. An important thing to keep in mind is that visual salience remains a *relative* property. For instance, a red house - which is a color known to grab attention - surrounded by other red houses will obviously not stand out from the environment. However, the main "advantage" of such salience is that the factors that contribute to its significance are quite similar from one observer to another [11]. Therefore, the computation of visual salience can be easily done by relying on specific attributes such as the *color* of the object, its *area* and *height*, and its *proximity to road* (cf. [9, 12, 13, 14]). As a complement, Winter introduced the notion of *advance visibility* by assuming that buildings highly visible from a long distance tend to grab travelers' attention [15]. The author proposed to combine the *visibility coverage* of the buildings and *their orientation compared to the road*.

Research around structural salience aimed to locate the ideal position of the landmark when a turn is required in the scheduled itinerary. Researchers clearly focused on landmark candidates located at *decision points* (i.e. Lovelace et al.'s choice points) since references to landmarks in people's route instructions are quite higher from those areas [7]. Specifically, Klippel and Winter significantly enriched Raubal and Winter's model [16]. According to them, venues located *before* the intersection and along the *same direction as the turn* are ideal structural landmarks. Those assumptions have already been empirically supported [17, 14]. Recently, Quesnot and Roche additionally found that the side where travelers move compared to the road also influences the landmark selection process. Indeed, the travelers' field of view varies according to this parameter and obviously interferes in the selection of landmarks.

The example of the red houses single-handedly summarizes the concept of semantic landmarks. Indeed, a red house surrounded by other houses of the same color will not grab the observer's attention, unless he (she) is familiar with this particular house. In this way, unlike visual and structural saliencies, semantic salience is based upon subjective features that are often recognized by a small group of people or even one person. It deals with people's mental representations of space. Measuring this salience is therefore more complex than the two other saliencies; which remain perceptual *per se*. Consequently, the measure of landmark semantic salience has been limited for a while to specific indicators, especially the *historical and cultural significance* of a place (e.g. [9]), its *function* (e.g. [12]), its *name brevity*, and its *ubiquity and familiarity* (e.g. [13]). With the advent of Volunteered Geographic Information (VGI) [18], researchers extended the notion of semantic salience by adding the social dimension (cf. [19]). Semantic landmarks remained a theory-based suggestion until recently. Their usefulness is now empirically supported (cf. [20, 14]).

2.3   Automatic Landmark Detection Systems

GIScientists relied on the conceptual framework previously presented to design systems that automatically detect landmarks (ALDS). They notably used Raubal and Winter's formal model of landmarkness to reach this goal ([9]). Concretely, ALDS are usually based on a *route* knowledge approach. They provide travelers relevant landmarks along an itinerary, especially at decision points (i.e. where a turn is scheduled). The landmark extraction is divided into three main steps. The first one consists in performing a neighborhood analysis at each decision point. Once potential landmark candidates selected, an analysis of their attributes is then performed. The last step is the selection of the outlier, i.e. the candidate of which attributes stand out the most from the others [19].

Two main generations of ALDS succeeded. The first one typically relied on a GIS that was connected to a spatial database. This database contained geographic features with sufficient attributes to compute landmark saliencies. I consider the solution proposed by Elias as the first generation of ALDS ([12]). Thanks to a cadastral database, Elias had an access to several building properties (e.g. size, height, orientation to road, etc.) for performing relevant salience scores. In this case, the outlier was selected by using Quilan's ID3 algorithm. Actually, this approach was limited to a GIS installed on a *single* computer. It was therefore not suitable for a web deployment. The second generation of ALDS attempted to overcome this gap by exploiting web map servers (e.g. Geoserver) and web map clients (e.g. *OpenLayers*). These technologies allow developers to display geographic features on a web map, but also - and most importantly - to perform several spatial queries just as a GIS would do. The work of Duckham et al. [13] remains the most representative example. They assigned a landmarkness score to each top-level category associated with a set of 170,000 POIs (e.g. Gas station). Their algorithm, named Core Landmark Navigation Model, was implemented on the Australian route service *Whereis*. By relying on the pre-established landmarkness scores, this platform was able to pick-up relevant landmarks from the POI database. Until its recent update, Whereis was the only web mapping platform that provided landmark-based route instructions.

These solutions remain a significant achievement in the field of spatial cognitive engineering but they still suffer from several drawbacks. Sadeghian and Kantardzic [21] listed six shortcomings that affect ALDS: (1) ALDS focus on objective attributes and neglect subjective factors; (2) those systems work on the assumption that the salience indicators are all equivalent whereas it is not the case (see [14]); (3) they only focus on buildings and ignore other types of object (e.g. trees); (4) ALDS only provide landmarks at decision points whereas both on-route and off-route landmarks are also useful (see [7]); (5) the issue of "false landmarks" is not addressed, and (6), experiments carried out to assess the reliability of the ALDS remain perfectible. It is important to notice that half of the listed issues is directly linked to the *data* used to measure the landmarkness (issues 1, 3, and 5). Exploiting *relevant data* is decisive in the automatic landmark detection context. Thus, I review in the following section the main (geographic) data that can be harvested to perform meaningful salience scores and to extract reliable landmarks accordingly.

3 Using Geographic Data for Landmark Extraction

3.1 Proprietary Data

Most of the spatial data usable for the automatic detection of landmarks are currently more *closed* than open. These proprietary data are now accessible from application programming interfaces (APIs) but their usages are restricted at the same time. The purpose of this subsection is not to provide an exhaustive list of these restrictions. Instead, I will focus on three companies that provide a large part of the geographic data that could be efficiently used to detect landmarks, namely: *Google*, *Foursquare*, and *Facebook*.

Google launched *Google Map Maker* in June 2008. This service allows Internet users to update the database of Google Maps. Like *OpenStreetMap* (OSM), contributors are able to add points, lines, polygons, and specify basic information (e.g. the name of the entity, its category, etc.). The main difference between the two platforms is that once created, geographic data become an exclusive property of Google. Before any online publishing, Google systematically verifies data freshly produced. Plus, they are not retrievable from the Google API. They are actually downloadable from a single hyperlink. For the moment, data from 64 countries are available; of which 62 are located in Africa and South-East Asia (the two remaining are Haiti and Chile). In parallel, Google proposes to retrieve useful information about its georeferenced places (e.g. name, location information, address, phone number, review ratings, etc.) through the *Google Places* API. These data are useful for computing both visual and structural salience scores. Unfortunately, information related to Google Plus check-ins cannot be harvested. Furthermore, the copy and the export of Google data are highly restricted. Saving content to a third party service or use it to create a personal database is strictly prohibited by the Terms of Service of the API.

The Location-Based Social Network (LBSN) Foursquare was created in 2009. The company launched Swarm in 2014, a complementary platform that now hosts the entire geosocial component of Foursquare (especially the check-in feature). The database of Foursquare currently contains 65 million of venues. It is constantly enriched by a community of 55 million of users who published more than 7 billion of check- ins. Useful data about venues can be easily harvested through the Foursquare API. The location information of the venue, its name, its address, and its category, as well as the number of check-ins, geolocated likes, and tips are all retrievable. As demonstrated by Quesnot and Roche [14, 19], these data are not limited to buildings and can be exploited to compute relevant semantic salience scores. The platform policy of Foursquare is less restrictive than Google. However, developers are not allowed to combine Foursquare data with any other location data. For instance, one cannot mix

Google Plus and Foursquare check-ins to compute a single check-in score. In the same vein, Facebook allows its users to publish check-ins and geolocated likes. Those place-based data are also retrievable through its API (Facebook Graph API). Nonetheless, Facebook Policy remains more flexible than the two others. It only engages developers to keep Facebook data up to date and forbid them to sell these data to any third party.

3.2   Open Data

Useful geospatial information can be harvested from open databases. Open data are released either by governments or by citizens (VGI). The *data.gov* US Government's website is one of the most important open data repository. It has initiated a movement that is now followed by other countries (e.g. Australia, Canada, China, France, Germany, Japan, Russia). Among the 158,000 US datasets currently available, almost 101,000 are *geospatial*. Given the size of this repository, I will not list all the datasets that can be exploited for extracting landmarks. Having said that, one must keep in mind that these data are not *uniformly* released. On the one hand, some themes are only available for few states. On the other hand, the data structure associated with a specific theme might differ from one state (or city) to another. Therefore, designing a database fed by these datasets might be complex. Because current ALDS are based on a single database, they cannot rely on such datasets for the moment.

Table 1: Relevant attributes of OSM *Buildings* and their occurrences for computing salience scores (July 2015).

Key	Description	Occurrence	Salience
levels	Number of floors	4,941,217	Visual
roof:shape	Shape of the roof	682,129	Visual
use	Function	627,286	Semantic
material	Material of the facades	435,935	Visual
roof:colour	Color of the roof	261,888	Visual
roof:material	Material of the roof	212,056	Visual
part	Noticeable part of the building	188,922	Semantic
colour	Color of the facades	177,256	Visual
height	Actual height (meters)	40,811	Visual
architecture	Building historically remarkable	7,968	Semantic
shape	Global shape of the building	901	Visual

OSM is the most advanced open cartographic platform on the Web. It provides a huge amount of geographic data that are all based on the same structure. Plus, they are distributed under the Open Data Commons Open Database License since 2012. They can be modified but on the other hand, they must be released under the same license. In my opinion, this platform remains the most relevant open data provider for computing salience scores, especially the visual and semantic ones. Concretely, *buildings* are a specific OSM map feature of which attributes can be efficiently exploited for the detection of landmarks. They are associated with several useful *keys* (i.e. attributes) that are summarized in Table 1. As shown, 3 of these 11 keys can contribute to the measure of the semantic salience (cf. [9, 12, 19]) whereas the others are more appropriate for the visual one. In addition, other relevant OSM features such as *historic, natural, places, shop* and *tourism* can be similarly exploited. Alternatively, Richter and Winter attempted to engage OSM users in the enrichment of a landmark database [22]. They developed *OpenLandmarks*, an OSM add-on that allows contributors to mark up any object that could serve as a landmark. However, this initiative did not succeed because landmark-based route instructions are not enough publicized.

3.3 Issues and Limitations

Current ALDS solutions systematically rely on a *single* spatial database (cf. [13]). The computation of landmark saliencies requires the combination of various types of data. For instance, data that contain information about buildings (e.g. from OSM) are essential for computing visual salience scores whereas place-based data (e.g. geolocated Facebook Likes or Foursquare check-ins) are more appropriate for the semantic salience. Yet, combining such geographic data into a *single* spatial database is a hard task. First of all, the combination of data that come from different providers is rather limited, or even forbidden (cf. section 3.1). Also, depending on the provider, the same place can be associated with different location information (lat/long), even if the data are georeferenced in the same coordinate reference system. In addition, these data might not necessarily belong to the same geometry type. For instance, Foursquare only provides point-based information while OSM also releases lines and polygons.

The issue of data quality also needs to be risen. Unlike Google, Foursquare does not verify the location accuracy of the content when it is created. In practice, the coordinates of the venue are first determined through the user's device. The accuracy depends on several parameters; in which the quality and the type of network. Actually, users are able to manually adjust the position of the venue on a base map. However, they do not necessarily care about the accuracy of the location information because their main goal is to communicate through places. They are producing data about places and not data centered on the location information [23]. This issue is less encountered with Facebook data since the position of the place is first geocoded from the address specified by the user.

Conflicts are not limited to locations and geometries. It is not unusual to come across two or more geographic entities that refer to the same *place*. This conflict is mostly related to either *language-based* or *label-based* issues (cf. Table 2). Specifically, a place can be named differently according to the language used (e.g. English *versus* French) and the label used (e.g. ten *versus* 10). Finally, another issue that I call *"set of scales"* [19] should also be addressed here because juggling with multiple scales cannot be avoided in the context of landmark detection. For example, a mall that hosts different shops is actually the most relevant landmark candidate because it is the only building visible from outside. However, users usually publish check-ins about the shops located inside the mall. This issue is complex to bypass because the system is not aware of the relationship between the shops and the mall.

To conclude, it is important to remember that landmarks are far from being limited to a place in its wholeness. Indeed, any observable item (e.g. small objects or specific parts of buildings) might be used as a landmark while navigating. For instance, this could be a remarkable signboard, a flag, or any other noticeable signs associated with a venue. OSM provides such type of information but to my best knowledge, it remains the only available source.

Table 2: Label-based and language-based issues: the example of the *Le Jules Verne* restaurant (Paris). Facebook data were harvested through the Graph API V2.3 on 3 April 2015.

Facebook Label	Check-ins	Likes
Restaurant Le Jules Verne au Somment De La Tour Eiffel	26465	872
Restaurant Jules Verne on top of the Eiffel Tower	3622	402
Restaurant Jules Vernes, En Haut De La Tour Effeil !	522	37
Jules Verne Eifell Tour Paris	52	10

4   Exploring the Web of Data to Detect Landmarks

4.1   What Are (Geo)Linked (Open) Data?

Nelson's hypertext concept was notably applied by Berners-Lee when he invented the *World Wide Web* by linking *documents* on the Internet. The architecture of the Web is composed of three interrelated components: (1) *HTTP* (Hypertext Transfer Protocol) is a way among others to ensure the communication between web browsers and servers, (2) *HTML* (Hypertext Markup Language) is the common representation language of the web documents, which are (3) identified and located by *URLs* (Unified Resource Locator). The initiative of *linked data* explores both the techniques and the technologies that can be used to link, structure, and publish *data* on the web.

Concretely, URLs are used to locate and identify *documents* that exist on the web. In the field of linked data, URIs (Universal Resource Identifier) are used to identify on the web any *entity* that exists *elsewhere* (e.g. a person, a building, etc.). The main objective is to link together entities identified by their URIs so anyone can reuse them. Resources on the web of data need to be identified but also *represented*. *RDF* (Resource Description Framework) is a language and a model used to reach that goal. Once published, linked data are retrieved by using a query language named *SPARQL* (Sparql Protocol And RDF Query Language). *Reasoning* about the links between data and their *semantics* is also crucial. In this way, *RDF-S* (Schema) and *OWL* (Web Ontology Language) are both languages used to design *ontologies*. Finally, *PROV is* used to produce structured metadata for tracing the *origin* of the linked data.

In this context, the *open data* movement is closely related to the initiative of linked data. Obviously, proprietary data can also be linked, but the ideal would be that linked data remain open at the same time. According to Berners-Lee, a "good" linked open data should be: (1) available on the web under an *open license*, (2) available as *machine-readable* structured data, and (3) as *non-proprietary* formats. In addition, he recommends users to (4) use *open standards* from W3C (RDF and SPARQL) to identify things, and (5), *link* their data to other people's data [24]. In the field of geographic information, GeoSPARQL, which is an OGC standard, proposes an ontology that supports both the representation of *geometries* and *features* and the spatial queries with the respect of *topological relationships* [25].

4.2   The Potential of the Web of Data for Landmark Extraction

Combining multiple kinds of geographic data is conceivable on the web of data. Therefore, I argue that the GIScience community should explore the potential of linked data for the landmark detection. The first generation of ALDSs relied on isolated architectures (e.g. [12]). The second one picked up landmarks from *a* (POI) database and pushed them on a web map platform; especially through verbal instructions (cf. [13]). In my opinion, the third generation might exploit the giant collaborative database of the web of data. Indeed, for computing relevant salience scores, ALDSs must pick up useful data from different providers without storing them into a single database (cf. section 3.3). For instance, the LinkedGeoData initiative makes the OSM information available in RDF and attempts to link it to other knowledge databases. Facebook also releases its data in the RDF format through its Open Graph API. Anyone who has an access token can retrieve the properties of each Facebook page in RDF *via* HTTP URIs (http://graph.facebook.com/URI). Check-ins, likes, "talking about" counts, and place categories are available and can be exploited for computing meaningful semantic salience scores. In addition to the *owl:sameAs* property, OSM and Facebook data can be linked together through *Silk* [26].

However, beyond the computation of the landmarkness scores, contextual parameters first need to be assessed. According to Richter and Winter, *"being a landmark is not a global characteristic of an object, but a function of parameters such as the individual that perceives and memorizes an environment, the communication situation, the decision at hand, and the time. The latter argument means that even prototypes cannot be considered prototypes in all cases, since there might be no such thing that is always, i.e., in any context a well- suited landmark."* ([27] p. 7). This quoted paragraph highlights the biggest challenge related to the development of systems that attempt to automatically detect landmarks. Indeed, a landmark is a *feature* that is *not absolute*. In this way, one cannot conceive an ontology that would formally establish relations so that feature A, compared to feature B, would be considered as a better landmark in every case. Features A and B are both *potential* landmarks *per se*. Otherwise, a global landmark database would already exist.

Research on landmark saliencies conducted over the past twenty years showed that landmarkness is firstly *contextual*. It clearly depends on the traveler's way of arriving and the turn scheduled in the route planed (cf. [16, 17,

15]). Personal spatial knowledge also impacts on the landmark selection (cf. [20, 14]). In addition, *time* is a decisive parameter since a place highly visible during daytime might be completely invisible at night [28]. These parameters must be taken into account *before* the computation of the landmark salience scores. In this way, *dynamically linking* data is the most relevant approach for extracting landmarks.

4.3   A First Step Toward the Detection of Landmarks through Linked Data

I will use Figure 1 to support my discourse. It represents a sketch of a fictional route followed by a pedestrian. Since the detection of landmarks is firstly context-dependent, one should first of all focus on this parameter. Except the mode of traveling, I distinguish the *traveler-based* from the *route-based* context. Actually, the way people travel (i.e. by foot, by car, or by public transport) falls into both of these categories. It impacts on the traveler's field of view, but also influences the itinerary to be followed. As Quesnot and Roche highlighted [14], the side of traveling compared to the road plays a fundamental role in the landmark selection process. This side can be easily assessed through the web of data in a static situation (e.g. when an individual plans a trip from a computer). For instance, the system can rely on the open gazetteer *Geonames* to retrieve sensible information for car drivers (i.e. one country is associated with one sense of driving). Otherwise, the traveler's position can be evaluated from a device such as a smartphone.

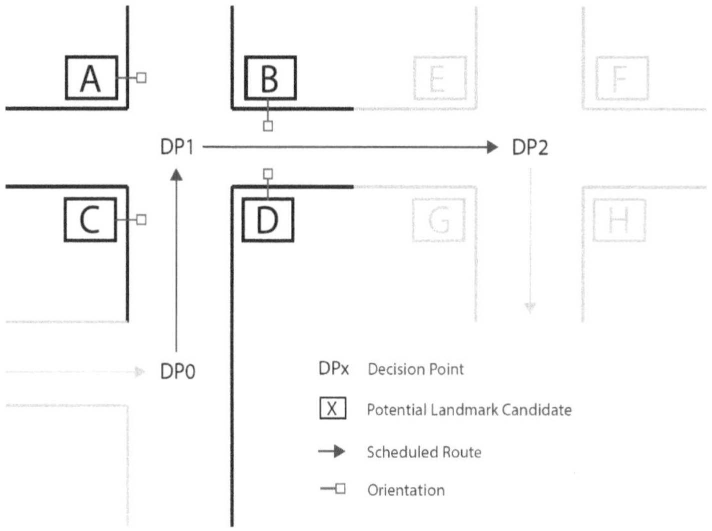

Figure 1: Fictional pedestrian route.

Hamburger and Röser [20] followed by Quesnot and Roche [14] empirically demonstrated that travelers' spatial knowledge interferes in the landmark selection process. The latter also found an association between the structural salience and the gender. Therefore, I propose to associate the traveler-based context with the traveler's *familiarity with the area* and the *gender*. Concretely, travelers and their attributes (i.e. gender, age, city, etc.) could be identified *via* an URI *per se*. For example, Facebook users are all identified by an HTTP URI. This statement rises up an issue related to the privacy that I will not cover here. Alternatively, that information could be directly picked up on the fly from the ALDS; with the user's consent.

The route-based context is also decisive. Studies conducted on the landmark structural salience ([16, 14, 17]) converge on the same conclusion: travelers favor landmark candidates located before the intersection and along the same direction as the turn. Therefore, the configuration of the route also needs to be assessed. To this end, I propose to define each portion of the route as a single triplet [*from-node,node,to-node*]. According to this proposition, the portion of the route related to the first figure is noted [*DP0,DP1,DP2*]. The couple [*DP0,DP1*] corresponds to the traveler's way of arriving whereas [*DP1,DP2*] represents the turn (a right turn in this case).

One may notice that each node of the route is actually a *decision point* (cf. Figure 1). In my opinion, one of the main challenges rests upon the implementation of the *Decision Point* class and its specification (cf. Figure 2). Indeed, decision points remain areas from where the references to landmarks are significant in people's wayfinding discourses [3]. Concretely, a decision point DP is firstly a geographic *feature*, i.e. an entity located in the physical world. This statement corresponds to [:DP → rdf:type → ogc:feature] in the abstract syntax of RDF graphs. Also, a decision point remains an *intersection* at the same time. According to the small taxonomy I propose in the third figure, the decision point DP0 is a T-intersection [:DP0 → rdf:type → its:T].

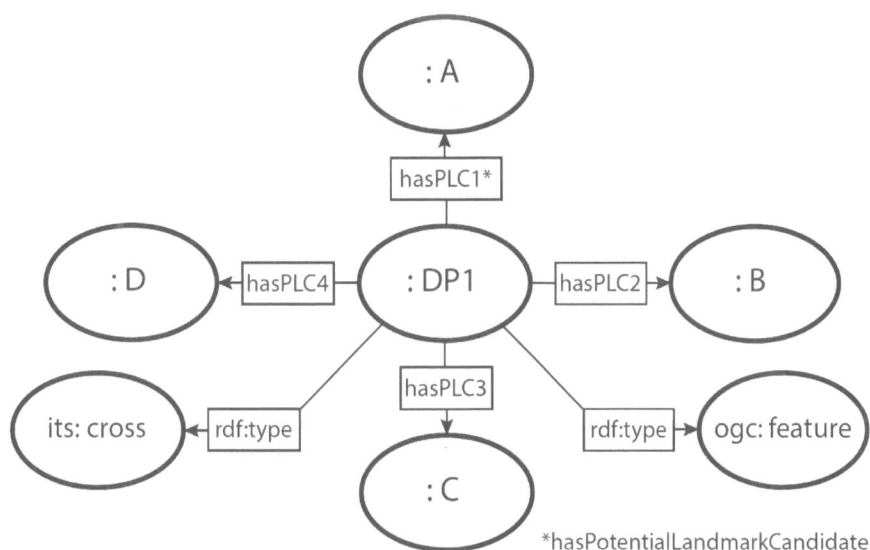

Figure 2: RDF graph of decision point 1 (abstract syntax).

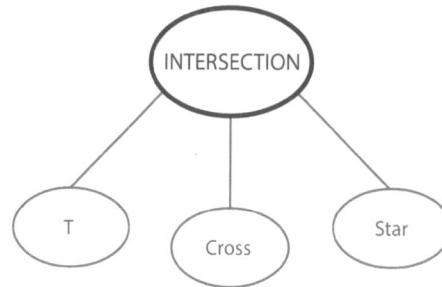

Figure 3: Taxonomy of the *Intersection* class.

In addition, I suggest selecting a limited number of potential landmark candidates according to the type of decision point. In this way, four landmark candidates should be selected for cross-like decision points whereas a T-intersection would only need three candidates. According to Figure 1, decision point 1 has four potential landmarks (A, B, C, and D). Like Elias's approach [12], I propose to select those candidates on the basis of their *proximity* to the decision point. Since each candidate of the set [A,B,C,D] is identified by an URI as a *geographic feature* ([ogc:feature]), one can easily access to its features. In this approach, the measure of both *visual* and *semantic* saliencies through OSM and Facebook linked data is clearly conceivable. Moreover, their relative position compared to the decision point (i.e. before or after it) and the direction of the turn (i.e. left or right) can be determined according to the route couples [*from-node,node*] (i.e. the way of arriving) and [*node,to-node*] (i.e. the turn). Those parameters are essential for the computation of the *structural* salience score and the *orientation score* of the landmark candidates. Unfortunately, the *visibility coverage* of the candidates cannot be computed with current spatial toolkits of the web of data. Therefore, the computation of the advance visibility score such as defined by Winter [15] is impossible for the moment.

To conclude this subsection, I summarized the proposed approach in the algorithm displayed on Figure 4. It works on the assumption that the traveler uses an ALDS on his (her) mobile device to plan a route. The selection of landmark candidates is made according to the user's attributes, the itinerary, and the salience scores. This algorithm is directly inspired from Quesnot and Roche's recent findings [14]. To sum up, their experiment consisted in asking participants to select landmarks along different intersections located in Quebec City. Participants followed predefined routes through Google Street View. They found that locals (i.e. people who knew the area) significantly favored semantic landmarks whereas strangers were more influenced by visual landmarks. Their results also show that women tended to focus on the places located along the same direction as the scheduled turn.

(i) Access to user's attributes through his (or her) personnal URI. **OTHERWISE**, ask user the appropriate information (i.e. the gender, the familiarity with the city, and the mode of traveling).

(ii) Generate a route R from the starting point to the arrival according to the mode of traveling.

(iii) **FOR EACH** turn scheduled in R:

    a. generate a street name-based route instruction STRI associated with the decision point (e.g. *Turn left on the Street X*);

    b. access to the attributes of each potential landmark candidate (PLC) from the Decision Point (DP) class;

    c. **FOR EACH** PLC, compute a visual salience score (VIS) and a semantic salience score (SEM);

    d. select the oustanding VIS (O-VIS) and the outstanding SEM (O-SEM);

    e. **IF** there is neither O-VIS nor O-SEM, **THEN** stop;

    f. **IF** there is no O-VIS and **IF** the user is a *stranger*, **THEN** stop;

    g. **IF** the user is *familiar with the city*, **THEN**:

        - **IF** there is no O-SEM, **THEN** the landmark candidate (LC) is the PLC with the O-VIS;

        - **OTHERWISE**, LC is the PLC with the O-SEM.

    h. **IF** the user is a *stranger* and a *male*, **THEN** LC is the PLC with the O-VIS;

    i. **IF** the user is a *stranger* and a *female*, **THEN**:

        - **IF** the PLC with the O-VIS is located at the *opposite* direction of the turn, **THEN** stop;

        - **OTHERWISE**, LC is the PLC with the O-VIS.

    j. Add ", at LC" to STRI (e.g. *Turn left on the Street X, at LC*).

Figure 4: Linked Landmark algorithm.

5 Conclusion and Future Work

I attempted to explore the web of data as an alternative to traditional ALDS approaches. Now that OGC standards and the *ad hoc* spatial query language GeosSPARQL are supported, I am convinced that one should focus on both the exploitation of linked data and the development of new techniques for the automatic extraction of relevant landmarks. Since data, tools, and standards related to the sphere of linked data are still in their early stages, I believe that the next generation of ALDSs will only appear in the medium term. Obviously, my position around the automatic detection of landmarks through linked data should be considered as a *starting point* and a way to encourage GIScientists to delve further into that issue. The ideas developed in the last section, especially the *Decision Point* class and the Linked Landmark algorithm are led to be updated (for example through an OWL ontology) or modified.

Acknowledgments

This chapter is a part of my Ph.D. research project. It is supported by the *Social Sciences and Humanities Research Council of Canada* (SSHRC) and the *Geothink* project thanks to my Ph.D. advisor *Stéphane Roche,* who is full professor at the Laval University Department of Geomatics. I would also like to sincerely thank *Stephan Winter* from the University of Melbourne for his valuable suggestions on the initial version of this chapter.

References

[1]   MARI, M. *Top global smartphone apps, who's in the top 10.* https://www.globalwebindex.net/blog/top-global-smartphone-apps, Accessed on 2015/04/02, 2013.

[2]   GIFFINGER, R., FERTNER, C., KRAMAR, H., KALASEK, R., PICHLER-MILANOVIC, N., AND MEIJERS, E. *Smart cities: ranking of European medium-sized cities.* Vienna, Austria: Centre of Regional Science (SRF), Vienna University of Technology, 2007.

[3]   DENIS, M., AND FERNANDEZ, G. The processing of landmarks in route directions. In *Representing space in cognition: interrelations of behaviour, language, and formal models,* T. Tenbrink, J. Wiener, and C. Claramunt, Eds. Oxford University Press. 2013, pp. 42-55

[4]   LYNCH, K. *The image of the city.* MIT Press, Cambridge, 1960.

[5]   SIEGEL, A. W., AND WHITE, S. H. The development of spatial representations of large scale environments. In *Advances in child development and behavior,* W. H. Reese, Ed. New-York, 1975.

[6]   GOLLEDGE, R. G. Representing, interpreting and using cognized environments. *Papers and proceedings of the Regional Science Association,* 41, (1978), 169-204.

[7]   LOVELACE, K. L., HEGARTY, M., AND MONTELLO, D. R. Elements of good route direction in familiar and unfamiliar environments. In *Spatial Information Theory. LNCS, vol. 1661,* C. Freksa and D. Mark, Eds. Springer, Berlin, 1999, pp. 65-82.

[8]   SORROWS, M. E., AND HIRTLE, S. C. The nature of landmarks for real and electronic spaces. In *Spatial Information Theory. LNCS, vol. 1661.* C. Freksa and D. Mark, Eds. Springer, Berlin, 1999, pp. 37-50.

[9]   RAUBAL, M., AND WINTER, S. Enriching wayfinding instructions with local landmarks. In *Geographic Information Science. LNCS, vol. 2478,* Egenhofer, M.J. and Mark, D. M., Eds. Springer, Berlin, 2002, pp. 243-259.

[10] JANZEN, G., AND VAN TURENNOUT, M. Selective neural representation of objects relevant for navigation. *Nature Neuroscience,* 7, (2004), 673-677.

[11] ITTI, L. Visual salience. *Scholarpedia,* 2, 9, (2007), 3327.

[12] ELIAS, B. Extracting landmarks with data mining methods. In *Spatial Information Theory. LNCS, vol. 2825,* Kuhn, W., Worboys, M. F. and Timpf, S., Eds. Springer, Berlin, 2003, pp. 243-259.

[13] DUCKHAM, M., WINTER, S., AND ROBINSON, M. Including landmarks in routing instruction. *Journal of Location Based Services,* 4, 1, (2010), 28-52.

[14] QUESNOT, T., AND ROCHE, S. Quantifying the significance of semantic landmarks in familiar and unfamiliar environments. In *Spatial Information*

Theory. LNCS, vol. 9368, Fabrikant, S.I., Raubal, M., Bertolotto, M., Davies, C., Freundschuh, S., Bell, S., Eds. Springer, Berlin, 2015, pp. 468-489.

[15] WINTER, S. Route adaptive selection of salient features. In *Spatial Information Theory. LNCS, vol. 2825*, Kuhn, W., Worboys, M. F. and Timpf, S., Eds. Springer, Berlin, 2003, pp. 349-361.

[16] KLIPPEL, A., AND WINTER, S. Structural salience of landmarks for route directions. In *Spatial Information Theory. LNCS, vol. 3693*, Cohn, A. G. and Mark, D. M., Eds. Springer, Berlin, 2005, pp. 347-362.

[17] RÖSER, F., HAMBURGER, K, KRUMNACK, A., AND KNAUFF, M. The structural salience of landmarks: results from an on-line study and a virtual environment experiment. *Journal of Spatial Science*, 57, 1, (2012), 37-50.

[18] GOODCHILD, M. F. Citizens as sensors: the world of volunteered geography. *GeoJournal*, 4, (2007), 211-221.

[19] QUESNOT, T., AND ROCHE, S. Measure of landmark semantic salience through geosocial data streams. *ISPRS International Journal of Geo-Information*, 4, 1, (2015), 1-31.

[20] HAMBURGER, K. AND RÖSER, F. The role of landmark modality and familiarity in human wayfinding. *Swiss Journal of Psychology*, 73, 4, (2014), 205-213.

[21] SADEGHIAN, P., AND KANTARDZIC, M. The new generation of automatic landmark detection systems: challenges and guidelines. *Spatial Cognition & Computation*, 8, (2008), 252-287.

[22] RICHTER, K. F., AND WINTER, S. Harvesting user-generated content for semantic spatial information: the case of landmarks in OpenStreetMap. In *Proceedings of the Surveying & Spatial Sciences Biennial Conference*. Wellington, NZ, 2011, pp. 75-86.

[23] QUESNOT, T., AND ROCHE, S. Platial or locational data? Toward the characterization of social location sharing. In *Proceedings of the 48th Annual Hawaii International Conference on System Sciences*. IEEE Computer Society Press, Washington, DC, 2015, pp. 1973-1982.

[24] BERNERS-LEE, T. *Linked data*. http://www.w3.org/DesignIssues/LinkedData.html, Accessed on 2015/04/02, 2009.

[25] BATTLE, R. AND KOLAS, D. Enabling the geospatial semantic web with parliament and GeoSPARQL. *Semantic Web - On linked spatiotemporal data and geo-ontologies*, 3, 4, (2012), 355-370.

[26] VOLZ, J., BIZER, C., GAEDKE, M., AND KOBILAROV, G. Discovering and maintaining links on the web of data. In *The Semantic Web - ISWC 2009. LNCS vol. 5823*, Bernstein, A., Karger, D. R., Heath, T., Feigenbaum, L., Maynard, D., Motta, E., and Thirunarayan, K., Eds. Springer, Berlin, 2009, pp. 650-665.

[27] RICHTER, K. F. AND WINTER, S. *Landmark: GIScience for intelligent services* Springer, Cham (Switzerland), 2014.

[28] WINTER, S., RAUBAL, M., AND NOTHEGGER, C. Focalizing measures of
      salience for wayfinding. In *Map-based Mobile Services*, Meng, L., Reichenbacher, T.,
      and Zipf, A., Eds. Springer, Heidelberg, 2005, pp. 125-139.

Place Properties

Maria Vasardani and Stephan Winter

Department of Infrastructure Engineering, The University of Melbourne, Parkville, Victoria 3010, Australia

Abstract: Place and space were antagonists in geographic information science for a long time, but not anymore. Place, it is argued here, is a location (in an environment, not in an empty space) with properties that give it 'shape and character' and which enable conversations about place. To realize this argument, place can be characterized by Alexander's theory of centers, where 15 structural properties that characterize a whole are assembled. This paper investigates these properties and their relationship to place by identifying theories within geographic information science that can be employed for their formalization. We argue therefore that we already have some tools to observe these properties for characterizing places, while many traditional issues with modeling place — for example, their typical lack of crisp boundaries, their subjective notion, and their reliance on context — may no longer pose a problem.

Keywords: Place, wholeness, centers, spatial cognition, spatial concept formalization.

1 Introduction

Philosopher Jeff Malpas argues that "...place is such a central and ubiquitous concept across so many disciplines [...] in the arts, humanities and social sciences in the twenty-first century" [40]. Indeed, place is an important term in the disciplines of geography and Geographic Information Systems (GISs) as well. While it is a key geographical concept, place with its non-quantifiable character has in the past largely escaped GISs, which since their inception, represent and manipulate measurable features in spatial form. However, and due to recent technological advances, the importance of the concept of place in everyday life is evident and ever growing. The merging of mapping software and social media apps provides constant streams of information about where people or things are, in what is in essence information about 'place'. Think for example of Foursquare: a popular app whose premise is based entirely on the concept of place. The resurface of the importance of place in GIS has not gone unnoticed by GIS scholars. Sui and Goodchild debate that:

> "Formalizing place in the GIS context will be both interesting and challenging; until recently, place has been off the intellectual radar screen of GIScientists, many of whom appear to use the two terms *place* and *space* somewhat

interchangeably [...], yet in GIScience, we still do not have an overarching theory of place or how to work with the concept."[48, pg. 1744]

The above-stated realization asserts that no matter how ubiquitous in its use — as a word that people use daily in the English-speaking world — place is not well defined in academic terms. While fundamental in many disciplines, it is a concept planted in common sense, thus evoked in many different ways. Tim Cresswell in his book 'Place: an introduction' offers a wide coverage of the different definitions of place and its centrality in both everyday life and interdisciplinary academic endeavor [12]. Definitions of the word *place* go as far back as Aristotle and Plato, who introduced the terms *chora* and *topos* — what in a free English translation one would think of as *region* and *place*, respectively — with the second term being the obvious root of geographic terms such as topography and topology. However, each discipline, including GIScience, provides different definitions of the concept of place, none of which seems to be all-encompassing given its commonsensical nature. In this work we pose the following question: Rather than focusing on an all-encompassing definition of the concept of place, can we, instead, provide a set of 'properties of place', which would allow its formalization and realization in different contexts and applications in GIS?

To start answering this question, we go back to Malpas' [41] approach of *interdisciplinarity* not as a featureless mélange of research related to place, but rather as research which has, in a sense, its own topography — locations with properties that give them 'shape and character' and which enable conversations about *place*. Fittingly then, our approach combines theories from GIScience with a toolset borrowed from the field of architecture: the theory of centers [2]. In this theory, Alexander assembles 15 structural properties that characterize a whole (see Table 1) — wholeness, in this theory is any living order or structure that exists in things and which people can feel. Such felt orders are factual and independent of individual cognition. These 15 properties can help generate a variety of 'good' patterns with this so-called living structure [23, 50]. As an architect, Alexander developed the theory of centers in an effort to make shared values and human senses part of science. He believed that existing science based on the positivists' mechanical view of the world, cannot layout a scientific foundation for architecture, whose goal should be to create structures and places where life can be sustained and people can feel connected to.

Table 1 Alexander's 15 Properties of Wholeness [2]

1. Levels of scale	2. Strong Centres
3. Boundaries	4. Alternating Repetition
5. Positive Space	6. Good Shape
7. Local Symmetries	8. Deep Interlock and Ambiguity
9. Contrast	10. Gradients
11. Roughness	12. Echoes
13. The Void	14. Simplicity and Inner Calm
15. Not separateness	

Observing these 15 properties through GIScience lenses, one can see that most, if not all of them, can be immediately identified as properties that already exist in theories developed for formalizing place in the discipline. In the remaining of this paper, we examine these theories and analyze how these 15 properties already correspond to characteristics of places. Our aim is to create a dialogue within GIScience for developing a set of place properties, with which any place can be uniquely identified in various contexts, depending on the domain of the properties' values. Such a properties set frees GIScientists from adhering to a specific definition of the concept of place, which would necessarily need to change according to different application fields.

2   Properties of Places

Much like Christaller developed central-place theory in geography [11], concerned with the size and distribution of central places (or settlements) within a system in an effort to explain how central places of different sizes are located in relation to, and affecting each other, Alexander's theory of centers [2] attempts to measure the degree of life in structures by the number of fundamental structural properties they comprise. The notion of centers, therefore, is an important one in any such framework concerning the spatial organization of elements. Having this concept in mind, the remaining of this section discusses how some of Alexander's 15 properties of wholeness can be already identified in place related theories in GIScience and can, therefore, be used to uniquely characterize and perhaps formalize places.

2.1   Levels of scale

Formations within and across places can exhibit different scales. Place attachment is a term used to describe the emotional ties people experience with places of different scale [38], such as their room/residence [7, 16], neighborhood, suburb, city [37], region, or country, places such as landscapes [29], forests, lakes, summer houses [53], or beaches etc. Apart from place attachment, terms such as place identity, sense of place, place satisfaction and others are used to name people's relations with places of different scale, and it is still debatable whether the concept itself is a multi or single dimensional one (for a review see [16]). However, what is perhaps more interesting in our discussion is the fact that scale is one of the fundamental place properties, which affects people's cognition and perception of their surrounding environment and as a result, their place attachment. For example, there is evidence of a curvilinear relationship between scale of place and strength of place attachment. When places of three different scales where measured, i.e. home, neighborhood, and city, emotional attachment was shown stronger at the two extremes, home and city than to the midpoint of the scale where neighborhood is typically found [21] (see [38] for a review of empirical case studies on the effect of place scale on place attachment). In GIScience and geography there is no shortage of research on mathematical models of scale in natural or artificial structures, from nature's self-organization [4, 10], to fractal theory and *ht*-indices of geographic phenomena and cities [5, 19, 26, 36], to scale of topological patterns of street networks [24], or general accounts of scale in geography and GIS [18, 43]. So whether the domain is geography, sociology, urban planning, humanistic geography, architecture or philosophy, scale is one of the fundamental properties of place, expressed in a plethora of models and terminologies in a variety of contexts, and one that affects people's perception and sense of place.

2.2   Strong centers, contrast, boundaries, gradients, non-separateness, deep interlock and ambiguity.

As has been already stated, at the heart of Alexander's theory is the concept of the existence of centers in any living structure. We argue that the existence of centers is also at the heart of the place properties set. In any 'place' formation, there exists at least one, and in most cases multiple centers of varying sizes, which support each other. This concept is clear in the central-place theory in geography [11] and its later modifications [8, 30]. However, when dealing with centers in geographic reality, one has to consider the notions of membership (i.e., belonging to a center vs. not part of the center), gradient membership (a more fuzzy interpretation of belonging and not-belonging), as well as boundaries. Therefore, the properties of gradients and boundaries are also studied together with the centers property. Places such as metropolitan areas, wetlands, and cultural regions have gradual boundaries in contrast to places with well-defined boundaries such as buildings. There are many models for representing and reasoning with geographic objects with either crisp or gradient boundaries. The latter are mostly based on fuzzy sets [3, 55], rough sets [1, 13, 45], or supervaluation [6, 34] to deal with gradient and boundaries (for a collection of edited papers see also Burrough and Frank's book [9]).

Recently, there have been attempts within the GIScience community to explain structures in verbal place descriptions and to localize features without committing to boundaries, crisp or otherwise. Winter and Freksa [54] use contrast sets to capture sufficiency of places by explicating their contrast to other places, based on the claim that cognition and communication about places in spatial environments is a matter of perceiving one place as sufficiently different from another. Contrast, a fundamental principle in sensing and understanding [17], and one of the organizing principles of perception in Gestalt theory, focuses on the core instead of the fridges of concepts. No matter how one chooses to represent and reason with places, however, it is clear that centers, boundaries and contrast are properties utilized in human perception to recognize and differentiate one place from another.

Places are hardly ever perceived as separate entities that exist in isolation. Rather, people recognize them as collections of entities and the relations between them, and in relations with other places. Even map sketches, the graphical externalizations of places as they are perceived and stored in memory, represent configurations of places and relations between them. These relations exist in various granularities and hierarchies, and exist within and across places. Freksa and Barkowsky [14] argue that what type of entities and relations people will choose is task-dependent. Therefore places exhibit the property of non-separateness as relations between within-place centers or across different places. These relations strengthen the ties between centers in places, as each one gets support from centers of equal or lesser size around it and equally supports larger centers. As a whole then, the entities that form a place and places them selves, exhibit centers, that can be contrasted to each other, may have distinct boundaries or gradients that create harmonious transitions between contrasting centers and they all belong to the same whole structure, experiencing what Alexander calls deep interlock and ambiguity. In Gestalt theory, this is the figure-ground reversal phenomenon, where distinct parts of a whole interpenetrate each other and create ambiguity in visual perception [52], just like the layout of the building blocks and the spaces between them in a city. When observed as a whole, these various distinct parts blend, creating ambiguity from a visual perception point, but are ultimately experienced as a 'place' in human cognition.

As an example, think of a city with its central district and the local suburban centers. Within these various size centers exist other centers such as public transport stations, malls, stadiums, parks and centers for various other activities. Between all these exist relations in the forms of street networks and paths. Similarly, the city itself is connected with other cities via land, air and water pathways that form together larger metropolitan areas and countries. The center of each hierarchical level and granularity has borders, some of them distinct, some others gradient, but together they blend in, creating non-separated places. Considering this example, one can clearly distinguish the resemblance of this group of properties with many of the five elements of Lynch's mental maps [39]. *Nodes* and *districts* are equivalent to smaller (local) and larger centers, while *edges* relate to perceived boundaries, especially explicit ones such as riverbanks. And then of course, the connections or relations between them are represented as *paths* such street networks and other travel channels.

2.3   Good shape, local symmetries, echoes, roughness, alternating repetitions, positive space

These six properties together all deal with the internal structural organization of place elements, which give each place its distinctive, yet familiar identity. They are all perceived in human cognition both at the conscious and subconscious levels and mostly described qualitatively in natural language place descriptions. These properties are, however, mathematical in nature and can, therefore, easily lend themselves to formalization. In particular, they adhere to fractal theory and self-similarity and they are responsible for the patterns that make various places look similar, but yet distinct. Local symmetries are experienced in both natural and artificial places where different foci create symmetrical neighborhoods around them. Alternating repetitions are common in places with self-similarity patterns such as coastal places or forests. Positive spaces are what differentiate the figure from the ground in Gestalt theory and they are usually associated with the convex footprints of spatial features especially in the built environment, vs. the background space that surrounds them. This pattern is evident in the layout of a city for example [25]. Roughness has to do with the irregularities and imperfections in any place configuration, as the result of organic generative process of development that do not adhere to perfect geometric symmetries. This development pattern is most common in the expansion of most neighborhoods and cities around the world, where urban sprawl for example does not follow strict geometric alignments, but depends on other factors such as accessibility, demand due to increasing popularity of place, and others. Then the property of good shape of a place is the result of the cumulative good shape of its parts, such that if the individual centers and their surroundings are characterized by good shape by experiencing a few or all the aforementioned properties, then a place as the sum of its parts is also in good shape. Finally, echo is the property of a place when its whole structure is reminiscent of another place, or the sense of familiarity that people some times experience in a place, even when they visit it for the first time, due to its similarity with other places of similar properties. Echoes can be internal, as similarity of the elements within a place, or external, characterizing a place as a whole when compared with other places.

While, to the best of our knowledge, there are no current models for the potential formalization of this subgroup of mathematical, in nature, properties, Jiang's hierarchical graph for modeling the 15 wholeness properties [25] is a good starting point, even though the author does not specify how, in this model, each of these properties is distinctly measured. The existence of patterns in this group of properties brings in mind spatio-temporal image schemata and how they capture common structures from people's repeated experiences of properties such as containment, linkage or contact [27, 35]. The regularity and recurrent patterns or shapes identified in schemata make them good candidates for formalizing local symmetries, echoes and alternating repetitions. In fact, Kuhn's work [31] on ontologies of spatio-temporal phenomena, which uses image schemata for their spatial nature and their ability to allow conceptual mappings and to construct abstract categories, could be a good first step toward such formalizations.

2.4   Void, simplicity and inner calm

Finally, the property of void is the one that exists in all places, natural and artificial, rural or urban, in micro- or macro-scales. It is that of empty space, a requirement for any place configuration through which people can move around, where space is not completely filled. It is also one of the properties that allows for people to use each place according to their needs at any given context. Take parks for example, maybe one of the place categories where void is an obvious property. It is also one of the properties of parks that make them so attractive to people. The void, emptiness or openness of the space in such places allows for its creative and individualized use, be it for recreation, sport, a meeting, or a picnic among others. And inherently related with the void is also the property of simplicity and inner calm. This property is a more abstract one perhaps, but one well understood and agreed upon, nonetheless, when describing places of preference, of which it more often than not, is a characteristic. It abides to the notion that simplicity offers a feeling of calmness, or that places function better when they are not overloaded with elements or functions, or both. Think of the words one uses when describing shopping malls. Usually, and depending on the previous experiences, expressions such as 'crowded', 'busy', 'difficult to navigate through', 'confusing', or 'tiring', often appear in the descriptions for such places where many needs and many functions are attempted to be accommodated, such as shopping for various categories, eating, resting, recreation and others in one single place. On the contrary, places where categories of functions, or to use a word closer affiliated with theories in GIScience, of affordances are kept to a minimum, experience a higher degree of simplicity and inner calm.

3   Discussion

Our basic premise in this paper has been that the concept of place, rather than defined in a precise manner that is bound to be different according to application domain and context, can rather be identified via a set of properties that are encoded in it, much like philosophers argue that abstract concepts can be identified by the properties they encrypt [49]. Recently, Jiang [25] also used Alexander's theory in order to 'capture the nature of space' in hierarchical graphs, from nations to buildings. Jiang argues along the same line that these properties are helpful to understand (and in the future formalize) patterns in space. Jiang, in the end, is more focused on the structure of a graph of centers, providing *ht*-indices from which number of centers and level of scale can be identified, but is not concerned much with how the rest of the properties could be measured. We leave the question for specific measures deliberately open: we can think of a range of alternative measures, and of different agencies using different measures for the same properties.

Accordingly, this paper addresses this identified gap of a higher-level discussion of the phenomenon itself: places characterized by properties. This ontological rather than quantitative approach should allow comparing patterns/places when they are described by different agencies, or when they are used in different communication contexts. As revealed in Turk and Mark's study [42] of how people categorize place elements in an Australian indigenous language vs. in English, there are fundamental differences at the basic levels of conceptual systems in different backgrounds and languages, supporting the idea that people may use a variety of categories for the same geographic elements. We argue that by not defining places, but rather describing them using a set of properties, we do not have to adhere to equivalent categories between different groups. Instead we postulate that it suffices to provide an agreed upon understanding of the value range of each property between the different domains or communication contexts.

An approach by a theory of centers is also relating and supported by other work. One is Kuhn's [32] postulate of spatial core concepts. These concepts are formed by *location*, *neighborhood, field, object,* and *network*. He identifies *location* as relation, not a property: "All location descriptions express spatial relations between figures to be located and chosen grounds" (p. 2271). This view of a figure on a ground is compatible with *strong centers, positive space* and *contrast*, and further supported by his *neighborhood*, which he calls the "natural companion concept to location" (also p. 2271). "When grounds become salient, as in the case of places, they tend to be thought of as 'locations' in the sense of objects" (p. 2271). *Object* "implies boundedness, but this does not mean that the object's boundaries need to be known or even knowable" (p. 2272), linking to Alexander's *boundaries*, and Kuhn's *network*, capturing the relationships between objects, closes the loop to Alexander's *non-separateness*.

Another suggested ontological approach to place has been built from affordance [28, 33, 46]. Affordance theory [15] adds an interesting view to this discussion, because it takes a stance from an individual's perception, capabilities and intentions, in contrast to Jiang's search for universal measures. Applying an approach grounded in affordances the above properties by Alexander finally get contextualized. A place, characterized by these properties, will be different between individuals, and even for an individual at different times (intentions). For example, in "let's meet at the market" the market is not an objective, positivist object, but a concept in the mind of the speaker (which could be described by the above properties) and in the mind of the listener (which could be described by the above properties, but potentially differently). Further expanding this example, "let's meet at the market" will most likely lead to a different description of *market*, used here with the intention of meeting, i.e., calling for a strong center point, compared to "at the market you can find produce from all over the region", used with the intention of shopping, i.e., calling for levels of scale (a place of places) and alternating repetition (many stalls).

4 Conclusions

This paper attempts to fill a gap in GIScience: it approaches places as 'locations with properties' that give them 'shape and character', and along the way points to a range of existing, but disconnected knowledge in GIScience that, combined together, provides a powerful tool to capture this elusive, subjective, and context-dependent concept. The framework for combining this knowledge has been provided by Alexander's theory of centers. This theory formulated 15 properties (of centers, or of wholeness) that this paper transferred to geographic places, namely from a GIScience perspective, not from a philosophical or human geography perspective. This transfer provides sufficient links to scattered knowledge to fill the properties with meaning in this particular context of place.

The paper focuses decidedly on the concept of *place*, a concept of emerging interest in GIScience. It does so in contrast to other work, e.g., Jiang's study whether *space* can be characterized by measures of these 15 properties. We deliberately do not commit to particular measures, arguing that in different context different measures of particular properties may be applied. Having said this, the same place characterized by different people or in different circumstances may assign different values to these properties.

The paper provides an ontological approach to place, in the way that it postulates an agreed set of properties (and property names), preparing the ground for a conceptual modeling. This conceptual modeling is compatible with the emerging research on place databases that model places as the nodes of property graphs [51]. In this scenario, a node `Place` would have properties, which values depend on a set of measurements chosen according to context.

As a very rough first draft how this can look like consider the following definition using 15 properties a to o:

```
data Scalelevel = Global | Environmental | Vista | Tabletop
data Centerstrength = Prototype | Smooth | None
...
data Place a ... o = Place {a :: Scalelevel,
                            b :: Centerstrength,
                            ...,
                            o :: NotSep}
```

Note that a place defined by these 15 properties has no reference to a location in an absolute spatial reference frame. While this is different from, for example, gazetteers [22] — databases of geographic placenames that also come with a place type from the gazetteer's taxonomy, and a georeference such that each placename can be pinned to a map — this design can be defended in various ways. The first argument is formal: Alexander's theory is about structure, not about location. The second argument is related, in as much Alexander's properties are perceptual properties: The way places are experienced by people, with their body senses, forms their memory about a place, including the relations to other places (neighborhood). One can argue that place memory is primarily spatial knowledge relative to other spatial knowledge, not absolute. This is supported by research from cognitive science (e.g., the landmark and route knowledge of Siegel and White [47]) as well as from neuroscience, which found a distinction between place cells and grid cells [44]. It goes without saying that places characterized this way in a place database can also have a link to a geometric representation, or even multiple, given their context-dependency. However, this link would again open the well-known can of worms that hindered for a long time to introduce places as a type in GIS: Places do not have crisp boundaries in many cases [54]. The suggested ontological approach avoids the symbol grounding problem [20] that many other ontologies seem to fall in – that semantics of symbols in an ontology are often determined by using another symbol system. Rather than deferring the problem of defining 'place' to coming up with equivalent place categories between different domain schemata, we suggest to use Alexander's set of wholeness properties, on the agreed upon value ranges of which place communication can be grounded.

References

[1] AHLQVIST, O., KEUKELAAR, J. and OUKBIR, K. 2000. Rough classification and accuracy assessment. *International Journal of Geographical Information Science*. 14(5), 475–496.

[2] ALEXANDER, C. 2002. *The Nature of Order: An Essay on the Art of Building and the Nature of the Universe, Book 1 - The Phenomenon of Life*. Routledge.

[3]   ALTMAN, D. 1994. Fuzzy set theoretic approaches for handling imprecision in spatial analysis. *International Journal of Geographical Information Systems*. 8(3), 271–289.

[4]   BAK, P. 1996. *How Nature Works*. Springer New York.

[5]   BATTY, M. and LONGLEY, P. 1994. *Fractal cities: a geometry of form and function*. Academic Press Professional, Inc.

[6]   BENNETT, B. 2001. Application of Supervaluation Semantics to Vaguely Defined Spatial Concepts Spatial Information Theory. D. Montello, ed. Springer Berlin / Heidelberg. 108–123.

[7]   BONAIUTO, M., AIELLO, A., PERUGINI, M., BONNES, M. and ERCOLANI, A.P. 1999. Multidimensional perception of residential environment quality and neighborhood attachment in the urban environment. *Journal of Environmental Psychology*. 19(4), 331–352.

[8]   BRADFORD, M.G. and KENT, W.A. 1977. "Central place theory: Christaller's model." *Human Geography: Theories and their Applications*. Oxford University Press. 6–27.

[9]   BURROUGH, P.A. and FRANK, A. 1996. *Geographic Objects with Indeterminate Boundaries*. CRC Press.

[10]   BUTTENFIELD, B.P. 1989. Scale-Dependence And Self-Similarity In Cartographic Lines. *Cartographica: The International Journal for Geographic Information and Geovisualization*. 2(1), 79–100.

[11]   CHRISTALLER, W. 1966. *Central places in southern Germany*. Prentice-Hall.

[12]   CRESSWELL, T. 2014. *Place: An Introduction*. John Wiley & Sons.

[13]   DUCKHAM, M., MASON, K., STELL, J. and WORBOYS, M. 2001. A formal approach to imperfection in geographic information. *Computers, Environment and Urban Systems*. 25(1), 89–103.

[14]   FREKSA, C. and BARKOWSKY, T. 1996. On the relation between spatial concepts and geographic objects. *Geographic objects with indeterminate boundaries*. P.A. Burrough and A. Frank, eds. Taylor and Francis, London. 109–121.

[15]   GIBSON, J. 1977. The theory of affordances. In R.E. Shaw & J. Bransford (eds.) *Perceiving, Acting, and Knowing*. Lawrence Erlbaum Associates.

[16]   GIULIANI, M.V. 2003. Theory of Attachment and Place Attachment. In M. Bonnes, T. Lee and M. Bonaiuto (eds.) *Psychological theories for environmental issues*. Aldershot: Ashgate, pp. 137–170.

[17]   GOODALE, M.A. and MILNER, A.D. 1992. Separate visual pathways for perception and action. *Trends in Neurosciences*. 1(1), 20–25.

[18]   GOODCHILD, M.F. 2011. Scale in GIS: An overview. *Geomorphology*. 130, 1-2, 5–9.

[19]   GOODCHILD, M.F. and MARK, D.M. 1987. The Fractal Nature of Geographic Phenomena. *Annals of the Association of American Geographers*. 77(2), 265–278.

[20]   HARNAD, S. 1990. The symbol grounding problem. *Physica D: Nonlinear Phenomena*. 42, 1-3, 335–346.

[21] HIDALGO, M.C. and HERNÁNDEZ, B. 2001. Place attachment: Conceptual and empirical questions. *Journal of Environmental Psychology*. 21(3), 273– 281.

[22] HILL, L. 2006. *Georeferencing: The Geographic Associations of Information*. MIT Press.

[23] ISHIKAWA, S. and SILVERSTEIN, M. 1977. *A Pattern Language: Towns, Buildings, Construction*. Oxford University Press.

[24] JIANG, B. 2007. A topological pattern of urban street networks: universality and peculiarity. *Physica A: Statistical Mechanics and its Applications*. 384(2), 647–655.

[25] JIANG, B. 2015. Wholeness as a Hierarchical Graph to Capture the Nature of Space. *International Journal of Geographical Information Science*, 29(9), 1632-1648.

[26] JIANG, B. and YIN, J. 2014. Ht-Index for Quantifying the Fractal or Scaling Structure of Geographic Features. *Annals of the Association of American Geographers*. 104(3), 530–541.

[27] JOHNSON, M. 1987. *The Body in the Mind: The Bodily Basis of Meaning, Imagination, and Reason*. The University of Chicago Press.

[28] JORDAN, T., RAUBAL, M., GARTRELL, B. and EGENHOFER, M.J. 1998. An Affordance-Based Model of Place in GIS. 8th *International Symposium on Spatial Data Handling* (SDH'98), 98–109.

[29] KALTENBORN, B.P. and BJERKE, T. 2002. Associations between landscape preferences and place attachment: A study in Røros, Southern Norway. *Landscape Research*. 27(4), 381–396.

[30] KING, L. 1984. *Central Place Theory*. Sage, Beverly Hills

[31] KUHN, W. 2007. An Image-Schematic Account of Spatial Categories. In S. Winter, M. Duckham, L. Kulik, and B. Kuipers (eds.) *Spatial Information Theory*, Springer Berlin Heidelberg. 152–168.

[32] KUHN, W. 2012. Core Concepts of Spatial Information for Transdisciplinary Research. *International Journal of Geographical Information Science*, 26(12), 2267–2276.

[33] KUHN, W. 2001. Ontologies in support of activities in geographical space. *International Journal of Geographical Information Science*, 15(7), 613–631.

[34] KULIK, L. 2001. A Geometric Theory of Vague Boundaries Based on Supervaluation. *Proceedings of the International Conference on Spatial Information Theory: Foundations of Geographic Information Science* (London, 2001), 44–59.

[35] LAKOFF, G. 1987. *Women, Fire, and Dangerous Things - What Categories Reveal about the Mind*. The University of Chicago Press.

[36] LAM, N.S.N. and QUATTROCHI, D.A. 1992. On the issues of scale, resolution, and fractal analysis on the mapping sciences. *Professional Geographer*. 44(1), 88–98.

[37] LEWICKA, M. 2008. Place attachment, place identity, and place memory: Restoring the forgotten city past. *Journal of Environmental Psychology*, 28(3), 209–231.

[38] LEWICKA, M. 2010. What makes neighborhood different from home and city? Effects of place scale on place attachment. *Journal of Environmental Psychology*, 30(1), 35–51.

[39] LYNCH, K. 1960. *The Image of the City*. MIT Press.

[40] MALPAS, J. Place Research Network. Progressive Geographies, 2010.
      http://progressivegeographies.com/2010/11/04/place-research-network/
      Accessed: 2015-02-26.

[41] MALPAS, J. Thinking Topographically: Place, Space, and Geography, 2013,
      http://jeffmalpas.com/wp-content/uploads/2013/02/Thinking-
      Topographically-Place-Space-and-Geography.pdf Accessed: 2015-02-26.

[42] MARK, D.M. and TURK, A.G. 2003. Landscape Categories in Yindjibarndi:
      Ontology, Environment, and Language. Spatial Information Theory. In W. Kuhn,
      M.F. Worboys, and S. Timpf (eds.) *Foundations of Geographic Information Science*.
      Springer Berlin Heidelberg, 28–45.

[43] MONTELLO, D.R. 2001. Scale in geography. In N.J. Smelser and B. Baltes (eds.)
      International Encyclopedia of the Social and Behavioral Sciences, 13501–13504.

[44] MOSER, E.I., KROPFF, E. and MOSER, M.B. 2008. Place Cells, Grid Cells, and the
      Brain's Spatial Representation System. *Annual Review of Neuroscience*. 31(1), 69–
      89.

[45] PAWLAK, Z. Rough sets. *International Journal of Computer and Information
      Sciences*, 11, 341–356.

[46] SCHEIDER, S. and KUHN, W. 2010. Affordance-based categorization of road
      network data using a grounded theory of channel networks. *International Journal
      of Geographical Information Science*, 24(8), 1249–1267.

[47] SIEGEL, A.W. and WHITE, S.H. 1975. The development of spatial
      representations of large-scale environments. In H.W. Reese (ed.) *Advances in
      Child Development and Behavior*, New York: Academic Press.

[48] SUI, D. and GOODCHILD, M. 2011. The convergence of GIS and social media:
      challenges for GIScience. *International Journal of Geographical Information Science*,
      25(11), 1737–1748.

[49] SWOYER, C. and ORILIA, F. 2014. Properties. In E.N. Zalta (ed.) *The Stanford
      Encyclopedia of Philosophy*.

[50] THOMPSON, D.W. 1992. *On Growth and Form*. Cambridge University Press.

[51] VASARDANI, M., TIMPF, S., WINTER, S. and TOMKO, M. 2013. From
      Descriptions to Depictions: A Conceptual Framework. In T. Tenbrink, J. Stell, A.
      Galton, and Z. Wood (eds.) *Spatial Information Theory - Proceedings of 11th
      International Conference* (COSIT'13), Scarborough, UK, September 2-6, Springer
      International Publishing, 299–319.

[52] WAGEMANS, J., ELDER, J.H., KUBOVY, M., PALMER, S.E., PETERSON, M.A.,
      SINGH, M. and von der HEYDT, R. 2012. A Century of Gestalt Psychology in
      Visual Perception I. Perceptual Grouping and Figure-Ground Organization.
      Psychological bulletin. 138(6), 1172–1217.

[53] WILLIAMS, D.R. and MCINTYRE, N. 2001. Where heart and home reside:
      changing constructions of place and identity. In Luft, K. and MacDonald, S.
      (comps.) *Trends 2000: Shaping the Future*, September 17-20, Lansing, MI, East
      Lansing, MI: Department of Parks, Recreation and Tourism Resources, Michigan
      State University, 392–403.

[54] WINTER, S. and FREKSA, C. 2012. Approaching the Notion of Place by Contrast.
      Journal of Spatial Information Science, 5, 31–50.

[55]   ZADEH, L.A. 1965. Fuzzy sets. *Information and Control.* 8, 338–353.

Spatial Networks in Epidemiological Studies

Ling Bian

Department of Geography, University at Buffalo, Amherst, NY 14068, USA

Extended Abstract

---

1 Introduction

This discussion attempts to formalize the spatial network model, as an alternative to the social network model, in epidemiological studies. Conceptual issues discussed include the composition of spatial networks, representation of their dynamics, and their application challenges.

In recent years, network-based models have received increasing interests in epidemiological research [1, 2, 3, 4]. Communicable diseases spread across space and time as a consequence of human interaction and mobility. The interactions between individuals at a location facilitate infections within a local network. The mobility of individuals between locations connects the local networks into a population-wide network and spreads infection throughout an area over time.

2 Social Networks and Spatial Networks

A network consists of nodes and links. The properties of individual nodes and links, along with the topology of the network as a whole, determine the ability of the network to transmit various tangible or intangible properties across it, including diseases.

Motivated by the need to identify the pathways of disease transmission between individuals, most current network models are focused on a human–network where individuals are nodes and the social contacts between them are links. Location and time characteristics associated with individuals are treated as attributes of the nodes. a secondary property of the network. They cannot be analyzed directly without first analyzing the social network.

Disease transmission is inherently a spatial and temporal process. An alternative to the social network model is the spatial network model where locations are treated as nodes and the mobility of infection cases between locations as edges. The spatial network can easily represent the spatial and temporal dynamics of the transmission process and address spatially oriented issues, such as the pathway, speed, direction, and extent of disease 'flow' in an epidemic. Individuals and their characteristics, such as infection vulnerability and health outcome, are attributes of the location nodes and are considered a secondary property of the spatial network.

The distinction between a social network model and a spatial network model can draw upon the analogy of the difference between Eulerian vs. Lagrangian views of motion [5]. In the Lagrangian view, the focus is on a moving object (e.g. a moving individual), while the background environment (e.g. streets or in-door settings) moves with the object. In the Eulerian view, the focus is on a fixed frame in space, while objects move around within the frame.

In the context of spatial representation, the social network model is most analogous to the Lagrangian view of motion. The individual of interest, as a node in the network, is in the center of space. The background environment, i.e. in this case the local network around the individual, changes with the individual spatially and temporally. This model is best suited for estimating the individualized vulnerability and health outcomes in a networked population.

In contrast, the spatial network model is more similar to a Eulerian view of motion. A network is fixed in space, while infection cases move around within the network. This model is more effective in representing the spatial temporal dynamics of an epidemic in a network-formed environment.

Properties of individual nodes, links, and the topology of the network can be measured and expressed at different scales by a rich set of parameters and analytical tools. These include those that measure the position, role, clustering, and structure of individual nodes, clusters of nodes, and the entire network. These tools are rooted in graph theory and have been enriched by social network studies through the past decades. They are intended to study social relationships and influences and are not intended for spatial analysis [6]. Currently in health studies, these measurements are mostly applied to social networks.

For a given population and area, the social network and spatial network have distinct node properties, link properties, and network topology. Presently, social networks are the predominant model to simulate disease transmission in health studies. Only in the past decade has the spatial network been explicitly presented and distinguished from the social network [1]. Spatial networks and their associated challenges and opportunities have been much less studied.

3   Criteria of Spatial Networks

A spatial network does not guarantee spatial analysis. Having spatially oriented features, such as location and mobility, explicitly represented as the nodes and links of a network seems to be a necessary, but not a sufficient condition to define spatial networks. Summarized from the literature, there seem to be three levels of approaches to the utility of spatial network.

The simplest level is to treat a spatial network as a social network. The network has a spatial form but does not support spatial analysis. The set of parameters and analytical tools commonly used to analyze social networks are directly applied to the spatial network. It is possible that for this type of studies, the network data are collected by geographic location or region, making it impossible to build a social network. The subsequent analysis must deal with a spatially formed network while its spatial characteristics are not a concern.

The second level of utility of a spatial network exploits the spatially explicit information of a spatial network in order to address spatial questions. In addition to the basic analysis, such as transmission pathways, speed, direction, and extent of disease flow, many other spatial characteristics, such as spatial dependence in the flow, have been explored [7]. This type of analysis requires additional, spatially oriented tools beyond the existing tools offered by conventional social network analysis.

The third level of utility of spatial network requires spatial constraints in addition to representing locations as nodes and mobility as links. Most typically, the location of nodes or the length of links must be associated with a cost or reward [8]. Thus far, this is the most restricted definition of a spatial network. Many flows show spatial dependence or the distance decay effect, but not all do. This rather restricted definition raises further questions regarding the criteria of a spatial network model, the advantages and limitations of the spatial network model, and its relationship with the social network model. These issues warrant further investigations.

References

[1]   Eubank S, Guclu H, Kumar V S A, Marathe M V, Srinivasan A, Toroczkai T, and Wang N 2004 Modeling disease outbreaks in realistic urban social networks. Nature 429: 180–83.

[2]   Ferguson N M, Cummings D A T, Fraser C, Cajka J C, Cooley P C, and Burke D S 2006 Strategies for mitigating an influenza pandemic. Nature 442: 448–52.

[3]   Salathé M, Kazandjieva M, Lee J W, Levis P, Feldman M W, and Jones J H 2010 A high-resolution human contact network for infectious disease transmission. Proceedings of National Academy of Science 107: 22020–25.

[4]   Bian L, Huang Y, Liang M, Lim E, Lee G, Yang Y, Cohen M, and Wilson D 2012 Modeling individual vulnerability to communicable diseases - a framework and design. Annals of the Association of American Geographers 102(5): 1016-1025.

[5]   Maidment D R 1993 GIS and hydrologic modeling. In Environmental Modeling with GIS, M.F. Goodchild and L.T. Steyaert, Eds. Oxford University Press, New York, 1993, pp. 147–167.

[6]   O'Sullivan D 2014 Spatial Network Analysis. In Handbook of Regional Science, M.M. Fisher and P. Nijkamp, Eds. Springer, New York, 2014, pp. 1253-1273.

[7]   Guo D 2008 Regionalization with Dynamically Constrained Agglomerative Clustering and Partitioning (REDCAP). International Journal of Geographical Information Science 22(7): 801-823.

[8]   Barthélemy M 2011 Spatial networks, Physics Reports 499(1–3): 1-101.

Developments Within Geospatial Technologies for the Support of Urban Sustainability Towards Smart Cities

Lars Bodum

Department of Development and Planning, Aalborg University, Vestre Havnepromenade 5, 9000 Aalborg, Denmark

Extended Abstract

Abstract: Four important environmental and societal challenges are identified and investigated within this presentation. In each of the four areas, examples of technologies that can support and enhance the sustainability of the urban environment that were invented and in some cases implemented (most of them in Denmark) are discussed.

Keywords: Urbanization, urban sustainability, smart cities, geospatial technologies, water management, waste management, energy management, 3D object orientation, mobility management, CityGML.

1 Introduction

Urbanization is a growing phenomena and more than 54% of the World population in 2015 lives in urban areas. This number is expected to grow to 66% in 2050 according to the United Nations (UN). This means that more than 2.5 billion will be added to the urban population in 2050 with more than 90% of the growth related to Asia and Africa [16]. To be able to deal with this intense growth and to handle the environmental and societal challenges coming from this scenario, it is important to prepare our cities for this invasion. There is a need for technologies that can enhance and support the urban sustainability. These technologies are to a certain degree the same technologies that many developers, authorities and other organisations today promote for the course of transforming our urban areas to smart cities. Geospatial solutions are in many ways the facilitator of these technologies and works as the cornerstone of the documentation, distribution and services coming from smart cities.

The technology behind the mapping of almost any kind of infrastructure of an urban area has gone from printed 2D paper maps with an update frequency of several years to a live map of the current service situation in 3D sometimes incorporated with live video from the location. In this abstract four important environmental and societal challenges have been selected and investigated. Examples of technologies that can support and enhance the sustainability of the urban environment in each of these four areas invented and in some cases implemented (most of them in Denmark) will be shown. In each of the problem areas presented there will be a specific focus on the use of geospatial technology as a tool for monitoring, collecting or spreading information. This is also what is normally called a spatial data infrastructure (sdi).

2 Water Management

Water management is important from a supply perspective, but it is also important to know how your water grid is performing or to give the citizens incentives to save water in the daily household. On a global level the 2030 Water Resources Group (2030WRG) expect the demand for fresh water to grow in every part of the world. This will lead to water scarcity and the need for technologies that can help maintain a sustainable water supply situation [1]. Some cities around the world have already had a long and successful tradition for saving water. In Copenhagen they successfully cut the yearly water consumption from 100 million m3 in the late 1970's to 55 million m3 in 2014 [9]. This has been achieved through a combination of an active policy towards each individual household and better knowledge about the grid. By increasing and taxing the price and installing meters in every household the city managed to communicate their strategy of seriously cutting the consumption of water from 170 litres per capita in 1987 to 108 litres per capita in 2010. At the same time another smart technology was introduced in the form of intelligent water pumps that monitors the actual water consumption through grid use patterns and remote sensors and thereafter automatically adjusts the water pressure accordingly using an algorithm developed by the Danish company Grundfos [8,9]. This reduces both water and electricity consumption by up to 20% and prolongs the lifetime of the pipes. The information related to each individual part of the water grid (age of the pipes, number of consumers and total consumption of water) helps to plan the renovation of the grid. Each year up to 1% of the total grid is changed and that corresponds to approximately 6.8 km of pipes. This renovation has helped to reduce the total loss of water in the grid to just 7%, which is very low compared to other urban areas [9].

3 Waste Management

Waste management will become more important than ever because of the urban growth. There are two dominant factors that determine the amount of waste from a society. First it is the population size and second it is the consumption patterns of that society. There is no doubt that the population growth will happen in countries where a rise in the Gross Domestic Product per Capita (GDP/c) also should be expected. The global average GDP/c around 2050 is expected to be fourfold of the present [13]. The amounts of waste generated will therefore grow, which again will call for innovative solutions to the problem of getting rid of the waste. Where the bad news is the amount of waste, the good news is that a global rise in the GDP/c will also automatically lead to more advanced solutions to the waste management. Globally there are two trends in the innovation of waste management. The first is the reservation of larger land fills near urban areas and organised with a combination of sorting in different types of waste and in some cases also complemented with a large incineration plant for the type of waste that can be burned and used for energy production (heat and/or electricity). This will most likely be the chosen technology in the majority of urban areas in Africa, Asia and the Americas. The greater City of Copenhagen, which is predicted to increase to around 1.35 million citizens in 2020, have decided to cut the number of incineration plants to two and the newest of them (under construction until 2017), called Amager Bakke, is planned to deal with 400,000 tons of waste every year. The plant will at this capacity yearly deliver 444,000 MWh (18% of the total yearly electricity consumption) and 5,240 TJ in heating (15% of the total yearly heating demand) for the larger urban area. The most interesting part of the design of the incineration plant, and the reason why Amager Bakke has become famous is due to the fact that the outside of the plant will work as a year-round alpine ski slope for the support of the experience economy.

Even though this modern facility is still under construction, the long-term goal for Denmark will be to phase out fossil fuels by 2050. That means also a close of all incineration plants in Denmark because 33% of the waste burned there is categorized as fossil fuel due to the large amount of plastic materials in the garbage. The second trend in waste management is the rise in recycling. According to the waste plan from the Danish Government the share of recycling should be 50% by 2020 [14]. This is an ambitious goal and it will only be possible to reach this by using advanced technology to sort out organic/biological waste, plastics and other materials. That is one part of the recycling plan and this alone will claim huge economic investments. The other part is the contribution from the public. Every household is supposed to start the recycling at home through reducing the total amount of household waste and begin to see each wasted item as a resource that could be used again maybe in the same household or maybe in another household. There are two major technological trends that can support the effort of increasing the recycling. The first trend is closely related to the theory behind the Internet of Things (IoT). By using tags of some sort and make a geospatial reference, it suddenly becomes interesting to follow items that once were in your possession. One example of this technology is the Tales of Things project from CASA [5]. The main idea of that project was to tag things and combine it with personal tales about the things. Then it was possible to follow the things in time and space. New projects are regularly launched with the same type of idea. The other dominant technology trend in recycling is a combination of joint ownership and rental sharing.

Through dedicated websites or through social media, users can either offer a joint ownership of specific equipment or rent out their machines, silverware or clothes. There are even sites where you can swap your goods for other things and thereby completely renew your possessions. This way the use of equipment, which normally has a low usage percentage, becomes much more efficient and eventually will lead to a lower consumption rate in society. Needless to say an important technology behind this boom in IoT have been the easy access to geospatial information and the help users get to navigate between each other through online maps and driving directions. This trend is a part of a global transition towards sharing economy [6] (sometimes also referred to as the collaborative economy), which again is a part of the movement towards circular economy [3].

4 Energy Management

Energy management is traditionally the first association that comes to mind when the talk is about smart cities. The smart grid technology has an enormous potential and lives from the dream of making distribution of energy (electricity and heat) more intelligent. If you are able to control production of energy directly from input generated by the consumers (or the appliances of consumers), then it becomes much more efficient to live in an urban area. This will also allow urban planners to come up with better alternatives to the traditional energy management, which for many countries mainly are based on fossil fuel or nuclear driven plants. In a future sustainable energy management the smart grid evolves to become a smart energy system [12]. The object-orientation of a 3D city model will also provide an important tool for the future and the combination of 3D geometry of the city and detailed information of the energy transmission network will provide enough information to reduce both the energy and heat consumption of individual households and also generate the correct mix of production of electricity and heat from renewable energy sources. The city of Frederikshavn in the northern part of Denmark announced itself as EnergyCity in early 2005 and with ambitions of becoming 100% renewable energy dependent before 2015. Even though they failed to succeed, they learned a lot during the years of the project and one of the main technological elements was the use of an object-oriented 3D city model used for visualisation of the energy system and for the interactive modelling of this in both space and time [11]. One of the big challenges in energy management of the future is the transition of heating and cooling of domestic housing from individual electricity based systems to integrated systems supplied from e.g. district heating and/or cooling produced with a combination of biomass, wind, solar and heat pumps. The energy that comes out of industrial production from e.g. water-cooling can be used as a renewable source of energy and reduce both the carbon footprint and the costs in an urban area. One of the largest data centres in Europe is planned to be build by Apple in a rural location in Jutland, Denmark. From 2016, when construction of the centre is planned to begin, this facility will only be powered from renewable energy sources (wind, water, solar) and at the same time the excess heat from the centre will be transmitted to the nearby city of Viborg (60,000 inhabitants) to cover the district heating demand in that urban environment [4].

5 Mobility Management

Mobility Management is an important element of a smart and sustainable city. The traffic congestions of modern cities are both environmental unsustainable and a threat to the future climate. In some cases the best policy against private car traffic is taxation. There are many examples of this in Europe. The congestion zones in London, Oslo and Stockholm are good examples of this policy. In line with this are more active technologies where cars are taxed through registration of their whereabouts. The road-pricing systems and other adaptive traffic control systems require very efficient mapping and tracking technologies [2]. But when it comes to providing future cities with hope of a more clean and less congested traffic situation, the only effective solution is to design the inner part of cities for pedestrians, cyclists and public transport solutions such as busses powered by non-emission fuels, light-rail and metro-systems [7]. It is very important for future cities to use geospatial technologies in smart manner, which means as a supporting technology for those people who are living, using, working and visiting the city.

6 Conclusions

Can these environmental and societal challenges be connected to the development of a future geospatial data infrastructure in smart cities? At Open Geospatial Consortium (OGC) they have launched a white paper on Smart Cities with the title Spatial Information Framework [15]. The purpose of the white paper is to promote the value of geospatial information for use within the framework of smart cities. A lot of technological solutions are already at hand and combined with the principles of theopen information technology standards this could open the way for new solutions in a future where organisations, authorities, public and private companies together with the citizens all feed the information systems. They both feed them and subscribe to the many different solutions and services that keep them updated about the city and how it performs. This is done with a reference to the long list of relevant indicators that constantly measures the performance of cities and the quality of life in the city. A great deal of these indicators is also indicators that would be used to find out how the city performs in relation to sustainability. When it comes to the platform for integration of the many different data types and processing of the private and public geospatial databases the most obvious choice will be the CityGML standard provided by OGC [10]. Developed continuously over the last 10 years, this standard has shown itself to be robust and future-proof both in relation to the diversity in spatial modelling but also in relation to the complex semantic modelling of cities.

References

[1]   2030 Water Resources Group.2030 Water Resources Group.
       http://www.2030wrg.org/.

[2]   Agerholm, N. and Olesen, A.V. Adaptive Traffic Control Systems in a medium sized Scandinavian city. I E T Intelligent Transport Systems, (2015).

[3]   Andersen, M.S. An introductory note on the environmental economics of the circular economy. Sustainability Science 2, 1 (2007), 133–140.

[4]   Apple. Press Info - Apple to Invest €1.7 Billion in New European Data Centres. 2015. https://www.apple.com/pr/library/2015/02/23Apple-to-Invest-1-7-Billion-in-New-European-Data-Centres.html.

[5]   Barthel, R., Leder Mackley, K., Hudson-Smith, A., Karpovich, A., de Jode, M., and Speed, C. An internet of old things as an augmented memory system. Personal and Ubiquitous Computing 17, 2 (2013), 321–333.

[6]   Gansky, L. The Mesh: Why the Future of Business Is Sharing. Penguin Books, New York, 2010.

[7]   Gehl, J. Cities for People. IslandPress, Washington DC., 2010.

[8]   Grundfos. Grundfos Demand Driven Distribution part II. 2012.
       https://youtu.be/Wcx64gS0dYM.

[9]   Grundfos. Smart cities secure water supplies while risks loom. 2014.
       http://www.grundfos.com/about-us/news-and-press/news/smart-citiessecure-water-supplies-while-risks-loom.html.

[10] Gröger, G. and Plümer, L. CityGML – Interoperable semantic 3D city models. ISPRS Journal of Photogrammetry and Remote Sensing 71, (2012), 12–33.

[11] Kjems, E. and Bodum, L. Object Oriented Visualization of Urban Energy Consumption. Proceedings of 11th conference on Computers in Urban Planning and Urban Management, ESRI Press (2009).

[12] Lund, H. Renewable Energy Systems. Academic Press, 2014.

[13] Mavropoulos, A. Waste management 2030+. Waste Management World, 2010. http://www.waste-management-world.com/articles/print/volume-11/issue-2/features/waste-management-2030.html.

[14] Miljøministeriet. Danmark uden affald. 2013. http://mim.dk/arbejdsomraader/danmark-uden-affald-ii/danmark-udenaffald/.

[15] Open Geospatial Consortium. Smart Cities Spatial Information Framework. 2015.

[16] United Nations, Department of Economic and Social Affairs, Population Division. World Urbanization Prospects: The 2014 Revision, Highlights (ST/ESA/SER.A/352). 2014.

Ontology-based Geo-spatial Knowledge Reasoning System

Kejin Cui[1], Thomas Bittner[1,2,3]

1 Department of Geography, State University of New York at Buffalo, Buffalo, NY 14260, USA
2 Department of Philosophy, State University of New York at Buffalo, Buffalo, NY 14260, USA
3 National Center for Geographic Information and Analysis (NCGIA), State University of New York at Buffalo, Buffalo, NY 14260, USA USA

Extended Abstract

---

1 Introduction

Ontological modeling [18] has been widely applied in current GIScience. For example, ontology can be used in analyzing natural language information to describe human activities [16]. When focusing on a specific geographic processes, an ontological model can be created to describe casual-like relationships amongst states, events and processes [2]. Ontological analysis can also be used in classifying geographic features [8].

Ontology describes an entity based on its attribute and its relationship with other entities, and its reasoning is based on logic [18]. Thus, when more and more pieces of knowledge are added into the ontology, a logic based formal model can be formed, which can also be seen as a network composed by different logic chains. From this logic network formal model, more knowledge can be discovered by reasoning.

This paper presents a conceptual system model to integrate many aspects of geo-spatial knowledge, including geographic categories, geographic process, geographic representation, qualitative spatial reasoning, then introduces how to apply this reasoning system in those four aspects.

2 Model description

Potential areas to apply the reasoning system are as follows:

2.1 Geographic categories

In ontological analysis of geographic concepts, a cognitive study was presented to distinguish the relationships among different geographic categories [20]. Also a semantic reference system was developed to describe relations between sub-concept and super-concept

in hydrological modeling [1]. To further analyze geographic concepts, more relationships need to be considered. For instance, the concepts "Island" can be classified as "Continental Island" and "Oceanic Island". So we can create a relation of "Lie on" between "Continental Island" and "Continental Shelve", and also between "Ocean" and "Oceanic Island". We can also build a relation that "Continental Island" and "Oceanic Island" are mutual exclusive. Therefore, by adding more relationships and attributes, the semantic power of the ontology model is enhanced, and more potential relationships amongst geographic concepts can be found.

2.2   Geographic process

In macro perspective, ontology modeling in earth system sciences is a potential area. In current research, the concept of system has been widely applied in climate change [15] and ecology study [3]. In this context, the system is divided by many components. Each component has some state attributes or variables, and each component can interact with other components with relationships such as "positive coupling" or "negative coupling". Thus, this characteristics of systems makes it appropriate to apply ontological modeling. However, when applying ontology in earth systems, two problem need to be discussed. First, in a system, the relationships between states in different components can be linear, logarithmic, exponential, or some more complex function curves. How can ontology modeling deal with the quantitative relations like that? Second, in a system, several couplings can form a feedback loop, and then how can ontology reason the possible result in a feedback loop? These questions need to be answered in future.

In micro perspective, focusing on a small geographic phenomena, ontological modeling can be applied to describe casual relationships amongst states, events and processes [2]. Then based on the result of spatial data mining, we can get the value of spatial variables with its probability and the associated rules between different variables. By apply this information into designed ontology model, we can find which direction of casual relationship for this geographic process. On the other hand, qualitative process theory [9], which was a form of ontology, was developed to simulate physical processes. This idea in modeling physical processes can also be applied in describing geography processes. There are also two problems to be solved. Firstly, compared with physical phenomena, which only has physical variables, geographic processes need to deal with spatial variables plus its location and time. This will enhance the complexity of ontological modeling. Secondly, after modeling, one can test the sensitivity of spatial variables by changing their values, spatial range, or time scale. Then how this sensitivity analysis should be done in the reasoning system is also a question.

2.3   Geographic representation

Geographic representation is a research topic on how to use appropriate data model or method for spatial analysis in different conditions [12]. Discrete-object and continuous-field conceptualizations are two key perspective of geographic representation [13]. Much attention is focusing on the essence, distinction and unifying of field and object models, such as Geo-atom [14], General Field[17], and Object-field[6]. Methods to extend field-view and object-view with temporal attributes are also developed [21]. On the other hand, formal logic model has been applied to describe object and field representation with their relationships [12]. So the next step will be using ontology-based logic model to describe the relationships between object and field geographic representation according to the achievements above.

2.4 Qualitative spatial reasoning (QSR)

Qualitative spatial reasoning is a research field on how to provide calculi which allow a machine to represent and reason with spatial entities without resort to the traditional quantitative techniques, such as computer graphics [5]. Many achievements have been made to identify spatial relations such as topology [7], direction [11], distance [10], and shape [4]. Since QSR uses logic to reason new information, it can be easily integrated into the ontological systems discussed above. Firstly, it can be a key part in spatial analysis, and it can enhance the power of analysis functions [20]. Second, in sensitivity analysis of ontological models for geographic processes, QSR can be applied to answer what will happen if the spatial relations among two or more entities changes. Third, it can also be integrated into geographic representation models to identify the potential relationship between object and field models. For example, Egenhofer's nine-intersection [7] can be defined on raster data to create a hybrid raster model [20].

3   Conclusions

This paper discusses the design of ontology-based reasoning system for geo-spatial knowledge. Potential applications in four major areas are discussed. New knowledge can be discovered by reasoning from one area, or combination of knowledge from different areas. For example, knowledge in geographic concepts and geographic processes can be integrated together to discover the function of different geographic concepts in their corresponding geographic processes. Knowledge in geographic representation and geographic process can also be linked to identify which data model is the best one to describe the specific geographic phenomena. Thus, future work will be designing reasoning systems based on different geo-spatial problems.

References

[1]   BIAN, L., AND HU, S. Identifying components for interoperable process models using concept lattice and semantic reference system. International Journal of Geographical Information Science 21, 9(2007), 1009-1032.

[2]   BLEISCH, S., DUCKHAM, M., GALTON, A., LAUBE, P., AND LYON, J. Mining candidate causal relationships in movement patterns. International Journal of Geographical Information Science, 28, 2(2014), 363-382.

[3]   BROWN, M. T. A picture is worth a thousand words: energy systems language and simulation. Ecological Modelling 178, 1(2004), 83-100.

[4]   CLEMENTINI, E., AND DI FELICE, P. (1997). A global framework for qualitative shape description. GeoInformatica 1, 1(197), 11-27.

[5]   COHN, A. G., AND HAZARIKA, S. M. Qualitative spatial representation and reasoning: An overview. Fundamenta Informaticae 46, 1(2001), 1-29.

[6]   COVA, T. J., AND GOODCHILD, M. F. Extending geographical representation to include fields of spatial objects. International Journal of Geographical Information Science 16, 6(2002), 509-532.

[7]   EGENHOFER, M. J., AND FRANZOSA, R. D. Point-set topological spatial relations. International Journal of Geographical Information System 5, 2(1991), 161-174.

[8]   FENG, C. C., AND BITTNER, T. Ontology-based Qualitative Feature Analysis: Bays as a Case Study. Transactions in GIS 14, 4(2010), 547-568.

[9]   FORBUS, K. D. Qualitative process theory. Artificial intelligence 24, 1(1984), 85-168.

[10] FRANK, A. U. Qualitative spatial reasoning about distances and directions in geographic space. Journal of Visual Languages & Computing 3, 4(1992), 343-371.

[11] FRANK, A. U. Qualitative spatial reasoning: Cardinal directions as an example. International Journal of Geographical Information Science 10, 3(1996), 269-290.

[12] GALTON, A. A formal theory of objects and fields. In Spatial Information Theory(2001), 458-473. Springer Berlin Heidelberg.

[13] GOODCHILD, M. F. Geographical data modeling. Computers & Geosciences 18, 4(1992), 401-408.

[14] GOODCHILD, M. F., YUAN, M., AND COVA, T. J. Towards a general theory of geographic representation in GIS. International journal of geographical information science 21, 3(2007), 239-260.

[15] KUMP, L. R., BRANTLEY, S. L., AND ARTHUR, M. A. Chemical weathering, atmospheric CO_2, and climate. Annual Review of Earth and Planetary Sciences 28, 1(2000), 611-667.

[16] KUHN, W. Ontologies in support of activities in geographical space. International Journal of Geographical Information Science 15, 7(2001), 613-631.

[17] LIU, Y., GOODCHILD, M. F., GUO, Q., TIAN, Y., AND WU, L. Towards a General Field model and its order in GIS. International Journal of Geographical Information Science 22, 6(2008), 623-643.

[18] SMITH, B. Ontology, 2003.

[19] SMITH, B., AND MARK, D. M. Geographical categories: an ontological investigation. International journal of geographical information science 15, 7(2001), 591-612.

[20] WINTER, S., & FRANK, A. U. Topology in raster and vector representation. GeoInformatica 4, 1(2000), 35-65.

[21] YUAN, M. Representing complex geographic phenomena in GIS. Cartography and Geographic Information Science 28, 2(2001), 83-96.

Spatial Preposition Specification for Improved Small Scale Indoor Navigation

Stacy A. Doore

NCGIA and School of Computing and Information Science, University of Maine, 5711 Boardman Hall, University of Maine, Orono, ME 04469-5711, USA

Extended Abstract

Abstract: Improving natural language descriptions of scenes and spatial localization of objects in indoor environments is critical to creating effective dialogue-based indoor navigation systems. One approach is to map context-based natural language (NL) classifications directly to concepts in a linguistically-motivated spatial ontology to generate NL spatial expressions. However, this approach may oversimplify important aspects of spatial prepositions and their context dependencies based on assumptions made about the relative weight given to the spatial configuration vs. functional interaction and the relationships between these two factors. This pilot study explores the influence of multiple factors in an existing scene description dataset in order to better understand spatial preposition semantics within indoor scene descriptions. Future work will investigate rules to allow for multi-level semantic detail and spatial preposition substitutions to improve semantic flexibility and precision in indoor navigation systems.

Keywords: Indoor spatial data models, navigation systems, spatial context, spatial prepositions, spatial linguistic analysis, spatial networks.

---

1 Introduction

Spatial concepts expressed in prepositions and other elements of language are relatively imprecise in describing non-metric qualitative regions, distances and directions. Likewise, most spatial terms are dependent on various aspects of context for their interpretation. The question about how to best specify context dependencies inherent in the interpretation and use of spatial prepositions attempts to resolve the "basic question" regarding the nature of spatial prepositions [8, 10]. In some cases, spatial prepositions can be characterized as strictly an expression of 'spatial configuration', while in other cases, they express a 'functional interaction' between two objects in space [8]. Spatial expression form and interpretation are also highly impacted by culture and native language of the observer [9].

Indoor space presents unique challenges for navigation support as it differs in scales, dimensions and structural boundaries from outdoor spaces. The aim of this research is to determine what types of formal ontological structures might enhance existing frameworks used for reasoning in indoor space through NL scene description analysis. The result of this analysis will provide more information about the context cues used in indoor settings, which can then be specified and formalized in a 'helper' ontology for existing frameworks. The expected contribution is a 'smart' thesaurus to support spatial preposition usage in NL descriptions of indoor space.

2   Related Work

A number of researchers have conducted experiments using spatial prepositions such as in, on, over and beside [2, 4]. These studies concluded that knowledge about how objects interact with each other contributes to the representation of functional relations, which, in turn, determines prepositional usage; and extrageometric factors contribute to models of spatial preposition use and comprehension. In most cases, the primary usage of prepositions is 'spatial configuration' versus interaction function, however, there are questions about our current ability to capture the functional as easily as spatial [8].

Spatial ontologies have been evaluated for inter-annotator reliability and spatial logics using a number of spatial language corpora [1,3,5]. However, most studies focused on the validation of spatial semantics over identification of spatial vs. function factors based on context. Other studies used an unrestricted NL parser to convert descriptions into spatial triples and a 2D spatial property graph using spatial annotation and formal models [7,11]. Their approach differed in its focus on outdoor space as opposed to indoor space. In related work [6], indoor scene descriptions were analyzed for word frequency and spatial object relations but were not formally mapped to a spatial linguistic annotation schema. These analyses also did not distinguish between moveable objects versus boundary structures (i.e., walls or floor).

3   Pilot Study

Indoor scene description data from a previous study [6] was converted to corpus style utterances and annotated using spatial linguistic ontology concepts [1,7]. The data were analyzed using a variety of linguistic and spatial network analysis methods to identify semantic patterns, spatial structures, and context dependencies. Finally, an additional analysis was conducted to extract evidence of anthropomorphic aspects and spatial vs. functional roles [10].

The number of utterances and number of spatial triples used in each description showed substantial consistency. Moveable objects dominated the trajectory position and boundary structures were most frequently employed in the landmark position in the extracted spatial triples and the spatial prepositions on, about, and in were the most frequently referenced relations. Linguistic differences were detected between room descriptions based on small contextual shifts. In the first setting, observers were more likely to use an intrinsic relative perspective ("you") and move through the description in either a dominant near/far or far/near access pattern. In the second setting, observations did not begin from an intrinsic perspective but instead SpSpatial preposition specification for improved indoor navigation 3 from the right side of the observer. There was little evidence of entities described according to their functional roles over simple spatial configurations.

Both test rooms exhibited spatial networks of a similar size and density and patterns of connectivity between specific objects/structures as well as groups of objects/structures. The spatial preposition on was used most frequently and almost exclusively in the Contact sense (e.g., TR (mobile object) on LM (structure)) rather than the Support sense. Semantically similar spatial prepositions were mapped to complex primitives in order to better understand the level of detail necessary to constrain or expand spatial relations based on user comprehension, perception limits and task dependencies. In some cases, simple spatial expressions may be sufficient to construct a simple cognitive model, however, a more complex task (object location or navigation) the relation may require more detail.

4   Discussion

Preliminary results suggest scene description studies need to consider both moveable and fixed structural objects within indoor settings to fully capture the range of object relations within built environments. This study suggests that indoor navigation NL models might benefit from a set of rules that build spatial descriptions from spatial triples of moveable objects as trajectors, boundary structures as landmarks and relations based on semantic similarity (i.e. spatial relation thesaurus). There is also some evidence that rules could guide the classification and grouping of object/structures as well as account for latent functional properties.

Additional questions raised by this study include:

- What level of semantic clarity is lost or gained when one spatial preposition is selected as the spatial relation vs. a semantic synonym?

- What critical factors influence user spatial expression choice/preference within different types of indoor environments (small scale vs large scale)?

- To what degree are user expression choices task dependent? Is using the most linguistically appropriate or correct spatial preposition important in some tasks but not others?

Future work will include additional human subject experiments to test native English speakers choice/preference of scene descriptions generated from rules based on the findings of the pilot study. These experiments will address the questions above in a variety of settings such as a 3D virtual indoor space, small and large scale indoor spaces, and in task based indoor scenarios. A practical application of this work is the creation of classification and organization rules for a NL scene description system. This type of system could be used in conjunction with image capture and interpretation systems designed for indoor environments, analogous to current mobile device GPS and NL navigation assistants for outdoor space.

References

[1]   BATEMAN, J., HOIS, J., ROSS, R., AND TENBRINK, T. A linguistic ontology of space for natural language processing. Artificial Intelligence 174 (2010), 1027-1071.

[2]   COVENTRY, K., Function, geometry and spatial prepositions: Three experiments. Spatial Cognition and Computation 1 (1999) 145-154.

[3]   ELAHI, M., SHI, H. BATEMAN, J., EBERHARD, K. AND SCHEUTZ, M. Classification of localization utterances using a spatial ontology. In Proceedings of the International Workshop on Place related knowledge acquisition research (P-KAR'2012) pp. 13-18.

[4]   EVANS, V. A Unified Account of Polysemy within LCCM Theory. 157 (2015) Lingua. 100-123.

[5]   HOIS, J. Inter-annotator agreement on a linguistic ontology for spatial languagea case study for GUM-Space In 7th International Conference on Language Resources and Evaluation.(LREC'10) pp. 3464-3469. ELRA.

[6]   KESAVAN, S. Indoor scene knowledge acquisition using natural language descriptions. Master's thesis University of Maine , Orono, Maine. (2013).

[7]   KORDJAMSHIDI, P., VAN OTTERLO, M., AND MOENS, M. Spatial role labeling: Towards extraction of spatial relations from natural language. ACM Transactions on Speech and Language Processing, 8, 3, (2011). 1-36.

[8]   LANGACKER, R. Reflections on the functional characterization of spatial prepositions. CORELA - Numéros thématiques I Espace, Préposition, Cognition. (2010). http://corela.edel.univ-poitiers.fr/index.php?id=999

[9]   SMITH, B. AND MARK, D. Do mountains exist? Towards an ontology of landforms. Environment and Planning B (Planning and Design) 30, 3, (2003). 411– 427.

[10] VANDELOISE, C. (2006) Are there spatial prepositions? In Space in Languages: Linguistic Systems and Cognitive Categories, M. Hickmann and S. Robert, Eds. John Benjamins, Philadelphia, 2006. 139-154.

[11] VASARDANI, M., TIMPF, S.,WINTER, S. AND TOMKO, M., From descriptions to Depictions: A conceptual framework. In T. Tenebrink, J.G. Stell, A. Galton and Z. Wood Eds. Conference on Spatial Information Theory, Proceedings of COSIT 2013. 8116, (2013). 299-319) Heidelberg: Springer Verlag.

Spatiotemporal Autocorrelation Analysis for Pattern Recognition on Geospatial Big Data

Song Gao

Department of Geography, University of California, Santa Barbara, 1832 Ellison Hall, UC Santa Barbara, CA93106-4060, USA

Extended Abstract

Abstract: Expeditions on the spatiotemporal analytical techniques can contribute to the future development of space-time GIS and thus play an important role in GIScience. In this research, we investigate three statistical measures which extend the classic spatial association indices for the spatiotemporal autocorrelation analysis (STAA). Experiments are conducted using large-scale mobile phone data in a city. The spatial order of weighted matrix was found to have more significant effects than the temporal neighbors on influencing the autocorrelation strength of hourly phone-call patterns. The analytical methods introduced in this paper can be applied in other geospatial datasets (e.g., infectious diseases, crimes, and GPS tracks) for facilitating data mining and knowledge discovery in geoinformatics and social sciences.

Keywords: Space-time, spatiotemporal analytics, spatiotemporal visualization, spatiotemporal autocorrelation analysis, geospatial big data.

---

1 Introduction

Despite that humans have keen ability to discover patterns hidden in small-scale data; they may find it difficult for large-scale data that often vary over both space and time. Researchers have made great effort on spatial data mining and spatiotemporal visual analytics to raise the cognitive ceilings which often prevent the interpretation of large-scale geospatial datasets. Recently, with the widespread use of location-awareness devices, it is possible to collect large-scale location-awareness datasets, such as mobile phone data, GPS-enabled taxi trajectories, and social media data, for sensing complex human activities and human-environment interactions. Although human movements and activities may vary over time across different regions, the observed activity hotspots and information flow might exhibit a pattern of spatial dependence. Also, ignoring the temporal dimension would not be sufficient to discover underlying spatiotemporal dynamics. For instance, urban governors might hope to understand patterns of human movements by observing the neighboring regions in previous time periods. To this end, there need some studies towards developing spatiotemporal autocorrelation measures for analyzing spatiotemporal Big Data.

2   Spatiotemporal Autocorrelation Analysis

Analyzing the spatiotemporal autocorrelation structures of geospatial big data would be helpful to understand the underlying dynamic patterns in space and time simultaneously. In statistics, autocorrelation can be taken as the correlation of a variable with a lagged specification of itself (Box et al., 2008). For instance, the temporal autocorrelation can be defined as the correlation of the same variable X between values at different time s and t.

$$R(s,t) = \frac{E[(X_t - \mu)(X_s - \mu)]}{\sigma^2} \quad (1)$$

While E is the expected value operator, μ is the mean of the observation values and σ^2 is the variance. The temporal autocorrelation can be used to explore the time-series autocorrelation patterns.

With regard to the spatial dependence, spatial autocorrelation (association) statistics have been used to analyze the degree of dependency among observations in a geographic space (Cliff & Ord, 1973). These measurements can be divided into two categories: global indices and local indices. Classic global indices of spatial autocorrelation include Moran's I (1950), Geary's C (1954), and Getis-Ord's General G (1992), while local indices of spatial association (LISA) can be established by transforming the global indices into corresponding local measurements based on different measures of similarity (Anselin, 1995). All of these spatial autocorrelation statistics require a spatial weighted matrix that reflects the intensity of the geographic relationship between observations and their neighbors, e.g., the distance-to-neighbor matrix or the binary matrix in which the element value is 0 or 1 determined by whether there is a shared boundary between the observation location and its neighbors. As suggested by Hardisty & Klippel (2010), adding the temporal neighbors into the spatial weighted matrix would be one approach to extend the traditional spatial autocorrelation measurements. Griffith (2010) gave an overview of spatiotemporal modelling techniques including autoregressive-integrated-moving average models, space-time autoregressive models, geostatistical models, and panel data models, as well as proposed spatial filtering models. All of those models have been motivated by considering the spatiotemporal associations simultaneously. Cheng et al. (2012) further extended both global and local spatiotemporal autocorrelation analysis onto the road network data for complex traffic analysis.

Here, we present three extended versions of global measures of spatiotemporal association analysis (STAA) regarding the Moran's I, Geary's C, and Getis-Ord's General G:

$$I_{st} = \frac{\sum_{i=1}^{N}\sum_{j=1}^{N} w_{ij}[z_i(t) - \bar{z}_t][z_j(t+\tau) - \bar{z}_{t+\tau}]}{\sigma_t \sigma_{t+\tau} \sum_{i=1}^{N}\sum_{j=1}^{N} w_{ij}} \qquad (2)$$

$$C_{st} = \frac{\sum_{i=1}^{N}\sum_{j=1}^{N} w_{ij}[z_i(t) - z_j(t+\tau)]^2}{2\sigma_t \sigma_{t+\tau} \sum_{i=1}^{N}\sum_{j=1}^{N} w_{ij}} \qquad (3)$$

$$G_{st} = \frac{\sum_{i=1}^{N}\sum_{j=1}^{N} w_{ij} z_i(t) z_j(t+\tau)}{\sum_{i=1}^{N}\sum_{j=1}^{N} z_i(t) z_j(t+\tau)} \qquad (4)$$

Where I_{st}, C_{st}, and G_{st} can be taken as different formats of space-time cross-correlation (or cross-product) models (Getis, 1991); Z is the target variable of interest; i and j are indices of total N spatial units; w_{ij} is an element of the k-order-neighbor spatial weighted matrix ($1_{st}, 2_{nd}, ..., k_{th}$); $\bar{z}_t$ and $\bar{z}_{t+\tau}$ are the means of variable Z within a time lag τ, while σ_t and $\sigma_{t+\tau}$ are the variances. The local measures of spatiotemporal autocorrelation can be derived by decomposing a global measure into particular spatial neighboring units. Similar to the spatial autocorrelation plot and mapping, the geovisualization of spatiotemporal autocorrelation analysis results extends the space-time cube in 3D GIS with volume rendering using a 3D (x, y, t) voxel structure, which has been used in spatiotemporal density representations (Brunsdon et al., 2007; Demšar & Virrantaus, 2010; Gao et al. 2013; Delmelle et al., 2014).

The chosen spatial weighted matrix (spatial neighbor) has been identified as an important factor that affects the spatial autocorrelation analysis results (Ord & Getis, 1995). In order to address this issue, in the experiment section, we will evaluate how different spatial and temporal neighbors (lags) affect the results of three spatiotemporal autocorrelation measures in geospatial data analytics.

3 Experiments

In this research, a large-scale geospatial datasets which contains a week of about 74, 000,000 anonymized mobile phone call detail records (CDR) in a city has been used. The CDR data lists the information of caller, receiver, mobile location, date, time, duration and so on. Every time when a user made a call, he/she was geo-referenced to a corresponding mobile base station that has a unique longitude & latitude coordinate. The coverage area of each mobile base station can be expressed as a Voronoi polygon for call activity analysis and termed as a "cell". In this Voronoi partition, all phone calls within a given polygon are closer to the corresponding mobile base station than any other stations. Generally, urban central regions have a higher density of mobile cells (the coverage area of each cell is smaller) than the outer suburb regions and vice versa.

The phone-call volume was aggregated into the Voronoi cells by hour in the data processing step in order to calculate the region-based autocorrelation statistics.

The study of spatiotemporal autocorrelation structure of mobile phone calls in urban areas can help to understand the citizens' dynamic mobile communication patterns and associated urban structures. Using the methodology introduced in Section 2, we implement three global spatiotemporal statistics of STAA with different spatial and temporal neighbors for analyzing hourly phone-call patterns across all cells. The variable is the total count of phone calls in a cell at the given time. Examining the STAA results reveals two key findings (See Figure 1b). First, the strength of global Moran's I like spatiotemporal autocorrelation measure (I_{st}) for hourly phone calls is temporally dynamic and there is a positive-association peak between 6 AM~7AM. Second, the I_{st} measure is more sensitive to the spatial orders (See Figure 1a) than the temporal neighbors. A higher-order of spatial weights generally results in higher strength of spatiotemporal autocorrelation structure. In addition, it is found that the hourly autocorrelation trends of the global Geary's C like STAA measure C_{st} measures are more similar to the I_{st} measures (Figure 1c). But using the Getis-Ord's G like STAA measure G_{st} measure didn't reveal the temporal dynamics of autocorrelation strength in this dataset. The G_{st} statistic is also sensitive to the spatial-order of weighted matrix (Figure 1d).

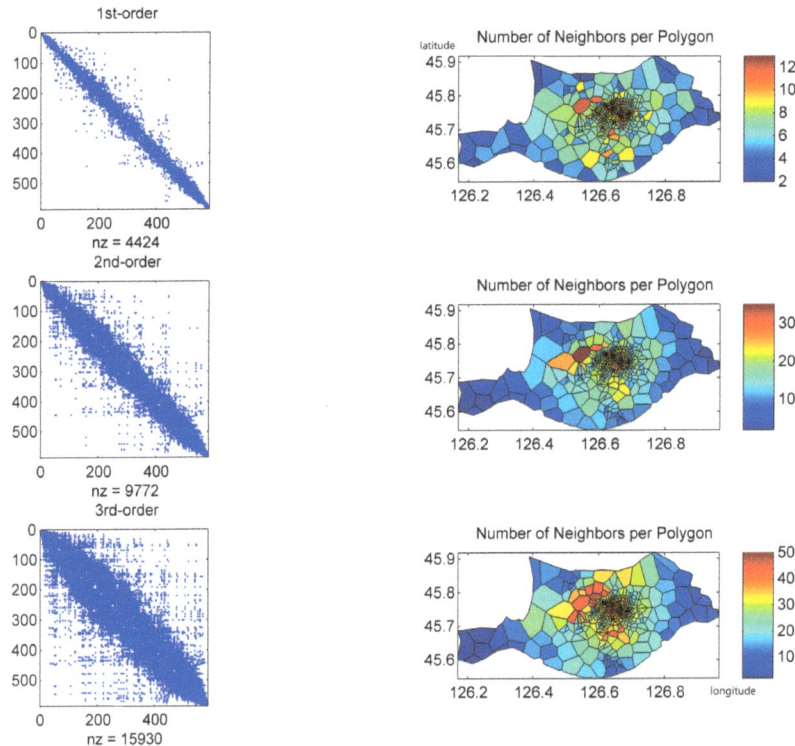

(a)

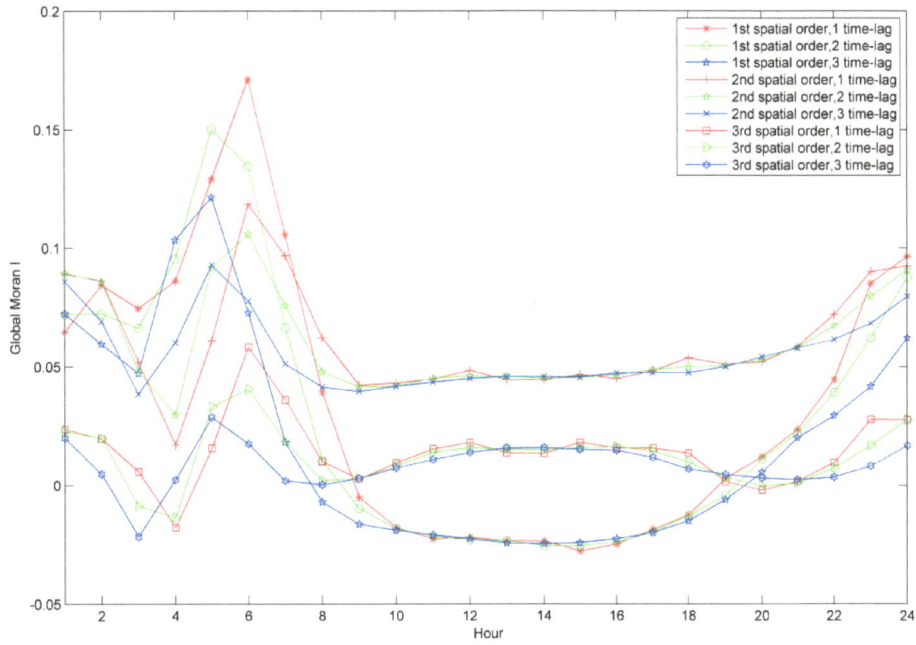

(b)

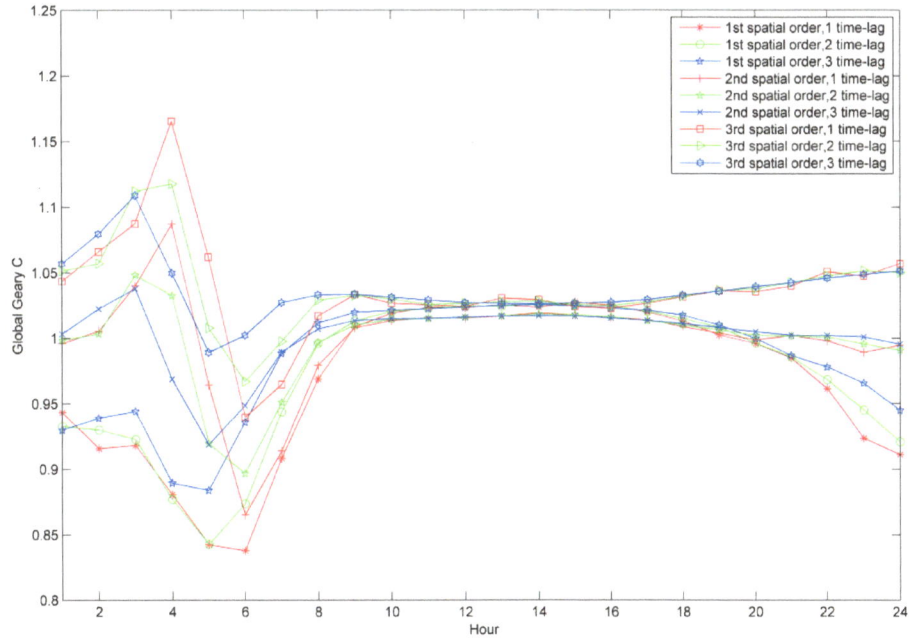

(c)

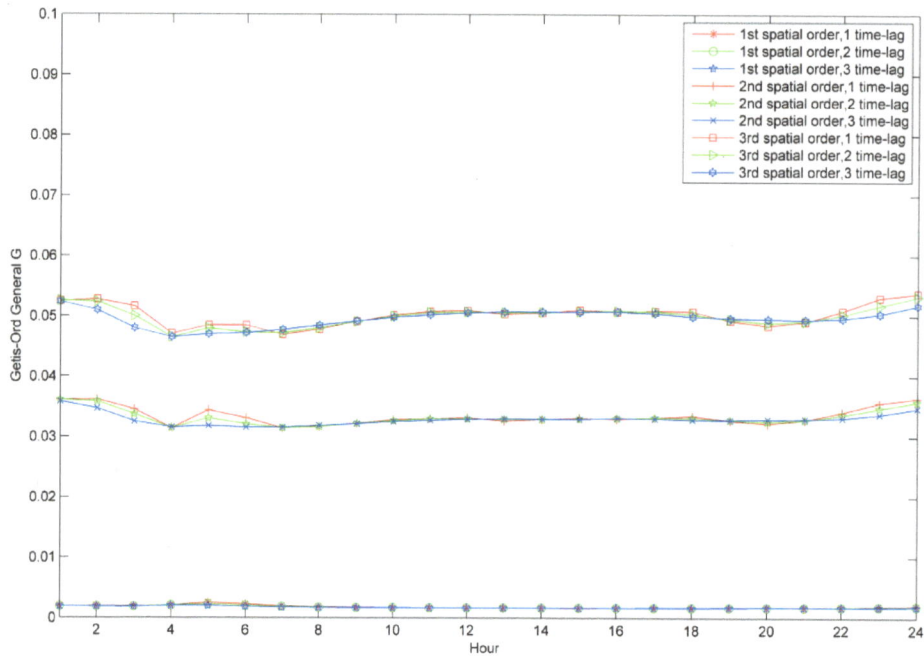

(d)

Figure 1. Three global measures of spatiotemporal association with different combinations of spatial weights (spatial orders) and temporal neighbors (1 time-lag: 1 hour; 2 time-lag: 2 hours; 3 time-lag: 3 hours) for hourly phone-call patterns: (a) the spatial adjacency matrix (a dot means the weight between the two cells is 1; otherwise is 0) and the corresponding distributions of neighbors for each mobile cell; (b) I_{st}; (c) C_{st}; and (d) G_{st} STAA measures.

4   Conclusions

In this work, we investigate three spatiotemporal statistical measures (I_{st}, C_{st} and G_{st}) which extended the classic spatial association indices for the spatio-temporal autocorrelation analysis. The spatial order of weighted matrix was found to have more significant effects than the temporal neighbors on influencing the autocorrelation strength of hourly phone-call volume in the experiments. The analytical methods introduced in this paper can be also generalized to other study areas and applied in other geospatial datasets (e.g., infectious diseases, crimes, and GPS tracks) for facilitating knowledge discovery and decision support in urban informatics and social sciences in the era of Big Data. Note that Big Data carries four important characteristics (i.e., volume, velocity, variety and veracity). The development of high-performance computing infrastructure can speed up the processing procedures (Gao et al. 2014), which deal with the volume and velocity challenges. But the variety and veracity issues need more discussion. For example, the uncertainty of actual user location beyond the cell tower needs to be studied when zooming into the individual trajectory mining and activity analysis. In addition, the temporal neighbors could be extended in two directions (past and future) or just one direction (past) to the given timestamp during the spatiotemporal autocorrelation analytics, which might rely on the purposes, e.g., historical data mining vs. online analytical processing.

References

[1] ANSELIN, L. Local indicators of spatial association—LISA Geographical analysis 27.2 (1995): 93-115.

[2] BOX, G. E., JENKINS, G. M., AND REINSEL, G. C. Time series analysis: forecasting and control. John Wiley & Sons, 2008.

[3] BRUNSDON, C., CORCORAN, J. AND HIGGS, G. Visualising space and time in crime patterns: A comparison of methods. Computers, Environment and Urban Systems 31.1 (2007): 52-75.

[4] CHENG, T., HAWORTH J., AND WANG J.Q. Spatio-temporal autocorrelation of road network data. Journal of geographical systems 14.4 (2012): 389-413.

[5] CLIFF, A. D., AND ORD, J. K. Spatial autocorrelation (Vol. 5). London: Pion, 1973.

[6] DELMELLE, E., DONY, C., CASAS, I., JIA, M., AND TANG, W. Visualizing the impact of space-time uncertainties on dengue fever patterns." International Journal of Geographical Information Science 28.5 (2014): 1107-1127.

[7] DEMŠAR, U., AND VIRRANTAUS, K. Space–time density of trajectories: exploring spatio-temporal patterns in movement data. International Journal of Geographical Information Science 24.10 (2010): 1527-1542.

[8] GAO, S., HU YJ, JANOWICZ, K., AND MCKENZIE, G. A spatiotemporal scientometrics framework for exploring the citation impact of publications and scientists. In Proceedings of the 21st ACM SIGSPATIAL International Conference on Advances in Geographic Information Systems, pp. 204-213. ACM, 2013.

[9] GAO, S., LI, L., LI, W., JANOWICZ, K., AND ZHANG, Y. Constructing gazetteers from volunteered big geo-data based on Hadoop. Computers, Environment and Urban Systems, doi:10.1016/j.compenvurbsys.2014.02.004

[10] GEARY, R. C. The contiguity ratio and statistical mapping. The incorporated statistician (1954): 115-146.

[11] GETIS, A., AND ORD, J. K. The analysis of spatial association by use of distance statistics. Geographical analysis 24.3 (1992): 189-206.

[12] GRIFFITH, D. A. Modeling spatio-temporal relationships: retrospect and prospect. Journal of Geographical Systems 12.2 (2010): 111-123.

[13] HARDISTY, F., AND KLIPPEL, A. Analysing spatio-temporal autocorrelation with LISTA-Viz. International Journal of Geographical Information Science 24.10 (2010): 1515-1526.

[14] MORAN, P. AP. Notes on continuous stochastic phenomena. Biometrika (1950): 17-23.

[15] ORD, J. K., AND GETIS, A. Local spatial autocorrelation statistics: distributional issues and an application. Geographical analysis 27.4 (1995): 286-306.

Semantic Challenges for Geographic and Spatial Reasoning

Torsten Hahmann

School of Computing and Information Science and National Center for Geographic Information and Analysis, 5711 Boardman Hall, University of Maine, Orono, ME 04469-5711, USA

Extended Abstract

---

1 Semantics and Ontologies in GI Science

Over the last 20 years, semantics, and ontologies as specific tools for capturing semantics, have played an increasingly significant role in Geographical Information Science as predicted in some early work [8, 9]. Since then much progress has been made in analyzing, understanding, and formally describing common geographic features, such as mountains and rivers [3, 22], and the foundational spatial relationships that underlie common sense descriptions of geographic space in the sense of [8], including qualitative relations that capture topology, direction, or shape (see [18] for an overview). This has significantly advanced the realization of a "Naïve Geography" [8], envisioned as consisting of two complementary sources:

> (1) the cognitive and linguistic approach, investigating the terminology people use for spatial concepts; and (2) the formal approach concentrating on mathematically based models, which can be implemented on a computer.

Much of the ontological research in GI Science can be thought of as being guided by this idea of a naïve geography necessary for formalizing (in a computer-accessible representation) and automating the kind of common sense spatial reasoning that humans accomplish effortlessly.

2 Changing Requirements for Semantics of Geographic Terms

But since 1995, the requirements for semantically-enabled geographic representations have significantly evolved, due to the explosion in available geographic data for which semantics are needed in order to not only access and find the data, but also to support the increasingly automated selection, comparison, integration, and reasoning about the data. Examples include high-precision Lidar data of Earth surface as well as detailed land-use and transportation network data, and volunteered data about both natural and artificial (engineered) geographic features. This wealth of data has stretched the limits of simple common sense spatial reasoning that relies on fairly small, hand-crafted representations of spatial knowledge as common in the literature on Qualitative Spatial Reasoning [7, 18]. Instead, data-driven approaches – foremost machine learning – are now considered the holy grail of spatial intelligence. While early work using machine learning approaches tried to do without semantics by recognizing patterns in data or by integrating heterogeneous data sources without knowledge or respect of the underlying semantics, the results are incomprehensible to humans and thus offer little insights into how geographic objects or features are classified. Consequently, recent work on semantics for geographic terms has focused on injecting semantics into these data-driven approaches in order to obtain more meaningful and human-understandable results. Most notably, work on geographic data within the realm of the "Semantic Web" has focused on developing data standards for geographic data and on general patterns applicable to many data sources to facilitate integration and semantically conformant reasoning. However, much of the analysis and formalization of the necessary semantics has remained on a fairly general level by trying to accommodate all possible linguistic senses (meanings/uses/interpretations) of spatial relationships such as "in contact", "contains", "inside", "meets", or "overlaps", and of geographic terms such as "stream" or \mountain" instead of formally disambiguating between them.

We believe that even more rigorous analysis, disambiguation, and formalization of semantics for spatial and geographic terms is needed – not necessarily for enabling data standardization and exchange, but for selecting appropriate senses of a specific uses of spatial and geographic terms. Human spatial and geographic language is highly ambiguous and dependent on specific contexts [1]; the more important it is to more precisely understand all the different senses and contextual conditions in which a specific spatial term is used1. We will outline three promising and interrelated challenges that need to be addressed to support semantically richer (semi-)automated geographic data integration and more sophisticated geographic reasoning and spatial intelligence. These critical challenges are motivated by the barriers/limitations we have encountered in our own attempts and closely related work [14, 15, 16, 21] about more sophisticated geographic representations of water bodies and water flows. They include:

   1. Complementing semantics of two-dimensional abstract spatial concepts by semantics of physically-based spatial concepts, which requires a fuller integration of the vertical spatial dimension;

   2. Developing computational spatial semantics separate from, yet in close relationship to, semantics of linguistic/cognitive uses of spatial terms as formalized in, e.g., [1];

   3. Developing computational ways to reason with multiple conceptualizations of space, in particular with different dimensional abstractions of physical/geographic space.

While this may go beyond narrower definitions of what constitutes geographic reasoning, which could be described as cartographic reasoning, we believe these are necessary for computationally solving many common sense spatial reasoning tasks that humans easily accomplish. The second and third challenge in particular emphasize the computational aspects of semantics of geographic and spatial terms as opposed to the linguistic/cognitive aspects. The remainder will explain the three challenges in more detail.

2.1 Complementing Semantics of Two-Dimensional Spatial Concepts by Semantics of Physically-Based Spatial Concepts

This challenge aims at expanding the scope of naïve geography by eliminating two assumptions from [8], namely the restriction of naïve geography to essentially two (or 2 1/2) dimensions and the related assumption that for the purposes of naïve geography the Earth is flat. The reason for this expansion is that the third, vertical dimension encodes much of the physics that governs space, such as when things stay put in place or fall, or where water collects and flows. To address this challenge, pure geographic (*abstract spatial*) knowledge must be joined with basic hydrographic, hydrologic, geologic, and physical knowledge, thereby enriching the spatial terms grounded in a two-dimensional abstraction of space by what the terms mean with respect to the physical terrain. First attempts such as [14, 15, 16, 21] are promising, but still need richer, explicit semantics that encodes what terrain features such as peaks and pits, ridge and slope lines, and channels in terms of what is "cartographically" (two-dimensionally) and physically possible or impossible: Where can these features be located and how do they spatially and physically relate to one another?

2.2 Developing Computational Spatial Semantics

Traditionally, the emphasis of ontological work within GI Science has been on representing the exterior reality [9], which manifests itself in geographic terminology and language, as opposed to ontologies that create a digital reality. However, nowadays the digital reality is often more important than the exterior reality: what is not represented in a digital representation (such as a database, a digital map, or a collection of observations) of the world does, for many purposes, not exist: a stream that is not recorded is usually not called a stream and an unnamed mountain or mountain peak is not explicitly displayed as a peak on a map. However, if we understand the semantic intricacies and possible distinctions of terms such as "stream", "peak", or "mountain" to such a level of detail that we can encode them in a computer-understandable representation, we can also design corresponding algorithms to automatically extract them from digital representations such as the USGS National Map. Such extraction algorithms already exist, but their semantics is not explicitly represented outside the algorithms, so that the semantics of the extracted features remain detached from the implied semantics that underlie the algorithms. But developing algorithms based on explicit representations of the semantics of geographic features, we would no longer need to rely on humans to label these features as we currently do and we would no longer need to try to guess or infer which sense of a term such as "stream" or "mountain" was originally meant – the algorithms' underlying semantics are explicit about it. This would complement the currently applied techniques used to extract features, such as roads, buildings, or surface water from satellite or areal imagery by computationally identifying and describing more subtle geographic features. While these descriptions may not always match human descriptions, at least they are uniformly applied and thus comparable across the landscape.

A prime example of how this could be accomplished could be set by linking the recently developed parallel treatment of various notions of spatial containment/surrounding from [2, 15]. Their explicit linkage could yield linguistically grounded formal models of relations that express some form of spatial containment or surrounding.

2.3 Developing Computational Ways to Reason with Multiple Spatial Conceptualizations

This challenge is closely related to the observation that people often use multiple conceptualizations of space in different contexts or even simultaneously [8]. This seems to be one of least understood and maybe most complicated aspects of human spatial and geographic reasoning, which has not yet been addressed satisfactorily. The related observation that humans often use multiple levels of detail in different contexts or simultaneously is now much better understood, thanks to work such as [4, 5, 20]. However, these two aspects must be treated in unison: different conceptualizations of space are often tied to specific scales at which they are applied. This is exhibited most clearly in how humans conceptualize geographic features dimensionally different based on application or required level of detail. For example, finding a route from A to B can be accomplished using a fairly coarse representation, whose elements are individual segments between intersections of the road networks, without any information about the width of the road or the change in elevation. But for finding a hiking route, the elevation may contain critical information that needs to be incorporated as a third dimension. Equally, when planning a route for an oversized truck, the width of roads is important, requiring not just a linear but a full three-dimensional model that incorporates distances, width and height clearance above the roads. As one prerequisite for this challenge, formal spatial semantics for these dimensionally varying conceptualizations of space are necessary. Early explorations of the role of dimension in spatial relations [19, 6, 10, 11] showed some promise but were not further pursued. In recent work, we picked up this line of research [17, 13] and showed that cognitive simple yet powerful sets of relations that respect and incorporate the different dimensions of spatial features can be formally defined and hold significant potential for modeling the ubiquitous geographic features represented using point, vector/line, or polygonal/region representations.

References

[1]   Bateman, J. A., Hois, J., Ross, R., and Tenbrink, T. A linguistic ontology of space for natural language processing. Artif. Intell. 174, 14 (2010), 1027–1071.

[2]   Bennett, B., Chaudhri, V., and Dinesh, N. A vocabulary of topological and containment relations for a practical biological ontology. In Conf. on Spatial Inf. Theory (COSIT-13) (2013), Springer.

[3]   Bennett, B., Mallenby, D., and Third, A. An ontology for grounding vague geographic terms. In Conf. on Formal Ontology in Inf. Systems (FOIS-08) (2008).

[4]   Bittner, T. Granularity in reference to spatio-temporal location and relations. In Florida Artif. Intell. Research Society Conf. (FLAIRS-15) (2002), pp. 466–470.

[5]   Bittner, T., and Smith, B. A theory of granular partitions. In Foundations of Geographic Information Science, M. Duckham, M. F. Goodchild, and M. F. Worboys, Eds. Taylor & Francis, 2003, pp. 124–158.

[6] Clementini, E., Di Felice, P., and van Oosterom, P. A small set of formal topological relationships suitable for end user interaction. In Symp. on Large Spatial Databases (SSD'93) (1993), LNCS 692, Springer, pp. 277–295.

[7] Cohn, A. G., and Renz, J. Qualitative Spatial Representation and Reasoning. In Handbook of Knowledge Representation, F. van Harmelen, V. Lifschitz, and B. Porter, Eds. Elsevier, 2008.

[8] Egenhofer, M. J., and Mark, D. M. Naive Geography. In Conf. on Spatial Inf. Theory (COSIT-95) (1995), LNCS 988, Springer, pp. 1–15.

[9] Frank, A. U. Spatial Ontology: A Geographical Information Point of View. In Spatial and Temporal Reasoning, O. Stock, Ed. Kluwer, 1997, pp. 135–154.

[10] Galton, A. Taking dimension seriously in qualitative spatial reasoning. In Europ.Conf. on Artif. Intell. (ECAI-96) (1996), pp. 501–505.

[11] Gotts, N. M. Formalizing commonsense topology: the INCH calculus. In Int. Symp. On Artif. Intell. and Math. (1996), pp. 72–75.

[12] Gruninger, M., Hahmann, T., Hashemi, A., Ong, D., and Ozgovde, A. Modular first-order ontologies via repositories. Applied Ontology 7, 2 (2012), 169–209.

[13] Hahmann, T. A Reconciliation of Logical Representations of Space: from Multidimensional Mereotopology to Geometry. PhD thesis, Univ. of Toronto, Dept. of Comp. Science, 2013.

[14] Hahmann, T., and Brodaric, B. The void in hydro ontology. In Conf. on Formal Ontology in Inf. Systems (FOIS-12) (2012), IOS Press, pp. 45–58.

[15] Hahmann, T., and Brodaric, B. Kinds of full physical containment. In Conf. on Spatial Inf. Theory (COSIT-13) (2013), Springer.

[16] Hahmann, T., Brodaric, B., and Gruninger, M. Interdependence among material objects and voids. In Conf. on Formal Ontology in Inf. Systems (FOIS-14) (2014), IOS Press.

[17] Hahmann, T., and Gruninger, M. A naive theory of dimension for qualitative spatial relations. In Symp. on Logical Formalizations of Commonsense Reasoning (CommonSense 2011) (2011), AAAI Press.

[18] Hahmann, T., and Gruninger, M. Region-based Theories of Space: Mereotopology and Beyond. In Qualitative Spatio-Temporal Representation and Reasoning: Trends and Future Directions, S. M. Hazarika, Ed. IGI, 2012, pp. 1–62.

[19] McKenney, M., Pauly, A., Praing, R., and Schneider, M. Dimension-refined topological predicates. In Conf. on Advances in Geographic Information Systems (GIS-05) (2005), ACM, pp. 240–249.

[20] Rector, A., Rogers, J., and Bittner, T. Granularity, scale and collectivity: When size does and does not matter. J. Biomed. Inform. 39 (2006), 333–349.

[21] Sinha, G., Mark, D., Kolas, D., Varanka, D., Romero, B. E., Feng, C.-C., Usery, L. E., Liebermann, J., and Sorokine, A. An ontology design pattern for surface water features. In 8th Int. Conf. on Geographic Information Science (GIScience 2014) (2014).

[22] Smith, B., and Mark, D. M. Do mountains exist? Towards an ontology of landforms. Environment and Planning B 30, 3 (2003), 411–428.

Spatial Data and Map Service Development: Mirroring the Path of a Discipline

Indy Hurt

Independent Researcher – San Francisco, CA

Extended Abstract

---

1 Introduction

Today's web map services are developed by collections of software engineers, database engineers, content and sourcing teams, data scientists, cartographers, geographers, planners, researchers, and editors. There are clear parallels between research themes that have developed over time in the discipline of geography and the development of web map services. Some challenges and criticisms that accompanied periods of geography continue to manifest themselves. The compressed timeline associated with web map development can amplify some challenges while advancing technologies and globalism can eliminate others. More cross-pollination between industry and academia could prove to be a fruitful partnership with respect to addressing challenges. To succeed, the academy must be up to the challenge of preparing students for these opportunities. Open source development enables transparency, while open data aims to encourage community around a shared resource. There are some barriers associated with the current reward system in academia that make it difficult to participation in the agile software development commonly associated with open source software [1]. While traditional publishing track records currently dominate the tenure-track review process, the overall number of tenure positions is declining [2, 3]. Graduate students are taking notice and considering other career opportunities for this and may other reasons [4].

2 Trajectory of Map Services

Web map services are advancing rapidly, fueled by an ever-growing list of players. In 2016, MapQuest's web service celebrates a 20-year anniversary. Google Maps celebrated 10 years in 2015. OpenStreetMap reached this same milestone in 2014.

Other notable services include Nokia's Here, and Microsoft's Bing Maps both changing hands entirely or in part in 2015 with a consortium of German car makers [5] and ride share app Uber [6], respectively. TomTom and Apple Maps have a data partnership while both maintain independent web map services. Russian search engine Yandex also offers a global map service; while countless other web map services like Géoportail, MapMyIndia, and Arealis provide specialized local content.

Global web map services are an interesting subset. A common first step to building one begins with a data model that can be populated with spatial and tabular data. A web map service might be a series of services that work collectively to provide various types of routing, flexible search able to return addresses and features, personal reminders, display of personalized data, and other useful location based features. Reminiscent of classical geography identified as the period between 600 BC and 1770 AD, today's players focus on general and regional geography as the foundation for their service when they enter the playing field. This is commonly referred to as the basemap.

One significant challenge during the classical geography period revolved around limitations in mobility. While mobility is not as much of a challenge today, collecting and maintaining the fundamental basemap data on a global scale presents new challenges. A comprehensive map of the world grows in complexity with each added theme of information. Errors in sparsely populated areas garner as much visibility and potentially negative publicity as any other area. Examples include routes that end in the middle of nowhere [7], routes to points of interest that end at residential addresses [8, 9], and numerous examples of missing localities or inaccurate representations of borders and place names [10, 11]. A fierce competition is on to secure market share, and a significant component to winning the hearts and minds of users is the ability to continuously present accurate reliable spatial data. Unfortunately, the users of these data are most concentrated in economically viable regions leaving other areas without a user base to demand rich content. Public participatory GIS and volunteered geographic information efforts have made contributions in this area. While some of these efforts suffer from data quality issue [12], the Humanitarian OpenStreetMap Team continues to address feedback and supports further development of rich content during and long after crisis events [13].

The era of modern geography, characterized as the period between 1770 and 1970, ushered in the dawn of university geography departments. This time period, strengthened by standardized empirical observations, took place alongside the period of the Enlightenment. A strong emphasis on the value of science has filtered its way into the map service development activities of today, but not just any science. Today's activities revolve around data science specifically targeted towards big data. With web map services, there are opportunities for geographers and other spatially oriented domain experts to conduct the kinds of analyses they have been doing for years, just on a much larger scale [14].

Is today's spatial data analytics the reincarnation of the quantitative revolution of the 1950's and 1960's? There are some interesting similarities. The quantitative revolution saw analysis conducted with tools and data that were not easily accessible to the general population. Desktop and web based GIS software environments with graphical user interfaces were not yet developed. Big data is similarly inaccessible to store on a personal computer, most cannot be accessed freely in the cloud, and it cannot be manipulated without a reasonable amount of technical skill. For this reason, data scientists often double as software engineers. They contribute to a large codebase, build web applications, store and retrieve large datasets, and employ statistical methods with proprietary and open source tools.

Data contributed by individuals in the form of data logs from sensors onboard personal devices remains an incomprehensible mystery to most. These logs help drive analysis and improvements to maps in many ways. They uncover patterns, reveal collective behaviors, and help businesses target goods and services more effectively in ways that are often tied to profitability. Large spatial data providers like TomTom boast probe data consisting of 6 trillion data points with an additional 6 billion new data points collected every day from their community of users and other sources [15]. Applications like Waze initially turned street data acquisition into a game. As the user base grew, users voluntarily agreed to share personal tracking information to improve traffic and routing analytics. These closed systems provide a traffic service in exchange for the data, but users have no way to download and process their own personal data. As the commodification of web map services continues to grow, an effort to identify exploitative activity around the collection and dissemination of spatial data and services remains an important area of inquiry. Acceptance of terms of service agreements does not mean that privacy is dead. Data from the Pew Research Center indicates that people do care about privacy and how their personal data is used [16].

Critical GIS was the response to the quantitative revolution, and this history continues to repeat itself. Through publications and continued scholarship, the Friday Harbor meetings of 1993 and 2014 lend voices to issues that remain prominent today. The 1993 meeting was sponsored by the NCGIA and was organized by Nick Chrisman, John Pickles, Tom Poiker and Eric Sheppard [17]. Notable publications from the 1993 meeting include Ground Truth: the social implications of Geographic Information Systems edited by John Pickles, and a special issue of Cartography and GIS featuring papers from the meeting. The 2014 meeting returned to Friday Harbor to revisit these topics and renew engagement between the scholars of critical GIS and quantitative spatial analysis. Humanist, Marxist, feminist, poststructuralist, postcolonial, antiracist, and queer geographers cautioned against quantitative geography and its inability to effectively address several areas of concern that could not be understood from a purely mathematical approach [18].

We could be turning the page. The open source community is attracting a broader audience by putting data back in the control of contributors. Open source analysis tools are becoming easier to use. While access to cloud computing still comes at a cost, the cost is declining at a rate of 33% each year and data storage costs are declining at a rate of 38% each year [19]. Amazon Web Services has made all Landsat 8 scenes from 2015 available through a joint effort with the U.S. Geological Survey and NASA. Could the opportunity for individuals to capture, access, and analyze the extensive amount of personal data they generate also become accessible in the same manner? Advanced technical skill sets are still key to interpreting information in an endless supply of data, but the potential to overcome this barrier is easier to imagine. GIS went through a similar transformation, and continues to become more accessible.

3   Conclusion

The similarities between the evolution of the discipline of geography and the trajectory of individual web map services are evident. Entities embark on the task of building a basemap. This stage is dominated by data discovery of regional geographies.

Simultaneously or in close succession, services are built on top of the basemap. These services include real time traffic, transit, multi-modal routing, spatially oriented personalized advertising, location sharing, and many others. Data collected from onboard sensors enhance these services while bringing privacy concerns to the surface. Data scientists sift through an endless sea of data looking for patterns and opportunities. The individuals contributing the data are often far removed from the analysis and decisions being made as a result of the analysis. These activities lend strength to critical GIS discussions and the support of a more equitable distributed system. Are we closer to this goal than we were 20 years ago? Arguably yes, we are, based on the advances in the development and distribution of open source data and tools. The final piece of the puzzle requires more inroads into the development process. Geographers familiar with critical GIS research themes and statistical methods specific to spatial data have a lot to contribute to the fast paced industry growing around web map services. Software engineers with computer science backgrounds are dominating the landscape of web map service development. Opportunities to change this must start with earlier engagement between geographers, computer scientists, and designers. While software engineering skills are highly valuable, it should not be a requirement for participation. The ability to communicate with software engineers presents a tremendous amount of value. Application building benefits from the cohesive relationship between both software engineering and design.

4 References

[1]   SUI, D., Opportunities and Impediments for Open GIS. Transactions in GIS, 2014. 18(1): p. 1-24.

[2]   JASCHIK, S. The Disappearing Tenure-Track Job. 2009 5/12/2009 [cited 2015 8/27/2015]; Available from: https://www.insidehighered.com/news/2009/05/12/workforce.

[3]   KEZAR, A. AND D. MAXEY. The Changing Academic Workforce. 2013 [cited 2015 8/27/2015]; Available from: http://agb.org/trusteeship/2013/5/changing-academic-workforce.

[4]   MASON, M.A., M. GOULDEN, AND K. FRASCH, Why graduate studetns reject the fast track. Academe, 2009. 95(1): p. 11-16.

[5]   BARTZ, D. German carmakers win U.S. antitrust approval to buy Nokia maps. 2015 9/2/2015 [cited 2015 9/10/2015]; Available from: http://www.reuters.com/article/2015/09/02/us-nokia-here-automakers-antitrust-idUSKCN0R21SO20150902.

[6]   WILHELM, A. Uber Acquires Part of Bing's Mapping Assets, Will Absorb Around 100 Microsoft Employees. 2015 6/29/2015 [cited 2015 9/10/2015]; Available from: http://techcrunch.com/2015/06/29/uber-acquires-part-of-bings-mapping-assets-will-absorb-around-100-microsoft-employees/ - .acdjk8:yvg4.

[7]   THOMPSON, N. Apple Maps flaw could be deadly, warn Australian police. 2012 12/11/2012 [cited 2015 8/12/2015]; Available from: http://www.cnn.com/2012/12/10/tech/apple-maps-australia-flaw/.

[8]   BURNHAM, K. 6 Memorable Google Maps Mishaps. 2011 7/27/2011 [cited 2015
       8/12/2015]; Available from: http://www.cio.com/article/2405903/internet/6-
       memorable-google-maps-mishaps.html - slide2.

[9]   REED, B. Apple's iOS Maps pushes woman to brink of madness. 2014 2/28/2014
       [cited 2015 8/12/2015]; Available from: http://bgr.com/2014/02/28/worst-
       apple-maps-mistakes/.

[10]   SUTTER, J. Google Maps border becomes part of international dispute. 2010
       11/5/2010 [cited 2015 8/12/2015]; Available from:
       http://www.cnn.com/2010/TECH/web/11/05/nicaragua.raid.google.maps/.

[11]   REED, B. Apple, Google map apps inflame international feud between Japan and
       Korea over tiny disputed island. 2012 11/4/2012 [cited 2015 8/12/2015];
       Available from: http://bgr.com/2012/11/04/apples-maps-app-korea-japan-
       island-dispute/.

[12]   AMERICAN RED CROSS, OpenStreetMap Damage Assessment Review
       Typhoon Haiyan (Yolanda) Interim Report. 2014, American Red Cross: American
       Red Cross. p. 8.

[13]   SODEN, R. AND L. PALEN, From Crowdsourced Mapping to Community
       Mapping: The Post-earthquake Work of OpenStreetMap Haiti, in COOP 2014 -
       Proceedings of the 11th International Conference on the Design of Cooperative
       Systems, 27-30 May 2014, Nice (France), C. Rossitto, et al., Editors. 2014, Springer
       International Publishing. p. 311-326.

[14]   WRIGHT, D., Have I Been a Data Scientist from the Start?, in Esri Insider. 2015,
       Esri: Esri.

[15]   TOMTOM. Custom Probe Counts - Traffic density information for location-based
       analysis. 2012 6/2012 [cited 2015 9/9/2015]; Available from:
       http://www.tomtom.com/lib/doc/licensing/I.CPC.EN.pdf.

[16]   MADDEN, M. Privacy and Cybersecurity: Key findings from Pew Research. 2015
       [cited 2015 8/1/2015]; Available from: http://www.pewresearch.org/key-data-
       points/privacy/.

[17]   CRAIG, W., T. HARRIS, AND D. WEINER. Empowerment, Marginalization and
       Public Participation GIS. Report of Varenius Workshop 1998 2/1/1999 [cited
       2015 9/8/2015]; Available from:
       http://www.ncgia.ucsb.edu/varenius/ppgis/PPGIS98_rpt.html.

[18]   KWAN, M.-P. AND T. SCHWANEN, Quantitative Revolution 2: The Critical
       (Re)Turn. The Professional Geographer, 2009. 61(3): p. 283-291.

[19]   HAGEL, J. KPCB Internet Trends 2014. [SlideShare] 2014 5/28/2014 [cited 2015
       9/9/2015]; Available from: http://www.slideshare.net/kleinerperkins/internet-
       trends-2014-05-28-14-pdf.

An Ontology-based Geospatial Database for Identifying Geographical Change

Jeon-Young Kang[1], Jinmu Choi[2], Thomas Bittner[1]

1 Department of Geography, University at Buffalo, Buffalo, NY, USA
2 Department of Geography, Kyung Hee University, Seoul, South Korea

Extended Abstract

Abstract: This paper aims to explore the spatiotemporal change of administrative units of Seoul. We built a domain ontology for administrative units of Seoul based on BFO 2.0, and integrated the ontology with geospatial database. In particular, formal ontology was used to clarify administrative units, their properties, and their relative processes. Formal relations of spatiotemporal changes were considered, as well. The ontology-based geospatial database can contribute to identifying geographical changes over time via SPARQL.

Keywords: Geographical Changes, BFO 2.0, Formal Ontology, Geospatial Database.

1 Introduction

Geographical entities change over time, so do their appearance and/or properties. Interestingly, administrative units in new urban areas, which look static at first glance, also undergo changes over time; some units are expanded, shrank, destroyed, and newly established. These changes may give a rise to change units' properties (e.g., name, postcode, area) and parthood relations to others.

Geospatial database and formal ontology have been used to identify and trace such changes. Geospatial databases play an important role in recording changes of geometry through time. Recorded changes then can be accessed by using spatiotemporal queries [5, 11, 12]. Geospatial database also serves to keep track of the identity of geographical entities that may undergo significant changes (e.g., merge, split) [10]. Formal ontology has been used to clarify specifications of geographical entities and their changes over time by providing classification schemes for entities, their relationships to others, as well as changes of class membership and relations through time. Formal relations of such changes, defined by formal ontology, can play a role in linking between two time stamps: start and end points of a particular changes. It facilitates a better understanding of particular changes [8, 9, 14]. Therefore, combining geospatial database and formal ontology helps to trace and identify geographical changes in a formal manner.

This paper takes Seoul, South Korea as a case for identifying changes of administrative units over time. As Seoul has been dramatically developed, it is somewhat difficult to clarify its changes. The purpose of this paper is threefold: 1) to describe the changes of administrative units of Seoul, 2) to integrate ontologies and geospatial database, and 3) to keep tracking such changes.

2   Geographical Changes

2.1   Geographical Changes

Much attention has been paid to clarifying geographical entities [1, 2, 3, 4] and phenomena [6, 7]. Basic Formal Ontology (BFO) 2.0 contains the ontologies of SNAP (or a snapshot view) and SPAN (or spanning time), which represent an object (continuant) and a phenomenon (occurrent), respectively [9, 13]. Geographical changes refer to quantitative and structural changes. For instance, changes in population or in parthood across a given region [9].

2.2   Administrative Units and Their Relative Processes

According to the BFO 2.0, each administrative units and a series of processes of the units are thought of as continuants and occurrents, respectively. The axioms for units are as follows:

$$\text{AdministrativeUnit}(X) \rightarrow \text{Continuant}(X) - \text{AXIOM1}$$

$$\text{AdministrativeUnit}(X) \rightarrow \exists t.\text{existAt}(X,t) - \text{AXIOM 2}$$

$$\text{AdministrativeUnit}(X) \rightarrow \exists c \ \text{hasSubAdministrativeUnit}(X,C) - \text{AXIOM 3}$$

$$\text{DependentEntity}(D) \rightarrow (\forall t.\text{existAt}(D,t) \rightarrow \exists X \ \text{dependsOn}(D,X)) - \text{AXIOM 4}$$

For all administrative units are continuant entities (AXIOM 1). X exists at some temporal regions t (AXIOM 2). X has a sub-administrative unit C (AXIOM 3). Some dependent entities D exist at some temporal region t, and depends on X (AXIOM 4), and so on.

All processes for administrative units consist of expanding, shrinking, newly establishing, and destroying. Since SPAN entities are associated with SNAP entities [9], such processes occupy administrative units. The axioms for processes are as follows:

$$\text{Process}(P) \rightarrow \text{Occurent }(P) - \text{AXIOM 5}$$

$$\text{Process}(P) \rightarrow \exists t \ \text{exsitAt}(P,t) - \text{AXIOM 6}$$

$$\text{Process}(P) \equiv (\forall t.\text{existAt}(X,t) \rightarrow \exists X \ \text{hasPaticipant}(P,X)) - \text{AXIOM 7}$$

For all process P are occurrent entities (AXIOM 5). P exists at some spatiotemporal regions t (AXIOM 6). P has participant X that exists at some temporal regions t (AXIOM 7).

3 Building Domain Ontology and Geospatial Database

3.1 Subtopic

As described upon, this paper deals with continuants and occurrents. Figure 1 shows continuants and occurrents in the ontology. Administrative units are continuants including its dependent entities (e.g., role, name). A series of processes such as expanding, shrinking, destroying, and newly establishing are occurrents.

Figure 1: Classes for Administrative Units (Left) and Related Processes (Right)

In general, each country has its own system of administrative units. For a better understanding of Korean administrative units, each unit is presented corresponding to American units. They refer to the same level of administrative unit. For instance, 'si' is a equivalent class of city.

3.2 Building Geospatial Database of Administrative Units of Seoul

Sub-administrative units of Seoul have experienced dramatic changes in 1884, 1914, 1936, 1949, 1963, 1973, and 2014 (Figure 2). Thus, the geospatial database consists of the eight tables and corresponding eight polygon *.shp files.

1884	1914	1936	1949
Hanseong-bu, Yongsan-bang, Seogang-bang	Goyang-si, Hanji-myeon, Yonggang-myeon	Gyeongseong-bu	Gyeongseong-bu, Yongsan-bu
1963	**1973**	**1995**	**2014**
Seoul, Yongsan-gu	Seoul, Yongsan-gu	Seoul, Yongsan-gu	Seoul, Yongsan-gu

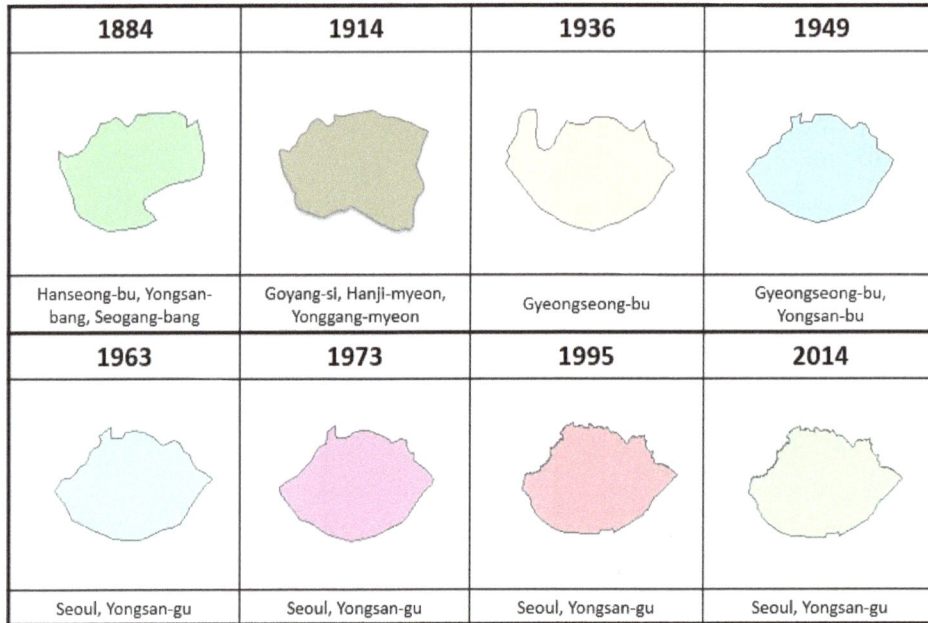

Figure 2. The Changes of Administrative Units of Seoul (e.g., Yongsan-gu)

Table 1 indicates geospatial database for Seoul in 2014. Geospatial database is composed of structured FID; a serial number of each spatial object in *.shp file, Shape; geometric features of spatial object in *.shp file, names of administrative units, the categories used in GeoNames, and the length and area.

Table 1. Geospatial Database for Administrative Units of Seoul (e.g., 2014)

FID	Shape	English name	Korean division name	English division name	Category of Geonames	First order division	Second order division	Third order division	Shape Length	Shape Area
1	Polygon	Seoul_Dongdaemun	Gu	District	Second order division	Seoul	Dongdaemun	-	32716.64	33633743.40
2	Polygon	Seoul_Jongno	Gu	District	Second order division	Seoul	Jongno	-	13498.98	10511816.16

4 Integrating Ontologies with GeoSpatial Database

4.1 Integration

The process of integrating ontologies with geospatial database consists of three steps. Initially, administrative unit ontology was built based on BFO 2.0. It was merged the ontology with GeoSPARQL, and GeoSpatial database, which is called ontology-based geospatial database. The database was ported into D2RQ. GeoSPARQL is OGC standard for querying geospatial data on the Semantic web. D2RQ is a widespread platform for ontological mapping, which makes relational database to access to a RDF-based system. Figure 3 shows 'Goyang_Wondang-myeon' unit via D2RQ mapping.

Property	Value
bfo:BFO_0000083	<http://localhost:2020/resource/sde/SPATIAL_REGION/1>
db:vocab/admin_division	<http://localhost:2020/resource/sde/ADMIN/Gyeonggi>
db:vocab/cat_geoname	<http://localhost:2020/resource/sde/GEONAMES/Third_order_administrative_division>
db:vocab/is_Site	<http://localhost:2020/resource/sde/SITE/Township>
Rdfs:label	SEOUL_MERGE #1
db:vocab/sde_SEOUL_MERGE_OBJECTID	1 (xsd:integer)
db:vocab/sde_SEOUL_MERGE_area	40351459.2021369 (xsd:double)
db:vocab/sde_SEOUL_MERGE_endyear	1914 (xsd:integer)
db:vocab/sde_SEOUL_MERGE_kor_d_name	Myeon
db:vocab/sde_SEOUL_MERGE_name_eng	Goyang_Wondang
db:vocab/sde_SEOUL_MERGE_second_ord	Goyang
db:vocab/sde_SEOUL_MERGE_third_ord	Wondang
db:vocab/sde_SEOUL_MERGE_year_	1884 (xsd:integer)
rdf:type	vocab:sde_Seoul_Merge

Figure 3. An Example of D2RQ Mapping

4.2 Exploration of the Changes of Administrative Units

For an application of ontology-based geospatial database, this paper used SPARQL, which is one of query languages for a RDF/OWL. It enabled to explore the changes of parthood relationship of Seoul. Figure 4 shows query syntax that which units had included in Seoul from 1973 to 1995 including its name and area, and results.

```
SELECT DISTINCT ?entity ?name ?area (?beginyear as ?year)
WHERE {
        ?entity vocab:admin_division http://localhost:2020/resource/sde/ADMIN/Seoul> .
        ?entity http://localhost:2020/resource/vocab/sde_SEOUL_MERGE_year_> ?beginyear .
FILTER (?beginyear <=1995)
?entity http://localhost:2020/resource/vocab/sde_SEOUL_MERGE_endyear> ?endyear .
FILTER (?endyear>=1973)
        ?entity vocab:sde_SEOUL_MERGE_area ?area.
        ?entity vocab:sde_SEOUL_MERGE_name_eng ?name.)
```

entity	name	area	year	year2
db:sde/SEOUL_MERGE/129	"Seoul_Dobong"	80720931.0018301	1973	1995
db:sde/SEOUL_MERGE/130	"Seoul_Seongbuk"	23813676.2257119	1973	1995
db:sde/SEOUL_MERGE/131	"Seoul_Jongno"	10664415.2164647	1973	1995
db:sde/SEOUL_MERGE/133	"Seoul_Dongdaemun"	32208275.5508674	1973	1995
db:sde/SEOUL_MERGE/134	"Seoul_Seongdong"	182711227.868282	1973	1995
db:sde/SEOUL_MERGE/136	"Seoul_Jung"	6032901.20232512	1973	1995
db:sde/SEOUL_MERGE/137	"Seoul_Yongsan"	21587559.7037717	1973	1995
db:sde/SEOUL_MERGE/138	"Seoul_Mapo"	11510549.6185603	1973	1995
db:sde/SEOUL_MERGE/139	"Seoul_Sodaemun"	73679978.1826024	1973	1995
db:sde/SEOUL_MERGE/144	"Seoul_Yeongdeungpo"	117376155.059354	1973	1995
db:sde/SEOUL_MERGE/148	"Seoul_Gwanak"	47164604.8887924	1973	1995

Figure 4: A Query Syntax and Its Result

5 Conclusion

This study attempted to integrate ontologies with geospatial database. It shows how BFO 2.0 can be used as a framework to define geographical entities and their changes.

It finds out in what ways ontology-based geospatial database can be utilized in tracing geographical changes through time. This study carried out spatiotemporal exploration as well. The approach of this study contributes to formally identifying administrative units' changes over time, and supporting such changes.

References

[1]   BITTNER, T. From top-level to domain ontologies: Ecosystem classifications as a case study, Spatial Information Theory, (2007), 61-77.

[2]   BITTNER, T., DONNELLY, M. AND SMITH, B. A Spatio-temporal ontology for geographic information integration, International Journal of Geographical Information Science 23, 6 (2009), 765-798.

[3]   BITTNER, T. On the integration of Regional Classification and Delineation Systems into The National Map, Catographica: The International Journal for Geographic Information and Geovisualization 45, 2 (2010), 127-139.

[4]   BITTNER, T. Vagueness and the trade-off between the classification and delineation of geographic regions-an ontological analysis, International journal of Geographical information Science 25, 5 (2011), 825-850.

[5]   CHOI, J., SEONG, J. C., KIM, B., AND USERY, L. Innovations in Individual Feature History Management- The Significance of Feature-based Temporal Model. GeoInformatica 12 (2008), 1-20.

[6]   GALTON, A. Space, Time, and the Representation of Geographical Reality. TOPOI 20, (2001), 173-187

[7]   GALTON, A. On What Goes On: The Ontology of Processes and Events, Formal Ontology in Information Systems. In FOIS '06: Proceedings of the 4th International Conference on Formal Ontology in Information Systems (Baltimore, MD, USA, 2006), IOS Press, pp. 4-11

[8]   GANGEMI, A. GUARINO, N., MASOLO, C., OLTRAMARI, A. AND SCHNEIDER, L., Sweetening Ontologies with DOLCE, AI Magazine 23, 3 (2003), 13-24

[9]   GRENON, P. AND SMITH, B. SNAP and SPAN: Towards Dynamic Spatial Ontology, Spatial Cognition and Computation 4, 1 (2004), 69-103.

[10]   HORNSBY, K. AND EGENHOFER, M. J. Identity-based change: a foundation for spatio-temporal knowledge representation, International journal of Geographical Information Science 14, 3 (2000), 207-224.

[11]   KAUPPINEN, T., VAATAINEN, J. AND HYVONEN, E. Creating and Using Geospatial Ontology Time Series in a Semantic Cultural Heritage Portal, In ESWC '08: Proceedings of the 5th European Semantic Web Conference (Tenerife, Canary Islands, Spain, 2008), Springer Berlin Heidelberg, pp.110-123

[12]   SENGUPTA, R. AND YAN, C. A hybrid spatio-temporal data model and structure (HST-DMS) for efficient storage and retrieval of land use information, Transactions in GIS 8, 3 (2004), 351-366.

[13]   SMITH, B., ALMEIDA, M., BONA, J., BROCHHAUSEN, M., CEUSTER, W., COURTOT, M., DIPERT, R., GOLDFAIN, A., GRENON, P., HASTINGS, J., HOGAN, W., JACUZZO, L., JOHANSSON, I., MUNGALL, C., NATALE, D.,

NEUHAUS, F., ROVETTO, A.P.R., RUTTENBERG, A., RESSLER, M., SCHULZ, S. Basic Formal Ontology 2.0 Draft, (2012)

[14]   WORBOYS, M. F. Modelling and Changes and Events in Dynamic Spatial Systems with Reference to Socio-economic Units. In Life and Motion of Socio-Economic Units, ESF GISDATA series, A. U. Frank, J. Raper, and J.-P. Cheylan, Eds. Taylor and Francis, London, 2001, pp. 129-138

Geospatial Resource Management in Disaster Stricken Area in Chile: A GEOSS Approach

Lucia C. Lovison-Golob

Afriterra Foundation, 400 Commonwealth Avenue, Boston, 02425, MA, U.S.A.

Extended Abstract

Abstract: The management of geospatial resources in Chilean areas stricken by disasters within GEOSS (Global Earth Observations System of Systems), a framework of content providers and a source of decision-support tools for geospatial data users, is presented. The GEO (Global Earth Observations) program, to which GEOSS belongs, encompasses nine societal benefit areas, one being the disasters area. The Architecture Implementation Pilot (AIP- GEOSS) project for disasters in Chile allows geospatial data and their associated metadata to be accessed, searched, and discovered through a geoportal, based on a distributed service-oriented architecture (SOA), called GEOSS Common Infrastructure (GCI). The project involves the following research areas: data sharing and collaboration among people, management of large volumes of data, their ontologies and models, as well as inclusion of geospatial standards from Earth observation sensors into augmented reality, disaster robotics, and virtual reality applications as a means to reduce societal vulnerability to disasters.

Keywords: GEOSS (Global Earth Observations System of Systems), disasters, geospatial products, and interoperable web services.

---

1 Introduction

The GEO (Global Earth Observations) program, to which GEOSS (Global Earth Observations System of Systems) belongs, started in 2005 and encompasses nine societal benefit areas: agriculture, biodiversity, climate, disasters, ecosystems, energy, health, water, and weather. The Chile Architecture Implementation Pilot (AIP-GEOSS) project covers one of the societal benefit areas, with several disaster scenarios in Chile, and involves the capacity-building of technical experts to decrease the vulnerability of Chile to disasters [5]. Chile was the site of the world's strongest earthquake – a magnitude 9.5 event in 1960 [9], and is the region of the largest number of active volcanoes in the world – 105 [1].

A wide range of national agencies and institutions in Chile collaborate with international organizations in the area of disaster response. Those national agencies and institutions include the following: IDE-SNIT (Infrastructura de Datos Geospatiales de Chile – Sistema Nacional de Información Territorial, Ministerio de Bienes Nacionales), Ministry of Foreign Affairs of Chile, ONEMI (Oficina Nacional de Emergencias de Ministerio del Interior y Seguridad Pública de Chile), SAF (Servicio Aerofotogramétrico de la Fuerza Aera de Chile), SHOA (Servicio Hydrográfico Oceanográfico de la Armada de Chile), CSN (Centro Sismologico Nacional, Universidad de Chile), Sernageomin (Servicio Nacional de Geologia y Mineraria de Chile), MeteoChile (Dirección Meteorológica de Chile), and the Universidad de Santa Maria in Santiago, Chile. International organizations, such as National Aeronautics and Space Administration (NASA), National Oceanic and Atmospheric Administration (NOAA), ConnectinGEO, and Afriterra Foundation, participate in the GEOSS framework called Common Infrastructure (GCI). The Chile AIP-GEOSS project encouraged the adoption of ISO and OGC Geospatial standards, including the Catalog Service of the Web (CSW) by IDE-SNIT (Chile) and the GEO Discovery and Access Broker (DAB) by ConnectinGEO for metadata services. A collaboration between SAF and NASA was also fostered. Several models were searched, discussed, and developed ultimately as web processing services (WPS).

2   Objective

The goals of the reported AIP-GEOSS Chile project are focused on disasters: to alert communities; to search, discover, and exchange data and services through interoperable interfaces; to develop and test components and services within GCI; and to assist and collaborate with decision makers, scientists, and users.

3   Materials and Methods

The Chile AIP-GEOSS project (Figure 1) covers two scenarios related to regions with earthquake and tsunami risk management issues (Talcahuano and Iquique); three scenarios related to areas with volcanic activity (Copahue, Villarrica and Calbuco); and one scenario related to wildfires (Valparaiso).

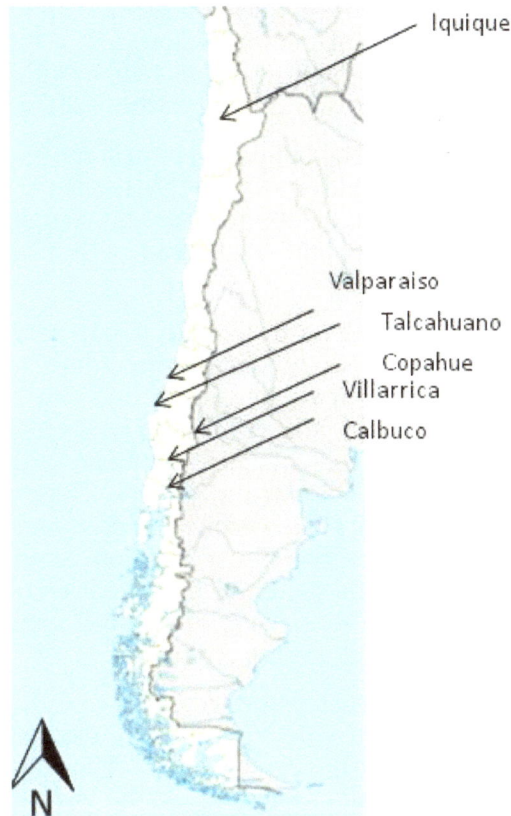

Figure 1 -- Testing areas of the Architecture Implementation Pilot of the Global Earth Observation System of Systems (AIP-GEOSS) in Chile.

On February 27, 2010, a magnitude 8.8 earthquake struck Talcahuano and generated a 2.30-meter tsunami. About 500 people were killed, and about $30 billion in damage was caused [5]. In Iquique, a magnitude 8.2 earthquake occurred on April 1, 2014, triggered a 2.1-meter tsunami, but only partially ruptured the seismogenic fault [3] . Volcanic activity occurred in Copahue on May 27, 2013, and additional volcanic activity was observed in October and December 2014; the Villarrica volcano erupted on March 3, 2015, causing mudslides and snow melts near Pucon; and the Cabulco volcano started to erupt on April 22, 2015, after about 41 years of dormancy [7]. This volcanic activity resulted in the evacuation of about 3,000 people living within a 25-kilometer radius from the volcano in the south rim of Copahue; of about 3,500 people from Villarrica, although about 15,000 people living in rural areas near Villarrica suffered from water shortages; and of about 4,000 people in a 20-kilometer radius around the Calbuco volcano. The wildfires in Valparaiso adversely impacted several endemic flora and fauna and, in May 2015, covered an area of about 11,428 hectares [6]. About one year earlier, on April 15, 2014, wildfires in urban Valparaiso killed at least 16 people.

4 Discussion

The life cycle of risk management for disasters areas is characterized by three phases: prevention, response, and recovery. In the Chile AIP-GEOSS project, these three phases of disasters are considered within a GEOSS framework for metadata and geospatial data. For each area, four levels of alerts are used: green, yellow, amber, and red. At the amber alert level, the mobilization of people exposed to a disaster is triggered, and people are evacuated. The Chilean emergency agency, ONEMI, makes broadcasts of alerts and notifications using all means, including radio, VHF, and social media.

The Chile AIP-GEOSS project was established to suggest more effective approaches for making alerts in relation to the scale and type of disasters. For example, the AIP-GEOSS project has recommended that alerts include the visualization of the geospatial data, with the adoption of geospatial standards, and with a basic map of the disaster event.

The Chile AIP-GEOSS project works on four main subareas: increasing people skills and knowledge in the geospatial field, developing metadata, imagery, and models. In addition, the project works to improve harmonization and increase integration of geospatial data. In fact, these data are originally in different types and formats dependent on the different sensor characteristics, and are afterwards converted into interoperable web services through standard interfaces. The project also estimates the hazards in the test areas and includes socio-economic data and services. These aspects are very important in relation to the rapid urbanization of once remote regions. The goal of this project is to prove that service oriented architecture (SOA) can be successfully and effectively applied to disaster areas, and to reduce the disaster risks for the benefit of societies in a rapid changing environment.

Furthermore, Chile AIP-GEOSS focuses on the research that needs to be undertaken to address disaster response models for wild fires; and for estimating volcanic risk. With respect to seismic and tsunami risks, the Chile AIP-GEOSS project includes prevention, response, and recovery policies and scenarios. In the prevention phase, the major emphasis is on capacity building, while in the response phase of the disaster cycle, mobilization starts with alerts and notifications, followed by the increasing mobilization of all resources at local, regional, national and international level. Depending of the type of disaster, there it will be necessary to classify as soon as possible the affected areas as total or partial losses, and to designate the shelter areas. With respect to volcanic risk, more research needs to be undertaken on evaluating the timing and exact location of the hazard, whether an eruption, ash cloud, mudslide, or episode of lake acidification, and on assessing the vulnerability of urban and rural populations. In this way, decisions can be made about the extent of the area to be evacuated and the duration of the evacuation. For urban and rural populations, the project plans to use the population density grid and the urban settlement points with the 2010 census for Chile [4, 5]. The goal of this effort is to estimate the web services and geospatial products that need to be registered to GEOSS Common Infrastructure (GCI) in order to reduce the magnitude of disaster risks and to suggest additional policies for managing disaster responses. Ultimately, the Chile AIP-GEOSS project will develop applications and services useful in responding to disaster events, some already available at the Group on Earth Observations geoportal [2].

Future activity of the Chile AIP-GEOSS project for disasters will probably be part of an initiative for Disaster Risk Reduction and the Sustainable Development Goals (SDGs), which will be lead by the Japanese government as part of the post-2015 development agenda, and will involve other countries in the Americas.

Part of the Chile AIP-GEOSS project is to address the parameters needed to measure different GEOSS activities for each type and scale of disaster. While many governments, non-profit and academic organizations as well as private entities will focus on providing data and services in case of disasters to users through networks such as internet and radio, people will see during the upcoming decades, especially in the private sector, the offering of Virtual Reality (VR) devices and services, such as Facebook Oculus, Google Cardboard, Microsoft HoloLens, Sony Morpheus, and China's Baofeng Mojing. Chile AIP-GEOSS project already shows the direction, although needs to integrate the data and services from "humanitarian" drones, as demonstrated in the 2015 Nepal earthquake [8], in order to provide more timely and comprehensive data and services for humanitarian actions and decision making. The project also shows the increased need for GIScience to implement augmented reality applications, such as GEOSS-type applications with a graphic layer added to a map or an image on mobile devices, such as Google and/or SONY glasses.

5   Conclusions

The effort of the Chile AIP-GEOSS project for disaster risk reduction will benefit not only Chile but also other countries stricken by disasters. So far, the Chile AIP-GEOSS project has resulted in strengthening the knowledge and skills of disaster relief experts while respecting cultural differences; in developing better policies in the management of disasters; and in developing and sharing geospatial resources and associated metadata to decrease the vulnerability of potential victims and property. In the future, pilot projects will be focused on building more geospatial applications and products, on managing increasingly large volumes of data and on including geospatial data from Earth observation sensors within a framework, currently represented by GEOSS, into augmented reality, disaster robotics, and virtual reality applications as a means to reduce our vulnerability to disasters worldwide. GIScience can nurture knowledge and skills of people who increasingly will not have a formal education on the management of geospatial data and products. For example, there is an increasing number of mobile users who want to manage their imagery even during a disaster: these people wants both to develop maps and applications with a geospatial component, and to generate themselves geospatial data. For more technical people, GIScience needs to focus on developing new ontological, spatio-temporal, software architecture models that also take into account privacy; on proposing and testing integration and analysis of big volumes of data, while experimenting with new technology and sensors.

References

[1]   GLOBAL VOLCANISM PROGRAM, http://volcano.si.edu/reports_weekly.cfm (last accessed 2015-05-09).

[2]   GROUP ON EARTH OBSERVATIONS, http://www.geoportal.org/web/guest/geo_home_stp (last accessed 2015-05-09).

[3]   HAYES, G.P, HERMAN, M.W., BARNHART, W.D., FURLONG, K.P., RIQULME, S., BENZ, H.M., BERGMAN, E., BARRIENTOS, S., EARLE, P.S., AND SAMSONOV, S. Warning signs of the Iquique earthquake. Nature, 512 (2014), 295-298.

[4]   ISTITUTO NACIONAL DE ESTADISTICAS,
       http://www.ine.cl/canales/chile_estadistico/familias/censos.php (last accessed
       2015-05-09).

[5]   LOVISON L., L. PARODI, A. MONETT, P. DUEÑAS, S. FRYE, S. NATIVI, and
       M. SANTORO, A GEOSS Architecture Implementation Pilot Project for Disasters
       in Chile, submitted to PE & RS, (2015) ASPRS.

[6]   ONEMI, http://www.onemi.cl/incendio-en-valparaiso/ (last accessed 2015-05-
       09).

[7]   SERNAGEOMIN, http://www.sernageomin.cl/volcan.php?iId=3 (last accessed
       2015-05-09).

[8]   SKY NEWS, https://www.youtube.com/watch?v=WwIw1-
       voHKQ&ab_channel=SkyNews (last accessed 2015-05-09).

[9]   U.S. GEOLOGICAL SURVEY,
       http://earthquake.usgs.gov/earthquakes/world/events/1960_05_22_articles.ph
       p (last accessed 2015-05-09).

Using Geo-Spatial Knowledge for Good Governance

Laxmi Ramasubramanian

CUNY Institute for Sustainable Cities, Hunter College, City University of New York, 695 Park Avenue, Room 1217 Hunter East, New York, NY 10065

Extended Abstract

Abstract: Although GIS applications to support collaborative planning and problem solving have greatly expanded information access and individual empowerment, the democratizing power of GIS continues to create new contradictions and tensions as it continues to be deployed across institutional settings. Both technical and non-technical barriers limit the use of geo-spatial knowledge in engaging ordinary citizens to participate in real world planning and policy-making. In addition, participatory processes themselves have moved online, further complicating how geospatial technologies and methods are used. The abstract highlights some of these contradictions and challenges GIScientists to develop better tools for participatory planning both in face-to-face and online settings.

Keywords: Participatory GIS, co-production, community, empowerment.

---

1 Introduction

The process of engaging citizens in planning and policy-making is fraught with difficulties. In the United States, as citizen participation has become more institutionalized, it has become disconnected from its original goals of increasing access and larger questions of social justice and is often used to fulfil procedural obligations or requirements [2, 7]. From the outset, many GIScience scholars have proposed and demonstrated the use of GIS principles, methods and geo-visualization to explain (and solve) complex socio-spatial problems. A smaller cohort of scholars has examined the social, political, and institutional aspects of GIS use in different realworld settings [1, 4, 5]. In addition to the academic discourse [6, 11], a Community of Practice (CoP) loosely defined as Public Participation-GIS (PPGIS) has also emerged [10]. Both academics and practitioners aligned with this CoP have emphasized the democratizing power of GIS while highlighting some of the contradictions associated with its use.

Nearly twenty years after the first discussions about GIS and Society debates [3], some of the tensions associated with GIS use in democratic decision-making have been resolved at the same time that new contradictions have emerged. This extended abstract examines some of these contradictions and suggests some directions for future research in this area. In particular, the focus of this abstract is planning and policymaking across spatial scales in big cities, wherein planning includes city management and heterarchic governance processes.

2   GIS and the Rise of Accidental Activists

Over the past decade, geo-visualization and communications technologies have created a virtual space for accidental activists. The phrase, "there's an app for that" is more than a cute tagline – it exemplifies how individuals are using their creative abilities and technological prowess to identify and create new niche markets. The power of an application like See, Click, Fix for instance, is situated in its promise of immediate gratification in practical and emotional terms. The end user with a smart phone can vent or complain about something that disturbs their sense of well-being while navigating their everyday urban environment. The application is designed for reporting of non-emergency issues such as potholes or non-functioning street lights. End users can demand accountability from a variety of government agencies with a single click of a button and feel personally empowered because they are able to act for themselves and their fellow citizens, albeit, with minimal effort. Both practising planners and GIS experts recognize See, Click, Fix, as one of the many examples of planning apps that use the power of GIS, GPS, as well as digital photo/videography to solve urban problems. The app, its purpose, and its deployment offer a lot of promise allowing citizens and responsible government agencies to quickly identify trouble spots and distribute scare resources in a timely manner. But, if one pauses to consider the issue a little longer, more difficult questions emerge, highlighting some of the contradictions created by the new ubiquitous, all pervasive, yet invisible, GIS.

See, Click, Fix represents only one particular aspect of planning and should not be confused with the complexity of the planning enterprise as a whole. Some questions that need to be answered include: Who has access to skills or the expertise to use See, Click, Fix? Does personal information provided by the end user (knowingly or unknowingly) get recorded and stored? Will it be used to keep track of end users? Are government agencies more sensitive to complaints about certain types of problems? Are they more responsive to problems that occur in certain locations? Are digital tools being developed only to make our citizens hyper-aware about the failures of government (when things don't work)? If so, what are the consequences? For instance, a recent NYC council hearing on the shooting death of an unarmed man by a police officer in a public housing complex cited neglect of routine maintenance on NYCHA (NYC public housing) properties. In these situations, does it demoralize members of a particular segment of public to realize that they can complain and complain about some problems and nothing will get fixed? Alternatively, does it make them believe the popular American refrain that government itself is somehow the problem? More importantly, how do these and other digital tools shape the larger democracy project that is presently being shaken and transformed in a myriad of ways that are both exhilarating and confusing?

3 Community Empowerment Remains Elusive Goal

The past two decades have seen rapid shifts in GIS adoption and use in different institutional settings, coupled with changes in the production, consumption, and use of GIS-data. While hyper-connected netizens use their "smart" phones to write emails, send text messages, "tweet", update their FaceBook profiles, and use the built-in GPS systems to find their way around strange cities and towns, low-skilled workers looking for work in the service sector will find that their jobs are far away from their places of residence; their commutes are long; and that the kind of work they do precludes tele-commuting. In the quest to find affordable housing and transportation or dependable child care options, these workers know that there is very little to be gained from getting onto a computer, even if they had access to one. At the most, these workers could find out bus routes and schedules, but the service on the ground is unlikely to be prompt or reliable. It can be argued that GIS-based decisions have done little to overcome deep and enduring barriers of race, class, gender, age, and privilege.

It is true that in 2015, societies around the world have made great strides in providing data access. We operate in a data-rich environment which can be mined because of cheap computing power. However, information access does not automatically encourage participation or civic engagement. Participation takes motivation, commitment, time, specialized skills, and above all, trust or confidence that the act of participating will make a difference in the resolution of the problem.

Geo-spatial tools developed for the public to encourage them to be involved in planning or policymaking are still not the norm. The dominant tools or apps are focused on recreation, gaming, or adventure, and have limited benefit in addressing socio-spatial inequalities. Government-funded tool developments such as the *Climate Resilience Toolkits* are actually not easily used in community conversations. Sophisticated geodesign software extensions such as *CommunityViz* have a steep learning curve and typically require skilled experts to conduct and explain the analyses to citizens. Twenty years on, the most rigorous spatial analysis techniques, the fanciest computers, and the best data are still no match to combat institutional inertia, interdepartmental rivalries, and other non-technical barriers to successful GIS implementation to solve community problems.

4 The Challenge to the GIScientists

The origins of geospatial science are grounded in a set of beliefs about planning and policy-making. Chief among them is the value placed on examining problems holistically, within particular spatial and temporal contexts. Geospatial science research has also valued the analysis of diverse types of data and information. Last but not the least, is the belief among geospatial scientists that decisions made using GIS can ensure transparency and accountability.

As geospatial science and technologies have grown and matured, the early ideals of the GIScientists are finally coming to fruition. The new genre of geospatial tools are user friendly and accessible, increasing opportunities for active citizen involvement. Citizens in the USA, western Europe, as well as many other countries of the global south have become sophisticated consumers of information and producers of highly localized data and information about their own neighborhoods and communities. Rather than accept the results for "official" studies, today's citizens are more likely to use social networks to assemble and gather data to confirm or refute official analyses and make rational counter-arguments when necessary. Citizen activism is now educational and affordable. It appears to empower individuals more than groups, but there is progress being made [9].

Yet, the nature of planning and policy-making is changing, with much of the "work" moving online. The emphasis in government-led planning is on e-participation and the idea that there are highly customized approaches to engaging different publics – a laudable goal. Technical (manipulating the technologies) and non-technical (group communication) skills associated with the use of online tools affect e-participation. Citizens require some technical skills to participate in processes that actively use information technologies and their by-products such as maps or graphic renderings. At the local level, the absence of technical skills is often countered through a well designed group process that is educational and informative. In many instances, group processes with marginalized communities use popular education techniques. In small groups, an individual's lack of a particular technical skill (for example, reading a land use plan) can create some collaborative moments as other participants explain and share their understanding, thereby fulfilling one of the goals of a participatory decision making process, i.e., to develop the capacity of the participants to organize, analyze, and discuss concepts to the level required by the particular endeavor in which they are involved. It is unclear how this problem will be managed with physically dispersed population that may come together only virtually (e.g., through site-to-site video conferences).

It is reasonable to speculate that inter-personal and group communication skills are critical in facilitating and managing e-participation processes. The staff in planning agencies has to be trained to meet the new demands and challenges associated with e-participation. While techno-enthusiasts abound, the technology cannot be used to drive the planning process. Thus, the facilitator (agency staff person or hired consultant) must be able to determine the needs of the planning process and identify the appropriate technology to suit that purpose. A technical expert unable to speak the language of community groups further compounds these problems, which results in the breakdown of already fragile participatory processes [8].

It may be reasonable to explore the idea of a set of principles that should be included in e-participation applications for planning.

E-participation applications should:

1. use stable technologies and be available free or at low cost to end users;

2. be easily understandable to potential users;

3. recognize and accommodate different levels of technical and spatial literacy, specifically allowing for individual users to learn at their own pace;

4. allow citizens to "interact" with the data with as much freedom as possible in order to generate different scenarios and alternatives, wherein the underlying models and formulas governing application design can also be scrutinized;

5. include the capability for citizens to download data and analyses from the official planning organization's website to their own computers.

6. include the capability for citizens to upload their own data sets. Application must allow upload of photographs, audio clips, video, sketch maps, or computer-rendered designs;

7. link scenario developments, wherever possible, to outcomes and impact assessments that can be described in quantitative and qualitative terms;

8. contain robust context-sensitive help that facilitates peer to peer information sharing and assistance in real-time; and,

9. allow and support extensive archiving and documentation.

References

[1]   ELWOOD, S. Information for Change: The social and political impacts of Geographic Information Technologies, PhD dissertation, Department of Geography, University of Minnesota. Available from University of Minnesota Libraries, 2000.

[2]   INNES, J., AND. BOOHER, D. Reframing Public Participation: Strategies for the 21st century, Planning Theory & Practice, 5, 4 (2004), pp. 419-436

[3]   HARRIS, T., AND WEINER, D. GIS and Society: The Social Implications of How People, Space, and Environment are represented in GIS. Scientific Report for the Initiative 19 Specialist Meeting, March 2-5, 1996, South Haven, Minnesota

[4]   MASSER, I., AND ONSRUD, H (Eds.) Diffusion and Use of Geographic Information Technologies. (Dordrecht, Netherlands, 1993), Kluwer

[5]   NYERGES, T., COUCLELIS, H., AND MCMASTER, R (Eds) The SAGE Handbook of GIS and SOCIETY, (London, England, 2010), Sage

[6]   OBERMEYER, N. The Evolution of Public Participation GIS, Cartography and GIS, 25, 2 (1998), pp.65-66

[7]   RAMASUBRAMANIAN, L., AND QUINN, A. Visualizing Alternative Urban Futures: Using Spatial Multimedia to Enhance Community Participation and Policymaking, in M. Campagna (Ed.). GIS and Sustainable Development. (Florida, USA, 2006), CRC Press, pp. 467-486

[8]   RAMASUBRAMANIAN, L. Nurturing community empowerment: Participatory decision-making and community-based problem solving using GIS, in Onsrud, H. and M. Craglia (Eds.) Geographic Information Research: Transatlantic Perspectives. (London, England, 1999), Taylor & Francis, pp. 87-102

[9]   RAMSUBRAMANIAN, L. GIS and Public Participation, (Heidelberg, Germany, 2010), Springer

[10] SAWICKI, D., & PETERMAN, D, 2002. Surveying the extent of PPGIS practice in the United States, in Craig, W, T. Harris & D. Weiner (Eds.) Community Participation and Geographic Information Systems (New York, NY, USA, 2002), Taylor & Francis, pp. 17-36

[11] SIEBER, R. Public Participation GIS: A Literature Review and Framework, Annals of the Association of American Geographers, 96,3 (2006), pp. 491-507

Geomorphological Delineation using Computer Vision to Support Automated Mapping

Paulo Raposo

Department of Geography, The Pennsylvania State University, University Park, Pennsylvania 16802, USA

Extended Abstract

Abstract: This article presents an automated workflow for finding generalized areas of relatively rough terrain using GIS, remote sensing, and computer vision techniques, taking a digital elevation model (DEM) as input. The method supports automated delineation of morphometrically self-similar areas as polygons and is demonstrated here using a portion of the Sahara Desert exhibiting large sand dunes, modeled in ASTER GDEM data.

Keywords: Geomorphometry, DEMs, terrain roughness, computer vision, segmentation, polygonization, labeling.

---

1 Introduction

Cartography has always benefitted from the evolution of graphic media, with clear examples seen in the invention of the printing press and, much later, computerization. Map media continue to evolve, seen in today's proliferation of location-aware smartphones. Maps and spatial data in the coming decades will take forms afforded by computational innovations. We predict that spatial data will be stored in increasingly decentralized repositories, and that it will increasingly not be stored at all, but generated on an immediate, as-needed basis from distributed sensor networks. Automated cartography of instantaneously synthesized data with become more and more important, as will computer or artificial intelligence (AI) interpretation of geography. While basic automated maps made today are of arguably passable quality (say, for GPS receivers used in car navigation), the methods programmed into GIS systems for producing instantaneous maps will have to improve to deal with the increase in diversity, resolution, and complexity we can expect from future data. GIS need to be better able to deal with fundamental cartographic modelling and design issues such as generalization, topological consistency, legibility, and feature detection. These challenges parallel many of those seen by researchers in computer vision, and methods used in that field seem promising for application in geographic information science (GIScience).

We present an automated workflow for finding generalized areas of relatively rough terrain using GIS, remote sensing, and computer vision techniques, taking a digital elevation model (DEM) as input. Specifically, we derive surface roughness and segment this image using mean-shift segmentation [11], a robust, non parametric, mode-seeking, iterative classification algorithm developed in information theory and adapted to pixel data in the computer vision context [7]. Our method allows for automated delineation of morphometrically self-similar areas as polygons. We believe this ability is useful in numerous applications, particularly with respect to computer-automated navigation (e.g., polygonal patches of rough land can be detected and avoided by computer navigation applications using simple point-in-polygon tests). The method also helps in a common contemporary map making problem, being the delineation of landforms [10] such as rock formations, mountain ranges, or canyons, as polygons. Having such areas polygonized is advantageous over points or lines in that automated label-placing algorithms are given greater legitimate, spatial flexibility [16, 2, 19]. Our method is automated using Python scripting in an open-source desktop GIS environment using The Geospatial Data Abstraction Library (GDAL version 1.7.0), Orfeo Tool Box (version 4.4), and QGIS (version 2.8.1), and is demonstrated here in a portion of the Sahara Desert exhibiting large sand dunes, modelled in ASTER GDEM data.

2 Background

Strong methodological similarities exist between raster GIS, remote sensing, and computer vision analyses. Image content can vary considerably between the fields in aspects including subject, acquisition method, and geometry (e.g., orthoimages vs. perspective images). Still, because analysis in all fields begins with pixels, analytical problems and algorithms nearly always take the form of mathematical calculations on fields of regularly-spaced values, taking the spatial relations between values as important context [12, 4, 3, 1]. For example, many GIS or remote sensing analysis procedures involve the "reclassification" of pixels (e.g., different kinds of land cover), while many computer vision procedures perform image "segmentation" to differentiate pixels in figure-ground relationships in a scene. Similarly, both fields make use of kernel operations on the premise that local pixels influence the variable being calculated at the pixel in question because their nearness, whether on the Earth's surface or in the visual scene, makes them important to the model. Geomorphometry and terrain generalization procedures to date have increasingly bridged methodological gaps between GIScience and related computer graphics fields. Several studies have presented methods for identifying landforms and classifying landscapes using DEM data [6, 18, 14, 8]. Other studies have devised and reviewed various derivative surfaces or surface parameters that can be used to characterize a surface [15, 17, 21, 20]. Methods in geomorphometry typically deal directly with elevation and its derivatives in the vertical and horizontal directions (i.e., slope, profile curvature, aspect, plan curvature) [9].

3 Demonstration

The present workflow is illustrated for a portion of the Sahara Desert modelled in
ASTER GDEM data, in Figure 1.

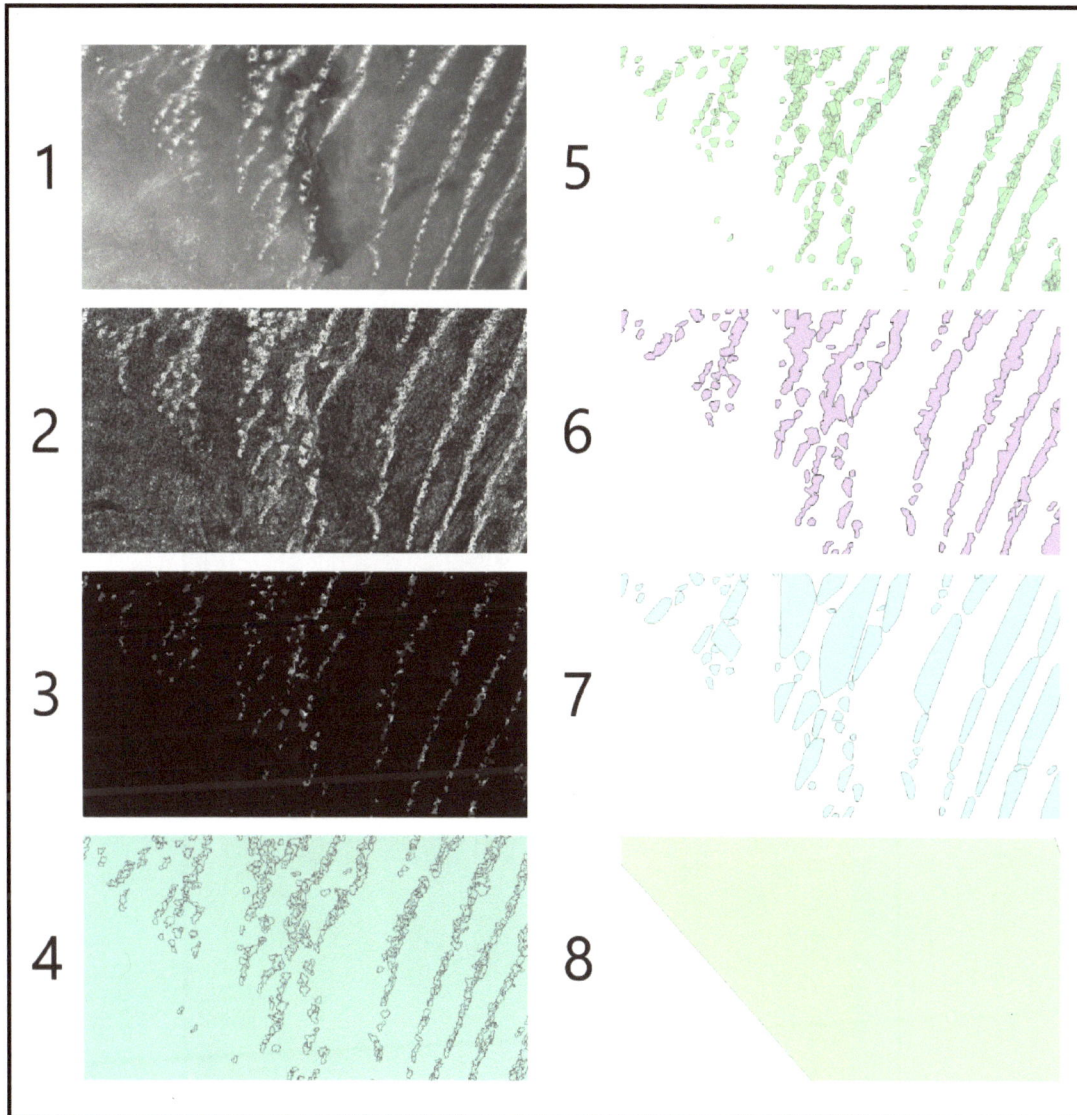

Figure 1: Illustrated steps in the workflow presented. From the DEM (1), the surface
roughness raster (2) is calculated, mean-shift segmented (3), and polygonized (4). The
largest single polygon is removed (5), and the union of all topologically disjoint
polygons above a certain area and sufficiently spatially clustered is computed (6). The
convex hull of these is computed (7), and, optionally, the convex hull of these is
computed (8) for further generalization. The area shown is a portion of the Sahara
Desert, measuring approximately 70 km across the longer side.

The sample area straddles the Erg Iguidi desert in Algeria, characterized by large longitudinal sand dunes, and the El Eglab Massif. The sample measures approximately 40 × 70 km. This area was chosen to exemplify the method's ability to detect and delineate the dunes from their surroundings, since the dunes have considerably complex morphology as expressed in surface roughness (Figure 2).

Figure 2: A subset of the sample area, for visualization of the dunes' relative morphometric complexity compared to their surroundings, illustrated as a slope map (top), a hillshade (middle), and in Google imagery (bottom; note that the orthoimage capture date differs from the DEM capture date relevant to the top images). Topographic roughness varies throughout the sample area (see Figure 1.2); the mean-shift segmentation algorithm successfully identifies the dunes by their greater spatial-statistical modes in the roughness raster.

Processing begins with generating surface roughness [20] using the *gdaldem* module of GDAL (Figure 2.1 and 2.2). Next, the roughness raster is segmented using the mean shift algorithm implemented in Orfeo ToolBox (Figure 1.3). The segmented (i.e., clustered) raster is polygonized (Figure 1.4) in QGIS such that each unique, contiguous region identified in the raster is given its own polygon, with individual features permitted to exist across multiple polygons (i.e., features are multi-part). The largest single polygon feature, representing the most common topographic roughness in the sample area and therefore the "ground" as opposed to the "figure", is removed from the polygon set (Figure 1.5). The remaining polygons are thresholded for area and proximity to other polygons (i.e., spatial clustering), and these have their convex hulls calculated. These hulls are unified into a single union polygon (Figure 1.6), and this multi-part polygon is dissolved into individual feature polygons for each topologically disconnected polygon. The convex hulls of the remaining polygons are computed (Figure 1.7), yielding generalized footprints of where anomalously rough terrain occurs in the sampled landscape. A further level of generalization of the rough area is achieved if the convex hull that surrounds the previous hull polygons is computed (Figure 1.8). The use of convex hulls ensures that dunes are "over-identified," meaning some portions of polygonized "dunes" do not exhibit the same membership to a local statistical mode as identified by the mean-shift algorithm. While convex hulls are one way to simplify the geometry of an object, they may not always be geographically appropriate, and other polygon simplification methods may be more appropriate.

The described workflow can be easily implemented with other derivative surfaces such as slope, openness [21], sky view factor [13, 5], terrain ruggedness index, or topographic position index [20]. These derived surfaces should be mathematically normalized, whether intrinsically or otherwise, so that the analysis is not as sensitive to the distribution of values in the sampled surface.

References

[1]   ATKINSON, P. M. (2004). Resolution Manipulation and Sub-Pixel Mapping. In S. M. De JONG & F. D. Van der MEER (Eds.), *Remote Sensing Image Analysis: Including The Spatial Domain* (pp. 51-70). Boston: Kluwer Academic Publishers.

[2]   BAE, W. D., ALKOBAISI, S., NARAYANAPPA, S., VOJTECHOVSKY, P., and BAE, K. "Optimizing map labeling of point features based on an onion peeling approach." Journal of Spatial Information Science 2. (2011) pp. 3-28.

[3]   BLASCHKE, T., LANG, S., and HAY, G. J., Eds. Object-Based Image Analysis: Spatial Concepts for Knowledge-Driven Remote Sensing Applications. Lecture Notes in Geoinformation and Cartography, Springer, (2008).

[4]   BLASCHKE, T. and STROBL, J. "What's Wrong With Pixels? Some Recent Developments Interfacing Remote Sensing and GIS." Geo-Informations-Systeme 14,6 (2001). pp. 12-17.

[5]   BOEHNER, J. and ANTONIC, O. Land-Surface Parameters Specific to Topo-Climatology. Geomorphometry - Concepts, Software, Applications. Developments in Soil Science. T. Hengl and H. Reuter, Elsevier. 33 (2009) pp. 195-226.

[6]   BOLONGARO-CREVENNA, A., TORRES-RODRIGUEA, V., SORANI, V. FRAME, D., and ORTIZ, M. A. "Geomorphometric Analysis for Characterizing Landforms in Morelos State, Mexico." Geomorphology 67 (2005) pp. 407-422.

[7]   CHENG, Y. "Mean Shift, Mode Seeking, and Clustering." IEEE Transactions on Pattern Analysis and Machine Intelligence 17,8 (1995) pp. 790-799.

[8]   COBLENTZ, D., PABIAN, F., and Prasad, L. "Quantitative Geomorphometrics for Terrain Characterization." International Journal of Geosciences 5 (2014) pp. 247-266.

[9]   EVANS, I. S. (1972). General Geomorphometry, Derivations of Altitude and Descriptive Statistics. In R. J. CHORLEY (Ed.), Spatial Analysis in Geomorphology (pp. 17-90). New York: Harper & Row Publishers.

[10]   EVANS, I. S. "Geomorphometry and Landform Mapping: What is a Landform?" Geomorphology 137 (2012) pp. 94-106.

[11]   FUKUNAGA, K. and HOSTETLER, L. "The Estimation of the Gradient of a Density Function, with Applications in Pattern Recognition." IEEE Transactions on Information Theory 21,1 (1975) pp. 32-40.

[12]   HARALICK, R. M. "Statistical and Structural Approaches to Texture." Proceedings of the IEEE 67 (1979) pp. 45-69.

[13]   HANTZSCHEL, J., GOLDBERG, V., and BERNHOFER, C. "GIS-Based Regionalization of Radiation, Temperature and Coupling Measures in Complex Terrain for Low Mountain Ranges." Meteorological Applications 12,1 (2005) pp. 33-42.

[14]   IWAHASHI, J. and PIKE, R. J. "Automated Classifications of Topography from DEMs by an Unsupervised Nested-Means Algorithm and a Three-Part Geometric Signature." Geomorphology 86 (2007) pp. 409-440.

[15]   MARK, D. M. "Geomorphometric Parameters: A Review and Evaluation." Geografiska Annaler, Series A, Physical Geography 57,3/4 (1975). pp. 165-177.

[16]   MARKS, J. and SHIEBER, S. The computational complexity of cartographic label placement. Cambridge, MA, Harvard University, (1991).

[17]   PIKE, R. J. "The Geometric Signature: Quantifying Landslide-Terrain Types from Digital Elevation Models." Mathematical Geology 20,5 (1988) pp. 491-511.

[18]   PRIMA, O. D. A., ECHIGO, A., YOKOYAMA, R., and YOSHIDA, T. "Supervised Landform Classification of Northeast Honshu from DEM-derived Thematic Maps." Geomorphology 78 (2006) pp. 373-386.

[19]   RYLOV, M. A. and REIMER, A. W. "A Comprehensive Multi-criteria Model for High Cartographic Quality Point-Feature Label Placement." Cartographica 49,1 (2014) pp. 52-68.

[20]   WILSON, M. F. J., O'CONNELL, B., BROWN, C., GUINAN, J. C., and GREHAN, A. J. "Multiscale Terrain Analysis of Multibeam Bathymetry Data for Habitat Mapping on the Continental Slope." Marine Geodesy 30 (2007) pp. 3-35.

[21]   YOKOYAMA, R., SHIRASAWA, M., and PIKE, R. J. "Visualizing Topography by Openness: A New Application of Image Processing to Digital Elevation Models." Photogrammetric Engineering & Remote Sensing 68,3 (2002) pp. 257-265.

Parallel Cartographic Modeling

Eric Shook

High-Performance Computing and GIS Laboratory, Department of Geography, Kent State University, Kent, OH 44242, USA

Extended Abstract

---

1 Introduction

The increasing volume, velocity, and variety of big spatial data combined with rapid technological advancements has motivated computational geographers and Geographic Information Scientists (GIScientists) to increasingly adopt parallel and high-performance computing (HPC) approaches. Yet, despite years of well-received research in the areas of Geoinformatics, GeoComputation, (Geo)Spatial Cyberinfrastructure, and CyberGIS, we still lack a general methodology—free from technical jargon and computational details—that captures the complex process of leveraging HPC infrastructures to solve spatial problems [1, 2, 8, 10]. This article establishes Parallel Cartographic Modeling as a general methodology for parallelizing spatial data processing, which extends the widely adopted spatial data processing methodology, cartographic modeling [7].

Cartographic modeling—one of many spatial data processing methodologies—consists of three primary components: procedures, layers, and locations; and two primary operators: operations and functions. For brevity, this article briefly reviews the primary components and operators defined as part of cartographic modeling, which will be used to describe parallel cartographic modeling. Interested readers are referred to a seminal text on cartographic modeling for further details [7]. Locations serve as the element unit of cartographic space in cartographic modeling. Map layers contain one or more locations. Functions provide data processing capabilities for cartographic modeling and are generally applied to each location in a map layer as part of an operation. Operations are applied to map layers to generate new map layers. Operations are generally classified as local, focal, zonal, and global based on which spatially proximate locations are used to calculate new values in a map layer ranging from the location itself (local) to all locations (global). An ordered set of operations is referred to as a procedure and is often visualized as a flowchart. While cartographic modeling is a flexible methodology for spatial data processing, the current suite of components and operators is ill suited for capturing parallel spatial data processing.

2 Parallel Cartographic Modeling

Parallel cartographic modeling is a general methodology for parallelizing spatial data processing. Unlike cartographic modeling, that is a data processing methodology, parallel cartographic modeling is a parallelization methodology. This distinction is important, because parallel cartographic modeling shifts the focus from *how to process spatial data* to *how to parallelize the process* for spatial data processing. To achieve this, the cartographic modeling framework is extended to include a subdomain component and four additional operators: scheduler, decomposition, executor, and iteration (shown in Figure 1 and detailed below).

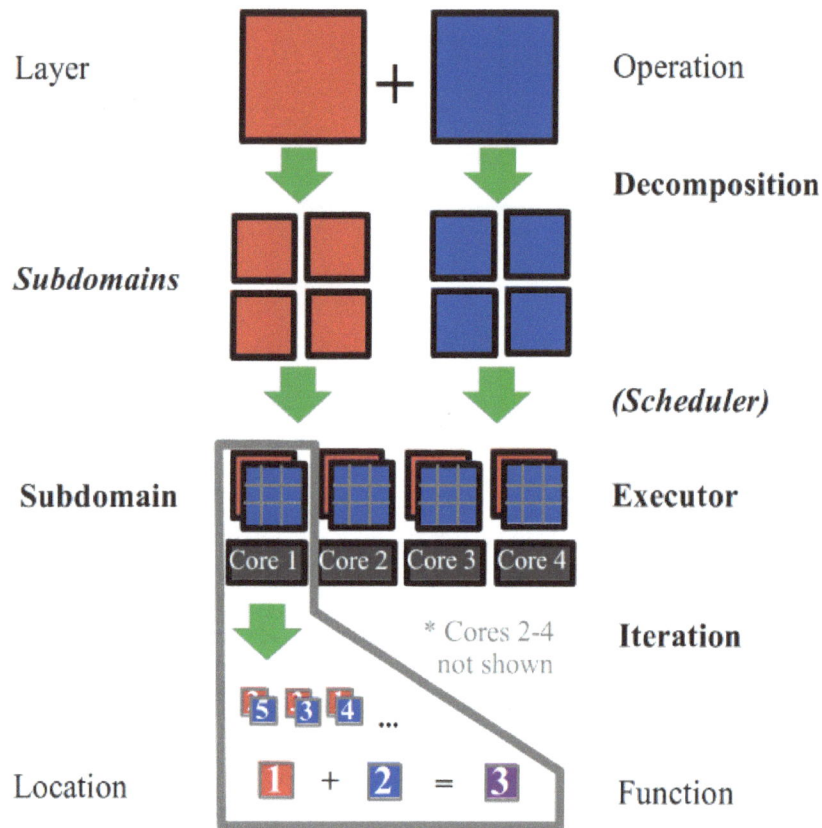

Figure 1: A conceptual framing of the parallel cartographic modeling methodology, which extends the cartographic modeling methodology.

Subdomains represent the elemental unit of parallel computation in parallel cartographic modeling. A subdomain is composed of a subset of locations in a layer that was partitioned using spatial domain decomposition [3]. The concept underlying a subdomain is not new and is well established under terms including the grain of parallelism, chunks, sub-cellspaces, or minimum bounding rectangles [3, 5, 6], which illustrates that parallel cartographic modeling does not contradict existing approaches, but rather builds on them to create a general methodology for parallelizing spatial data processing.

In Figure 1, novel model components (left side) and operators (right side) that capture the process of parallelization are in bold. This figure captures the methodological process of parallel cartographic modeling from the Sum operation applied to two layers, to functions processing individual locations (in parallel). At the core of parallel cartographic modeling is a novel component called a subdomain that serves as the elemental unit of parallel computation. Using subdomains, it is straightforward to capture the entire processing spectrum from serial data processing (decomposing a layer into a single subdomain) to completely parallel processing (decomposing a layer with N locations into N subdomains).

Schedulers manage the parallel execution of a procedure, which may include scheduling (1) two operations simultaneously (i.e. task-level parallelism); (2) the processing of multiple subdomains simultaneously (i.e., data-level parallelism as seen in Figure 1); or (3) both (i.e. data-task hybrid parallelism [5]). Schedulers, in conjunction with the rest of the framework, can be used to overcome challenges concerning HPC infrastructures (e.g., load-balancing, network bandwidth limitations, or memory constraints) or spatial problems (e.g., complex spatial or temporal dependencies).

Decomposition operators partition a layer into one or more subdomains (see Figure 1). Certain spatial problems or computational infrastructures may align themselves to certain decomposition strategies (see [3] for discussion), which may be guided by computational intensity representations to balance computational work- loads [8]. Parallel cartographic modeling does not favor or restrict any particular strategy whether row, column, recursive-bisection, quadtree, or a novel strategy.

Executors handle the execution of a function to process locations in a subdomain. Just as functions process locations and operations process layers, executors process subdomains. In essence, executors serve as a boundary of separation between parallel processing in the form of schedulers and decomposition and spatial data processing in the form of functions. This separation, using subdomains as the elemental unit of parallel computation, enables parallel cartographic modeling to simultaneously support parallel computing optimizations such as data-task hybrid parallelism as well as serial algorithmic optimizations for spatial-data processing.

Iteration operators control the order in which locations in a subdomain are processed by a function. Iteration orderings, as part of algorithmic optimizations, may help exploit data localities inherent in spatial data to improve utilization of disk, memory, or CPU cache thus improving performance [2, 9]. Numerous iteration orderings for rasters (e.g., row-prime), points (e.g., point quadtrees), and polygons (e.g., R-trees) have been proposed and could be used in parallel cartographic modeling [9].

Parallel cartographic modeling follows the tradition of cartographic modeling as being more a re-organization of existing ideas rather than all new ideas. Similarly, it captures the process of parallelization without being designed for a specific HPC infrastructure thus enabling it to be implemented in a variety of computational settings for spatial problem solving.

3 Case Study

A novel computing language named the Parallel Cartographic Modeling Language (PCML) has been developed based on the parallel cartographic modeling framework presented here. PCML is an open source language developed in Python that is freely available for download at the code hosting site GitHub (see https://github.com/HPCGISLab/pcml for further details and PCML code). This language was used in a CyberGIS course (Spring 2015) to teach fundamental parallel processing and spatial data processing concepts and approaches to undergraduate and graduate Geography students.

In this case study, we use PCML to demonstrate how parallel cartographic modeling and the novel operators including decomposition, executor, and iteration can be used to speedup processing time. Specifically, we apply the PCML FocalMean operation to one cell from the 3D Elevation Program that contains the City of Kent, OH as part of the United State Geologic Survey (USGS) National Map project. The raster dataset has a spatial resolution of 1/9 arc-second with dimensions 8,112×8,112 and is approximately 250 megabytes. Experiments were conducted using one node in the Resourcing Open Geo-spatial Education and Research (ROGER) computing resource at the CyberGIS Center for Advanced Digital and Spatial Studies, which consists of 2 Intel(R) Xeon(R) E5-2660 (2.60GHz) CPUs (totaling 20 processing cores) with 128 GB of memory.

Serial execution time using PCML is 348 seconds, and by leveraging the parallel processing capabilities that automatically apply decomposition, executor, and iteration operators we improved execution time by over ten-fold (Figure 2). Without modifying the FocalMean function, PCML also allows users to change the decomposition from the default Row decomposition to Column decomposition. Users can also change the iteration strategy from Row-major to Column-major iteration [9]. Further optimizations are available including Executor-level implementations of FocalMean that leverage a numerical library for dramatic performance improvements (see PCML code at GitHub page for details). In this way, PCML provides users a flexible methodological framework to experiment with different parallel techniques to optimize performance that are not available in the original formulation of cartographic modeling.

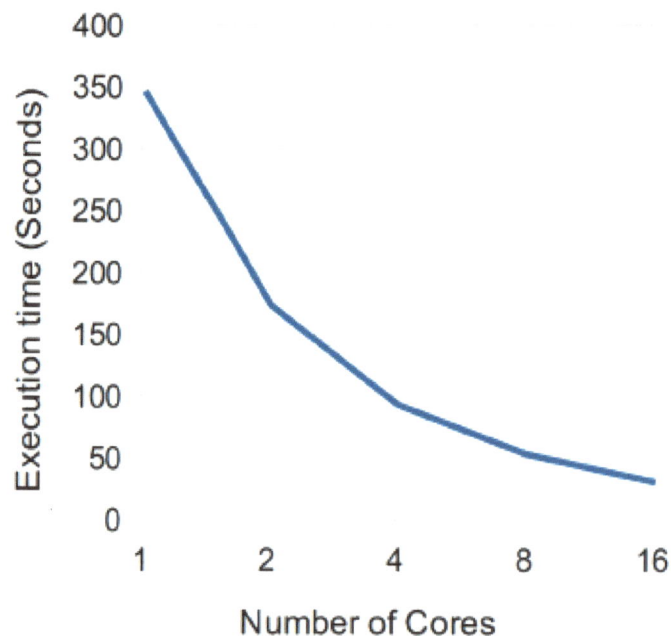

Figure 2: Execution times for a FocalMean operation when processing a 250 megabyte raster dataset using 1, 2, 4, 8, and 16 processing cores.

4 Concluding Discussion

As we reflect on the past and look toward the future of GIScience [4], it is pertinent to recognize that the rapid shift in technologies empowering much of GIScience introduces both opportunities and challenges for future research. While it can be challenging to look beyond the excitement of new *systems* including heterogeneous architectures, graphic processing units (GPUs), and many-core accelerators, the GIScience community has an opportunity to advance the *science* by surveying the rapidly shifting computational and geographical information landscape to identify new trends and approaches in spatial problem solving. Parallel cartographic modeling is one step in this scientific pursuit that captures the commonalities rather than uniqueness of parallel spatial data processing, which can be used to illustrate the general process and fundamental concepts underlying many parallel GIS.

5 Acknowledgments

Parallel cartographic modeling grew as a generalization of two interrelated projects. I would like to acknowledge Shaowen Wang, Michael Hodgson, Babak Behzad, and Kiumars Soltani for the original conception, design, and development of a PCML developed in C++ and for helping me extend that original work. I also acknowledge Zhengliang Feng for assistance in developing the Python-based PCML mentioned in the article. I appreciate the informative and engaging discussions with these individuals that helped lead to the creation of parallel cartographic modeling. This work used the Resourcing Open Geo-spatial Education and Research (ROGER) computing resource, which is supported by National Science Foundation grant number ACI-1429699.

References

[1]   ABRAHART, R., AND SEE, L. GeoComputation. CRC Press, 2014.

[2]   ARMSTRONG, M. Geography and computational science. Annals of the Association of American Geographers 90, 1 (2000), 146–156.

[3]   DING, Y., AND DENSHAM, P. Spatial strategies for parallel spatial modelling. International Journal of Geographical Information Systems 10, 6 (1996), 669–698.

[4]   GOODCHILD, M.F. Twenty years of progress: GIScience in 2010. Journal of Spatial Information Science, 1 (2010), 3–20.

[5]   GUAN, Q., AND CLARKE, K. A general-purpose parallel raster processing programming library test application using a geographic cellular automata model. International Journal of Geographical Information Science 24, 5 (2010), 695–722.

[6]   QIN, C., ZHAN, L., ZHU, A., AND ZHOU, C. A strategy for raster-based geocomputation under different parallel computing platforms. International Journal of Geographical Information Science 28, 11 (2014), 2127–2144.

[7]   TOMLIN, C. GIS and Cartographic Modeling. Esri Press, 2013.

[8]   WANG, S. A cyberGIS framework for the synthesis of cyberinfrastructure, GIS, and spatial analysis. Annals of the Association of American Geographers 100, 3 (2010), 535–557.

[9]   WORBOYS, M., AND DUCKHAM, M. GIS: a computing perspective. CRC press, 2004.

[10] YANG, C., RASKIN, R., GOODCHILD, M., AND GAHEGAN, M. Geospatial cyberinfrastructure: past, present and future. Computers, Environment and Urban Systems 34, 4 (2010), 264–277.

From Infection Cases to Infection Tree

Shiran Zhong and Ling Bian

University at Buffalo, the State University of New York

Extended Abstract

---

1 Introduction

The diffusion of communicable diseases, such as Influenza-Like Illness (ILI) is caused by interactions with the infectious at a place, while a population-wide propagation is the consequence of human mobility between places [5, 9]. Recently, an increasing effort has been devoted to developing models to understand spatial and temporal patterns of disease diffusion [6, 2]. These studies are mostly designed in either of the following two perspectives: spatial analysis in a static time frame [7] or temporal analysis on aggregated spatial data, such as classic Susceptible-Infectious-Recovered (SIR) models [1]. It is a common understanding that disease transmission processes are dynamic both spatially and temporally, but little research has focused on the analysis of spatial and temporal interactive patterns in disease transmissions.

The objectives of this study are twofold. Firstly, we construct an infection tree by mining the spatial and temporal co-occurrence information embedded in discrete ILI cases. Secondly, we identify "super-spreaders" and "super-receivers" from the infection tree in the context of spatial and temporal interactive transmission processes. The simultaneous accounting for both the spatial and temporal dynamics should reveal the processes observed during actual epidemics.

2 Study Area and Data

The study area is a metropolitan area in Midwest China. The dataset used for this study consists of 4,315 anonymous cases; each was clinically diagnosed as ILI during a 73 day period between September 1 - November 12. Each case is associated with a residential address (detailed to the level of residential community), a workplace (location identified to the census block group level in the U.S.), and the symptom onset date (self- reported at diagnosis). In this study, possible interactions occur among family members, colleagues, or neighbors who live within the same residential community. Interactions between family members or colleagues are sufficient to transmit seasonal influenza since they might have physical contact or share a close proximity at homes or workplaces every day. Neighbors residing in the same residential community also conduct certain amount of interactions, since they share the same community garden and other entertainment facilities (a common phenomenon in the metropolitan area of Midwest China). Their interaction activities, e.g. morning exercise in the garden, sharing the elevator, entertaining in the community center, or even walking together for grocery, also give rise to the probability of influenza transmissions.

Among the 4,315 anonymous ILI cases, there are 1,026 distinct locations that include predominantly schools and universities. The location and symptom onset date information is used to construct the infection tree. This dataset was obtained from the China Information System for Diseases Control and Prevention.

3   Methodology

A mining approach using spatial and temporal constraints is first developed and employed to identify the spatio-temporal co-occurrence information among the 4,315 ILI cases. An infection tree, defined as directed transmission paths between ILI cases, is then built based on this information. Secondly, characteristics of the tree are identified using clustering coefficient and in-degree and out-degree distributions. The latter is also used to detect the "super-spreaders" and "super-receivers".

3.1   Mining spatio-temporal co-occurrence

The spatio-temporal co-occurrence is explored by applying the spatial and temporal interactive constraints, as explained below:

An influenza case is denoted using the following formula:

$$Cn=(Tn, Rn, Sn),$$

where Tn denotes the symptom onset date of Case Cn; Rn and Sn denotes the residential address and school of Case Cn, respectively.

Ci and Cj spatially and temporally co-occur if:

$$(Ri \cup Si) \cap (Rj \cup Sj) \neq NULL,$$

$$and\ 0 < Tj-Ti \leq 7.$$

The first constraint identifies a pair of cases that spatially co-occur either at home or school (denoted by the union of Ri and Si). The second constraint identifies a pair of cases that temporally co-occur when Case j falls within the infectious period of Case.

According to the literature [8, 4], including a review of 71 influenza research [3], the length of seven days is adopted and it best supports the actual epidemic patterns.

3.2   Constructing infected and infecting list

Two lists, an "infected" list and an "infecting" list, are derived for each case from their spatio-temporal co-occurrence information. In an infected list, the given case plays a passive role of being infected by others, whereas in the infecting list the given case plays an active role of infecting others. The infected list of a given case includes all other cases who meet the above constraints and the symptom onset dates are within one week prior to that of the given case. The infecting list of a given case includes all other cases who meet the above constraints, but the symptom onset dates are during the week following that of the given case.

3.3   Constructing the infection tree

The infection tree is constructed by joining the two lists of each case and organized by symptom onset date of the cases. An infection tree consists of nodes and branches. Each node represents an ILI case, and each branch connecting two nodes represents a spatio-temporal co-occurrence between the two cases.

3.4   Analyzing tree characteristics

Clustering coefficient is a measure of transitivity in a connected graph. It is employed to reveal the parallel infection situation in the tree, in which one case might be infected by cases from multiple levels in the tree. The in-degree and out-degree of a node are the number of source cases it has been infected by, and the number of infection cases it has caused, respectively. In-degree and out-degree distributions are analyzed to identify the topology of the tree, and subsequently detect the "super-receivers" and "super- spreaders" by identifying nodes of high values of in-degree and out-degree.

4   Results and Discussion

4.1   The infection tree

Among the 4,315 cases, 3,270 cases have an "effective" (non-empty) infected list, while the rest do not have any cases considered as their infection sources. In total, 3,392 cases have an effective infecting list, while the rest do not contribute to the infection of other cases. By joining the two lists for all cases, the infection tree contains 3,106 cases (69% of 4,315) in total, which is shown as the largest connected graph in Figure 1. Other cases are either completely isolated (25%, not shown here) or in small groups (8%, those on the right hand side).

According to the circle size and branch density, the infection tree reveals two small peaks (early and late September) and one large peak (late October). Most cases during the first two small peaks occur at elementary schools. The large peak occurs in late October where most affected locations are universities, professional schools, and their associated dorms. Unlike students in elementary schools and high schools who interact only during school hours, students in universities or professional school interact during both the daytime and nighttime because these students reside in dorms on campus (a common practice in China). Their high frequency of spatio-temporal co-occurrence on campus gives rise to the significant transmissions during this peak.

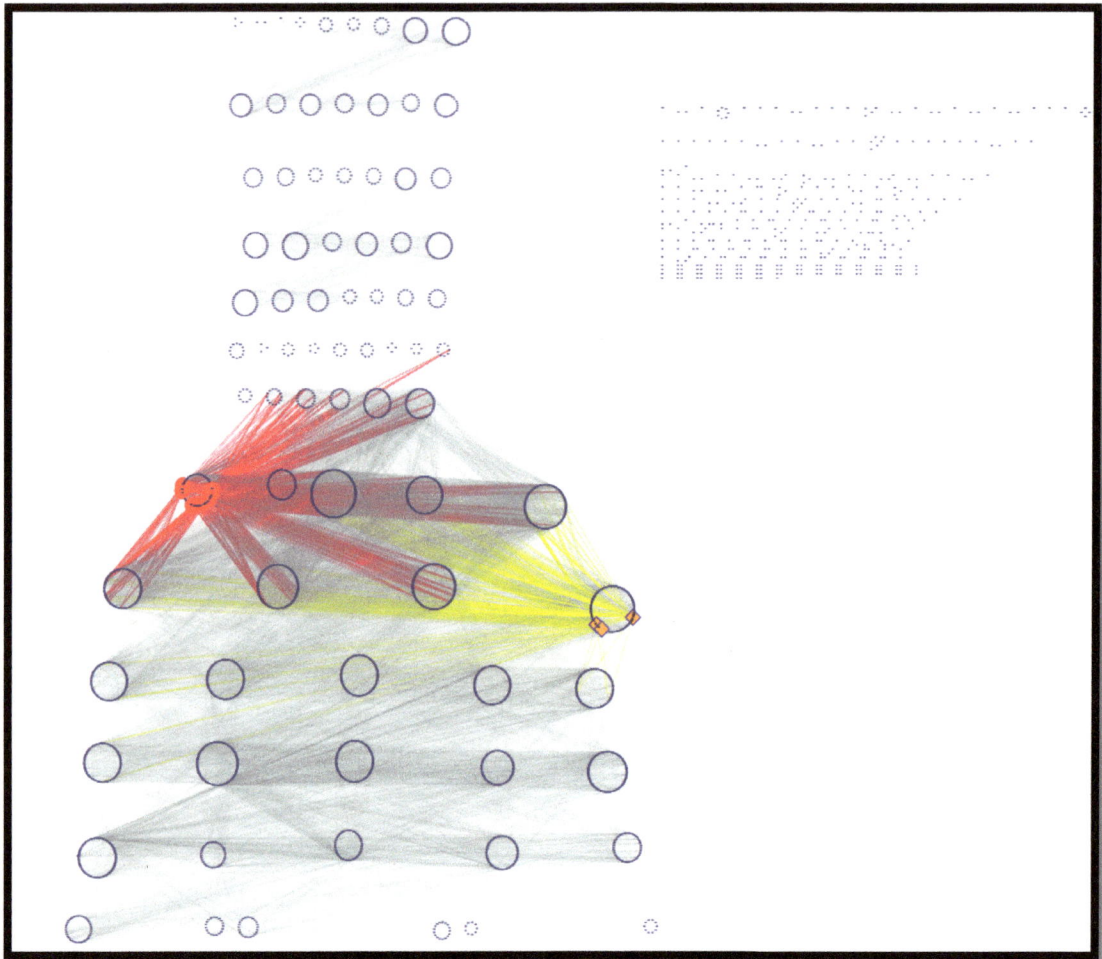

Figure 1. The infection tree and small connected groups. Cases with earlier dates are displayed at the top. Cases of the same symptom onset dates are displayed in the same circle. Larger circles indicate more cases. Red nodes and branches denote the "super-spreaders" and their contributions to others' infection. Yellow nodes and branches denote the "super-receivers" and their infection sources.

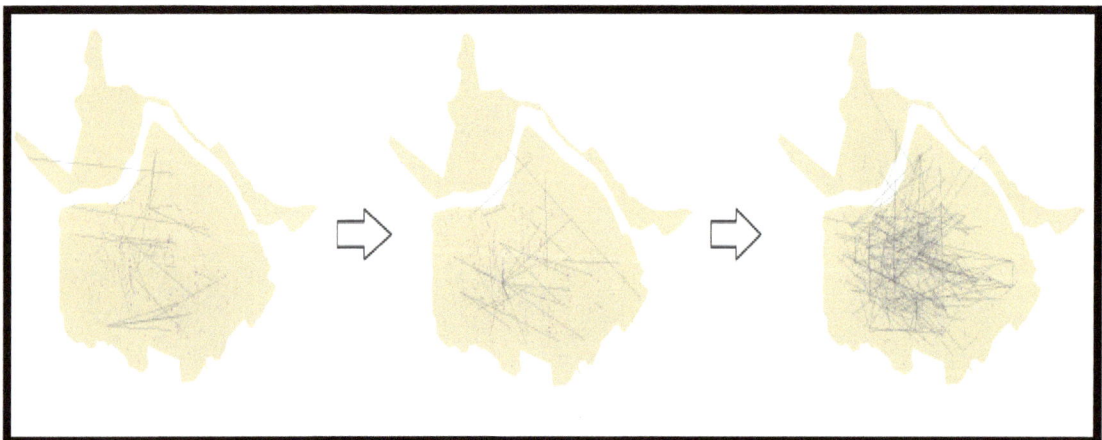

Figure 2. Snapshots of spatial and temporal interactive dynamics (Left and Middle: the first two small peaks in September. Right: the large peak in late October).

4.2 Clustering coefficient

The average clustering coefficient of 0.33 (Figure 3) illustrates the transitivity in the infection tree, which implies parallel infections among cases across multiple levels of the infection tree. If Case i contributes to the infection of Cases j and k, Case k might be the victim of both Case i and j if it spatially and temporally co-occurs with Case j. Thus, the possibility of Case k being infected is increased due to multiple parallel infection sources.

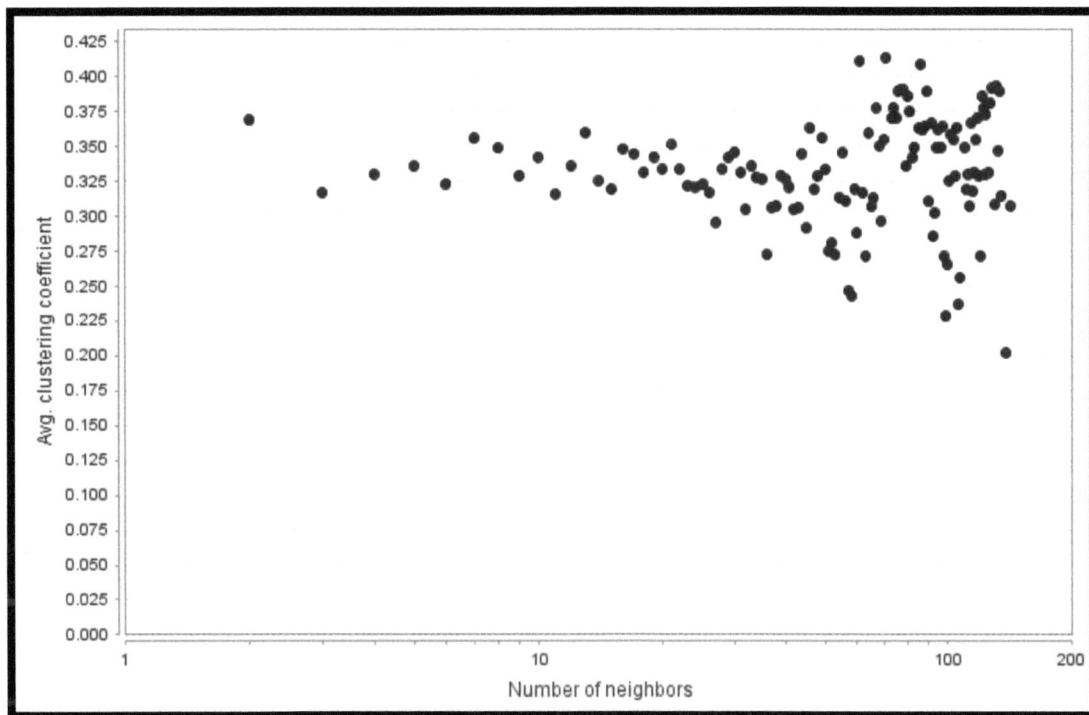

Figure 3. The clustering coefficient distribution of tree nodes.

4.3 In-degree and out-degree distribution

Both in-degree and out-degree distributions of the infection tree follow a power law distribution (Figures 4a. $\alpha=1.93$, p-value from the Kolmogorov-Smirnov test =0.93; Figures 4b $\alpha=1.83$, p-value from the Kolmogorov-Smirnov test =0.73). In the case of in-degree, a large number of cases (58%) are probably infected by less than ten cases. A few cases at the tail are probably infected by more than 100 cases, and thus are the "super-receivers".

330 Zhong and Bian

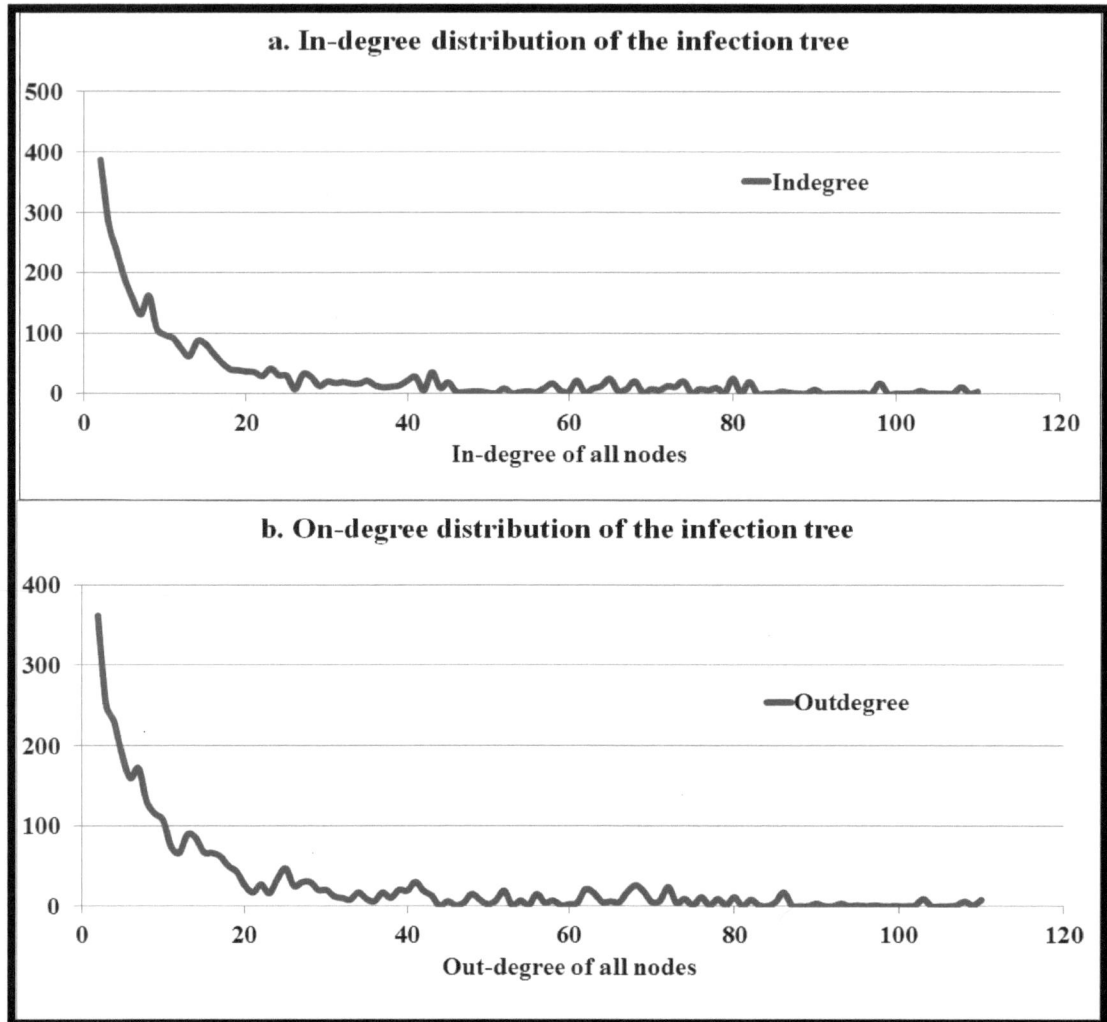

Figure 4. The in-degree (a) and out-degree (b) distribution of the infection tree.

Similarly, a large number of cases (50%) probably have contributed to the infection of less than ten cases. A few cases at the tail have contributed to the infection of more than 100 cases, and thus are the "super-spreaders".

4.4 Super-spreaders and super-receivers

Three cases are identified as "super-receivers", all with the highest in-degree of 109 (yellow nodes in Figure 1). They probably received an infection from the previous 109 cases within the past week. These are students from the same professional school and live in the dorms on campus. The high frequency of their spatio-temporal co-occurrence exposes themselves to a highly infectious environment, and thus they are highly vulnerability to infection.

Eight cases are identified as "super-spreaders", all with the highest out-degree of 125 (red nodes in Figure 1). They might have contributed to the subsequent infections of 125 cases within the following week. All of them are students from the same aforementioned professional school. This is an expected consequence in a highly infectious environment due to high frequency of spatio-temporal co-occurrence among cases.

5 Conclusion

The spatial and temporal interactive patterns that are reconstructed in this study are critical to improve our understanding of transmission dynamics of communicable diseases. Although not all individuals who have symptoms will visit hospitals to be included in the dataset, the spatial and temporal trend derived from the data available for this study is representative of the epidemic in retrospective.

References

[1]   ANDERSON, R. M., MAY, R. M. AND ANDERSON, B. Infectious diseases of humans: dynamics and control. Wiley Online Library, 1992. doi: 10.1111/j.1753-6405.1992.tb00056.x

[2]   BIAN, L., HUANG, Y., MAO, L., LIM, E., LEE, G., YANG, Y., COHEN, M. AND WILSON, D. Modeling individual vulnerability to communicable diseases: A framework and design. Annals of the Association of American Geographers, 102, 5 (2012), 1016-1025. doi:10.1080/00045608.2012.674844.

[3]   CARRAT, F., VERGU, E., FERGUSON, N. M., LEMAITRE, M., CAUCHEMEZ, S., LEACH, S. AND VALLERON, A.-J. Time lines of infection and disease in human influenza: a review of volunteer challenge studies. American journal of epidemiology, 167, 7 (2008), 775-785. doi: 10.1093/aje/kwm375.

[4]   CENTERS FOR DISEASE CONTROL AND PREVENTION (CDC). The 2009 H1N1 pandemic: summary highlights, April 2009–April 2010. Website: http://www.cdc.gov/h1n1flu/cdcresponse.htm. Accessed on August 2, 2011.

[5]   EUBANK, S., GUCLU, H., KUMAR, V. A., MARATHE, M. V., SRINIVASAN, A., TOROCZKAI, Z. AND WANG, N. Modelling disease outbreaks in realistic urban social networks. Nature, 429, 6988 (2004), 180-184. doi:10.1038/nature02541.

[6]   FERGUSON, N. M., CUMMINGS, D. A., FRASER, C., CAJKA, J. C., COOLEY, P. C. AND BURKE, D. S. Strategies for mitigating an influenza pandemic. Nature, 442, 7101 (2006), 448-452.doi: 10.1038/nature04795.

[7]   GOMES, M. F., Y PIONTTI, A. P., ROSSI, L., CHAO, D., LONGINI, I., HALLORAN, M. E. AND VESPIGNANI, A. Assessing the international spreading risk associated with the 2014 West African Ebola outbreak. PLoS currents, 6 (2014). doi: 10.1371/currents.outbreaks.cd818f63d40e24aef769dda7df9e0da5.

[8]   HEYMAN, D. Control of Communicable Diseases Manual. American Public Health Association. Washington, DC (2004).

[9]   SALATHÉ, M., KAZANDJIEVA, M., LEE, J. W., LEVIS, P., FELDMAN, M. W. AND JONES, J. H. A high-resolution human contact network for infectious disease transmission. Proceedings of the National Academy of Sciences, 107, 51 (2010), 22020-22025. doi: 10.1073/pnas.1009094108.

www.ingramcontent.com/pod-product-compliance
Lightning Source LLC
Chambersburg PA
CBHW050808220326
41598CB00006B/151